MANGROVE ECOSYSTEMS IN AUSTRALIA

Structure, function and management

Sponsoring Organisations

Australian Institute of Marine Science
Reserve Bank of Australia
(Rural Credits Development Fund)

MANGROVE ECOSYSTEMS IN AUSTRALIA

Structure, function and management

BF Clough Editor

Proceedings of the Australian National Mangrove Workshop
Australian Institute of Marine Science

Cape Ferguson
18-20 April 1979

Australian Institute of Marine Science
in association with
Australian National University Press
Canberra, Australia, London, England
and Miami, Fla., U.S.A.
1982

First published in Australia 1982

Printed & typeset in Hong Kong for the Australian National University Press, Canberra

National Library of Australia
Cataloguing-in-Publication entry

Mangrove ecosystems in Australia:
Structure, function and management

   Bibliography.
   Includes index.
   ISBN 0 7081 1170 x.

   1. Mangrove — Australia. I. Clough, B.F. II.
Australian Institute of Marine Science.

583′.42

Library of Congress No. 81-68098

United Kingdom, Europe, Middle East, and Africa: Books Australia,
3 Henrietta St, London WC2E 8 LU, England
North America: Books Australia, 15601 SW 83rd Avenue, Miami, Fla., USA
Japan: United Publishers Services Ltd, Tokyo

Printed by Colorcraft Ltd, Hong Kong.

Foreword

Interest in mangroves and mangrove communities has a long scientific history. Nonetheless, until quite recently, the ecological significance of these forests has not been well appreciated. Not many years ago there were even some in the scientific community who considered the mangroves as wastelands. Studies largely in the United States and in parts of the Caribbean, however, have been responsible for an abrupt change in attitude over the last decade and there is now an intensifying concern globally to develop a better understanding of these unusual and highly productive ecosystems. This interest has spread quite widely within Australia and to such an extent that the need to exchange views, take stock and consider future directions in the national mangrove research effort was clearly evident. This volume is the result. It is our hope that the material it contains will be of value and that it will encourage a wider interest in this field of research.

J.S. Bunt
Director
Australian Institute of Marine Science

Contents

Tables

Figures

Plates

List of Contributors and Discussion Leaders

T.J. Andrews, Australian Institute of Marine Science, PMB No. 3, Townsville MSO, Qld 4810

P.M. Attiwill, School of Botany, University of Melbourne, Parkville, Vic. 3052

M.M. Barson, School of Botany, University of Melbourne, Parkville, Vic. 3052

A.A. Benson, Scripps Institution of Oceanography, P.O. Box 109, La Jolla, California 92093, U.S.A.

E.C.F. Bird, Department of Geography, University of Melbourne, Parkville, Vic. 3052

K.G. Boto, Australian Institute of Marine Science, PMB No. 3, Townsville MSO, Qld 4810

P. Bridgewater, School of Environmental and Life Sciences, Murdoch University, Murdoch, W.A. 6153

J.S. Bunt, Australian Institute of Marine Science, PMB No. 3, Townsville Qld 4810

B.F. Clough, Australian Institute of Marine Science, PMB No. 3, Townsville MSO, Qld 4810

I.R. Cowan, Research School of Biological Sciences, Australian National University, P.O. Box 475, Canberra, A.C.T. 2601

R.M. Dowling, Queensland Herbarium, Meiers Road, Indooroopilly, Qld 4068

N.C. Duke, Australian Institute of Marine Science, PMB No. 3, Townsville MSO, Qld 4810

R.W. Galloway, CSIRO Division of Land Use Research, P.O. Box 1666, Canberra City, A.C.T. 2601

H.B. Gill, CSIRO Division of Wildlife Research, P.O. Box 84, Lyneham, A.C.T. 2602

E.J. Hegerl, Australian Littoral Society, 97 Lant Street, Fig Tree Pocket, Qld 4069

J. Imberger, Department of Engineering, University of Western Australia, Nedlands, W.A. 6009

K.F. Kenneally, Western Australian, Herbarium, Department of Agriculture, George Street, South Perth, W.A. 6151

I.J. Mason, CSIRO Division of Wildlife Research, P.O. Box 84, Lyneham, A.C.T. 2602

T.J. McDonald, Queensland Herbarium, Meiers Road, Indooroopilly, Qld 4068

N.E. Milward, Zoology Department, James Cook University of North Queensland, P.O., James Cook University, Townsville, Qld 4811

D.J. Moriarty, CSIRO Division of Fisheries and Oceanography, P.O. Box 120, Cleveland, Qld 4163

J. Oliver, Department of Geography, James Cook University of North Queensland, P.O. James Cook University, Townsville, Qld 4811

F. Olsen, Queensland Fisheries Service, 138 Albert Street, Brisbane, Qld 4000

J. Redfield, CSIRO Division of Fisheries and Oceanography, P.O. Box 120, Cleveland, Qld 4163

E.G. Rhodes, Australian Institute of Marine Science, PMB No. 3, Townsville MSO, Qld 4810

P. Saenger, C/— Queensland Electricity Generating Board, P.O. Box 1424, Brisbane, Qld 4000

R. Schodde, CSIRO Division of Wildlife Research, P.O. Box 84, Lyneham, A.C.T. 2602

S.C. Snedaker, School of Marine and Atmospheric Science, University of Miami, 4600 Rickenbacker Causeway, Miami, Florida 33149, U.S.A.

B.G. Thom, Department of Geography, Royal Military College, Duntroon, A.C.T. 2600

A.G. Wells, Department of Environmental Physics, University of Sydney, N.S.W. 2006

Preface

Mangroves are the only trees amongst a relatively small group of higher plants which have been remarkably successful in colonising the intertidal zone at the interface between land and sea. They occur characteristically along the more sheltered regions of tropical and subtropical coastlines, often being replaced at more temperature latitudes by saltmarshes composed of predominantly herbaceous species. In Australia, mangroves extend as a discontinuous coastal fringe from as far south as the temperate Victorian coastline, where they are restricted to a single species, to the tropical northern coastline where they form extensive tidal forests which are comparable in species diversity and luxuriance to the best developed tidal forests of South-east Asia.

There is now a considerable body of evidence, largely from research outside Australia, that mangroves play an important role in supporting a wide range of marine life in near-shore waters and in sustaining coastal fisheries. The recognition of their ecological significance, coupled with increasing urban and industrial pressures, has led in recent years to an increase in research on Australian mangroves. Much of this research, however, is fragmented and in many cases unpublished. Recognising this, a National Mangrove Workshop was held at the Australian Institute of Marine Science in April 1979. The objectives of the workshop were to review existing knowledge of Australian mangroves, to identify areas where further work is needed, and to explore ways of improving the exchange of information between research workers from different disciplines and geographic locations. In keeping with these objectives, a number of people were asked to prepare position papers on various aspects of mangrove biology and management to serve as a basis for discussion at the workshop.

This volume is the outcome of that workshop. It includes all position papers presented at the workshop, together with several papers which became available later. Most of the papers have been revised to include salient elements of discussion arising during the workshop, and therefore in a sense they represent the collective efforts of all participants at the workshop. Although special emphasis is given to the mangroves of Australia it is hoped that much of the information and many of the ideas presented in this volume will be of interest to readers outside Australia. For those readers who are unfamiliar with the geography of Australia key geographic markers may be found in Figure 3.1 on page 36.

Many of the staff of the Australian Institute of Marine Science made significant contributions to the organisation of the workshop and to the preparation of this volume. Special mention should be made of the efforts of

Ms A. Cerutti, Mr L. Brady and Mr L. Maza, and of Ms L. White who typed the manuscript. The Editor is particularly grateful for the assistance and guidance of Professor B. Thom, Professor I. Cowan and Dr J. Redfield who served on the Editorial Committee, and to Dr G. Walsh who undertook at short notice the onerous task of reviewing the entire manuscript. Partial support for the workshop was provided by the Reserve Bank of Australia through the Rural Credits Development Fund.

The plates in chapter 3 are reproduced with permission from the Division of National Mapping, Department of National Development and Energy.

Townsville, 1981   B.F. Clough

Part I
THE MANGROVE ENVIRONMENT

Introduction

B.G. Thom

The three chapters in the section 'Mangrove Environment' reflect different perspectives on the question of where mangroves occur. The nature of mangrove environments in Australia and overseas can be appreciated by using descriptive, experimental and modelling approaches. In a sense these three chapters demonstrate how these approaches can be applied to problems of mangrove distribution.

The first chapter in this section attempts to synthesise the various physical factors which influence mangrove distribution. A global perspective is adopted. The author believes that sufficient is known at this stage to at least tentatively examine the interaction of various factors on mangrove distribution. It is important to view these factors as they change in both time and space. However, such an approach must be treated with caution as further refinements will be required as our knowledge grows.

Professor Oliver has provided a review of the role of climatic conditions and their fluctuations on mangrove environments. He notes that of the various factors which may influence mangrove distribution 'the influence of climate, by contrast, is often less obvious and certainly not as well documented'. By examining the role of climate at various spatial scales, the author is able to highlight deficiencies in our knowledge of how mangroves as communities or individuals respond to climatic conditions. The need for more rigorous experimentation is obvious in a variety of environments.

The contribution by Dr Galloway is the first systematic attempt to document the distributional characteristics of mangrove communities in Australia. It is part of a broader inventory being undertaken by the Division of Land Use Research, CSIRO, of Australian coastal environments. Such a continent-wide study by a small group has many advantages over attempts to pool data from various sources. Although one might argue about the location of some boundaries or the emphasis placed on certain environmental attributes and not others, it is most useful to now have a descriptive account of mangrove environments at this scale.

It will be clear from these chapters that more research is necessary if we in Australia are to improve our understanding of interrelationships between mangroves and their environments. First, documentation of plant distribution in various physical settings can be improved with more detailed regional studies; there are still considerable gaps in knowledge of such phenomena as substrate properties, frequency of inundation, etc. Second, as Oliver demonstrates, there is the need for improved climatic data which relate specifically to mangrove habitats; there is an opportunity for short-term collection of data in an experimental context in a variety of settings. Finally, it is important to see Australian mangrove communities and environmental settings in their global context. More general models of environmental change are needed if our understanding of mangrove habitats and dynamics is to have a temporal perspective. The three approaches as represented in these chapters provide ideas for geographers, ecologists and others to investigate and thus contribute to coastal wetlands research.

1
Mangrove Ecology — A Geomorphological Perspective
B.G. Thom

Introduction

Besides the basic biogeographic question of why mangroves are where they are on a global and continental scale, physical geographers are also concerned with questions of mangrove ecology at the regional scale. Three interrelated questions are of interest:

(i)   What is the distribution of mangrove species and physiognomic types?
(ii) What factors influence the various distributional patterns?
(iii) What changes are these patterns experiencing at various time scales?

In order to answer these questions, it is useful to adopt the perspective of a geomorphologist interested in environments of deposition and resulting landforms. Whether one is process or historically oriented in geomorphology, it is inevitable that the geomorphologist will view habitats for plants in coastal regions as part of a constantly changing set of environments.

I have been impressed by the weight of literature adopting the classic successional view of mangrove dynamics (see Chapman, 1970, 1976; Walsh, 1974). This model emphasises biotic processes inducing soil accumulation and plant community change from pioneer through to climax stage. My training as a geomorphologist and experience (first in Tabasco and later elsewhere) has led to reservations about the general applicability of the classic model (Thom, 1967). Diversity in landform type, process and evolution from place to place suggested more complex physical environmental settings than that implied by the successional model. Species distribution and physiognomy seemed to be better explained by associating plant type directly with diverse and dynamic landform and substrate conditions. This suggests an alternative model whereby mangroves are viewed as opportunistic organisms colonising available substrate. In this context mangrove patterns are primarily seen as ecologic responses to external conditions of sedimentation, microtopography, estuarine hydrology and geochemistry.

Perspective of a geomorphologist

A physical geographer who specialises in coastal geomorphology is conscious of the vast array of landform types and combinations (assemblages of landforms) which occur in coastal regions. To the geomorphologist who is interested in coastal processes or dynamics these landform types represent a field laboratory in which hydrodynamic and sedimentologic processes interact to produce an ever-changing landscape at the interface of land and sea. Changes in the magnitude and frequency of processes at various time scales ranging from years to seconds creates a temporal perspective which must be appreciated if rates of landform change are to be understood. This leads on to the perspective of a geomorphologist who is more interested in the evolution of coastal depositional sequences, and for whom the array of landform types represents changing environmental conditions and process regimes over tens to thousands of years. The 'historical' as distinct from the 'process' oriented geomorphologist is often limited in his ability to measure and infer changes in geomorphic conditions, but both can provide useful information on the physical environmental characteristics which are significant to plant growth.

Plant habitat conditions in coastal regions may be defined by the geomorphic or landform settings in which the plants occur. The geomorphologist would recognise that the array of geomorphically-determined settings within a region would in turn represent the product of an array of interacting physical forces. These include forces operating at a global and continental scale, such as atmospheric and oceanic circulation and earth geophysical processes which affect continental geologic history and land tectonic and sea level movements. There are also factors operating at a regional scale which influence coastal landform development, including mesoscale climatic parameters, drainage basin geology and hydrology, and marine processes such as tidal and wave regimes. Coleman and Wright (1975) have shown how all these factors can be synthesised into meaningful groups which explain the spatial variability of coastal deltas at a global scale.

Therefore, the coastal geomorphologist brings to the study of mangrove ecology the perspective of one interested in environmental changes as they relate to landform development at various time and space scales. He views plant habitats as landform complexes which are subject to continual change as a result of processes (tides, waves, river discharge, sea level movements, etc.) varying in magnitude and frequency over time. The rate and direction of change may vary appreciably between and within regions, so that some understanding is required of the type, mechanisms of interaction and rate and direction of geomorphologic process and response before an appreciation of mangrove ecology is possible.

Mangrove ecology and geomorphology
The magnitude and rate of change in plant habitat conditions may vary in space and time both within and between localities. However, in order to understand the dynamics of various mangrove distributional patterns (i.e. species and structure), it is necessary to examine habitat change as a function of those processes which induce environmental change. The processes may be climatic, hydrologic, geophysical (sea level, tectonics), geomorphic or pedologic. The geomorphologist could argue that the emphasis in the mangrove literature on biologic processes leading to classic successional tendencies is habitat limited. That is, far from being the norm as proposed by Davis (1940), Chapman (1970, 1976), Macnae (1968) and others, successional tendencies are limited to particular localities by the dynamic nature of external forces which are constantly inducing changes to environmental gradients and plant habitats. Elsewhere the direct contribution of the plants to substrate elevations and

sediment properties, although ecologically important, is not seen as the prime initiator or controller of the rate or direction of community change.

In the areas studied by the writer (Thom, 1967, 1974; Thom *et al.*, 1975), the ecology of mangroves is examined in terms of the response of the plants to habitat change induced primarily by geomorphic processes. Given the climatic-tidal environment and a pool of mangrove species, each of which possesses a certain physiological response to habitat conditions, it is considered that the history of land surface, and contemporary geomorphic processes, together determine the nature of the soil surface on which mangroves grow. Attributes of the substrate (moisture content, texture, salinity, redox potential, chemical composition) are to a large extent a function of past and present geomorphic processes. The writer subscribes to the view that, by obtaining an understanding of those processes and their landform products developed over time, it is possible to explain the particular pattern of mangrove distribution present in an area. Knowledge of the development of this pattern is useful in predicting future changes that existing communities may experience as a result of geomorphic change.

Changes in the type, magnitude and frequency of geomorphic processes in any area over time are inevitable. Often such changes accompany climatic change which may also directly influence mangrove ecology. However, geomorphic processes may operate independently of variations in climate. The rate at which landforms change may differ enormously (i) from one environment to another, (ii) from place to place within a region or area, and (iii) over time within an area. For instance, once the high-tidal flats developed in the Cambridge Gulf-Ord River region of Western Australia, and once the cemented platforms developed on windward sides of 'low wooded islands' in the Barrier Reef, it is envisaged that mangroves occupying these and adjacent habitats are sustained as stable communities over several millennia (Thom, 1974). In contrast, in areas of rapid seaward progradation of the shoreline or deposition of alluvium in estuarine channels, it is possible that observable habitat change may take place in less than 50 years (see Thom *et al.*, 1975, Fig. 9). Likewise in deltas such as those in Tabasco, where distributionary diversion is quite common, the sequence of mangrove development may be drastically altered following a shift in the centre of active sedimentation and freshwater discharge (Thom, 1967).

Any regional model developed to explain mangrove distribution on the basis of geomorphic processes, past and present, must consider not only long-term directional trends in landform evolution, but also the possibility and effect of localised interruptions to such trends. Such disruptions may result from a variety of causes (e.g. incidence of high energy waves from a particular direction during passage of a tropical cyclone). Human activities are also responsible for such changes. The regional impact of these localised interruptions is that various stages in the development of vegetation cover will be present at any given time. When mangrove dynamics are viewed from the geomorphic perspective, the possibility of distinguishing short-term aberrations from long-term trends is enhanced (Thom, 1974).

Environmental settings and mangrove ecology

On a global scale, mangrove ecology studies may appear to be a chaotic mess of special cases represented by unique combinations of climatic, hydrologic, geophysical, geomorphic, pedologic and biologic conditions. However, it is possible to identify an array of regional environmental settings defined by largely geomorphological conditions which are repeated at different scales on all continents where mangroves occur. These settings influence the course of mangrove establishment, growth and reproduction, as outlined above. Once identified and documented with respect to physical variation in time and space, these settings can be used as a basis for more specific biological studies of mangroves.

There are three major components to the environmental setting of any locality in which mangroves occur: geophysical, geomorphic and biologic. The first component is referred to as 'background geophysical'. It includes a variety of physical forces which operate from global to regional spatial scales. These forces interact to produce the geographic character of the locality. Sea-level change induced by a combination of land and sea-level movement is one such force. Every coastal locality has its own distinctive sea-level history resulting from the interaction of global or eustatic changes in the volume of ocean water and movements of oceanic and continental crust. Other distinctive 'geophysical' factors are climatic and tidal regimes. Undoubtedly, the climate of a locality (the macroclimate) will influence plant growth in some way, although the direct relationship between any given climatic parameter and mangrove distribution is difficult to determine (see chapter by Oliver in this volume). But the climatic regime also affects the volume and variability of river runoff, and hence the discharge of sediments into, and the salinity regime of, coastal estuaries, lagoons and deltas where mangroves grow. Tidal exchange and exposure/inundation of land surfaces also influence the environmental setting of mangrove growth, so that the particular tidal regime of a locality needs to be considered as part of the 'background geophysical' component.

The second component is essentially the product of the above geophysical forces. From the perspective of this writer, it is the dynamic history of the land surface and the operation of contemporary geomorphic processes which directly determine mangrove habitat conditions. Hence the environmental setting of mangroves must be considered in terms of an array of geomorphically-defined habitats. There are three levels of generalisation in the identification of environmental settings on the basis of geomorphology. At the macro level there is the recognition of two broad classes of depositional landforms. On the one hand there are areas where coastal depositional landforms are derived from the reworking of terrigenous sediments supplied to the coast from rivers or offshore (e.g. river deltas, coastal barriers and lagoons); on the other hand, there are areas where sediment accumulation is either from *in situ* growth of coral reefs or from the deposition of carbonate clastics or precipitates.

At the next level of generalisation of environmental settings based on geomorphology, there is the assemblage of landforms which constitute the product of particular processes in a given region. For instance, deltas can be sub-divided into those dominated by wave or river or tidal processes (Galloway, 1975; see also Coleman and Wright, 1975). A wave-dominated delta will possess a different combination of landform types and processes with distinctive sediment properties to a river or tide-dominated delta. In each case geomorphic processes and products will determine the specific array of habitats which will be utilised by plants.

How the landforms are 'felt' by the plants can be best appreciated by recognition of a third level of generalisation of environmental settings based on geomorphology. This is the expression of 'microtopography' of particular landforms (e.g. river levees, beach-ridge swales) on plant establishment, growth and regeneration. Land surface elevation, drainage and stability in combination with substrate or sediment properties (texture, composition, structure, etc.) and nutrient inputs will produce environmental gradients within the coastal region. Microtopography in this sense induces varying physiological responses of different species (or different ecotypes within a species). According to the physiological response of species to moisture and/or salinity stress conditions, there will be more or less favourable plant growth in a particular habitat. Thus landform properties and processes find expression in the variation in growth, morphology and metabolism of mangroves along environmental gradients. For example, Lugo et al. (1975) reported differential responses in the in situ gas exchange characteristics of three species distributed along a salinity gradient in Florida. Such variation in physiological responses to an environmental variable are major factors affecting development of zonation patterns.

The physiological optimum of a species as determined from laboratory studies seldom corresponds with the ecological optimum. The differences arise from interaction with the biological component of the environment, which includes the pool of mangrove species occurring in a particular region. Interspecific competition plays an important role in determining the species diversity and distribution patterns in a given area. The influence of physical factors of the environment, especially those controlling landform conditions, on the relative competitive abilities of mangrove species probably accounts for the distribution of mangroves in typical zoned patterns (Ball, 1980). Competition affects not only the number of species that can be dispersed to an area, but also the competitive response of different combinations of species in similar physical settings. In the former case, there may be a relative lack of competition during early stages of colonisation producing mixed seedling stands of shade-tolerant and shade-intolerant species living off cotyledonary or propagule reserves (M. Ball, personal communication 1979). However, as species reach maturity and compete for space and resources, the competitive abilities of certain species in a particular physical setting appear to be very important. The pool of species in Atlantic or 'New World' regions is much more limited than in parts of the Indo-Pacific province. As a consequence, Avicennia and Rhizophora occupy a broader range of habitats within any given area or depositional complex in the Atlantic province than is likely in species-diverse parts of the Indo-Pacific province. Thus a delta with certain physical conditions in the New World may have quite different distributional patterns to a similar delta in the Old World. However, even in the Indo-Pacific province near the limits of mangrove distribution (e.g. along the south-east coast of Australia), one species can grow in a variety of habitats. There may be quite marked physiognomic differences in species growth in such a case. In more equatorial areas this species may be restricted by competition to a more limited number of habitats.

Physical environmental settings for mangrove growth

The first two components of environmental setting, the geophysical and geomorphic, can be combined to produce an array of physical settings in which mangroves grow. This chapter will concentrate on terrigenous physical settings because on a global scale carbonate settings do not represent large areas of mangrove growth.

Comparisons of thirty-four major river systems by Wright *et al.* (1974) in terms of particular sets of physical environmental variables, such as river discharge, wave energy regimes, river-mouth morphology, delta-plain landform suites, revealed that deltas tend to cluster together into a relatively few delta groups or 'families' within which the individual delta members are mutually similar. Further generalisation (Coleman and Wright, 1975; see also Wright, 1978) resulted in the classification of a number of general delta types with each type reflecting a particular combination of processes and physical environmental controls. These types vary appreciably in size, but in this chapter they form the basis of a broader classification of coastal physical environmental settings in which mangroves grow. As will be shown later, it is through the recognition of such types that an insight is provided into the environmental factors which influence mangrove distribution and physiognomy in a coastal region.

Figure 1.1 illustrates five coastal settings in the form of generalised geometry and possible habitats for mangrove growth.

Setting I is characteristic of what are known as allochthonous coasts of low tidal range. In such cases river discharge of freshwater and sediment leads to the rapid deposition of terrigenous sands, silts and clays to form deltas. These deltas are building seawards over flat offshore slopes composed of fine grained pro-delta sediments. Such slopes help dampen wave energy and any tendency for longshore drift. The delta geometry consists of multiple branching distributaries forming elongate, finger-like protrusions. The result is a highly crenulate coastline with shallow bays and lagoons between and adjacent to distributaries. The active distributary region is predominantly an area of high freshwater discharge so that salt-tolerant plants are not common. However, there may be abandoned distributary regions within the deltaic plain into which saline waters intrude either seasonally or more frequently. The area marginal to these distributaries is also relevant to this setting as longshore drift of muds and wave reworking of sands and shells will influence plant establishment and generation (e.g. on chenier plains). Thus parts of the deltaic plain may contain

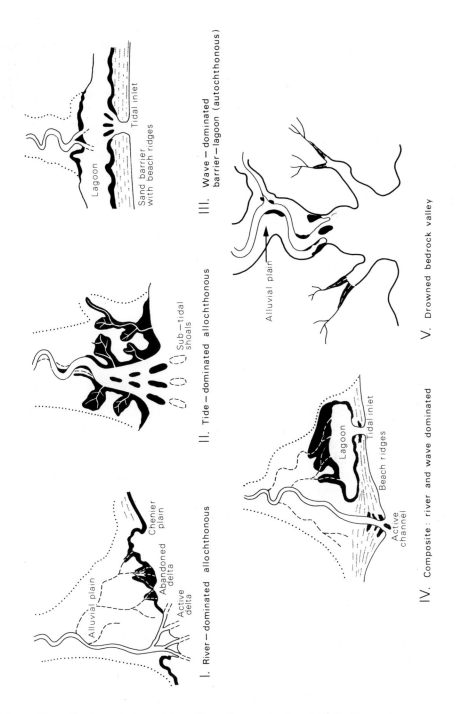

Fig. 1.1. Generalised environmental settings for mangrove colonisation and development (shaded). The five settings occur on coasts dominated by terrigenous deposition and reworking of sand, silt and clay sediments.

an array of habitats on which mangroves establish or are maintained. Such deltaic plains are subject to rapid rates of subsidence and switches in centre of freshwater discharge and deposition, so that this environmental setting is characterised by a high degree of morphologic diversity and rapid habitat change. One example is the Mississippi Delta and the adjacent chenier plain. The Orinoco Delta is another example.

Setting II is also associated with allochthonous coasts, only here the dominant physical process is high tidal range with associated strong bidirectional tidal currents. These currents are responsible for the dispersion of sediments brought to the coast by rivers, and in the offshore zone they form linear elongate sand bodies (Wright *et al.*, 1973). Wave power is often quite low because of frictional attenuation over broad intertidal shoals. Typically, the main river channels are funnel-shaped and are fed by numerous tidal creeks. These creeks are separated by extensive tidal-flat surfaces. Where relative sea level has been stable for 5000 or more years these channels appear to be fixed in position and the surfaces of the tidal flat accrete vertically to the high water spring tide level. They also prograde seawards along the promontories which separate the tidal channels. An example in a dry climate is the Ord River delta in north-west Australia, and in a wet climate an example is the Klang delta of west Malaysia.

Setting III is characterised by much higher wave energy and relatively low amounts of river discharge. The slope of the inner continental shelf in such a case would be steeper due to operation at different sea level of the high wave energy which reworks sediments delivered to the coast by rivers. This type of coast is referred to as autochthonous (Swift, 1976). Offshore barrier islands, barrier spits or bay barriers are typical of this setting. Barrier islands enclose broad elongate lagoons, whereas bay barriers enclose drowned river valleys. Small digitate deltas prograde into these water bodies without significant opposition from marine forces. The degree of tidal modification of landforms of this setting can be quite variable (see below). Salt-tolerant plants occur around the margins of the lagoon in a variety of habitats. An example of this setting is the linear barrier coastline of El Salvador or the bay barrier coastline of N.S.W.

Setting IV represents a combination of high wave energy and high river discharge. Sand debouched by the river is rapidly redistributed by waves alongshore to form extensive sand sheets. Much of the sand deposited on the inner continental shelf during lower sea levels is reworked landward during marine transgressions and subsequent sea-level 'stillstands'. The result is a coastal plain dominated by sand beach ridges, narrow discontinuous lagoons with an alluvial plain to landward. Salt-tolerant plants such as mangroves are concentrated in distribution along abandoned distributaries, and in areas near river mouths and adjacent lagoons. The Grijalva delta in Mexico is an example of this type. Here regional subsidence accentuates the development of environmental gradients, distributary diversion and lagoon expansion (Thom, 1967). The Purari delta of Papua New Guinea is a similar setting, but appears to lack the geomorphic (and habitat) diversity involving lagoon development.

Where the tidal range is greater and the climate drier, as in the case of the Burdekin delta of Queensland, there is a spread of saline habitats to inter-distributary areas which are periodically inundated by high spring tides.

Setting V can be described as a drowned river valley complex. The depositional setting is defined by a bedrock valley system which has been drowned (transgressed) by a rising sea level. Neither marine nor river deposition has been sufficient to infill what is an open estuarine system. However, the heads of valleys may contain relatively small river deltas which are little modified by waves. At the mouth of the drowned valley bordering the open sea, a tidal delta may occur composed of marine sand reworked landward during a marine transgression (Roy *et al.*, 1980). Broken Bay in N.S.W. is a good example; mangroves flourish in fine sediments at the heads of drowned tributary valleys, and in lagoons behind bay barriers near the mouth of the estuary. Missionary Bay, Hinchinbrook Island, may represent a type of this setting with the broad bedrock embayment serving as a sediment sink for mainland sediments.

It is not the purpose in this chapter to provide an exclusive list of physical environmental settings. Galloway (this volume) has demonstrated just how variable specific settings may be. Rather the five presented above should be seen as a means of identifying basic sets of process variables which will influence mangrove establishment, growth and regeneration. Through competition the plants will utilise favoured environmental niches within these settings, and thus create specific patterns of species zonation and community stability.

Physical processes and mangrove zonation and stability
Spatial variability
The interaction of processes and materials in producing distinctive patterns of landform assemblages, which can be interpreted as mangrove habitats, provides the investigator with a framework, or 'model', for conceptualising relationships between physical variables and plant behaviour in space and time. Table 1.1 attempts to integrate these relationships where physical variables vary spatially. Thus, for regions close to the equator (i.e. assuming no temperature constraints on mangrove growth), and of moderate (2-4 m) tidal range, the major process variables are seen to be rainfall, sediment input or discharge to the coastal zone, coastal water turbidity (a reflection of suspended load), and wave energy (to a large extent an inverse function between offshore slope and river sediment input). The geomorphic 'products' are shoreline stability and geomorphologic diversity (the array of landform and soil types present in a region). Characteristic settings are also shown in Table 1.1. The ecologic response to these process-response systems is indicated on the right-hand side of the table.

Clearly, areas of high geomorphologic diversity are also areas possessing a high degree of habitat variation. Within the distributary networks of settings I and IV there may be found complex distributional patterns of both saline and non-saline coastal plants. Furthermore, these areas are characterised by

Table 1.1 Geomorphic and ecologic responses to varying combinations of environmental process variables. Some attempt is made to quantify these variables for large river and open-ocean wave energy conditions (H = high; M = moderate; L = low).

SETTING	PROCESSES					GEOMORPHIC RESPONSE		ECOLOGIC RESPONSE		EXAMPLE
	Tide	Rainfall	River discharge	Turbidity	Wave power	Landform diversity	Shoreline stability	Zonation diversity	Community stability	
I	L	H	H	H	L	H	L	H	L	Mississippi
	M	H	H	H	L	H	L	H	L	Orinoco
II	H	H	H	H	L	M	M	M	M	Ganges
	H	L	M	H	L	L	L	L	H	Ord
III	M	M	L	L	H	L	H	L	H	El Salvador
	M	L	L	L	H	L	M	L	M	Senegal
IV	L	H	H	H	M	H	L	H	L	Grijalva
	M	H	H	H	M	M	M	M	L	Burdekin
V	M	M	M	M	H	L	H	L	H	Broken Bay

Tide	H > 4m	Rainfall	H > 1500mm	
	M 2-4m		M 700-1500mm	
	L < 2m		L < 700mm	
River discharge in m³/sec	H > 10000	Wave power in X10⁷ ergs/sec	H < 100	
	M 3000 to 1000		M 10-100	
	L < 3000		L > 10	

frequent switches in positions of freshwater discharge. Thus the influence of saltwater intrusion up active, atrophying and abandoned channels varies over time, producing 'unstable' environmental gradients. This means that conditions enabling the long-term maintenance of mangrove communities are restricted. For instance, I have observed the apparent invasion of a mangrove forest by a freshwater thicket along the Rio Gonzalez in Tabasco, following a distributary diversion (Thom, 1967).

In contrast, there are areas of sand barrier development along autochthonous coasts where sediment influx is limited, and where open-ocean coastal erosion or accretion has minimal impact on lagoonal wetlands to landward. This is the case along parts of the New South Wales coast as well as sand barrier coasts in more tropical regions (Setting III). There is not the high degree of diversity of zonation patterns in such areas as is characteristic of Setting I. However, it is possible to find local areas within the barrier-lagoon coastal type where rapid deposition or some other factor promotes considerable local diversity. In general, barrier-lagoon coasts may be shown to be areas of long-term community stability, especially where sea level has been stable for long periods, and where catastrophic storms/cyclones are infrequent. A high degree of community stability may also be favoured by a high tidal range in areas away from the major river channel (Thom *et al.*, 1975).

An interesting aberration in terms of community stability is the case of sand barriers which are rapidly eroding. Where the seaward face of these barriers is being redeposited as backbarrier or washover sand sheets, salt-tolerant plants fringing lagoons are subject to continual disturbance. This type is referred to as transgressive sand barriers. Zonation diversity and community stability are both low in this case (Table 1.1). Parts of the east coast of Malaysia may be experiencing rapid erosion. This is in contrast to the west coast where delta growth and vegetation change induced by mudflat accretion and freshwater swamp development is more significant (Watson, 1928; Coleman *et al.*, 1970).

The settings discussed above and illustrated in Figure 1.1 represent known examples which clearly demonstrate how physical processes through geomorphic responses interact to produce distinctive habitat conditions. However, there are combinations of processes which do not fit neatly into each setting. Western Malaysia is a good example. Here tidal processes influence distributary channel development and the seaward accretion of mudflats (Coleman *et al.*, 1970). The result is a combination of Settings I and II with a high degree of zonation diversity accompanying delta progradation and high tidal range. However, there are different degrees of community stability associated with invasion of freshwater forest and displacement mangrove zones on the one hand, and tidal channel stability and maintenance of channel-fringing communities on the other. Thus, for each case, it is important to evaluate the interaction of physical processes, landform-sediment products and ecologic conditions, and not simply try to fit a given area into the 'setting' classes outlined in this paper.

Temporal variability
Mangrove habitats are subjected to change in their characteristics over time as the landform assemblages evolve. In a geomorphic sense evolution involves both constructional and destructional aspects. Continuing with the Malaysian example, 'constructional evolution' refers to continued delta progradation into the Straits of Malacca producing sequences of new deposits both vertically and laterally. 'Destructional evolution' is manifested by erosion and redeposition of surfaces causing either the sudden or the gradual removal of plant communities from these surfaces.

In Table 1.1 the problem of community stability was related directly to landform types and physical environmental settings. One of the most challenging problems facing joint geomorphic-ecologic studies of coastal regions is the determination of types, rates, directions and causes of community change over different time scales. Such studies require well-documented depositional histories of landform assemblages of the quality known for very few areas of the world (e.g. Mississippi Delta). Until such studies are undertaken our ability to understand and predict community evolution is very limited.

Table 1.2 presents another approach to the problem of temporal variability of landform-plant zonation. A major variable influencing landform-habitat evolution is relative land-sea level movement. Both between and within areas there can be different trends associated with both continental scale differences in land-sea elevation, and regional scale differences such as the effect of compaction, subsidence, changing tidal regimes due to breaching or sealing of inlets, different wind-wave 'set-up' effects, etc. In Table 1.2 sustained trends operating over a decade or so are considered. These trends are generalised into three categories: still, rise or fall. Some attempt is made to differentiate rates of change on a very qualitative basis.

Table 1.2   The evolution of mangrove communities over time is related in this table to environmental setting (including tidal and climatic processes) and relative sea level change

Setting	Tidal range	Climate	Rel. sl. trend	Landform-Plant Zonation Evolution*	
				Initial deposit	Continued deposition
II	Macro (+4m)	Hot-wet	Still	Select sp.	Well zoned to RF peat (slow)
			Rise	Select sp.	Poor zoned mangrove peat
			Fall	Select sp.	Well zoned to RF peat (rapid)
		Seasonal dry	Still	Single sp.	Channel fringe (zoned) to bare flat
			Rise	Single sp.	Mixed sp. less well zoned
			Fall	Single sp.	Channel fringe (zoned) to bare to grass-scrub
I or IV	Moderate to Low	Hot-wet	Still	Select sp.	Zoned to RF peat (slow)
			Rise	Select sp.	Poor zoned to mixed sp. (tall) with peat
			Fall	Select sp.	Moderate zone to RF peat
III		Seasonal dry	Still	Single sp.	Channel fringe to dwarf to bare flat
			Rise	Single sp.	Mixed sp. poor zoned
			Fall	Single sp.	Channel fringe to bare flat to grass?
		Low temperature	Still	Single sp.	Single sp. (tall to dwarf zone) to SM (bare)
			Rise	Single sp.	Single sp. (tall) and SM peat
			Fall	Single sp.	Single sp. (dwarf) to SM (bare?) to fresh

* Applies to regions within both Indo-Pacific and Atlantic provinces but zonation pattern better developed in the Indo-Pacific province.

RF = rainforest; SM = saltmarsh.

It is suggested in Table 1.2 that patterns of community evolution respond to relative sea-level change in different ways depending on environmental setting. Climatic parameters, tidal regime, pool of species and geomorphic conditions are so interrelated that the course of past and future community evolution can only be understood against a background of sea-level change. For instance, a high tidal range area in a dry climate, which has experienced long-term stability in sea level, will be characterised by extensive tidal flats bare of vegetation. The Ord River-Cambridge Gulf region is such an area (Thom *et al.*, 1975). Vertical accretion is limited by a stillstand of the high spring tide elevation. In the dry season high evaporation rates lead to hypersalinity in the soils of these flats. Two factors mitigate against continued vertical accumulation of sediments above the limits of infrequent tidal inundation. One is wind deflation in the dry season leading to clay dune formation on the margins of the flats; the other is surface denudation by river runoff in the wet season. The Gulf of Carpentaria tidal flats exhibit the effects of both processes very clearly (Rhodes, 1980). In such a setting, once the flats have accreted to near H.W.S.T., mangroves form self-maintaining fringes particularly rich in shade intolerant species along the fringes of tidal creeks.

At another extreme, there are the well-zoned forests of mangroves in equatorial hot-wet climatic regions. In order to maintain zonation over time sea level must be relatively stable (e.g. west Malaysia; Coleman *et al.*, 1970). More complex mosaic patterns of species will reflect rising or falling sea levels. Where sea level is rising in areas of lagoon enlargement and local subsidence mangrove peats will accumulate (e.g. Tabasco; see also Florida where sea level is rising over a carbonate platform). However, where the distributary pattern is fixed and sea level is rising, regional subsidence and continued influx of fine-grained sediments will inhibit both mangrove and freshwater peat development. This is possibly the case in the Purari delta of Papua New Guinea. Zonation in this case is poorly developed as brackish water swamps merge along complex gradients with the more 'pure' *Rhizophora-Bruguiera* community to the west and rainforest inland.

The nature and direction of plant zonation evolution as suggested in Table 1.2 must be regarded as speculative at this stage. The table points to possible ways to predict sea-level trends from ecologic data. Such inferences must be undertaken with extreme caution as documentation of sea-level change for a given area must be obtained by independent methods.

Conclusion

Given the climatic-tidal environment and a particular pool of mangrove species for a specific region, it is considered that the history of the land surface and contemporary geomorphic and associated pedogenic processes together determine the pattern of mangrove growth. These factors combine to produce environmental gradients within any region, which, according to the physiological response of particular species to moisture and/or salinity stress conditions, will induce more or less favourable plant growth. Growth patterns will be reflected in species and structural distributional patterns as well as in gross and net productivity variation along the environmental gradients. It can be demonstrated in a number of regions that external forces are primarily responsible for promoting change in the physical properties of these gradients over time. Therefore, mangrove distribution (zonation ?) can be viewed as an opportunistic response of certain species to more or less favoured changing environmental conditions whose characteristics within a region are primarily controlled by past and present geomorphic processes.

It is possible to combine information on global-continental floristic distribution with knowledge of 'environmental settings', to produce models of mangrove evolution. These may be a substitute for the successional diagrams used by Chapman and others. A given model would take data on floristic composition, known physiological tolerance limits and growth behaviour of mangrove species. This information would be added to that on the physical properties of a particular area. Thus for a hot-wet, high discharge delta, which is slowly subsiding but protected from wave attack, in a floristic region containing ten or more mangrove species, we could expect a certain distributional pattern of mangroves which reflects geomorphologically controlled habitats and environmental gradients within the delta. Within such a delta mangrove species and structural diversity will primarily reflect dynamic geomorphic conditions.

Acknowledgments

The writer gratefully acknowledges the many individuals who have participated with him in discussions and field excursions into mangrove environments. Marilyn Ball kindly read this chapter prior to submission and made some helpful comments.

References

Ball, M.C., 1980. Patterns of secondary succession in a mangrove forest of Southern Florida. *Oecologia,* **44**, 226-35.

Chapman, V.J., 1970. Mangrove phytosociology. *Tropical Ecology* **11**, 1-9.

Chapman, V.J., 1976. *Mangrove Vegetation.* J. Cramer, Vaduz. 447 pp.

Coleman, J.M., S.M. Gagliano, and W.G. Smith, 1970. Sedimentation in a Malaysian high tide tropical delta. In J.P. Morgan (ed.), *Deltaic Sedimentation: Modern and Ancient.* Society of Economic Paleontologists and Mineralogists Special Publication No. 15, pp. 185-97.

Coleman, J.M. and L.D. Wright, 1975. Modern river deltas: variability of processes and sand bodies. In M.L. Broussard (ed.), *Deltas, Models for Exploration.* Houston Geological Society, Houston, pp. 99-150.

Davis, J.H., 1940. The ecology and geologic role of mangroves in Florida. Paper from the *Tortugas Laboratory,* Vol. 32, Carnegie Institute, Washington Publication No. 517, pp. 303-412.

Galloway, W.E., 1975. Process framework for describing the morphologic and stratigraphic evolution of deltaic depositional systems. In M.L. Broussard (ed.), *Deltas, Models for Exploration.* Houston Geological Society, Houston, pp. 87-98.

Lugo, A.E., G. Evink, M.M. Brinson, A. Broce and S.C. Snedaker, 1975. Diurnal rates of photosynthesis, respiration, and transpiration in mangrove forests of south Florida. In F. Golley and E. Medina (eds.) *Tropical Ecological Systems.* Springer-Verlag, New York, pp. 335-50.

Macnae, W., 1968. A general account of the fauna and flora of mangrove swamps and forests in the Indo-West-Pacific region. *Advances in Marine Biology* **6**, 73-270.

Rhodes, E.G., 1980. Modes of Holocene Coastal Progradation, Gulf of Carpentaria. Ph. D. thesis, A.N.U.

Roy, P.S., B.G. Thom, and L.D. Wright, 1980. Holocene sequences on an embayed high-energy coast: an evolutionary model. *Sedimentary Geology*, **26**, 1-19.

Swift, D.J.P., 1976. Barrier-island genesis: evidence from the central Atlantic shelf, eastern U.S.A. *Sedimentary Geology* **14**, 1-43.

Thom, B.G., 1967. Mangrove ecology and deltaic geomorphology, Tabasco, Mexico. *Journal of Ecology* **55**, 301-43.

Thom, B.G., 1974. Mangrove ecology from a geomorphic viewpoint. In G. Walsh, S. Snedaker and H. Teas (eds.), *Proceedings of the International Symposium on Biology and Management of Mangroves,* Institute of Food and Agricultural Sciences, University of Florida, Gainesville, Florida, Vol. II, pp. 469-81.

Thom, B.G., L.D. Wright and J.M. Coleman, 1975. Mangrove ecology and deltaic-estuarine geomorphology: Cambridge Gulf-Ord River, Western Australia. *Journal of Ecology* **63**, 203-32.

Walsh, G.E., 1974. Mangroves: a review. In R.J. Reimold and W.H. Queen (eds.), *Ecology of Halophytes.* Academic Press, New York, pp. 51-174.

Watson, J.D., 1928. Mangrove forests of the Malay Peninsula. *Malayan Forest Records* **6**, 1-275.

Wright, L.D., 1978. River deltas. In R.A. Davis Jr (ed.), *Coastal Sedimentary Environments.* Springer-Verlag, New York, pp. 5-68.

Wright, L.D., J.M. Coleman, and B.G. Thom, 1973. Processes of channel development in a high-tide range environment: Cambridge Gulf-Ord River Delta, Western Australia. *Journal of Geology* **81**, 15-41.

Wright, L.D., J.M. Coleman and M.W. Erickson, 1974. Analysis of major systems and their deltas: morphologic and process comparisons. *Coastal Studies Institute, Louisiana State University, Technical Report* **156**. 114pp.

2

The Geographic and Environmental Aspects of Mangrove Communities: Climate

John Oliver

Introduction

The distribution and ecology of mangroves is determined by many interrelated environmental and biological factors. The mangrove ecosystem is both complex and dynamic. In assessing the significance of climate it is important to understand the dynamics of the whole ecosystem, for climatic influences will take on a different significance as other elements in the ecosystem change. Care must be taken to avoid isolation of one group of factors, which may overemphasise their apparent importance, as well as distort a system that requires treatment as a whole. It is important to recognise, also, that past as well as present climatic conditions and their fluctuations will have helped shape the mangrove environment.

In many cases edaphic and geomorphological influences may well be more dominant than climate. Changes in sea level during and since the Pleistocene have resulted in alterations to the coastline and to mangrove distribution. The influence of climate, by contrast, is often less obvious and certainly not as well documented. The answer to the question 'To what conditions is the mangrove system most sensitive?' will provide the lead as to whether climate plays a major role in influencing the distribution and ecology of mangrove ecosystems. It is then necessary to determine whether the required climatic information is routinely available or whether specialised monitoring procedures must be established.

Climatic approaches

Climate will influence the mangrove environment over a wide range of temporal and spatial scales. Temporal scales may vary from long-period (30-year) normals to annual, seasonal or diurnal cycles. Spatial scales may range from broad regional features, through meso-scale (tens to hundreds of kilometres) differences, to local or even micro-climatic patterns, where the horizontal and vertical scales can be measured in centimetres. In interpreting the influence of climatic parameters, it is also necessary to consider biological scales which might range from communities, through individual species or plants, to differences in response at different stages in the life cycle of the plant or community.

Regional climatic relationships

At this level the main climatic parameters are temperature and rainfall. Whilst it is dangerous to assume that coincidence of distribution implies a causal relationship, it is relevant here to consider the distribution, in broad terms, of mangrove communities.

It is the commonplace generalisation that mangroves are associated with tropical coastlines. While it is certainly true that the greatest species diversity and most luxuriant mangroves are to be found along moist, warm coastlines, two species, *Avicennia marina* and *Aegicerus corniculatum,* extend well into temperate zones. In the northern hemisphere the extension beyond the tropics is somewhat less than in the southern hemisphere, but nevertheless reports indicate the extremes of 35°N at the south end of Kyushu island (Macnae, 1968) and to 32°N in Bermuda (Walter, 1971). The furthest spread in the southern hemisphere is related to the more southerly coastal areas that are available in Australia and New Zealand, at about 38°S. Whatever the definition of 'tropical' may be, clearly mangroves are not limited to such areas.

The one single factor that can be used to relate these distributional patterns is temperature. The literature lacks precise information on critical temperature thresholds. An upper threshold does not appear to be relevant. McMillan (1971) refers to seedlings being killed by 48 hours continuous exposure under experimental conditions at temperatures of 39-40°C. It is hard to envisage such conditions occurring with any frequency in coastal locations under mangrove shade for such a continuous period even in the hot arid subtropics, although in northern Queensland, leaves exposed to the sun may reach temperatures of 35-40°C for at least part of the day (B. F. Clough, personal communication 1979). Clough *et al.* (this volume) observed that leaf temperature is a key variable governing the photosynthetic physiology of mangrove leaves, with optimum leaf temperatures for photosynthesis well below 35°C.

A number of conflicting comments appear in different sources on the effect of minimum temperatures. West (1956) suggested that a coldest month mean temperature of over 20°C and an annual range of under 5°C provide the most suitable conditions for mangroves. While the number of species and their vigour of growth declines towards the colder limits of the distribution range, 'there is little in our current knowledge about the physiology of mangroves that helps explain their climatic distribution, particularly their absence from colder coastlines and their failure to adapt to frost' (Clough *et al.,* this volume).

The lower temperature threshold appears to lie within the range -4°C (Chapman, 1976, p. 222) to about +4°C (Macnae, 1968). Based on the Melbourne temperature record Macnae (1968) considers the latter threshold to apply to the southernmost extension of mangroves in Australia. He observes that the Melbourne absolute minimum is 0°C (the mean daily minimum for the coldest month is over 4°C; about 10 frosts occur each year). It is not certain whether the lower temperature threshold for mangroves is due to temperature *per se* or to the greater incidence of frost at the latitudinal extremes of their distribution. Walter (1971, p. 161) states that frost is an inhibiting condition and with reference to New Zealand noted that air temperatures below -2°C once in 5-10 years will act as a lower threshold. Walter (1977, p. 65) also suggests that the high salt concentration of the cell sap in *Avicennia* may afford this species some resistance to frost. Saenger (this volume) and Bird and Barson (this volume) have additional comments on the significance of frost.

Table 2.1 represents for selected Australian stations the pattern of maximum and minimum sea temperatures and compares them with air temperatures (Chapman, 1977). It should be observed here that many of the values quoted in the literature appear to be derived from the nearest official weather station. Quite apart from the fact that they will have been recorded in a Stevenson, or

Table 2.1   Selected climatic data for some coastal sites in Australia. Shown here are mean winter and summer sea surface temperatures and their departures from July (winter) and January (summer) mean air temperatures. The days of frost below 0° and between 0 and 2°C are also shown. All temperatures are °C.

	Sea surface temperatures		Departures from mean air temperatures		Frost days	
	Winter	Summer	Winter	Summer	<0°	0-2°C
Bunbury	17	20	+4	−1		
Geraldton	19	22	+4	−2		
Carnarvon	21	26	+4	−1		
Onslow	21	27	+3	−3		
Port Hedland	22	29	+2	−2		
Broome	23	29	+2	−1		
Derby	24	29	+2	−1		
Wyndham	23	28	−1	−3		
Darwin	25	28	0	−1		
Cape Don	25	28	+1	0		
Millingimbi	25	28	+1	0		
Gove	25	29	+1	+1		
Karumba	23	30	+1	0		
Weipa	26	30	+1	+1		
Thursday Is	24	29	+1	+1		
Cooktown	23	28	+1	0		
Cairns	22	28	+1	0		
Lucinda	22	27	+3	0		
Townsville	22	27	+2	−1		
Mackay	21	27	+4	0		0.8
Gladstone	20	26	+3	0		
Bundaberg	20	26	+4	0		
Brisbane	19	25	+4	0		
Coffs Harbour	18	23	+4	0	0.4	3.5
Newcastle	17	22	+4	0		
Sydney	17	22	+5	0		0.2
Westernport Bay (Stoney Point)	14	17	+4	−1	1.2	6.5
Port Lincoln	14	19	+2	−1		
Adelaide (Outer Harbour)	13	19	+1	−4		0.3

similar, screen, such weather stations are selected to be generally representative of the regional climate of the area in which they are located. As far as possible local climatic influences are avoided. It has yet to be determined what sort of weight should be given to air, water, mud or leaf temperature when examining the significance of temperature. The deficiency of data mentioned with respect to relevant air temperature records becomes much more acute when one's concern is with near-shore or within mangrove water temperatures, and information is virtually non-existent, outside of a few research based measurements, in the case of leaf and mud temperatures.

Mangrove communities grow, however, in a specifically local climate which incorporates the interface between a water surface and a land area. There is a marked temperature gradient over the zone from low water mark to a few hundred metres inland. As well as temperature, humidity, wind force and even radiation can change quite abruptly over this zone. Kenny (1974) has provided an interesting illustration of the way in which inshore shallow water temperatures vary. Air affecting a tropical coastal fringe, especially its intertidal zone, will be strongly influenced by the temperatures over the adjacent water. Table 2.2 summarises some of the available information which demonstrates the difference between the records taken of seawater temperatures, and the air temperature monthly means at the Garbutt weather station, Townsville, approximately 2700 metres away from the nearest shoreline.

It seems probable that most of the thermal correlations made are misleading because data are not available for the near coastal strip. It is to be expected that temperature range will be significantly less on the coastal fringe since the maxima will be lower and the minima higher. Especially in temperate areas and the poleward part of the subtropics, air mass temperatures can play a greater part in influencing the coastal fringes and thus partially obscure local influences on the temperature. If frost is a critical factor, are we dealing with air-frost (minima at or below $0°C$ in the screen) or ground frost when $2.2°C$ or below is conventionally assumed to be the threshold? So far as I am aware, nothing like a statement, 'so many hours consistently below a given minimum threshold' is available. What sort of index should we be seeking? Specific values such as mean or absolute minima may be far less indicative than accumulated values below (or in the case of growth periods, above) a threshold. There is no information on whether persistence or spells of particular values are of importance. Frequencies may be far more useful than averages. The problem becomes even more serious if there are considerable differences in behaviour and location of individual species.

Radiation, total or net solar radiation, or sunshine could be related to broad distribution patterns, but have not been closely examined in this context. More knowledge is required on the photosynthetic responses to the quality and amounts of radiation. Clough and Attiwill (this volume) point out the marked seasonal fluctuations in mangrove production. Sunshine totals differ considerably with latitude and regional cloud tendencies. Adelaide (dry season) with a January sunshine average of 10.0 hours per day can be compared with

Table 2.2   Comparison of sea and air temperature at Townsville (°C)

	J	F	M	A	M	J
Sea temperatures						
a) Absolute maximum*	32.4	31.9	31.4	29.8	26.5	23.7
b) Absolute minimum*	29.6	28.2	17.1	24.8	24.2	19.3
c) Mean*	31.2	30.5	28.8	26.9	25.4	22.1
Air temperatures Garbutt						
d) Mean[†]	27.6	27.4	26.8	25.4	22.9	20.9
e) Average minimum	24.5	24.2	23.3	21.4	18.5	16.6
f) Absolute minimum	18.7	17.9	16.7	11.7	6.2	4.5

	J	A	S	O	N	D
Sea temperatures						
a) Absolute maximum*	23.8	24.8	27.6	28.8	30.6	31.2
b) Absolute minimum*	20.4	20.6	23.1	25.2	25.7	27.6
c) Mean*	21.8	22.7	24.2	26.7	28.6	29.5
Air temperatures Garbutt						
d) Mean[†]	19.9	20.8	22.8	24.9	26.4	27.4
e) Average minimum	15.4	16.4	18.8	21.4	23.2	24.2
f) Absolute minimum	3.7	1.1	8.4	8.2	15.9	18.7

Notes: *   Sea temperatures were taken at the seaward end of the eastern breakwater of Townsville harbour over approximately 4 annual periods 1961-2, 1966-67, 1968-69 and 1971. 212 observations.

   [†]   The Garbutt values are from the standard Stevenson screen for the period 1926-65.

Darwin's 6.1 hours (wet season). However, in Adelaide's wet season the daily average value has dropped to 4.3 hours in July whilst Darwin (dry season) has recovered to a day average of 9.8 hours. It is hard to see a great deal of detailed progress being made in this direction, not least because of the lack of sufficient accurate information for coastal areas. The problem of insufficiency of long records of temperature for coastal margins is acute enough, these other parameters are even more sparse and fragmentary. The remarks made so far apply to air temperatures (or possible surrogates). No discussion has been offered about soil or water temperatures since I am not aware of any detailed inquiry into these aspects.

The broad distribution is not explained by rainfall distribution though this is not so when variations within the overall distribution are examined. Davis (1940) found no significant correlations between mangrove growth and annual and seasonal precipitation in Florida. Mangroves can be found on very humid and very arid coasts. Most authorities when considering the relevance of rainfall suggest that the most favourable conditions are those of well distributed and plentiful rainfall (Galloway, this volume), though, since mangroves grow under and are adapted to varying degrees of physiological drought, there is not a simple relationship between rainfall and distribution.

Shelter has often been emphasised as an important factor influencing distribution. The requirement for sheltered coasts also tends to be relevant at the next scale of analysis, though it can be observed that the easterlies of the tropics and their sub-tropical margins tend to be more constant and have higher average speeds than the westerlies of middle latitude. On the other hand middle latitude circulations, though less steady, have a higher energy potential than the low latitudes except at the time of such extreme though infrequent events as tropical cyclones. The wind parameter certainly is important for the differentiation between sheltered and exposed sections of the coast.

Meso-scale climatic variations
In this part of the discussion the emphasis is upon the factors and processes which contribute to the location of mangrove communities along some coasts and not others, or which result in varying degrees of impoverishment of the species making up a community.

Shelter
Mangroves are best suited to low energy coastal locations. Wind has several separate effects. Coastal water drift and tidal currents will be modified by wind directions and speed. Wave action is accentuated, especially at high tide, by stormy conditions. This wave action may cause undermining of the roots of mangroves. Both waves and water movements affect sediment transport, and strong onshore winds can cause greater penetration of waves and the deposition of sediment in or even, with extremely stormy weather, beyond the mangrove fringe. Stormy weather may drown the pneumatophores with sediment, but it was observed by Jennings and Coventry (1973) that, in the Fitzroy estuary where dune movement had overtopped the mangrove, it was still able to grow through 0.5 to 1.0 m of sand and gravel. Not all transports of sediment are unfavourable. For example, in Cairns Bay at the time of high spring tides, strong wave action deposits mud on flats adjacent to the existing mangroves which are then able to colonise them (Bird, 1972).

Deflation and deposition of sediment by wind may occur in very arid climates, or in periods when the coastal land surface dries out. Wind has a major part to play in causing evaporation and in the concentration of saline solutions. As well, it can cause physical damage to leaves, desiccate the foliage, and it may also influence the dispersal of seeds and hypocotyls.

Problems arise also with respect to the wind data available. Rarely, except over short periods of investigation, are those data recorded which directly relate to the local environment. General wind records at official weather stations are, in the majority of cases, for stations some kilometres at least away from the coast. The standard height of the anemometer is 10 in above ground surface, and, though theoretically it would be possible to make a partial correction to provide the wind at the canopy height, it would not be feasible to correct for local site roughness — especially in trying to evaluate the shelter at a particular locality. Variations in the growth habit of the community progressively change the shelter effect. Within the trunk space of the mangroves, shelter reduces wind speeds markedly and in most instances velocities decline below the levels at which physical damage is caused, while evapotranspiration losses are also minimised. Both horizontal and vertical wind components are of interest, and, if available, data on the extent of turbulence and gustiness would be useful. Much of this information is not available from a standard record. Often the horizontal wind information desirable is that for the dominant wind, i.e. that having the most influence on the growth conditions rather than the 8 or 16 points of the compass which are usually tabulated.

Exposure modifies the wind experience at particular sites. Lagoons, deltas, estuaries, tidal inlets, areas on the leeward side of shielding headlands or of islands or coastal orientations which cause the dominant winds to blow parallel or almost so to the coast offer favourable situations for the establishment of mangroves, as for example in Cairns Bay (Bird, 1972). Off-shore reefs, whilst not protecting the mainland coast from strong winds, have an important quietening influence, by reducing wave and wind fetch on wave action or tidal drifts. From this point of view the Great Barrier Reef plays a more effective part north of Cairns where it approaches closer to the coast. Lack of sheltered sites may be one reason for the absence of mangroves from more exposed parts of north-west and western coasts of Australia.

The ability of mangroves to withstand the infrequent but none the less very high energy winds generated by tropical cyclones has been commented on by Jennings and Coventry (1973), Stoddart (1962) and Chapman (1976). Though the frequency of such events at any one coastal location might be once in twenty or thirty years or more the rate of mangrove recovery is usually sufficient to enable even badly devastated stretches to recover before the next major storm. Whilst tropical cyclones do not usually determine the long-term pattern of colonisation they may affect the shorter-term fortunes of a mangrove community. Comments by Jennings and Coventry (1973) and Chapman (1976) on the considerable capacity of *Rhizophora* to withstand hurricanes seem to be at variance with the observation by Spenceley (1976) that *Rhizophora* suffered more than other species from tropical cyclone Althea which struck Townsville in 1971 (see also Hopley, 1974).

There seems little doubt that mangroves reduce the regression of coastlines under the onslaught of cyclonic winds, waves and even storm surges. There is more debate as to whether, after the storm, some individual trees at least suffered die-back from the damage they endured, including the erosion of sediments from around their roots. Just what wind velocity represents a critical damaging threshold is uncertain. When the effect is primarily a desiccating one then the combination of dry warm winds of continental origin and high velocities is involved. Australian coasts do not suffer on mangrove sectors from cold dry air-masses. The significance of excessive transpiration has not, so far as is known, been made the subject of a detailed inquiry, though it would add additional stress if the mangroves were growing at near the upper limits of salinity tolerance.

Salinity and evaporation In tidally inundated situations the frequency of flooding and evaporative losses are major factors determining soil salinity. Climatic factors such as humidity, wind velocity and high solar irradiance, together with the degree of plant cover, have a significant influence on evaporative losses from the mangrove environment. The most severe conditions characterise the arid or semi-arid seasonal rainfall climates of the subtropics and tropical margins. The inland margin of the mangroves is particularly prone to high evaporation losses and the drying out of saline stream discharges. In the humid tropics, rain wetting of leaf surfaces, cloud cover and high humidities will reduce the evaporative losses. The trade wind coasts, especially when the trade wind inversion is well developed, can experience quite strong and persistent winds from the south-east, sometimes accentuated in the day by sea-breeze effects. On the one hand they will pick up moisture according to the length of their track across the warm oceans. On the other hand they are least likely to be disturbed by rain producing perturbations in the winter months when lower air temperatures make the rainfall more effective and reduce evapotranspirative losses.

The sea surface is usually dynamically less mechanically and thermally rough so that wind speeds are greater than over the land. As winds flow from the sea across the shoreline the frictional drag of the changed nature of the surface reduces wind speeds, but this is a progressive process so that the mangrove zone tends to experience the speeds characteristic of the winds over the sea. Recording stations are often on the landward side of this sharp change in wind speeds from sea to land.

Salinities will also be affected by the amount of rainfall and the surface or through-flow of freshwater which can leach excess salts from the soil and discharge them out to sea. This aspect will be considered later.

Moisture supply The supply of moisture in the mangrove environment is influenced by rainfall, surface or through-flow of water on land and tidal flooding.

In terms of rainfall distribution, mangroves can be found over the whole range of rainfall conditions from desert to humid equatorial regimes, though the freshwater supply is restricted. Walter (1977, p. 65) suggests that rainfall conditions have an effect on the sequence of zones in the tidal region. *Rhizophora apiculata* seems to prefer a plentiful source of lower salinity groundwater, whereas other species like *Ceriops* spp. thrive better where land sources of water are available and they become stunted in drier (but more saline) environments. Where rainfall is well distributed and plentiful the number of species increases and zonation is better developed. This is apparent between Cardwell and Mossman on the north-eastern coastline of Queensland, where rainfall exceeds 2000 mm per annum and in places reaches double that amount. It also happens to be favoured by fertile soils derived from basalt lavas. The relative importance of rainfall and soil fertility has not been determined. The flushing effect, in this case, of the heavy rain keeps salinity in check, and bare salt flats on the landward margins of the mangrove are absent so that the vegetation change to the rainforest is sharp. Where the rain flushing is infrequent and short-lived, salts may still remain in the sub-surface layers into which the water does not have time to infiltrate. Strongly seasonal patterns of rainfall, even if considerable, permit bare hypersaline landward salt flats to become established as, for example, in north-eastern Queensland.

Freshwater discharges down the river estuaries, sometimes drawn from wetter catchments than the coastal rainfall would indicate, or through the different distributaries in the case of a delta, or through seepages which often come out just above or at mean sea level, can provide large volumes of freshwater which mixes at or near river mouths, modifying the tidal salinity. When heavy rains occur (for example in the rain depression stage of a tropical cyclone) large discharge volumes can greatly reduce the surface salinity up to a few kilometres offshore. These events are infrequent and short lived and seem unlikely to affect mangrove growth or location except through erosion or deposition of alluvial material. However, persistent freshwater inputs may influence the structure and ecology of mangrove communities which fringe channels and creeks.

A feature of subtropical rainfall is its high variability from year to year or even in its distribution within the rainy season, giving rise to parallel variations in salinity over the same time scale. Where rainfall, as distinct from tidal flooding, affects the height of the water table, this too will fluctuate in harmony with the rainfall pattern.

Local and microclimates
Although the line between some local climatic and meso-climatic contrasts is not clear cut, the question arises as to how far climatic conditions will have unique qualities which influence mangrove growth and location in particular areas. Unfortunately, suitable climatic data are generally lacking and standard meteorological records provide little guidance. For reliable results the period of special climatic records should cover at least a number of seasons in the case of local climatic investigations, though short period monitoring may meet the needs of a true microclimatic study. Few detailed climatic surveys of this sort are available to fill the gap. Far more work has been put into the monitoring of the changes in soil or water chemistry than into atmospheric sounding.

At a finer scale, 'mangrove forest expression and the dependent ecology is likely to be heavily influenced by local weather patterns, especially in concert with tidal movements' (Bunt, 1978). Weather patterns on this scale would require the detailed logging of short-term events within a wider framework of synoptic meteorology. The precise nature of the association between weather patterns and their ecological consequences also requires identification. In particular far more information is needed about the tolerance limits of individual species and whether being near the tolerance limits means that the plants are more susceptible to brief but marked climatic abnormalities. Tidal movements might well be understood much better within the framework of a detailed reconstruction of the wind field. The degree of gustiness and the strength of the tendencies to turbulence and instability may also be important. Some of the other weather sensitive relationships have hardly been explored yet. Ecologists have still to define what weather, as distinct from climatic, events are important.

Some basic concepts can be transferred from other studies of plant climates. The interior trunk space climate of other tree communities has been found by a number of investigators to differ from the climate outside the canopy. It is certain that within this part of a well developed mangrove community evaporation is reduced, specific and relative humidity are high, wind velocities are greatly reduced and so is turbulent flow. Not only is the radiation received much less, but the wavelengths of light of which it is comprised are different. Temperature variations are much less, whilst the overall average temperature is usually slightly decreased in the tropics. Rainfall is evaporated more readily from the canopy surface and plays a limited part in the rest of the ecological processes. Through-fall and stem flow modify the distribution of the rainfall at ground level. Few of these remarks can be supported quantitatively with respect to the mangrove environment, and even more serious is the fact that it is extremely difficult to incorporate these factors into ecological interpretations. It should be appreciated, however, that severe limitations are placed upon our understanding of the microclimate of mangrove communities by lack of data.

Shade is an important factor in the regeneration of mangroves.Seedlings of different mangrove species have different preferences for shade in their early period of establishment (Macnae, 1968; Wells, this volume; Saenger, this volume) and these may well differ from the requirements of the mature tree. These preferences for shaded or sunny sites may lead to changes in species composition following disruption of the canopy by storms, human activity or tree death. Breaks in the canopy can also result in a sharp increase in the ground level evaporation in the disturbed area (cf. Clarke and Hannon, 1969).

In the earlier part of their life cycle mangroves like other plants may be more sensitive to spells of unfavourable weather and less able to sustain themselves, for example, over dry periods which would hardly check mature trees. The early competition between seedlings takes place in a microclimate to which the whole community contributes and which is unlike many aspects of the regional climate.

Direct and indirect climatic effects
Figure 2.1 attempts to summarise the linkages between different factors in the mangrove community and has been slightly modified from that in Clarke and Hannon's paper (1969, p. 214).

The ecological system is characterised by a number of feedback loops. Establishment of a mature well developed community has modifying influences upon the very climatic, and other, factors which caused the initial

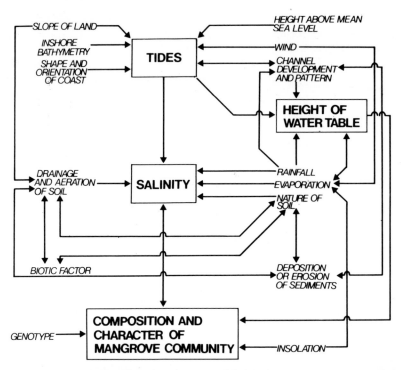

Fig. 2.1. Interrelationships of environmental factors in a mangrove community

development. It is not appropriate here to pursue this topic further, but climate has many indirect effects upon mangrove communities, particularly through its influence upon the nature and scale of operation of geomorphic processes as well as in the complex relationships associated with soil chemistry.

A representation such as Figure 2.1 is a good start for the identification of broad connections between parts of the ecosystem. It may, however, underplay the range of sensitivities and tolerances to climate of particular species and overstress the apparent similarities in the response of different mangrove communities to their environment.

Conclusion

This survey suggests the need for improved collection and availability of data which relate more specifically to the actual mangrove habitats in order to identify and to evaluate the direct and indirect effects of different climatic parameters. It is suggested that the climatic components of the environment could contribute, more than has been done so far, to an improved understanding of the environmental interrelationship, especially when the detailed analysis of the characteristics of a community is being undertaken.

References

Bird, E.C.F., 1972. Mangroves and coastal geomorphology in Cairns Bay, north Queensland. *Journal of Tropical Geography* **35**, 11-16.

Bunt, J.S., 1978. The mangroves of the eastern coast of Cape York Peninsula north of Cooktown. Paper delivered at the Workshop on the Northern Sector, Great Barrier Reef Marine Park Authority, Townsville.

Chapman, V.J., 1976. *Coastal Vegetation.* 2nd ed., Pergamon, Oxford, pp. 217-33.

Chapman, V.J. (ed.) 1977. *Ecosystems of the World. I. Wet Coastal Systems.* Elsevier, Amsterdam.

Clarke, L.D. and N.J. Hannon, 1969. The mangrove swamp and salt marsh community of the Sydney district. II. The holocoenotic complex with particular reference to physiography. *Journal of Ecology* **57**, 213-34.

Davis, J.H., 1940. The ecology and geologic role of mangroves in Florida. *Papers Tortugas Laboratory* **32**, 303-412.

Hopley, D., 1974. Coastal changes produced by tropical cyclone Althea in Queensland, December 1971. *Australian Geographical Studies* **12**, 445-56.

Jennings, J.N. and B.J. Coventry, 1973. Structure and texture of a gravelly barrier island in the Fitzroy Estuary, WA and the role of mangroves in shore dynamics. *Marine Geology* **15**, 145-67.

Kenny, R., 1974. Inshore surface sea temperatures at Townsville. *Australian Journal of Marine and Freshwater Research* **25**, 1-5.

McMillan, C., 1971. Environmental factors affecting seedling establishment of the black mangrove on the central Texas coast. *Ecology* **52**, 927-30.

Macnae, W., 1966. Mangroves in eastern and southern Australia. *Australian Journal of Botany* **14**, 67-104.

Macnae, W., 1968. A general account of the fauna and flora of mangrove swamps and forests in the Indo-West Pacific Region. *Advances in Marine Biology* **6**, 73-270.

Richards, P.W., 1952. *The Tropical Rainforest: An Ecological Study.* Cambridge University Press. 450 pp.

Spenceley, A.P., 1976. Unvegetated saline tidal flats in north Queensland. *Journal of Tropical Geography* **42**, 78-85.

Stoddart, D.R., 1962. Catastrophic storm effects in the British Honduras reefs and cays. *Nature (Lond.)*, **196**, 512-15.

Thom, B.G., 1967. Mangrove ecology and deltaic geomorphology. Tabasco, Mexico. *Journal of Ecology* **55**, 301-43.

Thom, B.G., L.D. Wright and J.M. Coleman, 1975. Mangrove ecology and deltaic-estuarine geomorphology: Cambridge Gulf-Ord River, Western Australia. *Journal of Ecology* **63**, 203-32.

Walsh, G.E., 1974. Mangroves: a review. In R.J. Reimold and W.H. Queen (eds.), *Ecology of Halophytes.* Academic Press, New York, pp. 51-174.

Walter, H., 1971. *Ecology of Tropical and Sub-Tropical Vegetation.* Oliver and Boyd, Edinburgh. 539 pp.

Walter, H., 1977. Climate. In V.J. Chapman (ed.), *Ecosystems of the World. I. Wet Coastal Systems.* Elsevier, Amsterdam, pp. 61-7.

West, R.C., 1956. Mangrove swamps of the Pacific coast of Columbia. *Annals of the Association of American Geographers* **46**, 98-121.

3

Distribution and Physiographic Patterns of Australian Mangroves

R. W. Galloway

Introduction

Existing accounts of mangrove distribution over extensive portions of the Australian coast include publications by Macnae (1966), Butler *et al.* (1977), Lear and Turner (1977), Saenger *et al.* (1977), Semeniuk *et al.* (1978), Wells (this volume), Dowling and McDonald (this volume) and Kenneally (this volume). There are also numerous local studies such as those by Bird (1972) and Graham *et al.* (1975) of mangroves near Cairns. The present study seeks to give a continent-wide view of mangrove distribution with emphasis on the general patterns rather than on individual taxa.

This chapter is based on an inventory of Australia's coastal lands in which the geology, landforms, vegetation, land use and population of a coastal strip 3 km wide have been examined. A dot grid with one dot per km^2 was used to measure the extent of mangroves on the mainland, which was defined to include islands less than 1 km offshore such as Curtis Island in Queensland; mangrove areas on more distant islands were estimated from maps and air photos. A complete cover of black-and-white air photographs, mostly at a scale of *c.* 1:85,000, was used to study the mangrove patterns.

Extent of mangroves

In round numbers mangroves cover 11,500 km^2 of the costal zone—nearly three million acres (Table 3.1). Ninety-five per cent lie in tropical Australia and 11 per cent on islands more than 1 km offshore. The total length of mainland coast fringed by mangrove is 6000 km. Island mangrove fringes would probably amount to a further 1000 km. The fringes range from narrow strips one or two trees wide to belts of several kilometres. If the mangroves that edge inshore waters were included the total length of coast with a mangrove fringe would of course be much greater.

Factors affecting mangrove distribution and patterns

Mangroves exist on most coasts except those of Tasmania and southern Western Australia; over such a vast area habitat factors and the resulting pattern may vary enormously. Habitat factors affecting mangrove distribution include climate, water temperature, sedimentation, tides, relief, shelter from wave attack, salinity and geological history.

Australian coastal environments can be divided into a tropical region north of the line joining Northwest Cape to Fraser Island and a warm temperate region to the south (Davies, 1977). The tropical coasts are mesotidal (mean spring tide range 2-4 m) or macrotidal (over 4 m), have relatively low wave energies except in

Table 3.1   Area of mangroves in each state (km²)

Queensland mainland*	4410
Queensland islands †	192
Northern Territory mainland*	3138
Northern Territory islands†	981
Western Australia mainland*	2430
Western Australis islands†	87
South Australia mainland*	195
South Australia islands †	6
New South Wales	99
Victoria	12
Total	11 550
Area in tropical Australia north of Northwest Cape-Fraser Island line	11 175

*Mainland includes all islands less than 1 km offshore.
†Estimates for islands less accurate than for mainland.

occasional cyclones, extensive intertidal flats and abundant inputs of fine sediment. The warm temperate coasts are microtidal with high wave energies, relatively steep intertidal slopes and limited input of fine sediments.

Climate
Mangroves develop best in warm to tropical climates even though some species extend into warm temperate regions. Most Australian mangroves occur on tropical coasts where size and species diversity correlate broadly with rainfall (Macnae, 1966); however, mangroves are not excluded by climate from even the driest localities. The largest number of species (nearly 30; Lear and Turner, 1977) occurs in the wet Ingham to Innisfail region of northern Queensland and the most extensive occurrences are on the tropical east coast of Cape York Peninsula, on islands adjacent to New Guinea, on Melville Island, in Van Diemen Gulf and along the well watered northern fringe of Arnhem Land. Species diversity and size decrease notably in temperate Australia until at the poleward limit in Victoria only shrubs of *A vicennia marina* (Forsk.) Vierh. exist. Frost is believed to be a factor in determing the poleward limit (Chapman, 1977).

Water temperature
Mean annual sea temperatures in tropical Australia are 24-29°C with annual ranges 6-8°C (Radok, 1976). At the poleward limit of mangroves open sea temperatures are substantially lower and air temperatures differ from one side of the continent to the other especially in winter (Chapman, 1977; Oliver, this

volume). However, summer temperatures of inshore waters in temperate Australia where the mangroves actually grow exceed those of the open sea and approach the tropical mean annual temperatures quoted above. Preliminary studies indicate that the poleward limit corresponds to peak monthly inshore water temperatures of about 21°C (Table 3.2). Thus in southern Australia the restriction of mangroves to sheltered inlets may reflect not only protection from wave attack but also the warmer water in summer compared to that on open coasts.

Table 3.2   Approximate summer surface water temperatures near the southern limit of mangroves in Australia (°C)

(a) Inshore waters with mangroves	
Clyde estuary, N.S.W.*	24-26
Moruya estuary, N.S.W.*	22-23
Westernport Bay, Victoria[†]	22
(b) Offshore waters[‡]	
Eden, N.S.W.	20-21
Queenscliff, Victoria	18-19
Port Lincoln, S.A.	18-19
Thevenard, S.A.	20
Albany, W.A.	21
Fremantle, W.A.	22

*   Unpublished data from Division of Land Use Research, CSIRO.
[†]   Unpublished data from Westernport Bay Environmental Study.
[‡]   From Radok (1976).

Sediments
Although poor stands of the hardier species can grow on gravelly or even rocky shores such occurrences are minor exceptions and soft, generally fine-grained substrates are necessary for proper mangrove development. Suitable sediments are much commoner in tropical Australia because of the relatively large silt load of the rivers and the moderate wave climates which reduce dispersion.

Establishment requires suitable sediment surfaces no lower than approximately mid-tide level. Obviously the area of mangroves is likely to be expanded where intertidal sedimentation rates are high — notably in estuaries and deltas. Once established, mangroves encourage further sedimentation leading to site modification, species succession and eventually the creation of supratidal surfaces too high for mangroves.

Tides and relief
Mangroves grow between mid tide and high tide levels and the tidal range in association with the intertidal slope determines their potential extent. The high tidal range and generally low intertidal slopes of tropical Australia offer larger sites than the steep, microtidal coasts to the south. Undoubtedly species

zonation within a mangrove is intimately related to the duration of tidal flooding and so to the tidal range, slope and altitude of the site (Macnae, 1966).

However, tidal range does not by itself determine mangrove patterns since similar features can occur in micro-, meso- and macrotidal environments and mangroves can even exist in totally atidal inland situations (Beard, 1967).

Shelter from waves

Even in the relatively low wave energy environments of tropical Australia shelter is essential for full mangrove development. It prevents waves from damaging the plants or eroding the substrate on which they grow and encourages deposition of fine sediments. Only in really sheltered situations do mangroves extend right to the open water; usually a wave-built barrier lies between them and the open sea. In most embayments in tropical Australia beach ridges are on the seaward side of the mangroves in exposed bay mouths but lie within or behind them in the more sheltered sites within the bay, and may even be absent entirely at the bay heads.

In places mangroves are colonising tidal flats in front of beach ridges, which implies that wave energies have been less in recent decades. However, there must be uncertainty about making such a deduction from air photo evidence alone since waves can sweep through mangroves, pile sand on ridges well back from the seaward edge and even drive shingle beds through them provided the roots are not seriously disturbed (Ward, 1967; Jennings and Coventry, 1973; Hopley, 1974; Thom *et al.*, 1975).

The intricate coasts of northern Australia offer many more favourable sheltered sites for mangroves than do the less indented coasts to the south. Furthermore, coral reefs and constructional features derived therefrom provide shelter on atolls and round islands and headlands. While the Great Barrier Reef certainly reduces the force of the Pacific surf it lies sufficiently far offshore to provide only limited shelter for mangroves on the east coast.

Salinity

Mangroves are usually regarded as facultative rather than obligate halophytes and salinity favours them by excluding competition. However, too high a salinity kills them. *Avicennia marina* can tolerate up to 90 parts salt per thousand in the groundwater (Macnae, 1968) but this corresponds to lower salinity in the tidal water. In Shark Bay, north-western Australia, mangroves die out where sea salinity is only 50 parts per thousand because salinities in the mud are substantially higher (Davies, 1970). Dying mangroves occur around bare areas in tropical regions of strong evaporation. In such areas particularly high groundwater salinities exist (Macnae, 1966; Spenceley, 1976). Absence of bare areas in especially high rainfall localities probably results from leaching of the salt by rainwater. However, high evaporation does not adequately explain all bare areas in mangrove zones: evaporation in the dry summers of South Australia is high yet bare areas are rare within the mangroves of that State.

Geological history
Even during the last 6000-7000 years when sea level has lain close to its present position, geological events must have had significant effects on mangroves. In particular, changes in the relative altitude of land and sea, whether caused by tectonism, sea-level fluctuations, changes in tidal range, compaction of sediments, erosion or deposition would have affected mangroves. Likewise even modest climatic changes could have had major effects on the extent and luxuriance of mangroves (Jennings, 1975). However, since mangrove patterns are themselves used as evidence for such changes, caution is needed to avoid circular arguments in a study such as this which is not based on detailed field work.

Regional description of mangroves
For convenience in description mangroves can be grouped into regions in which the patterns derive some unity from environmental factors. Many regional schemes could be erected according to the level of detail required; for the present study twenty-six regions have been recognised. These regions are meant to group extensive areas with similar patterns related to broadly homogeneous environments, but considerations of scale have meant considerable lumping of different types as on the coast of Arnhem Land for example. The distribution of the twenty-six regions is shown on Fig. 3.1 and some of the more important patterns are illustrated in the plates. Since patterns can recur in several localities there is some duplication in the following descriptions. Approximate areas of mangrove in each region are listed in Table 3.3. Changes in mangrove area are only impressions derived from the air photos and at this stage no rates of change can be determined.

1. Northwest Cape to Cape Keraudren
    This extensive region is mainly a flat depositional plain, 12-15 km wide in the south decreasing to 2-3 km in the north-east, sandy and silty near the major rivers such as the Ashburton and finer-textured elsewhere. Northwest Cape, the rocky peninsula at Dampier, numerous islands, reefs and aeolianite barriers combine to shelter most of the coast from onshore waves. Spring tidal ranges are 2-3 m and although cyclonic winds occasionally drive seawater far inland most of the plain is supratidal with sparse saltmarsh vegetation.
    Mangrove occurs as a fringe up to 5 km wide in the particularly sheltered waters of Exmouth Gulf where it grows right to the water's edge on the eastern coast and seems to be advancing slowly. The western coast of the Gulf experiences quite strong wave action at times of easterly winds and has no mangrove. North-eastwards, as exposure increases and the coastal plain steepens, the mangrove zone narrows and becomes confined to sites behind protective barriers such as beach ridges. They do not penetrate up the main rivers which are tidal only for very short distances and dry for most of the year but they do fringe short tidal creeks dissecting seaward parts of the coastal plain. A very narrow belt of mangroves fringes rocky shores in the Dampier Archipelago.

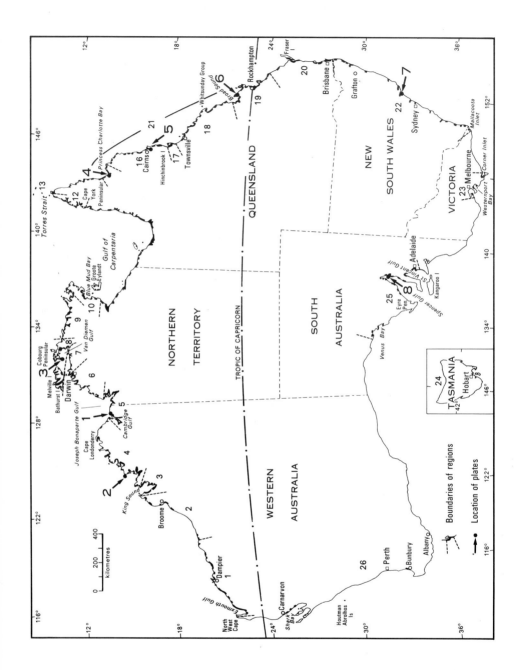

Fig. 3.1.   Distribution of mangroves and coastal regions as described in text

Table 3.3   Areas of mangroves in coastal regions (km²)

Region No.	Location	Area
1	Northwest Cape to Cape Keraudren	597
2	Cape Keraudren to Cape Leveque	117
3	Cape Leveque to Point Usborne	285
4	Point Usborne to Cape Dussejour	1064
5	Cape Dussejour to Pearce Point	847
6	Pearce Point to Cape Hotham	1269
7	Cape Hotham to Wangarlu Bay	486
8	Wangarlu Bay to Macquarie Strait (includes Melville and Bathurst Islands)	692
9	Macquarie Strait to Cape Wilberforce	913
10	Cape Wilberforce to Rose River	239
11	Rose River to Aurukun	1593
12	Aurukun to Cape York	609
13	Islands in Torres Strait	158
14	Cape York to Evanson Point	354
15	Evanson Point to Bathurst Head (Princess Charlotte Bay)	93
16	Bathurst Head to Cardwell	243
17	Cardwell to Port Hinchinbrook	216
18	Port Hinchinbrook to Clairview Bluff	645
19	Clairview Bluff to Bustard Head	498
20	Bustard Head to Tweed Heads	285
21	Islands off Queensland east coast	20
22	New South Wales	99
23	Victoria	12
24	Tasmania	0
25	South Australia	201
26	South and west coasts of Western Australia	15
	Total	11 550

2. Cape Keraudren to Cape Leveque

This exposed, sandy coast receives little sediment from the land and consists of almost continuous sand barriers or low cliffs. Tidal range increases northwards along the coast attaining 7 m (springs) at Broome. Mangrove reaches the coast only in the sheltered waters of Roebuck Bay and even there shows signs of wave damage. In the northern half of the region patches of mangrove lie around minor tidal creeks protected by strongly developed sand barriers. Behind the barriers there are fairly extensive salt flats and plains seamed by former tidal channels which look as if they once had mangrove fringes. Their abandonment may be due to recent uplift, to sedimentation or to alterations in the tidal prism induced by coastal changes. Within this region the area of mangroves is shrinking.

Plate 3.1.   Tropical deltaic pattern; false mouths of the Ord River, W.A.
             (1) Bare supratidal flats or saltmarsh
             (2) Main tidal channel with continuous mangrove fringe
             (3) Tidal creeks with narrow mangrove fringe
             (4) More extensive mangroves in low back swamps where sedimentation
                  is slower
             (5) Islands subject to rapid changes in area and in mangrove cover

3. Cape Leveque to Point Usborne

This region encompasses the sheltered coasts of King Sound where rivers bring in abundant fine sediment from the south and east and where spring tidal ranges exceed 10 m. The western shore of King Sound, with little sediment input, has only a narrow mangrove fringe that widens locally at valley mouths. The eastern and southern coasts consist of extensive deltas that mostly form bare supratidal flats occasionally covered by high spring tides. These flats are traversed by major estuarine channels and seamed by dendritic tidal creeks. In the major channels tidal erosion and deposition induce rapid changes in the extent of intertidal land and so of mangroves; in the tidal creeks headward extension (Jennings, 1975) may be accompanied by landward colonisation of mangroves. At the seaward margin of.the deltas the mangrove has advanced in step with the progress of sedimentation while at the upstream end rather poor stands grow on very low alluvial terraces and will presumably retreat downstream as fluvial deposition builds up the surface. On relatively more exposed coasts in this region, sand ridges exist in front of the mangroves and have even developed within them (Jennings and Coventry, 1973).

Similar patterns recur with minor variations at many places in northern Australia where major rivers debouch into sheltered waters as at the Ord (Plate 3.1), Roper, McArthur. Normanby and Fitzroy (Qld) Rivers. It occurs in both macro- and mesotidal situations. Comparison of air photos taken some 20 years apart demonstrates a net loss of mangroves in King Sound (Jennings, 1975) and a gain in Cambridge Gulf (Thom et al., 1975); no information is available for the other deltas.

About 6000-7000 years ago both here and at the mouth of the Ord mangroves were much more extensive than they are now (Jennings, 1975). Limited areas of denser mangrove on slightly lower sites behind the main locus of sedimentation on the deltas may be survivals of these earlier conditions (Plate 3.1 4).

Plate 3.2.   Pattern on dissected, hard-rock coast; Kimberleys, W.A.
(1)   Resistant bedrock providing little fine sediment
(2)   Pockets of mangrove fringing the coast
(3)   More extensive mangroves in sheltered inlets colonising tidal flats

4. Point Usborne to Cape Dussejour

This region occupies the steep and intricate drowned coast of the Kimberleys and the Buccaneer and Bonaparte Archipelagos. Over most of the region mangroves occur as a narrow, sporadic fringe at the foot of steep rocky coasts or as restricted patches in quiet inlets. In the latter situation the mangroves often form a woodland rather than the usual closed forest and appear to be extending seawards (Plate 3.2). Relatively extensive mudflats occur only around the heads of George Water and Walcott Inlet and here the pattern of bare flats with narrow mangrove fringes typical of King Sound reappears.

Throughout the region there are no beach ridges in front of or within the mangroves except on the exposed north-east-facing subregion from Cape Londonderry to Cape Dussejour where patches of mangrove are protected behind substantial dune barriers. Although some local erosion has occurred in exposed sites, in the region as a whole mangroves are colonising new areas both at the seaward fringe and in the tidal creeks and channels.

5. Cape Dussejour to Pearce Point

This region forms the broad southern end of Joseph Bonaparte Gulf into which several large rivers, notably the Ord and the Victoria, bring large quantities of fine sediments. The deltaic situation and mangrove pattern resemble those in King Sound (Region 3). Broad intertidal and supratidal mudflats are mostly bare or carry sparse saltmarsh. Mangroves are now confined to narrow strips along the banks of major tidal channels and narrow, dendritic tidal creeks (Plate 3.1), although they were formerly more extensive (Thom *et al.*, 1975). Upstream the mangrove grows on very low alluvial floodplains invaded by high spring tides. Within the main channels of the deltas mud islands form and disappear repeatedly thereby producing rapid changes in the extent of mangrove.

At the seaward margin, narrow beach ridges exist at the edge of and within the mangroves. As rapid sedimentation is continuing, it is reasonable to suppose that the mangrove is advancing seaward: there may also be some slight re-invasion of the bare supratidal flats along some creeks which are extending headward. However, extensive grass and saltmarsh plains at the upstream end of the delta show patterns of former tidal creeks which imply that mangrove was formerly more extensive there.

6. Pearce Point to Cape Hotham

This region is a mixture of four types of coast. The first type consists of exposed, north-west-facing coasts which have sand barriers and low cliffs but no mangroves.

The second type occurs in fairly sheltered broad bays with an almost continuous mangrove fringe a few hundred metres wide which often shows signs of storm damage and which has a beach ridge at its outer edge in exposed situations. Behind the mangroves lies a bare intertidal strip which passes back into extensive freshwater swamps and grassy plains on which old tidal channels can still be discerned and which probably supported mangroves a few thousand years ago. This type recurs on alluvial coasts as far east as Princess Charlotte Bay in north-east Queensland.

The third type of coast consists of intricate drowned valleys such as Port Darwin which provide very sheltered sites for mangroves that extend almost unbroken from the central tidal channel to the foot of surrounding higher ground where small bare areas may occur.

The fourth type of coast comprises islands and promontories shielded by coral reefs behind which well developed mangroves fill most of the lagoons, e.g. the Vernon Islands north-east of Darwin.

From the air photographs it appears that mangrove advance and retreat at the shoreline are roughly in balance for this region as a whole.

7. Cape Hotham to Wangarlu Bay

This mesotidal coastal region occupies the low, flat, alluvial south and east coasts of Van Diemen Gulf. Wave action inhibits the growth of extensive deltas, except at the more sheltered eastern end of the Gulf, despite abundant sediment brought in by large rivers. The coast is very smooth, fringed by a belt of mangroves up to a few hundred metres wide and backed by bare supratidal flats that give way to swampy plains inland. In places there are beach ridges in front of, within, or behind the mangroves. More extensive mangroves exist at the more sheltered eastern end of the Gulf, along large, rather straight, tidal channels and winding tidal creeks.

The major rivers such as the Mary and the South Alligator are tidal and bordered by mangroves for up to 80 km inland. These mangrove fringes are often no more than one tree wide but broaden to occupy concentric belts drained by radial tidal gutters on convex meander banks. This distinctive pattern of riverine mangroves recurs on all major rivers between here and the central Queensland coast. Mangroves do not penetrate far up tributary creeks into the surrounding alluvial plains or swamps although some old tidal creek patterns imply that they did so in the past.

Despite some sign of storm damage, mangroves on the whole appear to be advancing seawards in this region as exemplified by Field Island, where mangroves now border the entire coast and prevent waves from reaching youthful-looking sand ridges behind.

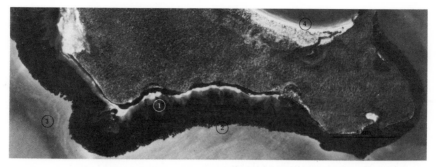

Plate 3.3.   Coral lagoon pattern; Greenhill Island, N.T.
(1)   Dense mangroves up to 16 m high with well developed zonation
(2)   Expanding fringe of mangroves
(3)   Approximate position of coral reef
(4)   Mangroves absent on coast without coral reef

8. Cobourg Peninsula, Melville Island and Bathurst Island

In this coastal region there is a marked contrast between the smooth, exposed, south-and west-facing coasts subject to considerable wave action and the deeply indented, sheltered inlets of the north-facing coasts. The south-facing coast is fronted by almost continuous beach ridges behind which are narrow strips of mangrove; there are also limited patches backed by bare supratidal flats along the few creeks. The north-facing coast has very extensive areas of mangrove in sheltered inlets and straits. Coral reefs around islands and exposed headlands provide shelter for well developed mangroves as at Greenhill Island (Plate 3.3). Here the trees attain heights of 14-16 m (according to stereoscopic measurements), zonation is well developed and the mangroves appear to be expanding out towards the reef.

9. Ilimanyi River to Cape Wilberforce

This region comprises the complex north coast of Arnhem Land. There are substantial variations in exposure to waves, in sediment supply and in topography plus indications of changes in high tide level relative to the land. Coral, however, is not an important factor.

Coasts with northerly or easterly exposures generally consist of bare rock or sand barriers and mangrove is absent or restricted to narrow strips between and behind sand ridges. However, at the head of deep bays even north-east-facing coasts are sufficiently sheltered for belts of mangrove a few hundred metres wide to grow to the open water's edge and form a fringe to bare tidal or supratidal flats. Straight drainage channels with mangroves cut across these flats and contrast with the usual meandering patterns of such features.

Some alluvial and estuarine plains that extend inland are now grassland and present-day tidal creeks with mangrove fringes are clearly incised into them. Former creeks discernible on these plains indicate that tidal influence and mangroves extended further inland during the Holocene. Other alluvial plains are somewhat lower and support sparse saltmarsh with mangroves along the tidal creeks and have fewer signs of former mangroves and tidal channels. Still lower plains have a more complete mangrove cover with only limited saltmarsh or bare patches.

Sheltered rocky coasts (e.g. Nalwarung Strait) have continuous if narrow mangrove fringes resembling those already described from the hard rock coast of the Kimberleys (Region 4).

As a whole the mangrove in this region is fluctuating or retreating slightly at the coast but it is advancing in the sheltered waters of eastern Cadell Strait where extensive intertidal mudflats provide potential sites.

10. Cape Wilberforce to Rose River

South-east winds blowing across the Gulf of Carpentaria subject this region to strong wave action. Consequently most of the coast consists of dunes and sand ridges with mangrove confined to narrow strips along occasional creeks and around lagoons behind these barriers. However, Blue Mud Bay lies in the lee of Groote Eylandt, Bickerton Island and various headlands and here more extensive mangroves exist. At the head of each sub-embayment of Blue Mud Bay extensive bare mudflats merge landwards into freshwater swamps and pass seawards into well defined mangrove belts up to 4 km wide. These flats and mangroves are crossed by remarkably straight tidal channels. Similar straight channels exist elsewhere, notably at Arnhem Bay, on the south coast of Van Diemen Gulf and at Roe Plains east of Broome, where their landward extensions are no longer reached by the tide and mangrove is now absent.

11. Rose River to Aurukun

This region encompasses the plains that fringe the southern two-thirds of the Gulf of Carpentaria, which is mesotidal and sufficiently extensive to generate considerable waves, especially during cyclones. This region could be sub-divided on the basis of sediment type and associated landforms and mangrove distribution. The eastern side of the Gulf and about half the southern side have sandy shores where mangrove near the coast is restricted to occasional strips behind sand ridges. Muddy shores predominate at the south-eastern and south-western corners of the Gulf where there is not only less wave action, but also large rivers such as the McArthur and Leichhardt reach the sea. On these muddy shores there is a more-or-less continuous belt of mangroves, usually a couple of hundred metres across, but widening to a kilometre in especially favoured sites and showing signs of seaward progression. On the other hand about 120 km of the coast west of Wellesley Island are severely eroded and the mangrove has been destroyed entirely in places.

Inland, mangrove extends along the tidal lower courses of the rivers especially at meander convexities. It also fringes narrow tidal channels that traverse bare tidal flats as on the Fitzroy and Victoria River deltas in Regions 3 and 5 far to the west. On the eastern side of the Gulf former tidal creeks occupy a plain between an outer Holocene beach ridge complex and an inner, Pleistocene complex; further north, in Region 12, these tidal creeks are still extant and bordered by mangroves. Islands in the Gulf have modest mangrove fringes in places, rarely exceeding 200 m in width, but sometimes occurring in surprisingly exposed situations.

12. Aurukun to Cape York

This is an exposed coast with Holocene and Pleistocene sand barriers separated by a plain some 2 km wide on which tidal creeks with mangrove fringes are interspersed with bare areas and saltmarsh. Several drowned valleys cut across these barriers and provide sheltered sites for mangroves up to 4 km wide. These mangroves have a complex zonation and occur as unusually wide fringes to tidal creeks. Air photo evidence indicates that the patterns are related to a Holocene history of sedimentation, dissection and renewed sedimentation at a slightly lower level where the mangroves are now growing. If there is sufficient fetch for wave action, beach ridges front the mangroves but in more sheltered inner recesses of the drowned valleys the mangrove edge is stable or advancing.

13. Islands of Torres Strait

Mangroves occur in two main patterns corresponding to the high rocky islands near Australia and the low mud islands near New Guinea. On the high islands (e.g. Badu) mangroves are confined to fairly narrow strips protected by coral reefs, have rarely expanded to occupy all the lagoon, and do not seem to be advancing. On the low islands (notably Saibai and Boigu) luxuriant mangroves grow to the water's edge. Stereoscopic measurements show that the mangroves attain a height of 25 or even 30 m.

Sassie and Turnagain Islands are transitional, being low islands with extensive mangroves but enclosed within a coral reef.

14. Cape York to Evanson Point

Although the Great Barrier Reef forms an almost continuous screen off this coast, wave energies are quite considerable and consequently shelter is important. Exposed coasts in the northern half have no mangroves and in the southern half they are confined to narrow strips behind recently formed sand spits and beach ridges.

On the other hand, mangroves are luxuriant in sheltered bays and inlets that face north. Around Newcastle Bay they include one of the largest single occurrences in Australia (c. 200 km^2). Here, and at Lloyd Bay to the south, the mangroves have a well developed species zonation associated with tidal creeks; limited bare areas and saltmarsh occur on sites furthest from the water. Although some mangrove colonisation may be continuing in tidal creeks, there are signs of wave damage at the seaward margin. Such damage is even more apparent at more open sites such as Temple Bay. In the region as a whole mangrove adjoining the sea is being cut back, presumably as a result of cyclones.

15. Princess Charlotte Bay

Princess Charlotte Bay has a sheltered northerly orientation and several rivers bring in considerable quantities of fine sediments. At the rather exposed north-western end a strip of mangrove lies behind a protective sand barrier. Moving eastwards round the bay the degree of shelter increases. There is first a

Plate 3.4.   Sheltered bay pattern; Princess Charlotte Bay, Qld
     (1)   Young outer mangrove fringe
     (2)   Inner, older, eroded mangrove fringe
     (3)   Bare supratidal flats
     (4)   Tidal river with mangrove fringe, widest on meander convexities
     (5)   Tidal creek with narrow mangrove fringe
     (6)   Former tidal creek in grassland

transition section where eroded mangroves at the water's edge alternate with narrow sand barriers, then the mangrove forms a continuous coastal strip that widens gradually from *c.* 50 m to 400 m at the most sheltered north-eastern end. The strip also widens locally near river mouths where sediment supply is greater.

Behind the coast, mangroves penetrate up to 25 km inland along the rivers which flow through grassy or swampy plains. Old tidal creeks imply that the community was more extensive in the past. Active channels with mangrove fringes still exist in the bare, lowermost, central part of these plains. In the region as a whole, mangrove is probably increasing slightly.

16. Bathurst Head to Cardwell

Along most of this wet, exposed coast the land falls steeply to the sea leaving no suitable space for mangroves. However, there are stretches with well developed beach ridge barriers behind which lie mangroves that grade into paperbark swamps away from the tidal creeks. Bare areas in the mangroves are absent presumably because the high rainfall prevents the groundwater from becoming too saline (Macnae, 1966). North-and north-east-facing open embayments provide limited shelter and have coastal mangroves a few hundred metres wide backed by supratidal flats into which mangrove-fringed tidal creeks are slightly incised. The coastal fringe shows signs of severe storm damage followed by partial regeneration.

The only really sheltered site, Trinity Inlet at Cairns, has well developed mangroves which cover some 45 km^2 and occupy almost the entire estuary apart from a central tidal funnel with narrow tributaries. There are also limited saltmarshes and beach ridges which were laid down before the mangrove filled the estuary at a time when the Barron River was probably furnishing more sediment (Bird, 1972). This pattern (Plate 3.5) could be regarded as typical for

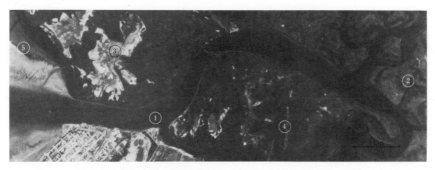

Plate 3.5.   Well developed tropical mangrove; Trinity Inlet, Cairns, Qld
              (1)   Main tidal channel
              (2)   Tidal creeks draining extensive mangroves with well developed
                    zonation
              (3)   Bare patches, partially caused by human interference
              (4)   Old beach ridges
              (5)   Young mangroves advancing seawards

well developed tropical mangroves and it exists in several sheltered sites in
northern Australia e.g. Port Darwin.

In the region as a whole, storm damage has prevented mangroves from
advancing seawards, but in the sheltered waters at Cairns mangroves are
advancing seawards on the eastern side of the inlet and constant 'weeding' of
seedlings is necessary to keep the esplanade clear (Graham *et al.*, 1975).

17. Hinchinbrook

This small region comprises the coasts of Hinchinbrook Island and Channel.
The steep, exposed seaward side of the island has only one patch of mangroves
behind a protective sand barrier but the sheltered western side has extensive
mangroves. At the north end of the island they extend up to 5 km in the lee of a
tombolo and have an unusual pattern of sub-parallel tidal channels. In the
quiet waters of Hinchinbrook Channel the mangroves have the more common
pattern of winding tidal channels and distinct zonation (See Plate 1 in Macnae,
1966).

18. Port Hinchinbrook to Clairview Bluff

This section consists of an alternation of steep headlands, north-facing bays
and exposed coasts with sand barriers. The headlands are devoid of mangroves
except in the intricate section in the lee of the Whitsunday Islands where
narrow fringes have developed in bay heads and occasionally behind coral
reefs. The north-facing bays have a variety of mangrove features according to
the degree of shelter and the nature of the plains that back them. In some open
embayments such as Abbott Bay beach, ridges front all the mangroves but in
more sheltered situations mangrove grows in front of the sand ridges which
may even be entirely absent. In accord with the greater evaporation here than in
wetter areas to the north, bare areas within the mangrove are common and the
community looks as if it is dying back at its landward edge thereby leaving bare
supratidal flats.

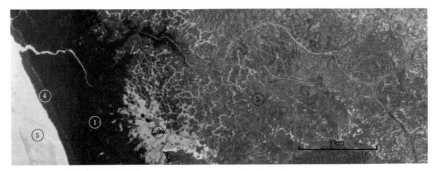

Plate 3.6.   Mangroves backed by former tidal creeks; Broadsound, Qld
    (1) Present mangroves
    (2) Supratidal flat with dying mangroves
    (3) Grassland with old tidal channels, formerly mangrove
    (4) Narrow seaward fringe of young mangroves
    (5) Low tidal flat—site for future mangroves

The coasts with sand barriers are found in exposed situations where there is a plentiful supply of sand. Behind the barriers that rim the Burdekin delta mangrove occupies very low terraces and directly abuts high alluvial surfaces with grassland or woodland. Elsewhere there are swamps in which mangrove areas near the rare tidal creeks grade into paperbark forests, saltmarsh and bare supratidal flats. Cape Bowling Green is a special case where the sand barrier has developed into a major spit behind which mangroves flourish. They risk destruction should waves destroy this narrow sand barrier as nearly happened during cyclone Althea in December 1971 (Hopley, 1974).

19. Clairview Bluff to Bustard Head

This is a complex stretch of coast with north—north-west trending peninsulas and islands separating shallow re-entrants and straits. Most of the section is mesotidal, but a macrotidal area extends from Mackay to Gladstone and is centred on Broadsound where mean spring tidal ranges attain up to 10 m.

Exposed coasts have no mangrove but limited patches exist behind barrier complexes as for instance north of Yeppoon. More extensive plains exist where larger valleys reach the coast. In the lee of Cape Capricorn there are coastal fringes of mangrove up to 500 m wide protected by sand barriers and backed by bare mud surfaces or saltmarsh. Former tidal creeks imply previously more extensive mangroves.

The most extensive plains fringe Broad Sound where mangroves now border most of the estuary in a belt up to 1.5 km wide and are backed by extensive grassy plains with well preserved former tidal creeks (Plate 3.6).

Burgis (1974) and Cook and Mayo (1977) have described how the mangrove has advanced towards the centre of this estuary during the last 6000 years. They attribute this progradation, which has averaged 11-12 cm per annum over the interval from 5000 to 1000 years ago, to local uplift (Cook and Polach, 1973) but the coincidence with macrotidal conditions suggests that alteration in the tidal prism may be responsible. The outer edges of the Broad Sound mangroves show recent signs of both cutting back and advance.

In Shoalwater Bay and sheltered parts of Port Clinton mangroves extend for as much as 3 km out from the shore to form continuous tracts broken only by tidal channels and small bare areas ringed by stunted trees. Mangroves are colonising low intertidal flats both here and at Rodds Bay to the south.

Patterns at the Fitzroy mouth resemble those on major tropical deltas. Winding tidal creeks with narrow mangrove fringes cross bare mudflats and saltmarsh. Broader tidal channels and the main estuary have mangrove borders up to 100 m wide while in the main river low mud islands with mangroves are subject to rapid formation and destruction. Upstream mangrove grows on very low surfaces of fluvial rather than estuarine origin and finally peters out as narrow fringes on the river banks. The sheltered strait between Curtis Island and the mainland is largely occupied by mangroves, which presumably flourish here because sedimentation has been insufficient to raise the surface above high tide level.

A consistent feature in this coastal section is a narrow bare strip up to a few hundred metres wide between the mangroves and adjacent solid land. The bare strip occurs sporadically elsewhere in both meso-and macrotidal situations but it is best developed here. Its origin is not apparent.

20. Bustard Head to Tweed Heads

This is a sand barrier coast. Where the barriers form the mainland coast mangroves are restricted to small occurrences at river mouths. Wave action is so strong that even the bigger rivers cannot build up extensive intertidal surfaces suitable for mangroves.

Where the sand barriers lie offshore from Fraser Island to South Stradbroke Island, the quiet waters of Great Sandy Strait and Moreton Bay in their lee provide sites for extensive mangroves with a distinctive pattern. Numerous low islands have a roughly concentric pattern of bare low-tidal flats, mangroves, saltmarsh and wooded sand cores. Mangroves also fringe the mainland coast especially near river mouths. Narrow bare strips lie between mangroves and higher ground but they are less prominent than in areas to the north and die out towards New South Wales. Mangrove is expanding onto low tidal flats as sedimentation builds them up. Its simultaneous development from a number of island nodes offers an alternative model to seaward progression of a single continuous coastal strip for the development of extensive mangroves.

This pattern is being severely modified by man's activities. According to Gutteridge et al. (1975) some 2200 ha of mangroves have been destroyed during the last thirty years and a further 1100 ha (8 per cent of the remaining resource) will be removed by projects already committed in the early 1970s. Still larger areas must have also been affected indirectly by such means as influx of agricultural chemicals.

21. Islands off the Queensland coast

Small areas of mangroves exist round high islands protected by coral reefs and in the lagoons of atolls. On Magnetic Island the mangroves are quite complex (Macnae, 1966) but they are usually fairly simple on other high islands

Plate 3.7.   Coastal rivers of N.S.W.; Hunter River delta
          (1) Distributaries and fluvial channels with mangrove fringe
          (2) Wider mangrove and paperbark fringe to lagoon
          (3) Former mangrove swamp now becoming freshwater grassland with
               a few mangroves still surviving along creeks

and are absent from the exposed Whitsunday Group. On atolls, the mangrove tends to develop at the windward end of the lagoon in the lee of debris ridges but there are cases where they have spread over most of the reef. Some of the atoll mangroves, as on Night Island, show severe storm damage.

Lord Howe Island, with a small patch of very low mangrove in its lagoon, is a southern outlier of this region.

22. New South Wales

Wave energies on the New South Wales coast are high and consequently mangroves are confined to sheltered sites well within estuaries. Furthermore, vigour and species diversity decline southwards and consequently fewer niches are available to the community. Towards the southern limit only stands of *Avicennia* exist and form a narrow fringe to very sheltered waters such as Wagonga Inlet (Bird, 1967; Owen, 1978). Mangroves extend as far as Mallacoota Inlet in Victoria (A. Fox, personal communication). Most of the New South Wales mangroves occur on estuarine sediments filling drowned valleys behind the general line of the coast. In such situations, as on the Clarence, Hunter and Tuross Rivers, there is a very narrow fringe of mangroves along the main channel while rather more extensive stands rim shallow lagoons that lie behind the main river levees (Plate 3.7). At their landward limit the mangroves are dying back, as for instance in Hexham Swamp on the Hunter River.

It is likely that in southern New South Wales the estuarine mangroves depend not only on shelter but also on the relatively warm waters in summer (Table 3.2).

23. Victoria

On the Victorian coast mangrove is confined to very small strips on muddy foreshores in Corner Inlet, Westernport Bay and Port Phillip Bay. *Avicennia marina* is the sole species and it barely exceeds two metres in height. The mangroves in this State form only one thousandth of the continental total but they have attracted considerable attention because of their high latitude, accessibility, convenience for study and biologic importance in environments

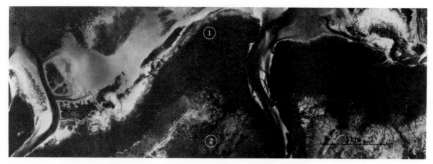

Plate 3.8. Pattern in South Australia Gulfs; near Port Pirie
  (1) Mangroves
  (2) Saltmarsh and algal mats
  (3) Mangrove woodland subject to wave attack
  (4) Tidal channel

that are coming under increasing stress. Even here, at their climatic limit, they have survived some man-induced changes in their habitat and have recolonised disturbed areas (Enright, 1973). The sites are protected and no signs of wave damage were detected on the small scale air photos.

24. Tasmania and islands in Bass Strait

Tasmania is now too cool to support mangroves and coastal sediments around Bass Strait laid down during the last 6000-7000 years contain no mangrove pollen (Hope, 1974, 1978; Ladd, 1979). However, even modestly higher temperatures in this region would have permitted mangroves to grow and archaeological evidence hints that they might have been present locally. Bones of the pied commorant (*Phalacrocorax varius*) are abundant in human occupation layers 450-2000 and 4000-5000 years old that occur on the floor of a cave at Rocky Cape, north-west Tasmania (J. van Tets and R. Jones, pers. comm.). These birds are now extremely rare visitors to Tasmania but are still common in South Australia where they nest mainly in the mangroves (*Avicennia marina*).

25. South Australia

In South Australia mangroves are confined to the sheltered and relatively warm waters towards the heads of the Gulfs and in lagoons round Eyre Peninsula. *Avicennia marina* is the sole species. Two clear sub-regions of mangroves exist: an extensive eastern one from Adelaide to Whyalla and a small western one from Venus Bay to Denial Bay. The eastern side of Eyre Peninsula forms a transitional sub-region.

The eastern sub-region occupies low shelving shores with moderate tidal ranges of 2-3 m and is occupied by dense uniform mangroves up to 600 m wide cut by widely-spaced and rather small tidal creeks. In relatively exposed situations low sand barriers front the mangroves but as a rule the latter grow right to the edge of open water and indeed are often colonising seawards. Perhaps the outstanding feature associated with the pattern is the extensive saltmarsh and algal mats behind the mangrove which appear almost equally dark on the air photos (Plate 3.8) and on satellite imagery and which look different from corresponding communities elsewhere.

In the western sub-region, running north-west from Venus Bay, wave energies are much higher and the occurrence of mangrove depends on the shelter of wave-built sand barriers. There are fewer signs of seaward colonisation and less saltmarsh behind the mangroves. The sediments on which they grow are rather coarser than in the eastern sub-region (Butler *et al.*, 1977) and contain marine and eolian sand.

The transitional sub-region south of Whyalla has strips of mangrove alternating with wave-built beach ridges and shows considerable signs of wave erosion. Even in the enclosed waters of Franklin Harbour waves have damaged the mangrove fringe.

26. South and west coasts of Western Australia

On the south coast there is no mangrove even where apparently suitable sites exist as at Albany. Water and air temperatures are probably too low but it would not require a great increase in temperature for *Avicennia* to survive. Perhaps it existed here in early to mid Holocene times.

On the west coast mangroves exist at Leschenault Inlet (Bunbury), Houtman Abrolhos Islands, Shark Bay and Lake Macleod. Most of the coast is too sandy and exposed for mangroves but they are missing even from the sheltered waters of the Swan River and Peel Inlet. Although the inner recesses of Shark Bay provide sheltered sites on suitable material, salinities of the interstitial water are too high (Davies, 1970) and mangroves are confined to the fresher waters nearer the mouth of the bay. The only extensive mangroves are at Carnarvon where there is a coastal belt some 800 m wide growing on deltaic sediments of the Gascoyne River. The other occurrences in Shark Bay and elsewhere are tiny patches in the lee of sand barriers.

Mangrove environments

Most of the environments represented in the above regions can be grouped into six broad classes homologous with the mangrove settings discussed by Thom elsewhere in this volume. Of course, overlaps and transitions exist between the classes and clear-cut distinctions are rare.

Alluvial plains

This class of environments comprises plains of riverine sediments derived from the adjacent land and is thus comparable to Thom's Setting I. However, in many cases fine sediments are also contributed by marine processes to give some affinity with Thom's second, tide-dominated setting. More locally, shelter may also be provided by narrow sand barriers at the seaward edge of the mangroves. In these environments mangroves form a continuous belt along the coast and narrow fringes along creeks and rivers extending inland to near the tidal limit. Examples include the eastern side of Exmouth Gulf (Region 1), the southern shore of Van Diemen Gulf (Region 7), the Gulf of Carpentaria (Region 11), Princess Charlotte Bay (Region 15) and the shores of the South Australian Gulfs (Region 25).

Tidal plains

In this class tidal processes extensively rework sediments supplied by rivers as in Thom's tide-dominated Setting II. The most distinctive examples include the deltas of the Fitzroy Rivers (W.A., Region 3; Queensland, Region 19) and the Ord River (Region 5). Here extensive mudflats have been built up to about high tide level and no longer support mangroves, which are confined to lower sites along tidal creeks, the main river channels and mud islands therein. Landwards the mangroves are restricted to very low alluvial terraces and meander convexities on the major rivers and ultimately peter out as narrow fringes along the river banks. Deltas of the Roper, McArthur and Normanby Rivers in Regions 11 and 15 as well as minor deltas in Region 9 have relatively more direct fluvial sedimentation and are intermediate between this class of mangrove environments and the preceding class of alluvial plains.

The low mud islands off New Guinea in Region 13, the shores of Broad Sound in Region 19, the mud islands and shores of Moreton Bay (Region 20) and the shores of Westernport Bay in Region 24 could also be allocated to this class.

Barriers and lagoons

Here shelter is provided by wave-built sand barriers behind which mangroves develop in lagoons and sheltered inlets (see Thom's setting III). The mangroves may form no more than a narrow fringe to lagoons as on the western side of the Gulf of Carpentaria (Region 10) or around the Eyre Peninsula in Region 25, or they may occupy most of a former lagoon and grade laterally into freshwater swamps as in parts of Region 16. Eventually sedimentation goes so far as to raise the surface above high tide level and the mangrove disappears leaving only traces of former tidal creeks.

Where the barriers project from the coast or link islands to the mainland, sheltered waters in their lee can provide sites for extensive mangroves if a sediment supply is available. Notable examples are at Cape Capricorn, Cape Bowling Green and Missionary Bay, all on the central Queensland coast.

Composite alluvial plains and barriers

This class of environments is equivalent to Thom's Setting IV and is particularly common on the east coast in mangrove Regions 16 to 22. Lagoons and swamps occur sporadically behind wave-built barriers, but in addition riverine features such as old distributaries and floodplains provide further sites for mangroves. Sediment inputs and marine action are considerable, leading to rapid changes in mangrove sites. An example is where mangroves are extending behind a very young sand spit fringing the Burdekin delta (Hopley, 1979). Deltas on the New South Wales coast (Region 22) also show combinations of lagoonal and fluvial environments; the higher wave energies dictate that the suite of forms occurs in bayhead situations rather than as protruding deltas.

Drowned bedrock coasts

In this class of sites mangroves range from narrow strips fringing steep bedrock slopes in the Kimberleys and parts of Arnhemland (Regions 4 and 9), through rias with wide mangrove fringes (e.g. Port Darwin in Region 16), to extensive flats with a network of tidal creeks and complex mangrove zonation such as in the Hinchinbrook Channel, at Newcastle Bay in Region 14 and at Shoalwater Bay in Region 19. Presumably because the rate of sediment supply is moderate the depositional surfaces have rarely been built up above high tide level and consequently mangroves can extend for greater distances between a central tidal funnel and the surrounding higher land. The most extensive occurrences of mangrove occur in this class.

Coral coasts

This class of site rarely supports extensive mangroves but nevertheless occurs quite frequently in the western half of the Northern Territory (Regions 6 and 8), on islands in Torres Strait and off the Queensland coast (Regions 13 and 21). Mangroves grow on terrestrial sediments behind fringing reefs or on coral sand, especially on platform reefs.

Discussion

This survey suggests that climatic and geomorphic factor, except salinity, combine to render tropical Australia a more favourable environment for mangroves than temperate Australia. Not only are air and water temperatures higher but wave energies are lower, tidal ranges and sediment supplies are greater and protected sites are far more abundant. While climate is the dominant factor determining continental distribution, shelter from wave attack is the main determinant of mangrove patterns at the regional and local scales.

The close correlation between mangrove patterns and habitat enables some present and former environmental conditions not directly apparent on the air photographs to be deduced. The presence of former mangrove swamps on coastal plains is strong evidence for progradation; bare areas within mangroves indicate high groundwater salinity. Detection of both storm damage and mangrove advance at the seaward margin should assist in determining whether tropical coasts, like temperate ones (Bird, 1973), are currently in a phase of retreat.

Acknowledgments

The text was constructively reviewed by Dr A.M. Gill and Dr K. Paijmans.

References

Beard, J.S., 1967. An inland occurrence of mangrove. *Western Australian Naturalist* **10**, 112-15.

Bird, E.C.F., 1967. Depositional features in estuaries and lagoons on the south coast of New South Wales. *Australian Geographical Studies* **5**, 113-24.

Bird, E.C.F., 1972. Mangroves and coastal morphology in Cairns Bay, North Queensland. *Journal of Tropical Geography* **35**, 11-16.

Bird, E.C.F., 1973. Physiographic changes on sandy shorelines in Victoria within the past century. Paper presented to International Geographical Union working group on Dynamics of Shoreline Erosion. (Department of Geography, University of Melbourne).

Burgis, W.A., 1974. Cainozoic history of the Torilla Peninsula, Broad Sound, Queensland. *Bureau of Mineral Resources, Geology and Geophysics, Australia.* Report 172.

Butler, A.J., A.M. Depers, S.C. McKillop, and D.P. Thomas, 1977. Distribution and sediments of mangrove forests in South Australia. *Transactions of the Royal Society of South Australia* **101**, 35-44.

Chapman, V.J., (ed.) 1977. *Ecosystems of the World. I. Wet Coastal Systems.* Elsevier, Amsterdam.

Cook, P.J., and W. Mayo, 1977. Sedimentology and Holocene history of a tropical estuary (Broad Sound, Queensland). *Bureau of Mineral Resources, Geology and Geophysics, Australia. Bulletin* 170.

Cook, P.J. and H.A. Polach, 1973. A chenier sequence at Broad Sound, Queensland, and evidence against a Holocene high sea level. *Marine Geology* **14**, 253-68.

Davies, G.R., 1970. Carbonate sedimentation, eastern Shark Bay, Western Australia. *American Association Petroleum Geologists Memoirs* **13**, 85-168.

Davies, J.L., 1977. The Coast. In D.N. Jeans (ed.), *Australia a Geography.* Sydney University Press, Sydney. pp 134-57.

Enright, J., 1973. Mangrove shores in Western Port Bay. *Victoria's Resources* **15**, 12-15.

Graham, M., J. Grimshaw, E. Hegerl, J. McNally, and R. Timmins, 1975. Cairns Wetlands. A Preliminary Report. *Operculum* **4**, 117-47.

Gutteridge, Haskins and Davey, 1975. *Coastal Management Queensland-New South Wales Border to Northern Boundary of Noosa Shire.* 4 vols. Co-ordinator-General's Department, Queensland.

Hope, G.S., 1974. The vegetation history from 6000 BP to Present of Wilsons Promontory, Victoria, Australia. *New Phytologist* **73**, 1035-53.

Hope, G.S., 1978. The late Pleistocene and Holocene vegetational history of Hunter Island, north-western Tasmania. *Australian Journal of Botany* **26**, 493-514.

Hopley, D., 1974. Coastal changes produced by tropical cyclone Althea in Queensland; December 1971. *Australian Geographer* **12**, 445-56.

Hopley, D., 1979. Australian Landform Example No. 35. Deltaic Barrier Spit. *Australian Geographer* **14**, 248-51.

Jennings, J.N., 1975. Desert dunes and estuarine fill in the Fitzroy estuary (north-western Australia). *Catena* **2**, 215-62.

Jennings, J.N. and R.J. Coventry, 1973. Structure and texture of a gravelly barrier island in the Fitzroy estuary, Western Australia, and the role of mangroves in shore dynamics. *Marine Geology* **15**, 45-167.

Ladd, P.G., 1979. A Holocene vegetation record from the eastern side of Wilsons Promontory, Victoria. *New Phytologist* **82**, 265-76.

Lear, R. and T. Turner, 1977. *Mangroves of Australia.* University of Queensland Press, St Lucia. 84 pp.

Macnae, W., 1966. Mangroves in eastern and southern Australia. *Australian Journal of Botany* **14**, 67-104.

Macnae, W., 1968. A general account of the fauna and flora of mangrove swamps and forests in the Indo-West-Pacific Region. *Advances in Marine Biology* **6**, 73-270.

Owen, P.C., 1978. Estuaries. In R.H. Gunn (ed.), *Land Use on the South Coast of New South Wales.* Vol. 2. *Bio-physical Background Studies,* pp. 100-17.

Radok, R., 1976. *Australia's Coast.* Rigby, Adelaide. 100 pp.

Saenger, P., M.M. Specht, R.L. Specht and V.J. Chapman, 1977. Mangal and coastal salt marsh communities in Australasia. In V.J. Chapman (ed.), *Ecosystems of the World.* I. *Wet Coastal Ecosystems.* Elsevier, Amsterdam.

Semeniuk, V., K.F. Kenneally, and P.G. Wilson, 1978. *Mangroves of Western Australia.* Handbook No. 12. Western Australian Naturalist's Club, Perth. 92 pp.

Spenceley, A.P., 1976. Unvegetated saline tidal flats in North Queensland. *Journal of Tropical Geography* **42**, 78-85.

Thom, B.G. L.D. Wright, and J.M. Coleman, 1975. Mangrove ecology and deltaic-estuarine geomorphology: Cambridge Gulf-Ord River, Western Australia. *Journal of Ecology* **63**, 203-32.

Ward, J.M., 1967. Studies in ecology on a shell barrier beach. I. Physiography and vegetation of shell barrier beaches. *Vegetatio* **14**, 241-97.

Part II
COMMUNITY CHARACTERISTICS

Introduction

P. Bridgewater

The six chapters presented in this section all reflect aspects of the vascular plant vegetation of mangrove communities, together with some consideration of other biota.

Although the first four chapters deal with vegetation in a regional context they also represent different but complementary approaches. For example, a major emphasis in Keneally's chapter is on distribution and taxonomy, Wells examines distribution with some ecological notes on species performance, Dowling and McDonald and my own chapter examine mangrove communities. All these studies are valid and worthwhile, but it is perhaps appropriate to examine briefly the roles of the different approaches.

First, it is clear we still need more information on the distribution and autecology of species. Wells has added considerably to our knowledge of this for northern Australia, and the recent publication of handbooks for eastern and western Australia ensures that workers on mangroves have up to date information. Nevertheless, it is important to consider the need for setting up a central source for distribution data that can be easily available to all.

Second, we need to be clear in our understanding of the nature of mangrove vegetation. Although extending into the marine environment it is nevertheless a terrestrial system, linked to the hinterland landform and vegetation. Because of the sharp environmental changes in the mangal it is always conspicuously zoned. It has always been tempting to describe the mangal in terms of these zones, but it is important to realise that zonations are peculiarly site specific, and therefore of little value as the basis of comparative studies. For such comparative studies the approach has to be based on a comparison of mangrove communities. Dowling and McDonald have emphasised the structural approach, which is particularly useful for mapping, but less useful for intersite comparisons.

Although the chapter by Keneally deals with some aspects of the mangrove fauna, Milward's chapter offers a detailed account of mangrove dependent biota. In some ways this serves to emphasise that while there are gaps in our knowledge of mangrove distribution, structure and floristics at community level these are small compared with our lack of knowledge of the dependent biota. The one group of dependent biota of which we have most knowledge is clearly the Avifauna, as the paper by Schodde *et al*. reveals. However, as the authors' *caveat* concedes, even here the few localities investigated suggest the need for considerably more data gathering.

These chapters emphasise the unevenness of our knowledge, both in terms of the species present, and the localities used for study. In particular, lack of knowledge of invertebrates and non-vascular plants offers a considerable handicap to understanding the function of mangal as an ecosystem.

Although it is perhaps invidious to quote from any chapter, two sentences from Milward's chapter form an excellent statement of the attitude we should adopt to descriptive studies of mangrove ecosystems.

> There is an urgent need not only for an intensification of research effort, but especially for an extension of it into the components of the biota that have been until now largely neglected. Equally critical however, *is the necessity for adopting a synecological approach, and conducting investigations over a long period of time.* (Italics mine)

These are timely words for all actual and potential investigations in the mangrove environment.

4

Mangrove Vegetation of Northern Australia

A.G. Wells

Introduction

A survey of mangrove communities across a wide area of northern Australia was commenced in 1975. To date, seventy-seven tidal river and creek systems have been examined, most of them at least twice. The survey area (Fig. 4.1) extends from the Kimberleys in the north-west of Western Australia, around the coastline of the Northern Territory to and including rivers and creeks entering the western and southern shorelines of the Gulf of Carpentaria.

It is the purpose of this paper to report primarily on the distribution of mangrove species in the survey area, and on the highest water salinities recorded for each species. Some comments are also included on the shade tolerance of different species based on extensive field observations.

Details of variation in density, girth and height of a number of mangrove species in different types of tidal rivers will be given in a series of papers now in preparation. Brief descriptions of fringing riverside mangrove vegetation along many tidal waterways in the study area have already been given in a series of monographs (Messel *et al.*, 1979).

Twenty-five species of mangroves were recorded in the Northern Territory, although one, *Nypa fruticans*, occurs only at one site on Melville Island. Fourteen species were recorded in the Kimberley region of Western Australia (Wells, 1981a). An additional species, *Scyphiphora hydrophyllacea,* has been reported in this area by Semeniuk *et al.* (1978). One species, *Avicennia officinalis,* has not been recorded previously in Australia. *Bruguiera sexangula, Ceriops decandra, Ceriops tagal, Rhizophora apiculata* and *Sonneratia caseolaris* are previously unrecorded in the Northern Territory, and *Xylocarpus granatum* has not been recorded previously in Western Australia.

Survey area

The area surveyed (Fig. 4.1) included several types of tidal river and creek systems. Rivers showing major structural control of drainage were covered in the north-west Kimberleys of Western Australia and parts of the Cambridge Gulf-southern Joseph Bonaparte Gulf regions of Western Australia and the Northern Territory. A detailed discussion of mangrove ecology and deltaic estuarine geomorphology for the Ord River (which lies within the survey area) is given by Thom *et al.* (1975). Other rivers entering Hyland and Anson Bays (N.T.) in this region meander across alluvial floodplains. Included also are the relatively short tidal river systems along the north coast of Melville Island (N.T.), the long meandering river systems flowing across the extensive alluvial floodplains that drain into Van Diemen Gulf, the admixture of drowned river valley systems and meandering rivers that occurs across the north coast of Arnhem Land (N.T.) and the relatively short tidal rivers that enter the western shores of the Gulf of Carpentaria. Within the survey area, the estuarine tidal portions of rivers draining the north-west Kimberleys experience a semi-diurnal tidal range of up to 11 m whereas rivers at the other extremity of the study area (western shores of the Gulf of Carpentaria) normally experience a diurnal tidal range up to 1.5 m.

Drainage basin characteristics, tidal ranges, currents, salinity regimes, climatic patterns and the variety of substrates suitable for colonisation and seedling establishment are considered to be major factors influencing the present distribution and abundance of mangrove species in the survey area.

Methods

The tidal river systems were surveyed from the University of Sydney's 21 m research vessel. A 5.5 m boat was used for work within rivers. All navigable tidal waterways in the river and creek systems in the survey area were examined and lists made of the mangrove species present. Mangrove swamps on the majority of rivers within the area were also surveyed from the air.

Locations were marked on maps prepared from aerial photographs (accurate to ± 0.1 km). Quadrats 100 m long and 20 m wide—or the maximum width of the mangrove forest if it was less than 20 m — were located on both banks at 2.5 km intervals on each tidal waterway. Within each quadrat, mangrove species were listed and their percentage cover assessed.

High and low tide salinity profiles were normally taken in the tidal waterway adjacent to each quadrat location. Measurements were made at the surface, midwater and bottom using an Autolab (Model 602) salinity/temperature bridge. Surface salinity was also measured with a refractometer (American Optical Co.). Up to three Foxboro tidegauges were used simultaneously on the various rivers in order to record tidal information.

Identifications were based on keys for mangroves in eastern Australia (Jones, 1971), in Sarawak, Malaysia (Chai, 1972, 1973) and in Sabah, Malaysia (Fox, 1970). Mangroves collected have been deposited at the Herbarium Australiense (Canberra), the John Ray Herbarium (University of Sydney) and the Northern Territory Herbarium (Darwin).

Regional distribution

Within the survey area, five broad biogeographical regions were distinguished on the basis of changes in species number, climate and geomorphological features. These regions are shown in Fig. 4.1.

Region 1: North West Kimberley Area.

This region is characterised by an extremely rugged coastline and a large tidal range of 8-11 m during spring tides. The lack of suitable sites for colonisation by many species is accentuated by steep topographic gradients along the banks of a number of coastal river systems. Rainfall (1000-1250 mm annually) is strongly seasonal, all falling during the summer monsoonal wet season. For the

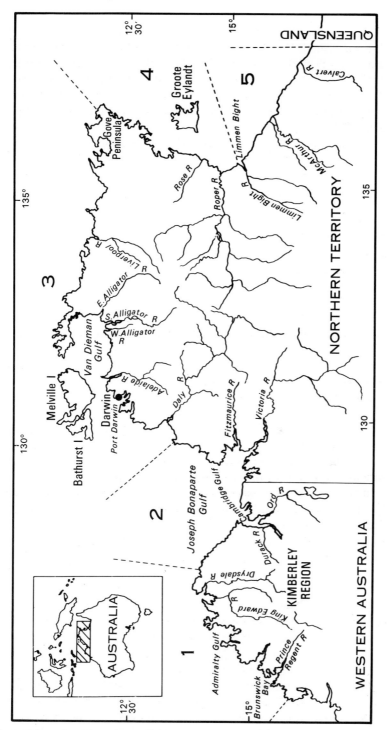

Fig. 4.1.   Map of northern Australia showing the survey area and the biogeographic regions into which it was divided

Table 4.1 Distribution of mangrove species in Biogeographic Regions of the survey area.

Family	Species	Region 1	Region 2	Region 3	Region 4	Region 5
Acanthaceae	*Acanthus ilicifolius*			X	X	X
Avicenniaceae	*Avicennia marina*	X	X	X	X	X
	Avicennia officinalis			X		
Bombacaceae	*Camptostemon schultzii*	X	X	X	X	
Combretaceae	*Lumnitzera littorea*			X	X	
	Lumnitzera racemosa	X	X	X	X	X
Euphorbiaceae	*Excoecaria agallocha*	X	X	X	X	X
Meliaceae	*Xylocarpus granatum*	X		X		
	Xylocarpus australasicus	X	X	X	X	X
Myrsinaceae	*Aegiceras corniculatum*	X	X	X	X	X
Myrtaceae	*Osbornia octodonta*	X	X	X	X	X

remainder of the year the climate is arid. Local climatic factors thus may influence the number of mangrove species colonising this area.

Fifteen species of mangrove have been recorded in this region (Wells, 1981a; Table 4.1.). Monospecific stands of *Bruguiera* are noticeably absent from this region. The occurrence of *Xylocarpus granatum* amongst the fringing riverside vegetation in the upstream reaches of the Prince Regent River (Wells, 1981a) is unusual and obviously reflects local site conditions; this part of the river remains brackish for most of the dry season. *Xylocarpus granatum* was not found at any other site in the Kimberley region.

Region 2: Ord River-Victoria River Area.

Straddling the Western Australian-Northern Territory border, this region, with an annual rainfall of 750-900 mm, is more arid than Region 1. The extremely seasonal rainfall pattern is likely to be a major factor influencing species diversity (Fosberg, 1975).

A total of thirteen species were recorded from this region (Table 4.1). Twelve species were found in the Ord River system (almost twice the number previously reported by Thom *et al.*, 1975), and ten and eleven species were recorded respectively in the Victoria and Fitzmaurice river systems.

Family	Species	Region 1	Region 2	Region 3	Region 4	Region 5
Plumbaginaceae	*Aegialitis annulata*	X	X	X	X	X
Rhizophoraceae	*Bruguiera exaristata*	X	X	X	X	X
	Bruguiera gymnorhiza			X	X	
	Bruguiera parviflora	X	X	X	X	
	Bruguiera sexangula			X		
	Ceriops decandra			X		
	Ceriops tagal var. *australis*	X	X	X	X	X
	Ceriops tagal var. *tagal*			X		
	Rhizophora apiculata			X		
	Rhizophora stylosa	X	X	X	X	X
Rubiaceae	*Scyphiphora hydrophyllacea*	X		X	X	
Sonneratiaceae	*Sonneratia alba*	X	X	X		
	Sonneratia caseolaris			X		

Region 3. Daly River-Gove.

This region has the highest annual rainfall (1100-1600 mm) of the five regions in the survey area. Although rain is restricted to the summer wet season, conditions over the remainder of the year are considerably less arid than in other regions within the survey area.

Although a total of twenty-four species were recorded for this region (Table 4.1), only 15-20 commonly occur within most tidal waterways. The greatest diversity (18-20 species) was found in Arnhem Bay where the tidal reaches of a number of tributaries feeding the bay remain fresh or slightly brackish throughout most of the year. The low salinity of these rivers affords greater scope for colonisation by species with a low tolerance to high salinity.

Region 4. Gove-Limmen Bight River.

This region of the coastline can be considered seasonally arid, with considerable evaporation during the latter half of the dry season. Annual rainfall is 750-1000 mm.

Sixteen species have been recorded for this region (Table 4.1), but two of

these, *Camptostemon schultzii* and *Bruguiera parviflora*, were found only on
the Limmen Bight River. Most tidal waterways in the region have 8-13 species.
The extreme aridity and increasing latitude of this section of the coastline may
account for the less diverse mangrove flora of this region.

Region 5: Limmen Bight River-Calvert River (Northern Territory/Queensland
Border).
    This is the most arid of the five regions within the survey area, receiving less
than 750 mm rainfall annually, most of which falls during the summer wet
season.
    Eleven species were recorded in this region (Table 4.1), though more
commonly only 7-9 species were found in a given river. As in the previous region,
the extreme aridity is probably the major factor limiting the number of species.
About 25 species of mangrove are found in the region of Cairns at a similar
latitude on the moist, humid east coast of Australia (N. Duke, personal
communication, 1979).

Species distribution and ecological features
Acanthus ilicifolius L. (Family Acanthaceae)
    Acanthus ilicifolius occurs as a small sparsely branched herb or small shrub,
1-2 m high. It has a restricted distribution in the survey area, being found on only
41 of the 77 tidal waterways examined.
    This species is commonly found colonising accreting portions of river
meanders. On such sites, it may form a monospecific understorey within pioneer
stands of *Sonneratia alba*, *Avicennia officinalis* or *Avicennia marina*. *Acanthus
ilicifolius* is frequently observed amongst understorey of fringing riverside
vegetation along tidal waterways particularly along portions of rivers that remain
brackish for a considerable period of the year.
    The species tolerates up to 7 months' inundation by freshwater annually but is
frequently observed along banks of tidal waterways that become hypersaline at
the end of the dry season. Within the survey area, *A. ilicifolius* was found in
areas inundated by waters of salinity up to 65 parts per thousand.

Australian distribution. The southernmost limits of distribution reported for *A.
ilicifolius* are the Daly River (13°10'S, 130°14'E) on the west coast of the
Northern Territory and St Lawrence, Qld (22°15'S) on the east Australian coast
(Jones, 1971).
    The species has not been recorded south of the Walker River (13°35'S,
135°53'E) on the east coast of the Gulf of Carpentaria (N.T.). It occurs at least
as far south as Weipa (12°40'S, 141°50'E) on the eastern shores of the Gulf of
Carpentaria, but is not abundant there (L. Love, personal communication,
1978). Saenger and Hopkins (1975) found the species at Tarrant Point (17°23'S,
139°25'E) in the south-eastern portion of the Gulf of Carpentaria.
    A closely related species, *Acanthus ebracteatus* Vahl., has been reported once
in Australia, at King River near Wyndham (15°30'S, 128°05'E) in Western
Australia (Semeniuk *et al.*, 1978).

Aegialitis annulata R. Br. (Family Plumbaginaceae)

This species grows as a herb or small shrub of up to 3 m height. It is widely distributed throughout the survey area and was found on 71 of the 77 tidal waterways examined.

Aegialitis annulata is frequently observed on rock/mud substrate in estuarine locations, particularly around headlands. It occurs as a shrub in mixed associations of *Avicennia marina, Excoecaria agallocha, Lumnitzera racemosa* and *Ceriops tagal* var. *australis* in the more landward, less frequently inundated zones. It may also occur as a monospecific community, principally on sand/mud substrates within estuaries. *Aegialitis annulata* often occurs as a carpet-like understorey beneath *Sonneratia alba* on consolidated muds in the Kimberley area of Western Australia and within Darwin and Bynoe Harbours. It is common as an understorey amongst fringing riverside vegetation (sometimes in association with *Avicennia marina*) in tidal waterways that become hypersaline by the end of the dry season. It is also often observed as a stunted shrub (height ≤ 0.5 m) on the periphery of saltpans.

Aegialitis annulata appears intolerant of long periods of inundation by freshwater and normally occurs only on substrates that are inundated by highly saline waters for most of the year. Within the survey area, the species was found in areas inundated by waters of salinity up to 85 parts per thousand.

Propagules of *A. annulata* are dispersed easily by the tides and colonise sites with high light intensities. Seedlings do not appear to survive in heavy shade. A dense seedling cover is often observed along riverbanks of hypersaline waterways.

Australian distribution. The southernmost limits of distribution reported for *A. annulata* are at Exmouth Gulf (21°53′S, 114°22′E) on the west Australian coast (Semeniuk *et al.*, 1978) and Fraser Island, Qld (25°30′S) on the east Australian coast (Jones, 1971).

Aegiceras corniculatum (L.) Blanco. (Family Myrsinaceae)

This species occurs as a shrub, up to 5 m high. It is particularly widespread and was found on 71 of the 77 tidal waterways examined.

Aegiceras corniculatum is frequently observed as understorey in fringing riverside tree associations along tidal rivers. The species colonises consolidated muds and may also form groves at the landward edge of swamps, particularly along portions of rivers that remain brackish for long periods during the dry season. In upstream areas of tidal waterways that become hypersaline by the end of the dry season, *A. corniculatum* may form an association with *Sonneratia alba* on soft unconsolidated muds, forming impenetrable thickets beneath the *Sonneratia* tree canopy. *Aegiceras corniculatum* forms associations with most mangrove species. It tolerates a wide range of environmental conditions, and can withstand up to 9 months of flooding by freshwater. It also occurs frequently in hypersaline waterways. Within the survey area, the species was found at sites inundated by waters of salinity up to 67 parts per thousand.

Dense crops of seedlings are often observed under mature shrubs fringing tidal waterways. The seedlings appear intolerant of heavy shade, but odd shrubs may occupy sites within the inner mangrove zones if the canopy is broken. Seedlings often establish along the exposed inner margins of mangrove swamps.

Australian distribution. The southernmost limits of distribution reported for *A. corniculatum* are at Cossack (20°1'S, 117°12'E) on the west Australian coast (Semeniuk *et al.*, 1978) and Merimbula, N.S.W. (36°53'S, 149°55'E) on the south-east coast of N.S.W. (P. Weate, personal communication, 1978).

Avicennia marina (Forsk.) Vierh. Syn. *A. eucalyptifolia* Zipp ex Miq. (Family Avicenniaceae)

This species occurs as a tree (canopy height ≤ 25 metres) to small shrub (canopy height ≤ 1 metre). It is widespread, being found on 76 of the 77 tidal waterways examined in the survey area.

Avicennia marina often forms a monospecific pioneer community on newly accreting mudbanks in estuaries. It may also be found in a mixed pioneer association with either *Sonneratia alba, Camptostemon schultzii* or both. *Avicennia marina* forms associations with all mangrove species but more commonly with *Rhizophora stylosa* and *Camptostemon schultzii* along riverside fringes. It also occurs in association with *Ceriops tagal* var. *australis* and *Excoecaria agallocha* in less frequently inundated, more landward sites, and with *Aegiceras corniculatum* in many upstream areas of tidal rivers that remain fresh for most of the year.

Avicennia marina also forms a paired association with *Aegialitis annulata*, typically in areas that are inundated infrequently. This association sometimes occurs as a fringe in rivers along the southern coastline of the Gulf of Carpentaria. It may also form a near monospecific woodland in the most landward mangrove zone where tidal inundation is infrequent and soil salinities rise to values greater than 70 parts per thousand by the middle of the dry season.

The species tolerates a wide range of environmental conditions. It has been observed growing in sites that are inundated by freshwater to a depth of over m for up to 3 months of the year. Within the study area, *A. marina* was found at sites inundated by waters of salinity up to 85 parts per thousand, and it probably tolerates even higher water salinities.

The propagule is dispersed by the tide. Seedlings initially establish throughout the mangrove forest in the wet season but most subsequently die apparently due to low light intensity on the forest floor. Other seedlings may initially colonise bare mudflats during the wet season but most die during the dry season. Successful seedling colonisation is most noticeable on bare muds of accreting banks and within the more landward mangrove zones.

Australian distribution. The southernmost limits of distribution of *A. marina* in Australia are at Bunbury (33°16'S, 115°42'E) on the west Australian coast and on the south-east Australian coast at Corner Inlet, Vic. (38°45'S, 146°30'E), the southernmost limit of mangroves in the world.

Avicennia officinalis L. (Family Avicenniaceae)

The growth form of *A. officinalis* varies from a shrub to small tree with a canopy height up to 7 m. The species is restricted in distribution and was found on only 15 of the 77 tidal waterways examined.

Avicennia officinalis colonises soft muds along banks of rivers in Region 3 (Fig. 4.1) that remain brackish for most of the year. There it is found frequently on accreting convex parts of meanders where it occurs as a pioneer shrub, often with *Sonneratia alba*. The understorey in this association is normally provided by *Acanthus ilicifolius*.

The restricted distribution of this species is unusual insofar as it is absent from many portions of river systems in the same latitudinal belt which appear to provide suitable habitat for colonisation. Seedlings of *A. officinalis* colonise bare mud on accreting portions of river meanders. They appear intolerant of shade and have not been observed amongst the understorey of fringing riverside vegetation on tidal waterways. Within the survey area, the species was found in areas inundated by waters of salinity up to 63 parts per thousand.

Australian distribution. This is the first record of this species in Australia. The restricted distribution of *A. officinalis* in terms of tidal waterways and the area surveyed and the habitat it occupies suggest that this species is at the southern limits of its geographical range. That it does not occur in rivers entering the north coast of Melville Island is also unusual as the species is quite widely distributed throughout South-east Asia (Chai, 1973; Chapman, 1975).

The species was not recorded west of Buffalo Creek (Shoal Bay, near Darwin), N.T. (12°20′S, 130°57′E) or east of the Clyde River (12°16′S, 135°03′E) in eastern Arnhem Land.

Bruguiera exaristata Ding Hou (Family Rhizophoraceae)

This species grows as a shrub to tall tree of up to 12 m in height. It is widespread throughout the survey area, being found on 64 of the 77 tidal waterways.

In the northernmost parts of its range in Australia, *B. exaristata* is found frequently along the riverside fringe in mixed association with other species. It sometimes occurs as monospecific stands but more commonly forms associations with *Bruguiera parviflora, Bruguiera gymnorhiza, Ceriops tagal* var. *australis, Avicennia marina, Rhizophora stylosa* and *Camptostemon schultzii.* It is sparsely represented in *Ceriops* dominated thickets.

Bruguiera exaristata normally colonises well drained sites that are regularly inundated by tides. It appears tolerant both of long periods of inundation by freshwater and of hypersaline conditions. Within the survey area, the species was found in areas inundated by waters of salinity up to 72 parts per thousand.

The light, relatively small propagules are dispersed by tides or floods. They quickly establish on muds throughout mangrove forests in the wet season but many seedlings within the forest die, probably due to the low light intensities on the forest floor.

Australian distribution. The southernmost limits of distribution reported for *B. exaristata* in Australia are at Cossack (20°41'S, 117°11'E) on the west Australian coast (Semeniuk *et al.*, 1978(and St Lawrence, Qld (22°15'S) on the east Australian coast (Jones, 1971). The species is reasonably well represented within these limits except along the west Australian coastline, where it is uncommon.

Bruguiera gymnorhiza (L.) Lamk. (Family Rhizophoraceae)
   The growth form of this species varies from a shrub to a large tree of up to 18 m in height. It was found on 32 of the 77 tidal waterways examined.
   Bruguiera gymnorhiza is frequently observed in backswamp areas that are inundated by spring high tides. The species occurs in association with most mangrove species and in particular with *Rhizophora stylosa, Rhizophora apiculata, Bruguiera exaristata, Lumnitzera racemosa, Camptostemon schultzii, Xylocarpus australasicus, Avicennia marina* and a strand plant, *Diospyros ferrea* var. *humilis*
   Bruguiera gymnorhiza is often abundant amongst the fringing vegetation along portions of tidal waterways that remain brackish for considerable periods of the year. It occurs most frequently on rock/mud substrates and on well drained soils having a high sand content, but may also occur on poorly drained soils. In estuaries, *B. gymnorhiza* may occur towards the landward edge of mangrove swamp, particularly in areas that receive considerable freshwater seepage throughout the year. It shows a preference for lower salinity sites and can tolerate up to 9 months of flooding by freshwater. Within the study area, the species was found in areas inundated by waters of salinity up to 37 parts per thousand.
   The propagules are dispersed relatively easily by the tides and appear to be shade tolerant. Seedlings frequently regenerate in areas where tidal inundation is infrequent. Seedlings of *Bruguiera gymnorhiza* have not been observed colonising sites beneath the canopy of mature trees of their own species.

Australian distribution. In the present survey, *B. gymnorhiza* was not recorded west of Darwin, N.T. (12°25'S, 130°48'E), but occurred eastwards of there to as far south as the Rose River, N.T. (14°17'S, 135°44'E) in the Gulf of Carpentaria. On the eastern shores of the Gulf of Carpentaria, it has been reported as far south as Tarrant Point (17°23'S, 139°25'E) by Saenger and Hopkins (1975). Along the east Australian coastline, the species has been recorded south to 29°25'S, 153°21'E on the Clarence River, N.S.W. (W. McCormick, personal communication, 1978).

Bruguiera parviflora (Roxb)W. & A. ex Griff. (Family Rhizophoraceae)
   The growth form of this species is variable, ranging from a shrub to a tree of up to 14 m in height. It was found on 56 of the 77 tidal waterways examined.
   Bruguiera parviflora often forms monospecific stands in mangrove zones that are not frequently inundated. It may occur in mixed associations, principally with *Bruguiera exaristata, Rhizophora stylosa, Rhizophora*

apiculata, Ceriops decandra, Camptostemon schultzii and *Avicennia marina.* The species is also found as isolated small trees or shrubs amongst fringing riverside vegetation on rivers that are of seawater salinity or higher by the end of the dry season. Monospecific stands on consolidated mud substrate have been observed at sites mainly inundated by brackish water and also on sites inundated by seawater for most of the year. The species thus appears to be tolerant of a wide range of salinity and has been found in areas inundated by waters of salinity up to 66 parts per thousand.

The propagules are dispersed by the tide. This species quickly establishes itself in cleared or open areas of forest or at sites along the riverine margins of the forest where ample light penetrates to the forest floor.

Australian distribution. The southernmost limits of distribution reported for *B. parviflora* in Australia are the Sale River (15°57′S, 124°33′E) on the west Australian coast (this study) and Proserpine, Qld (20°30′S) on the east Australian coast (Jones, 1971).

The species does not appear to be abundant on the southern or eastern shores of the Gulf of Carpentaria. Neither Saenger and Hopkins (1975) nor Specht *et al.* (1977) report the species at Tarrant Point (17°40′S, 141°50′E), and Weipa (12°40′S, 141°50′E), respectively, in the Gulf of Carpentaria, but specimens have been seen recently by the author at Port Musgrave (12°00′S, 141°54′E), 65 km north of Weipa.

Bruguiera sexangula (Lour.) Poir. (Family Rhizophoraceae)

This species occurs as a tree up to 12 m high. It is not common, being found in only two of the 77 tidal waterways examined.

On the Cato and Peter John Rivers in Arnhem Bay (N.T.), *B. sexangula* occurs within the fringing riverside vegetation in mixed association with *Rhizophora stylosa, Camptostemon schultzii, Bruguiera parviflora* and *Avicennia marina* over a wide range of sediment types and tidal regimes. *Bruguiera sexangula* was found at sites inundated by brackish water at the end of the dry season and tolerates long periods of inundation by freshwater. This species seems to prefer low salinity conditions and was not found at sites flooded by water with a salinity above 33 parts per thousand.

Australian distribution. Bruguiera sexangula is previously unrecorded in the Northern Territory (specimens which were labelled *B. sexangula* in the N.T. Herbarium, Darwin, are *B. exaristata).*

Within the survey area, the species was recorded only on the Cato and Peter John Rivers in Arnhem Bay, N.T. (12°15′S, 136°21′E).

On the eastern shores of the Gulf of Carpentaria this species has been recorded south to 12°00′S, 141°54′E at Port Musgrave (Wells, 1981b) while on the east Australian coastline, *B. sexangula* has been recorded south to 18°15′S at Hinchinbrook Island, Qld (N. Duke and J. Bunt, personal communication 1979).

Camptostemon schultzii Mas. (Family Bombacaceae)

The growth form of this species varies from a shrub to a large tree, of up to 25 m in height. It is widespread, being found on 63 of the 77 tidal waterways examined.

Camptostemon schultzii occurs in association with most mangrove tree and shrub species within the survey area, often on well drained sites. It frequently forms an association with *Rhizophora stylosa* and *Avicennia marina* as fringing vegetation along tidal waterways.

On accreting mudbanks to seaward, particularly in the Kimberley area of Western Australia (Region 1, Fig. 4.1), *C. schultzii* may form a pioneer association with *Sonneratia alba* (canopy height ≤ 8 metres). Such an association is unusual for *Camptostemon*. This species normally prefers to colonise well drained soils at sites that are inundated only by spring high tides. However, on the extensive gently sloping mudbanks of many of the embayments of the Kimberley region (Wells, 1981a) (particularly Port Warrender) the species is inundated up to twice per day by tides of up to 8 m that allow high tide waters to inundate all but the upper portions of the canopy of this association.

Camptostemon schultzii is quite common in estuarine localities and along the banks of hypersaline waterways. Within the study area, the species was found in areas inundated by waters of salinity up to 75 parts per thousand.

The seeds are dispersed by the tides and seedlings survive below forest canopies in fringing riverside swamps.

Australian distribution. Camptostemon schultzii is one of the few mangrove species that comes close to being endemic to Australia. It has a wide distribution around the far north Australian coastline as well as throughout rivers entering into the Gulf of Papua (Percival and Womersley, 1975; Floyd, 1977). The species has also been observed on Ambon Island in the Moluccas (Chapman, 1976). The southernmost limits of distribution reported for *C. schultzii* are Cape Bossut (18°43′S, 121°38′E) on the west Australian coastline (Semeniuk *et al.*, 1978) and the Pascoe River, Qld (12°31′S) on the east Australian coast (N. Duke, personal communication 1979). On the eastern shores of the Gulf of Carpentaria, it occurs at least as far south as 12°40′S at Weipa (Specht *et al.*, 1977). The species was not found on any river system entering the eastern shores of the Gulf of Carpentaria, nor was it recorded by Saenger and Hopkins (1975) at sites in the south-eastern part of the Gulf of Carpentaria.

Ceriops decandra (Griff.) Ding Hou (Family Rhizophoraceae)

This species grows as a shrub to small tree of up to 5 m in height. It is relatively common in the survey area and was found on 40 of the 77 tidal waterways examined.

Ceriops decandra typically occurs as an understorey in various mixed associations of fringing riverside trees. It is commonly found beneath mixed canopies of *Rhizophora stylosa, Camptostemon schultzii, Bruguiera parviflora, Bruguiera exaristata* and *Avicennia marina.* The species often occurs on consolidated muds on the riverine edge of stands dominated by either *Bruguiera parviflora* or *Ceriops tagal* var. *australis. Ceriops decandra* is also frequently observed as an understorey plant (mixed with *Aegiceras corniculatum* and *Aegialitis annulata*) on tidal waterways that become hypersaline by the end of the dry season. It appears intolerant of long periods of inundation by freshwater but more tolerant than *Ceriops tagal* var. *australis* or *Ceriops tagal* var. *tagal.* The species was found in areas inundated by waters of salinity up to 67 parts per thousand.

The small fluted propagules are easily dispersed by the tide. Seedlings appear intolerant of heavy shade.

Australian distribution. Ceriops decandra has not previously been recorded from the Northern Territory. In the present survey it was not found west of Darwin, N.T. (12°25'S, 130°48'E) or on any tidal waterway entering the western or southern shores of the Gulf of Carpentaria. The distribution of this species throughout the remainder of the Gulf of Carpentaria is largely unknown, although it occurs at least as far south as 12°00'S, at Port Musgrave on the eastern shoreline of the Gulf of Carpentaria (Wells, 1981b), and possibly as far south as Weipa (L. Love, personal communication, 1978). On the east Australian coastline, the species has been recorded as far south as 18°15'S at Hinchinbrook Island, Qld (Duke and Bunt, personal communication).

Ceriops tagal var. *australis* C.T. White (Family Rhizophoraceae)
This species occurs as a shrub to small tree up to 12 m high. The species is widespread, being found on 72 of the 77 tidal waterways examined.

Ceriops tagal var. *australis* frequently forms monospecific thickets in the landward, less frequently inundated zones. It is often in a mixed association with *Excoecaria agallocha, Avicennia marina,* and *Lumnitzera racemosa,* where it commonly forms the understorey. *Ceriops tagal* var. *australis* sometimes forms an association with *Bruguiera parviflora* on certain sites. Shrubs of *Osbornia octodonta* and *Bruguiera exaristata* may occur in the mixed *Ceriops* dominated association, particularly in thickets bordering portions of rivers that become hypersaline by the end of the dry season.

The species appears intolerant of long periods of flooding by freshwater. It is normally found on well drained consolidated clays in less frequently inundated zones of mangrove swamps. Within the survey area, the species was found at sites inundated by waters of salinity up to 72 parts per thousand.

Propagules are dispersed by the tide. Successful colonisation occurs only on sites infrequently inundated by tides. Seedlings are moderately shade tolerant. They often colonise bare saltpans during the wet season only to die during the dry season.

Australian distribution. The southernmost limits of distribution of *C. tagal* var. *australis* are at Exmouth Gulf (21°53'S, 114°22'E) on the west Australian coast (Semeniuk *et al.*, 1978) and the Tweed River, N.S.W. (28°11'S, 153°32'E) on the east Australian coast (Lear and Turner, 1977).

Ceriops tagal var. *tagal* (Perr). C.B. Rob. (Family Rhizophoraceae)

This species grows as a small shrub up to 3 m high. It is restricted in occurrence in the survey area and was found only on 7 of the 77 tidal waterways examined.

Ceriops tagal var. *tagal* occurs as an understorey in fringing riverside associations. It was observed with *Bruguiera gymnorhiza, Ceriops tagal* var. *australis, Excoecaria agallocha* and *Avicennia marina.*

The species colonises consolidated muds or rock/mud substrates, particularly in areas that are infrequently inundated. Within the survey area, the species was found at sites inundated by waters of salinity up to 36 parts per thousand.

Australian distribution. Ceriops tagal var. *tagal* was previously unrecorded from the Northern Territory. It has not been recorded in Western Australia or within the Gulf of Carpentaria.

In the study area, the species was not recorded west of the Goomadeer River, N.T. (11°50'S, 133°49'E) or east of the Cato River, N.T. (12°16'S, 136°21'E). In eastern Australia this species extends south to 24°01'S at Bustard Head, Qld (R. Dowling, personal communication, 1978).

Excoecaria agallocha L. (Family Euphorbiaceae)

The growth form of this species ranges from a shrub to a large tree of up to 10 m in height. It is widespread, being found on 73 of the 77 tidal waterways examined.

Excoecaria agallocha frequently occurs in association with *Ceriops tagal* var. *australis, Avicennia marina* and *Lumnitzera racemosa* on consolidated muds in the more landward, less frequently inundated zones. It also occurs as tall trees amongst fringing riverside vegetation along portions of tidal waterways that remain brackish for the greater part of the dry season. *Excoecaria agallocha* in association with *Avicennia marina* is a noticeable component of fringing riverside vegetation on all upstream portions of tidal waterways in the north-west Kimberleys (W.A.) the Ord (W.A.), and the Victoria and Fitzmaurice rivers in the Northern Territory. This association is inundated only by spring high tides. The large tidal range and rapidly increasing land gradients back from the river banks that occur within these areas may be largely responsible for the lack of suitable sites for colonisation by other mangrove species. High soil salinities towards the end of the dry season at sites colonised by the *Excoecaria/Avicennia* association may also be above the tolerance levels of most other mangrove species. It is likely that the occurrence of this association as fringing riverside vegetation in these areas is the result of complex interactions of several environmental factors. *Excoecaria agallocha* also appears to tolerate long periods of flooding by freshwater. Within the survey area, the species was found at sites inundated by waters of salinity up to 85 parts per thousand.

Propagules are dispersed by the tide. Seedlings are often found in peripheral localities at the landward edge of mangrove swamps, particularly in areas abutting saltpans. Seedlings of the species are also frequently observed on consolidated muds within fringing mangrove forests and appear tolerant of low light levels.

Australian distribution. The southernmost limits of distribution of *E. agallocha* are at Thangoo Station (18°16′S, 122°10′E) on the west Australian coast (Semeniuk *et al.*, 1978) and the Clarence River, N.S.W. (29°25′S, 153°21′E) on the east Australian coast (W. McCormick, personal communication, 1978).

Lumnitzera littorea (Jack) Voigt (Family Combretaceae)
This species was observed as a shrub to small tree of up to 8 m in height. By contrast it occurs as a tree of up to 25 m in many situations in Malaysia and the northern parts of Cape York Peninsula. This species is not common in the survey area and was found in only 8 of the 77 tidal waterways examined.

Lumnitzera littorea normally occurs as a shrub on rocky or muddy substrates, commonly in landward mangrove zones where it often forms an association with another shrub, *Scyphiphora hydrophyllacea.*

Lumnitzera littorea is found mainly on sites which are infrequently flooded by the tide. Within the survey area, the species was found in areas inundated by waters of salinity up to 35 parts per thousand.

Australian distribution. Lumnitzera littorea was not recorded west of the Johnston River on Melville Island, N.T. (11°18′S, 131°10′E). Along the western shores of the Gulf of Carpentaria, it was recorded south to the Rose River (14°17′S, 135°44′E). On the eastern shore of the Gulf of Carpentaria the species occurs at least as far south as Weipa (L. Love, personal communication, 1978) and it has also been recorded at Mornington Island (Woolston, 1973), and Tarrant Point (17°23′S, 139°25′E) (Saenger and Hopkins, 1975) in the south-eastern portion of the Gulf of Carpentaria.

On the eastern Australian coast, *L.littorea* is recorded south to 18°32′S on the Herbert River, Qld (Jones, 1971).

Lumnitzera racemosa Willd. (Family Combretaceae)
This species is commonly found as a shrub to small tree of up to 8 m in height. It is widespread and was found on 61 of the 77 tidal waterways examined.
Lumnitzera racemosa colonises the more landward less frequently inundated mangrove zones. It occurs amongst fringing riverside vegetation along portions of tidal waterways that remain fresh or slightly brackish for the greater part of the year. It sometimes forms nearly monospecific stands on the landward fringe of mangrove forests, particularly in areas where the landward fringe merges into a sedge swamp. *Lumnitzera racemosa* also commonly occurs in association with *Ceriops tagal* var. *australis, Excoecaria agallocha,*

Avicennia marina and *Aegialitis annulata* on consolidated muds in areas that are flooded infrequently. In seasonally flooded areas, it often grows in mallee habit (canopy height ≤2 m).

Lumnitzera racemosa can withstand considerable periods of flooding by freshwater, but can also tolerate extremely saline conditions. The species was found in areas inundated by waters of salinity up to 78 parts per thousand.

Australian distribution. The southermost limits of distribution of *L. racemosa* are Beagle Bay (16°56′S, 122°32′E) on the west Australian coast (Semeniuk *et al.* 1978) and Moreton Bay, Qld (27°30′S) on the east Australian coast (R. Dowling, personal communication, 1979).

Osbornia octodonta F.v.M. (Family Myrtaceae)

This species is found as a shrub to small tree up to 6 m high. It is widespread along the northern coastline and was found on 53 of the 77 tidal waterways examined.

Small trees or shrubs of *O. octodonta* are common on rocky headlands and in peripheral locations bordering sand beaches within estuaries. It also occurs, sometimes forming groves, along cutaway (concave) portions of meanders on waterways that become hypersaline by the middle of the dry season. It is common in *Ceriops* dominated thickets and is also found amongst mangrove species colonising the less frequently inundated inner zones. In the Kimberley area of Western Australia, *O. octodonta* commonly forms a closed shrub community bordering saline mudflats.

The species colonises sites that are inundated by waters of seawater salinity or greater on a wide range of substrates and appears to be absent from sites which receive more than 60 days flooding by freshwater annually. Within the survey area, the species was found at sites inundated by waters of salinity up to 56 parts per thousand.

Australian distribution. The southermost limits of distribution reported for *O. octodonta* are at Cossack (20°41′S, 117°11′E) on the west Australian coast (Semeniuk *et al.*, 1978) and Tin Can Bay, Qld (25°30′S) on the east Australian coast (R. Dowling, personal communication, 1978). Specht *et al.* (1977) record this species at Weipa (12°40′S, 141°50′E), but Saenger and Hopkins (1975) did not report its presence at Tarrant Point in the south-eastern portion of the Gulf of Carpentaria.

Rhizophora apiculata Blume (Family Rhizophoraceae)

The growth form of this species varies from a tall shrub to a small tree of up to 10 m in height. This species has a restricted distribution within the survey area, being recorded in only 8 of the 77 tidal waterways examined.

Rhizophora apiculata usually colonises estuarine areas that are inundated regularly. It normally occurs in mixed association with *Rhizophora stylosa, Camptostemon schultzii, Bruguiera parviflora, Bruguiera gymnorhiza* and *Avicennia marina*.

On Dongau Creek, Melville Island (N.T.), *R. apiculata* forms an association with *Rhizophora stylosa,* both species being stunted (canopy height ≤ 1.5 m). Imperfect tidal flushing and poor drainage may account for the stunted habit of this association. Although *R. apiculata* was found at sites inundated by water of salinity up to 65 parts per thousand the species normally colonises sites inundated by waters of 35 parts per thousand or less. It tolerates long periods of inundation by freshwater.

Propagules of *R. apiculata* are produced in large numbers on mature trees and either embed themselves in muds below the parent tree or are carried by tides to other areas. They appear to tolerate shade. As the propagule is shorter than that of *Rhizophora stylosa,* *R. apiculata* seedlings are carried into shallower waters and hence can establish themselves on higher ground than *R. stylosa.*

Australian distribution.

Rhizophora apiculata has not been previously recorded from the Northern Territory. It has not been recorded in Western Australia. The species has not been recorded west of Andranangoo Creek, Melville Island, NT (11°21′S, 130°51′E) or east of Gove NT (12°15′E). On the east Australian coastline, the species has been recorded south to Port Clinton, Qld (22°30′S) (N. Duke and J. Bunt, personal communication, 1979.

Rhizophora stylosa Griff. (Family Rhizophoraceae)

This species grows to a tall tree of 20 m in height. It is common within the survey area, being found on 71 of the 77 tidal waterways examined.

Rhizophora stylosa is the dominant species along the banks of tidal creeks, commonly growing in nearly monospecific stands. It may occur as a seaward pioneering species or, alternatively, form a band of variable width behind a pioneer community of *Sonneratia alba.* However, the species also occurs frequently on firm consolidated muds in more landward zones which are inundated less often. Along tidal rivers and creeks, *R. stylosa* often forms a mixed tree association with *Camptostemon schultzii* and *Avicennia marina.* It is also present in other mixed associations, chiefly with *Bruguiera parviflora, Xylocarpus australasicus, Bruguiera gymnorhiza, Bruguiera exaristata, Aegiceras corniculatum* and *Ceriops decandra. Rhizophora stylosa* grows to maximum proportions in sections of tidal rivers that remain brackish for most of the year and it tolerates a considerable period of inundation by freshwater. Within the survey area, the species was found in areas inundated by waters of salinity up to 74 parts per thousand.

The propagules are dispersed by water. The great length of the fruit compared to other species may limit its landward dispersal by water. Species that colonise the shallower landward areas, generally have small fruits, e.g. *Ceriops* spp., *Avicennia marina, Aegiceras corniculatum, Lumnitzera* spp. The species is rarely observed colonising sites more than a few hundred metres inland. Further inland it is apparently replaced by other species with smaller fruits.

Australian distribution. The southernmost limits of distribution reported for *R. stylosa* in Australia are at Yardie Creek (22°20'S, 113°51'E) on the west Australian coast (Semeniuk *et al.*, 1978) and the Richmond River, N.S.W. (28°31'S) on the east Australian coast (Jones, 1971). The species is common throughout this range.

Scyphiphora hydrophyllacea Gaertn. (Family Rubiaceae)

This species grows as a shrub up to 4 m high. It has a restricted distribution in the survey area, and was found in only 15 of the 77 tidal waterways examined.

Scyphiphora hydrophyllaceae occurs on mud/rock substrates, often forming a shrub layer along the banks of tidal waterways that are of seawater salinity or greater by the middle of the dry season. The species normally occupies sites that are inundated infrequently and appears intolerant of lengthy periods of inundation by freshwater. Within the survey area, the species was found in areas inundated by waters of salinity up to 63 parts per thousand.

Scyphiphora hydrophyllacea also appears intolerant of shady conditions. Sites on which it occurs (rock/mud substrates) appear unsuitable for colonisation by most other mangrove species.

Australian distribution. The limits of distribution reported for *S. hydrophyllacea* in Australia are at Cape Londonderry (13°48'S, 126°46'E), the most northerly point of Western Australia (Semeniuk *et al.*, 1978), and Townsville, Qld (19°12'S) on the east Australian cost (Jones, 1971).

Within this area of coastline, the distribution of *S. hydrophyllacea* is patchy. In the Northern Territory it was not found west of Darwin (12°25'S, 130°48'E) or on the west shore of the Gulf of Carpentaria. It has been reported as far south as Weipa (12°40'S, 141°50'E) on the eastern shore of the Gulf of Carpentaria (Specht *et al.*, 1977).

Sonneratia alba J. Sm. (Family Sonneratiaceae)

This species grows to a tree of up to 12 m in height. It is very common and was found on 57 of the 77 tidal waterways examined.

Sonneratia alba often occurs in monospecific stands or in mixed association with *Rhizophora stylosa, Camptostemon schultzii* and/or *Avicennia marina* on accreting mudbanks to seaward. Although a pioneering species, it occupies sites that are largely protected from strong wave action. In some rivers of the Kimberleys (W.A.), *Aegialitis annulata* forms a short carpet-like understorey beneath trees of *Sonneratia alba* (Messel *et al.*, 1977). *Sonneratia alba* occurs far upstream on some tidal rivers that do not receive a substantial freshwater input after commencement of the dry season (e.g. South Alligator River). In such saline rivers, it forms a shrub association with *Avicennia officinalis* on accreting mudbanks around convex portions of river meanders; *Acanthus ilicifolius* is often observed as understorey in this association.

Sonneratia alba colonises sites that are inundated by most high tides. It frequently occurs on consolidating soft muds and appears intolerant of long periods of exposure to freshwater. The species was found in areas inundated by waters of salinity up to 44 parts per thousand. Seedlings of *Sonneratia alba* are never prolific but always occur on bare newly-accreting mudbanks. The species was not observed regenerating under tree canopies and appears intolerant of shade.

Australian distribution. The southernmost limits of distribution of *S. alba* in Australia are at Cape Bossut (18°43′S, 121°38′E) on the west Australian coast (Semeniuk *et al.*, 1978), and Port Clinton, Qld (22°30′S) on the east Australian coast (N. Duke and J. Bunt, personal communication, 1979). The species was prevalent in estuarine areas within the survey area, but was not recorded on any river system entering the western or southern shores of the Gulf of Carpentaria. *Sonneratia alba* occurs at least as far south as Weipa on the eastern shore of the Gulf of Carpentaria (L. Love, personal communication, 1978).

Sonneratia caseolaris (L.) Engl. (Family Sonneratiaceae)

This species grows to a tree of up to 18 m in height. It is restricted in distribution, being found on only 12 of the 77 tidal waterways examined.

Sonneratia caseolaris occurs as a pioneering species on accreting mudbanks in some rivers that remain fresh or slightly brackish over most of the year. It normally colonises soft muds but may occur on firmer more consolidated muds. It is restricted to riverine sites that are inundated by most tides. *Sonneratia caseolaris* may form monospecific stands along riverbanks or occur throughout the river course. It often forms mixed associations with other pioneering species such as *Avicennia marina*, *Avicennia officinalis*, *Aegiceras corniculatum* and *Acanthus ilicifolius*. In some localities, the species may occur in a mixed association with *Sonneratia alba*. *Sonneratia caseolaris* is more abundant at sites inundated by brackish waters, but can tolerate higher salinities. The species was found in areas inundated by waters of salinity up to 35 parts per thousand. In the more saline areas, *Sonneratia caseolaris* is a shrub. It only attains tree dimensions in brackish or predominantly freshwater sites. This species only regenerates on accreting exposed bare mudbanks. Seedlings appear to be intolerant of shade.

Australian distribution. *Sonneratia caseolaris* has not been recorded in Western Australia and this is the first report of this species in the Northern Territory, where the most westerly occurrence of the species is on Andranangoo Creek, Melville Island, N.T. (11°21′S, 130°51′E). It is abundant on river systems entering Van Diemen Gulf (N.T.) and also occurs in certain rivers in Arnhem Bay (N.T.), but was not recorded east of the Peter John River, N.T. (12°15′S, 136°21′E). The species has not been observed on any river system entering the Gulf of Carpentaria. On the east Australian coast, it occurs south to the Murray River, Qld (N. Duke and J. Bunt, personal communication, 1978).

Xylocarpus australasicus Ridl. (Family Meliaceae)

Xylocarpus australasicus grows as a shrub to large tree up to 14 m high. It is widespread, being found on 72 of the 77 tidal waterways examined.

Xylocarpus australasicus is common amongst fringing riverside vegetation in Northern Australia. In portions of rivers that remain brackish for long periods of the dry season, *Xylocarpus australasicus* occurs as the dominant tree species in association with *Diospyros ferrea* var. *humilis, Bruguiera parviflora* and *Rhizophora stylosa*. The most extensive forest types of this nature occur on Andranangoo Creek, Melville Island and the Koolatong River (Blue Mud Bay, N.T.). *Xylocarpus australasicus* has not been observed as a pioneering species. The species can withstand long periods of inundation by freshwater (up to 8 months) and also tolerates limited periods of hypersaline conditions. Within the survey area, the species was found in areas inundated by waters of salinity up to 76 parts per thousand.

Seeds of *X. australasicus* are widely distributed by the tide but many are attacked by boring insects and fail to germinate. Seedlings appear to tolerate low light levels.

Australian distribution. The southernmost limits of distribution reported for *X. australasicus* are King Sound, Derby (17°19′S, 123°38′E) on the west Australian coast (Semeniuk *et al.*, 1978) and Gladstone, Qld (23°50′S) on the east Australian coast (Saenger and Robson, 1977).

Xylocarpus granatum Koen. (Family Meliaceae)

This species occurs as a shrub to small tree up to 9 m high. Its distribution within the survey area is very restricted, being found in only 2 of the 77 tidal waterways examined.

Xylocarpus granatum occurs on various substrates, but seems to prefer consolidated muds. It is often associated with *Rhizophora apiculata, Rhizophora stylosa, Bruguiera gymnorhiza, Xylocarpus australasicus* and the mangrove fern *Acrostichum speciosum*. It can withstand considerable periods of inundation by freshwater, but occurs most frequently in brackish water at sites that are flooded infrequently by seawater. The species was found at sites inundated by waters of salinity up to 34 parts per thousand.

Australian distribution. The southernmost limits of distribution reported for *X. granatum* are the Prince Regent River (15°27′S, 125°03′E) on the west Australian coast (Wells, 1981a) and Fraser Island, Qld (25°30′S) on the east Australian coast (R. Dowling, personal communication, 1979).

In the Northern Territory, it occurs on Andranangoo Creek, Melville Island (11°21′S, 130°51′E) and Yirrkala on the Gove Peninsula (Specht, 1958). Specht *et al.*, 1977 have also recorded the species at Weipa, and Saenger and Hopkins (1975) have reported the species at Tarrant Point, Qld (17°23′S, 139°25′E) in the south-eastern portion of the Gulf of Carpentaria, though in the latter case there is a possibility that *X. australasicus* has been misidentified as *X. granatum*. *Xylocarpus granatum* has not previously been recorded from Western Australia.

Acknowledgments

I thank in particular Professor Harry Messel, Head of the School of Physics, University of Sydney for assistance both in the field and in providing logistical and financial support.

Thanks are also due to all members of the University of Sydney and Territory Parks and Wildlife Commission's Joint Crocodile Research Project (in particular to Fred Duncan), to the Aboriginal people of Arnhem Land, to the officers of the West Australian Department of Fisheries and Wildlife (in particular Dr Andrew Burbidge), and to Ian Onley and Harry Rawlins.

I also wish to thank Drs Peter Myerscough, Bill Allaway and Bill Magnusson of the School of Biological Sciences, University of Sydney for assistance both in the field and in critical appraisal of this work, and Ms Corinne Tuttlebee for typing the manuscript.

References

Chai, P.K., 1972. *Field Key to the Mangrove Trees and Shrubs Occurring in Sarawak, Including a Brief Description of the Flora*. Forest Department, Sarawak. 25 pp.

Chai, P.K., 1973. *The Types of Mangrove Forest in Sarawak*. Forest Department,Sarawak. 34 pp.

Chapman, V.J., 1975. Mangrove biogeography. In G.E. Walsh, S.C. Snedaker and H.J. Teas (ed.), *Proceedings of the International Symposium on Biology and Management of Mangroves*. Institute of Food and Agricultural Sciences, University of Florida, Gainesville, Florida, Vol. I, pp. 1-22.

Chapman, V.J., 1976. *Mangrove Vegetation*. Cramer, Vaduz. 425 pp.

Chapman, V.J., 1976. *Ecosystems of the World, I. Wet Coastal Ecosystems*. Elsevier, Amsterdam. 428 pp.

Floyd, A.G., 1977. *Ecology of the Tidal Forests in the Kikori-Romilly Sound Area — Gulf of Papua*. Ecology Report No. 4, Division of Botany, Forest Department, Department of Primary Industry, Lae, P.N.G. 59 pp.

Fosberg, F.R., 1975. Phytogeography of Micronesian mangroves. In G.E. Walsh, S.C. Snedaker and H.J. Teas (eds.) *Proceedings of the International Symposium on Biology and Management of Mangroves*. Institute of Food and Agricultural Sciences, University of Florida, Gainesville, Florida, Vol. I, pp. 23-42.

Fox, J.E.D., 1970. Key to mangrove species. In *Annual Report on Forest Research*. Forest Department, Sabah, Malaysia. 126 pp.

Jones, W.T., 1971. The field identification and distribution of mangroves in eastern Australia. *Queensland Naturalist* **20**, 35-51.

Lear, R. and T. Turner, 1977. *Mangroves of Australia*. University of Queensland Press, *St Lucia, Queensland. 84 pp.*

Messel, H., A.A. Burbidge, A.G. Wells and W.J. Green, 1977. *The Status of the Salt-water Crocodile in Some River Systems of the North-West Kimberley, Western Australia*. Report No. 24, Department of Fisheries and Wildlife, Western Australia, pp. 1-50.

Messel, H., G.C. Vorlicek, A.G. Wells and W.J. Green, 1979. *Surveys of Tidal River Systems in the Northern Territory of Australia and Their Crocodile Populations. The Blyth-Cadell River System*. Monograph 1. Pergamon Press, Sydney. 400 pp.

Messel, H., C. Gans, A.G. Wells and W.J. Green, 1979. *Surveys of Tidal River Systems in the Northern Territory of Australia and Their Crocodile Populations. The Victoria and Fitzmaurice River Systems*. Monograph 2. Pergamon Press, Sydney. 51 pp.

Messel, H., C. Gans, A.G. Wells and W.J. Green, 1979. *Surveys of Tidal River Systems in the Northern Territory of Australia and Their Crocodile Populations. The Adelaide, Daly and Moyle Rivers.* Monograph 3. Pergamon Press, Sydney. 60 pp.

Messel, H., A.G.Wells and W.J. Green, 1979. *Surveys of Tidal River Systems in the Northern Territory of Australia and Their Crocodile Populations. The Alligator Region River Systems.* Monograph 4. Pergamon Press, Sydney. 68 pp.

Messel, H., A.G. Wells and W.J. Green, 1979. *Surveys of Tidal River Systems in the Northern Territory of Australia and Their Crocodile Populations. The Goomadeer and King River Systems and Majarie, Wurugoij and All Night Creeks.* Monograph 5. Pergamon Press, Sydney. 61 pp.

Messel, H., A.G. Wells and W.J. Green, 1979. *Surveys of Tidal River Systems in the Northern Territory of Australia and Their Crocodile Populations. Some River and Creek Systems on Melville and Grant Islands.* Monograph 6. Pergamon Press, Sydney. 63 pp.

Messel, H., A.G. Wells and W.J. Green, 1979. *Surveys of Tidal River Systems in the Northern Territory of Australia and Their Crocodile Populations. The Liverpool-Tomkinson River System and Nungbalgarri Creek.* Monograph 7. Pergamon Press, Sydney. 110 pp.

Messel, H., M. Elliott, A.G. Wells and W.J. Green, 1979. *Surveys of Tidal River Systems in the Northern Territory of Australia and Their Crocodile Populations. Some Rivers and Creeks on the East Coast of Arnhem Land, Gulf of Carpentaria.* Monograph 8. Pergamon Press, Sydney. 40 pp.

Percival, M. and J.S. Womersley, 1975. *Floristics and Ecology of the Mangrove Vegetation of Papua New Guinea.* Botany Bulletin No. 8, Division of Botany, Forest Department, Department of Primary Industry, Lae, Papua New Guinea. 96 pp.

Saenger, P. and M.S. Hopkins, 1975. Observations on the mangroves of the southeastern Gulf of Carpentaria, Australia. In G.E. Walsh, S.C. Snedaker and H.J. Teas (eds.), *Proceedings of the International Symposium on Biology and Management of Mangroves.* Institute of Food and Agricultural Sciences, University of Florida, Gainesville, Florida, Vol. I, pp. 126-36.

Saenger, P. and J. Robson, 1977. Structural analysis of mangrove communities on the central Queensland coastline. *Marine Research in Indonesia* **18**, 101-18.

Semeniuk, V., K.F. Kenneally and P.G. Wilson, 1978. *Mangroves of Western Australia.* Western Australian Naturalists' Club. Handbook No. 11, Perth. 89 pp.

Specht, R.L., 1958. The climate, geology, soils and plant ecology of the northern portion of Arnhem Land. In R.L. Specht and C.P. Mountford (eds.), *Records of the American-Australian Scientific Expedition to Arnhem Land. 3. Botany and Plant Ecology.* Melbourne University Press, Melbourne, pp. 333-414.

Specht, R.L., R.B. Salt and S. Reynolds, 1977. Vegetation in the vicinity of Weipa, North Qld. *Proceedings of the Royal Society of Queensland* **88**, 17-38.

Thom, B.G., L.D. Wright and J.M. Coleman, 1975. Mangrove ecology and deltaic-estuarine geomorphology; Cambridge Gulf-Ord River, Western Australia. *Journal of Ecology* **63**, 203-32.

Wells, A.G., 1981a. A survey of riverside mangrove vegetation fringing tidal river systems of Kimberley, Western Australia. In *Biological Survey of Mitchell Plateau and Admiralty Gulf, Kimberley, Western Australia. Part 3.* Records of the Western Australian Museum. Supplement. pp. 95-121.

Wells, A.G., 1981b. Range extensions of mangrove species in the vicinity of Cape York, Australia. *Royal Society of Queensland.* (Submitted)

Woolston, F.P., 1973. *Ethnobotanical Items from the Wellesley Islands, Gulf of Carpentaria.* Occasional paper, University of Queensland Anthropological Museum. No. 1, pp. 95-103.

5
Mangrove Communities of Queensland
R.M. Dowling and T.J. McDonald

Introduction

Mangrove communities form a conspicuous part of the flora of the Queensland coastline. In general the structure and floristics of these communities are poorly known. While accounts exist giving species lists for particular areas, only a few give details of structural forms, community composition or species distribution within Queensland estuarine systems. Accounts giving species lists for particular areas include Dredge *et al.* (1977), Graham *et al.* (1975), Hegerl and Timmins (1973), Hegerl and Tarte (1974), Shanco and Timmins (1975), McDonald and Elsol (1979), Shine *et al.* (1973), and Specht *et al.* (1975) while general accounts including structure and species composition are to be found in Dowling (1979), Macnae (1966), Pedley and Isbell (1971), Saenger and Hopkins (1975) and Saenger and Robson (1977). Detailed accounts of various estuaries giving species composition, structural form and maps of community distribution are to be found in Dowling (1980, 1981) Dowling and McDonald (1976), Durrington (1974 and 1977), Elsol and Sattler (1979), Elsol and Dowling (1978) and McDonald and Whiteman (1979). General descriptions of Queensland mangroves and the communities they form are found in Jones (1971), Lear and Turner (1977) and Saenger *et al.* (1979).

Distribution of mangrove communities

Mangrove communities occur along the Queensland coastline from the Queensland-Northern Territory border to the Queensland-New South Wales border. They do not, however, form a continuous band.

Along the coastline there are extensive areas of low lying coastal plains which have been formed in a number of ways including infilling of the mouths of streams and rivers, and by isostatic movements (Twidale, 1964, Gill and Hopley, 1972, Hopley 1974) or eustatic changes in sea level. The most extensive of these plains (Fig. 5.1A) are found around the southern and south-eastern coastline of the Gulf of Carpentaria, Princess Charlotte Bay, Broad Sound and the mouth of the Fitzroy River. Other less extensive areas occur around the coastline, notably at Weipa, Mackay, Fitzroy River to Bustard Head and to the area north and south of Townsville. Extensive areas of these plains are at, or slightly below, mean high water springs, making them suitable for colonisation by mangroves. While the substrates on the seaward edge and along creek banks are mainly silts and muds, most of the remaining areas consist of stiff marine clays. In general mangroves do not survive well on stiff clay soils but may grow well on clays which have a high organic content.

Because large areas of these plains are only flushed infrequently by the highest and least frequent tides, and are flat and subsequently poorly drained, there is a tendency for them to become hypersaline, especially in areas of low or seasonal rainfall and/or with high evaporation rates.

Two major factors affect the distribution of mangrove communities along the Queensland coastline. They are:

(i) mode of formation, nature and extent of the intertidal area; and

(ii) climate.

There is considerable interaction between these two factors and it is often impossible to separate the effects of one from the other.

Mode of formation, nature and extent of intertidal area

For the successful establishment of mangroves a suitable substrate and protection from strong wave action is necessary. Mangroves generally require soft marine muds, silts and clays to become established. The nature and extent of these substrates depends largely on the wave energy of the shoreline on which they occur and on the silt load of the water, with the most extensive mangrove development being found in low energy-high silt areas.

Most of the larger rivers and many of the smaller streams within Queensland carry suitable silt loads and where these streams discharge onto low wave energy shorelines, mangrove communities are usually formed. The major streams of Queensland are shown in Fig. 5.1A.

Mangroves may also be found well away from river mouths in areas protected from strong wave action, to which silts have been transported because of the low wave energy on that section of the coastline. Such areas include the lee of the larger offshore islands such as Hinchinbrook Island, Fraser Island, Moreton Island, North and South Stradbroke Islands or in the lee of headlands of promontories along the coastline. In general silts and muds form the predominant substrates in these areas but marine clays also occur, especially in the upper tidal areas.

Climate

The climate of Queensland coastal areas varies from tropical in the north to subtropical in the south, with the rainfall occurring mainly in the summer (State Public Relations Bureau, 1976).

Wind

Along the eastern Queensland coastline the prevailing winds are from the south-east. These winds are usually moisture laden and in general blow either approximately parallel to the coastline or slightly on shore. In the Gulf of Carpentaria, owing to the effects of the intertropic front in the summer months, the prevailing winds are from the north-west, while in the winter months they are from the south-east.

Mangrove communities are generally found in areas protected from strong wave action, which is usually associated with direction of the prevailing winds. Along the eastern coastline they commonly occur on the northern sides of headlands or in the lee or western side of offshore islands.

In the Gulf of Carpentaria mangroves are also found behind headlands protecting them from the onshore north-westerly winds. They may also be found on apparently more open coasts in the southern part of the Gulf, where some protection is afforded by the Wellesley Islands. The southern part of the Gulf of Carpentaria is also fairly shallow with an extensive gently sloping shoreline, so that wave action is moderated and allows the successful establishment of mangroves.

Rainfall and evaporation

The rainfall along the coastline is predominantly in the summer, often falling as a result of short duration summer storms and cyclonic activity. Along the southern parts of the coastline the rainfall is more evenly distributed though it is still predominantly in the summer. The 1500 mm isohyet for Queensland is shown in Fig. 5.2. Areas of higher rainfall occur from Cape Melville to Ingham, Bowen to Mackay and from Gympie to the Queensland-New South Wales border. These higher rainfall areas are found where the prevailing moisture laden south-east winds cross the coastline in association with mountain ranges. Elsewhere the prevailing winds blow more or less parallel to the coastline and the rainfall is lower.

Areas of higher rainfall occur on Cape York Peninsula as a result of the intertropic front which brings with it monsoonal rains in the summer months.

In general evaporation greatly exceeds precipitation over most of the State, though in the higher rainfall areas, especially in those areas where the rainfall is more evenly distributed throughout the year, the difference between precipitation and evaporation is not so great. The distribution of mangrove communities along the Queensland coastline (not including associated claypans), is shown in Fig. 5.1A.

Floristics

For the purpose of this study mangroves will be taken to be any woody plant that grows between the tidal limits.

The number of species listed for Australia varies with different authors. Macnae (1966) noted 21 species, Jones (1971) 27 species and Lear and Turner (1977) 29 species. A composite list for Queensland compiled from these sources consists of 32 different species (Table 5.1). This list can further be expanded as Tomlinson and Womersley (1976) report *Rhizophora lamarckii, Sonneratia caseolaris* and *Sonneratia ovata* also occur in the State; specimens of the latter two are now held in the Queensland Herbarium. The authors have also observed *Xylocarpus moluccense* growing on Cape York while it is obvious from field work that there are several undescribed species of *Sonneratia* and one undescribed species of *Xylocarpus* in the mangroves along the Queensland coastline. Further species, including some of those that occur in New Guinea and Indonesia, probably await discovery in the far northern parts of Queensland.

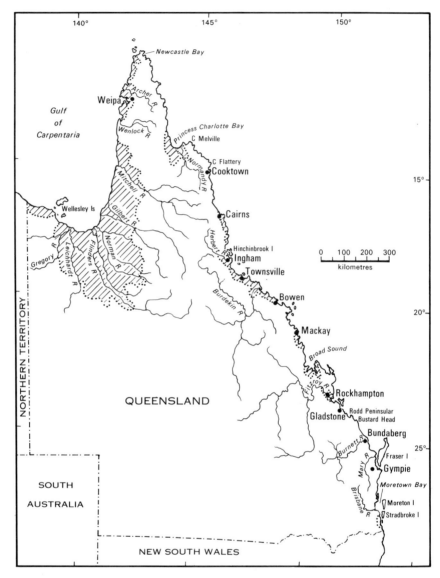

Fig. 5.1a.   Major rivers and low-lying coastal plains of Queensland, and localities
              mentioned in text

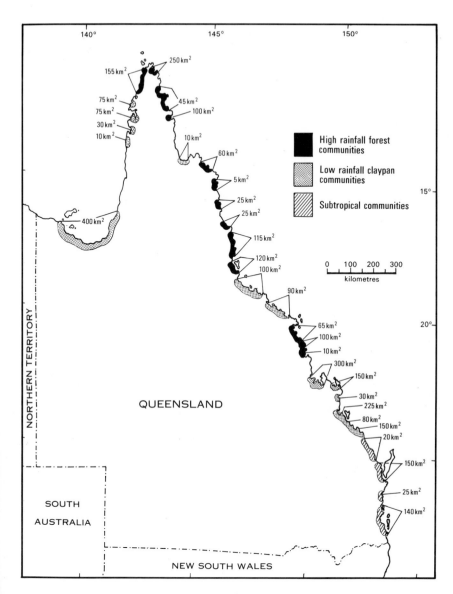

Fig. 5.1b.   Distribution and areas of major mangrove communities along the Queensland coast

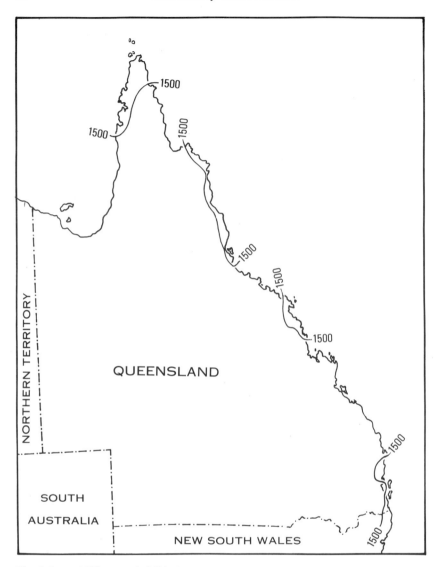

Fig. 5.2.   1500 mm rainfall isohyet

In some instances it is difficult to decide which species are 'true' mangroves and which are not. This problem mainly exists for marginal species that occur in brackish areas and which may occasionally behave as a 'true' mangrove in some situations and as land based plants in others, e.g., *Hibiscus tiliaceus, Thespesia populnea, Casuarina glauca.* Difficulties also exist with the synonymy of some species and in the taxonomic limits and delineation of others. Table 5.2 shows the occurrence of the Queensland mangrove species for a range of areas. This list is compiled from the available literature, Queensland Herbarium records and the authors' personal knowledge of these distributions. The names quoted in Tables 5.1 and 5.2 have been adjusted to conform with current Queensland Herbarium usage.

Table 5.1   List of mangrove species recorded from Queensland

Species	Macnae (1966)	Jones (1971)	Lear and Turner (1977)
Acanthus ilicifolius		x	x
Aegialitis annulata	x	x	x
Aegiceras corniculatum	x	x	x
Avicennia eucalyptifolia		x	x
Avicennia marina var. australasica	x	x	x
Bruguiera cylindrica		x	x
Bruguiera exaristata	x	x	x
Bruguiera gymnorhiza	x	x	x
Bruguiera parviflora	x	x	x
Bruguiera sexangula			x
Campostemon schultzii		x	x
Ceriops decandra	x	x	x
Ceriops tagal var. *australis*		x	x
Ceriops tagal var. *tagal*	x	x	x
Cynometra iripa		x	x
Excoecaria agallocha	x	x	x
Heritiera littoralis		x	x
Hibiscus tiliaceus	x		
Lumnitzera littorea	x	x	x
Lumnitzera racemosa	x	x	x
Nypa fruticans		x	
Osbornia octodonta	x	x	x
Pemphis acidula	x		
Rhizophora apiculata	x	x	x
Rhizophora mucronata		x	x
Rhizophora stylosa	x	x	x
Scyphiphora hydrophyllacea	x	x	x
Sonneratia alba	x	x	x
Sonneratia caseolaris			x
Thespesia populnea	x		
Xylocarpus australasicus	x	x	x
Xylocarpus granatum	x	x	x

Community description

Three broad types of mangrove communities are recognisable along the Queensland coastline. They are:

    (i)   high rainfall forest communities;
    (ii)   low rainfall claypan communities;
    (iii) subtropical communities.

These three community types result from the interaction of the mode of formation of the estuarine system and climate. For any given area it is possible to predict, in broad terms, from consideration of these factors, the type of community most likely to be found. The distribution of these community types is shown in Fig. 5.1B.

In the description of these communities the structural forms used are those proposed by Specht (1970).

Table 5.2 Occurrence of Queensland mangrove species

	(1)	(2)	(3)	(4)	(5)	(6)	(7)	(8)	(9)	(10)	(11)	(12)
ACANTHACEAE												
Acanthus ilicifolius		x		x		x						
PLUMBAGINACEAE												
Aegialitis annulata	x	x	x	x		x		x	o	x	o	
AVICENNIACEAE												
(Verbenaceae)												
Avicennia eucalyptifolia	x	x	x	o	x	o						
A. marina var. *australasica*		x	x	x		x	x	x	o	x	o	x
BOMBACACEAE												
Camptostemon schultzii		x	x									
COMBRETACEAE												
Lumnitzera littorea		x		o		x						
L. racemosa	x		x	o	x	x		x	o	x	o	x
Lumnitzera sp.				x								
EUPHORBIACEAE												
Excoecaria agallocha	x	x	x	x		x		x	o	x	o	x
LEGUMINOSAE												
Cynometra iripa				x		x						
LYTHRACEAE												
Pemphis acidula	x			o						x	o	
MELIACEAE												
Xylocarpus australasicus			x	o		x			o			
X. granatum		x		o		x		x			o	
X. moluccense				o								
Xylocarpus sp.				x			x		o		o	
MYRSINACEAE												
Aegiceras corniculatum	x	x	x	o		x		x	o	x	o	x
MYRTACEAE												
Osbornia octodonta			x	x	x	x	x	x	o	x	o	

	(1)	(2)	(3)	(4)	(5)	(6)	(7)	(8)	(9)	(10)	(11)	(12)
NYPACEAE												
Nypa fruticans				X								
PTERIDACEAE												
Acrostichum aureum						O						
A. speciosum					O	X				X	O	X
RHIZOPHORACEAE												
Bruguiera cylindrica				O								
B. exaristata			X	O		X						
B. gymnorhiza		X		O		X		X		X	O	X
B. parviflora		X		O								
B. sexangula				O								
Bruguiera sp.	X			X			X					
Ceriops decandra						X						
C. tagal var. *australis*				X		X			O	X	O	X
C. tagal var. *tagal*	X	X	X	O		O		X	O	X		
Ceriops sp.							X					
Rhizophora apiculata				X	X	X		X				
R. mucronata	X	X										
R. stylosa			X	X	X	X		X	O	X	O	X
Rhizophora sp.							X					
RUBIACEAE												
Scyphiphora hydrophyllacea			X	X		X						
SONNERATIACEAE												
Sonneratia alba				X	X	X						
S. caseolaris				O		O						
STERCULIACEAE												
Heritiera littoralis				X		X						

X Species as listed in available literature.
O Additional species known to occur in area from author's personal knowledge and Queensland Herbarium records.

(1) Wellersley Islands (Woolston, 1973)
(2) Tarrant Point (Saenger and Hopkins, 1975)
(3) Weipa (Specht *et al.*, 1975)
(4) Cape York (Pedley and Isbell, 1971)
(5) Cape Flattery (McDonald and Batianoff, in press)
(6) Cairns (Graham *et al.*, 1975)
(7) Magnetic Island and Townsville (Macnae, 1966)
(8) Capricorn Coast (Hegerl and Tarte, 1974)
(9) The Narrows
(10) Gladstone (Dowling, in press b)
(11) Wide Bay-Burnett
(12) Moreton Bay (Dowling, in press a)

High rainfall forest communities

High rainfall forest communities (e.g. Plate 5.1A) are associated with the higher rainfall areas of the state or in areas of localised heavy rainfall along the Queensland coastline such as the northern tip of Cape York, e.g. Newcastle Bay, Cape Melville to Ingham and Bowen to Mackay. They generally have over 1500 mm of rainfall per annum. Although the rainfall is predominantly in the summer in these areas there is usually adquate rainfall in the cooler winter months.

Within these communities the whole intertidal region is generally covered by mangrove vegetation. Though large areas may occur near the upper tidal limits, no extensive claypans are formed because the rainfall apparently washes away any build-up in surface salt, and the mangrove cover is generally continuous. In addition the vegetation cover adds considerable amounts of organic matter to the soils, especially the clay soils, and this tends to break them up and thus improves the growth of mangroves on soils that in drier conditions would be unfavourable to mangrove growth.

Structurally they consist of:
- (a) tall closed-forest;
- (b) tall open-forest;
- (c) closed-forest;
- (d) open-forest;
- (e) tall woodland; and
- (f) woodlands.

The structural forms (a)-(d) predominate. These communities may also include areas of low closed-forest, low open-forest, open-scrub, closed-scrub, low shrubland and low open-shrubland, especially towards the upper tidal limit, but they are generally neither common nor extensive. Small areas of claypan and saltmarsh may be present but they are usually not extensive.

Floristically the mangrove communities vary depending on where they occur. *Rhizophora* spp. and *Bruguiera* spp. are the most common species present and frequently form extensive pure stands which in many places constitute the bulk of the mangrove areas. However, in some areas *Ceriops* spp. is common and may cover large areas, mainly in the upper tidal limits. The mangrove communities in the area from Cooktown to Ingham appear to be the most floristically diverse, due mainly to the large number of species found at the landward margin of the mangroves or on high spots within them. However, the bulk of the remaining mangrove areas are generally floristically simple.

The landward margin species include *Acanthus ilicifolius, Aegiceras corniculatum, Cynometra iripa, Excoecaria agallocha, Heritiera littoralis, Lumnitzera littorea, Lumnitzera racemosa, Osbornia octodonta, Scyphiphora hydrophylaceae, Xylocarpus australasicus* and *Xylocarpus granatum.*

Low rainfall claypan communities

Low rainfall claypan communities (e.g. Plate 5.2) are found in the lower rainfall areas of the state, especially in those areas with a marked dry and wet season. They are characterised by extensive areas of claypan at the upper tidal

Plate 5.1. Newcastle Bay—example of high rainfall forest communities—note continuous cover of mangroves

Plate 5.2. Fitzroy River—example of low rainfall forest communities—note extensive claypan development

Plate 5.3. Moreton Bay—example of subtropical communities—note some claypan development

limits. Often mangroves only occur as a narrow fringe along the shoreline and creekbanks. The claypans are usually very extensive and may make up 50 per cent or more of the area from high water mark to the seaward edge of the mangroves. In places the claypan may form 90 per cent or more of this area.

The seasonality of the rainfall is probably the major causal factor in the formation of the claypans as it allows a build up of salt, especially in the higher tidal areas. These areas are only occasionally inundated and are poorly flushed by the tide, resulting in the formation of hypersaline claypan flats.

The high salt levels apparently restrict plant growth and this, in association with the clay soils often found at the higher tidal levels, serves to maintain the claypans. Because mangroves grow poorly in clay soils not enough organic matter is added to the soils to help break them down as in the higher rainfall communities. This also serves to maintain the claypans.

Areas of low rainfall claypan communities are common around the southern part of the Gulf of Carpentaria, Princess Charlotte Bay, Townsville, Broad Sound and the area from Rockhampton to Rodd Peninsula. The claypans are usually bare but may support samphires or *Sporobolus virginicus* grassland towards the upper tidal limits.

Structurally the mangrove communities associated with the claypans are predominantly open-scrub and closed-scrub but areas of closed-heath, open-heath, low shrubland and low open-shrubland are also commonly present, mainly on the landward edge of the mangroves where they back onto the claypan. Small areas of low closed-forest, low open-forest, low woodland, low open-woodland, tall shrubland and tall open-shrubland may also be present but they are not common. In many areas the mangroves form a narrow fringe 15 m or less wide along the creek banks, while in other areas they may be more extensive.

Floristically the communities vary in different areas. However, species that are commonly present include *Rhizophora stylosa, Avicennia marina* var. *australasica, Ceriops tagal* var. *australis, Lumnitzera racemosa, L. littorea, Excoecaria agallocha, Aegiceras corniculatum, Aegialitus annulata, Osbornia octodonta* and *Xylocarpus granatum*. Generally *Rhizophora stylosa* and *Ceriops tagal* var. *australis* are the only species that form pure stands over appreciable areas while the other species usually occur in various compositions in mixed stands. The mixed stands usually occur on the inner edge of the mangroves where they back onto the claypan, or as a narrow fringe on the landward side of the claypan especially in areas where freshwater seeps onto the claypan.

Subtropical communities

These communities (e.g. Plate 5.3) are intermediate in structural form between the high rainfall forest communities and the low rainfall area claypan communities. The area of mangroves is generally extensive but areas of the claypan and saltmarsh are also commonly present, often forming between 10 and 20 per cent of the area from high water mark to the seaward edge of the mangroves.

The subtropical communities mainly occur in southern Queensland from Bundaberg to the Queensland-New South Wales border where the rainfall is more evenly distributed throughout the year than in the north and the climate is cooler and evaporation rates are subsequently less. They may, however, be found in other parts of the state where conditions are suitable.

Structurally they consist mainly of low closed-forest, low open-forest, closed-scrub, open-scrub, tall shrubland, tall open-shrubland, low shrubland and low open-shrubland but may also contain areas of woodland, open-woodland, closed-heath and open-heath. Generally these latter types are not common.

Floristically the subtropical communities are less diverse than the other major mangrove types, mainly because they occur towards the southern distribution limit of many of the mangrove species. *Avicennia marina* var. *australasica, Rhizophora stylosa, Ceriops tagal* var. *australis* and *Aegiceras corniculatum* are the most common species present, often forming extensive pure stands. Other species also present include *Aegialitis annulata, Bruguiera gymnorhiza, Excoecaria agallocha, Lumnitzera racemosa* and *Osbornia octodonta* but they are usually found in mixed communities.

Because of the cooler, moister climate, hypersaline flats are not common; however, a claypan and/or saltmarsh may be formed in the upper tidal limits but it is usually not extensive and in many areas is not present at all. Often when a claypan is formed it is vegetated by samphires or *Sporobolus virginicus* grassland. In the southern ranges of this community type, e.g. Moreton Bay, extensive areas of *Sporobolus virginicus* grassland are formed.

Discussion

It can be seen from Table 5.2 that some species have a disjunct distribution along the Queensland coastline. The distributions merely reflect the sometimes subtle ecological differences that occur between estuarine systems and the ecological requirements of each of the species. Some species have broad ecological tolerances while others have narrow limits. In addition it is likely that some of the gaps apparent in the table will be filled as our knowledge on the distribution of mangrove species increases.

There is a general trend for the number of species to decrease from north to south within the state, with the greatest range of species being found in the wetter northern areas. This is mostly due to the increased number of species that occur in the upper tidal limits, especially at the landward margin of the mangroves. Some of the landward margin species, however, are scattered and rare.

In the main the recognisable mangrove communities are not more floristically complex in the wetter tropical areas than they are in the drier or cooler areas. Indeed in the latter areas the communities tend to consist of mixtures of several species while in wet tropical areas the communities tend to be monospecific. Similarly, the number of recognisable community types in the wet tropical areas is little different from the number in drier or cooler areas of the State, and in many cases it is considerably less.

Acknowledgments

We thank Mr F. Olsen of the Queensland Fisheries Service for information on areas of mangroves used in Fig. 5.1 and Mrs M. Saul for the preparation of the figures.

References

Dowling, R.M., 1979. The mangrove communities of Moreton Bay. In A. Bailey and N. C. Stevens (eds.), *Northern Moreton Bay Symposium.* Royal Society of Queensland, pp. 54-62.

Dowling, R.M., 1980. The mangrove vegetation. In Olsen, H.F., R.M. Dowling and D. Bareman *Biological Resources Survey (Estuarine Inventory) Round Hill Head to Tannum Sands.* Research Bulletin No.2, Queensland Fisheries Service, Brisbane, pp. 45-290.

Dowling, R.M., 1981. *Mangroves of Moreton Bay.* Technical Bulletin No.46 Botany Branch, Department of Primary Industries, Brisbane.

Dowling, R.M. and W.J.F. McDonald, 1976. *Moreton Region Vegetation Map Series: Brisbane.* Botany Branch, Queensland Department of Primary Industries, Brisbane. 20 pp.

Dredge, M., H. Kirkman and M.Potter, 1977. *A Short Term Biological Survey Tin Can Inlet, Great Sandy Strait.* Report 68, CSIRO Division of Fisheries and Oceanography, Cronulla. 26 pp.

Durrington, L.R., 1974. Vegetation of Brisbane Airport development and environs. In *Brisbane Airport Development Project Environmental Study.* Australian Government Publishing Service, Canberra. Vol. 3, pp. 19-46 and Vol.5, Fig. III-4.

Durrington, L.R., 1977. *Vegetation of Moreton Island.* Technical Bulletin No. 1, Botany Branch, Queensland Department of Primary Industries, Brisbane. 44 pp.

Elsol, J.A. and R.M. Dowling, 1978. *Moreton Region Vegetation Map Series: Beenleigh.* Botany Branch, Queensland Department of Primary Industries, Brisbane. 24 pp.

Elsol, J.A. and P.S. Sattler, 1979. *Moreton Region Vegetation Map Series. Caloundra.* Botany Branch, Queensland Department of Primary Industries, Brisbane. 23 pp.

Gill, E.D. and D. Hopley, 1972. Holocene sea levels in eastern Australia—a discussion. *Marine Geology* **12**, 223-33.

Graham, M., J. Grimshaw, E. Hegerl, J. McNalty and R. Timmins, 1975. Cairns wetlands—a preliminary report. *Operculum* **4**, 117-48.

Hegerl, E.J. and R.D. Timmins, 1973. The Noosa River tidal swamps. *Operculum* **3**, 38-43.

Hegerl, E.J. and D. Tarte, 1974. A reconnaissance of the Capricorn Coast tidal wetlands. *Operculum* **4**, 50-62.

Hopley, D., 1974. Investigations of sea level changes along the coast of the Great Barrier Reef. *Proceedings of the Second International Coral Reef Symposium.* Great Barrier Reef Committee, Brisbane, pp. 551-62.

Jones, W.T., 1971. The field identification and distribution of mangroves in Eastern Australia. *Queensland Naturalist* **20**, 35-51.

Lear, R. and T. Turner, 1977. *Mangroves of Australia.* University of Queensland Press, St Lucia, Qld. 84 pp.

McDonald, T.J. and G.N. Batianoff, 1980. Report on a visit to Cape Flattery. *Queensland Naturalist* **23**, 1-9.

McDonald, W.J.F. and J.A. Elsol, 1979. The vegetation of Bribie Island and environs. In A. Bailey and N.C. Stevens (eds.), *Northern Moreton Bay Symposium.* Royal Society of Queensland, pp. 47-53.

McDonald, W.J.F. and W.G. Whiteman, 1979. *Moreton Region Vegetation Map Series: Murwillumbah.* Botany Branch, Queensland Department of Primary Industries, Brisbane. 58 pp.

Macnae, W., 1966. Mangroves in eastern and southern Australia. *Australian Journal of Botany* **14**, 67-104.

Muller, J. and C.G.G.J. van Steenis, 1968. Do *Sonneratia caseolaris* and *S. ovata* occur in Queensland or the Northern Territory? *North Queensland Naturalist* **35**, 3-8.

Pedley, L. and R.F. Isbell, 1971. Plant communities of Cape York Peninsula. *Proceedings of the Royal Society of Queensland* **82**, 51-74.

Saenger, P. and M.S. Hopkins, 1975. Observations on the mangroves of the south-eastern Gulf of Carpentaria, Australia. In G.E. Walsh, S.C. Snedaker and H.J. Teas (eds.), *Proceedings of the International Symposium on Biology and Management of Mangroves.* Institute of Food and Agricultural Sciences, University of Florida, Gainesville, Florida, Vol. I, pp. 126-36.

Saenger, P. and J. Robson, 1977. Structural analysis of mangrove communities on the central Queensland coastline. *Marine Research in Indonesia* **18**, 101-18.

Saenger, P., M.M. Specht, R.L. Specht and V.J. Chapman, 1977. Mangal and coastal salt-marsh communities in Australia. In V.J. Chapman (ed.) *Ecosystems of the World. I. Wet Coastal Ecosystems.* Elsevier, Amsterdam. Vol. 1, pp. 293-345.

Shanco, P. and R. Timmins, 1975. Reconnaissance of southern Bustard Bay tidal wetlands. *Operculum* **4**, 149-54.

Shine, R., C.P. Ellway and E.J. Hegerl, 1973. A biological survey of the Tallebudgera Creek estuary. *Operculum* **3**, 59-83.

Specht, R.L., 1970. Vegetation. In G.W. Leeper (ed.), *The Australian Environment.* CSIRO and The University of Melbourne Press, pp. 43-67.

Specht, R.L., R.B. Salt and S.T. Reynolds, 1975. Vegetation in the vicinity of Weipa, North Queensland. *Proceedings of the Royal Society of Queensland* **88**, 17-38.

State Public Relations Bureau, Premiers Department, 1976. Climate. *Queensland Resources Atlas*, pp. 24-8.

Tomlinson, P.B. and J.S. Womersley, 1976. A species of *Rhizophora* new to New Guinea and Queensland, with notes relevant to the genus. *Contributions of Herbarium Australiense* **19**, 1-10.

Twidale, C.R., 1964. *Geomorphology of the Leichhardt-Gilbert Area.* CSIRO Land Research Series No. 11, pp. 115-24.

Woolston, F.P., 1973. *Ethnobotanical Items From the Wellesley Islands, Gulf of Carpentaria.* Occasional Paper University of Queensland Anthropology Museum No. 1, pp. 95-103.

6

Mangroves of Western Australia

Kevin F. Kenneally

Introduction

Mangroves in Western Australia form part of the discontinuous, fringing tidal community extending around much of the Australian coast. Those of the western coast may be remnants of a much wetter climatic regime (Jennings, 1975; Thom *et al.*, 1975) and are different from their northern and eastern counterparts in that they occupy a more arid climatic setting. This is reflected in the paucity of epiphytes within the communities and the development to landward of extensive salt flats lacking vegetation because of dry-season hypersalinity. Despite this arid setting Western Australian mangroves provide a habitat for one of the world's richest mangrove bird faunas, and there are early indications that, like other fringing tidal communities of Australia, they may prove to be important corridors for migrating wildlife.

Previous studies

Until the recent study by Semeniuk *et al.* (1978) mangroves in Western Australia had been largely ignored. Although the coastline was explored by Portuguese, Dutch, French and British navigators, few found interest in the mangroves.

One of the earliest references to Western Australian mangroves is that made by William Dampier in 1699, who spent five or six days at Shark Bay, visited several islands in the Dampier Archipelago and landed at La Grange Bay at the northern end of the Eighty Mile Beach. In his journal he referred to a 'small black mangrove-tree' along 'the sides of the creeks'. He did not collect a specimen and it is difficult to decide which of the species it could have been (George, 1971).

In 1821 Captain Philip Parker King in the *Mermaid*, while carrying out hydrographic surveys along the north coast, recorded that the Aborigines used mangroves to construct rafts. The botanist accompanying the expedition, Allan Cunningham, made a collection of a flowering specimen of *Ceriops tagal* from Careening Bay. His collections are housed in the Herbarium of the Royal Botanic Gardens, Kew, England. Cunningham also compiled what could be considered the first biogeographic list of plants (including mangroves) recorded from the shores of Australia that are common to India or South America (King, 1827). Further hydrographic surveys were carried out by Commander Stokes of the *Beagle* in 1838 (Stokes, 1846). The survey charts prepared by King and Stokes are most useful now in detecting areas of coastal erosion affecting mangroves.

Although botanical studies commenced soon after the founding of the Swan

River Colony in 1829 little interest was shown in the mangrove communities. The German botanist Ludwig Preiss collected *Avicennia marina* from Bunbury in 1839 (Miquel, 1844-45), while the naturalist John Gilbert collected it from the Abrolhos Islands in 1842, as did botanist Ferdinand von Mueller from Shark Bay in 1883.

It was not until Ludwig Diels (1906) published *The Plant World of Western Australia South of the Tropics* that the first detailed account of mangroves appeared. He noted that the mangroves of the tropical coast were an impoverished form of the Malayan, and that neither floristically nor biologically had they developed any special features of their own. He also observed that *Avicennia* was the most 'resistant element' in that it appeared to occur around the coast of Australia. Diels also recognised the arid setting of the Western Australian mangroves and distinguished them as follows:

> Immediately behind the Mangrove swamp in many of the more dry regions the formations of the interior are to be found. On the north west coast, however, a special strand-woodland formation can be distinguished, and on the more southern coasts dune and marsh formations bound the strand. The north-eastern strand woodland characterises the region of plenteous summer rain, and consequently extends from the Kimberley eastward up to Moreton Bay.

In the Pilbara and Kimberley regions C.H. Ostenfeld (1918) made collections and described the mangrove formations at Port Hedland, Onslow, Ashburton River and Broome. He commented:

> The Mangrove formation of W.A. is consequently poor; it does not make such a luxuriant impression as do the Malayan and the West-Indian Mangroves. Still, this evergreen fringe bordering the coast and estuaries refreshes the eye in these regions, where the other vegetation is far more reduced owing to the dry and hot climate.

The first detailed description of Kimberley mangroves is that made by C.A. Gardner (1923), who was attached to the Easton Kimberley expedition of 1921 as botanist. Gardner observed that mangroves were a feature of the coast, particularly in sheltered areas such as estuaries and creeks. He also noted root adaptations in *Rhizophora* and *Bruguiera* and related leaf xerophily to salinity of the soil. Gardner also recorded the occurrence of *Ceriops* and *Aegiceras* above high tide in the equinoctial tide zone.

The potential of mangroves as a topic of natural history study was recognised by Whitlock (1947) although his observations were primarily ornithological. It was not until many years later that Sauer (1965) published his studies on the seashore vegetation of the State which included studies on the mangroves at Port Hedland.

Several authors have made more recent references to mangroves in reconnaissance vegetation surveys (Beard, 1967; Miles *et al.*, 1975; Burbidge *et al.*, 1978; George, 1978).

Floristics and ecology

The floristics and ecology of Western Australian mangorves have been described in some detail by Semeniuk *et al.* (1978), and much of the following account
is derived from this work.

The mangroves of Western Australia are distributed in the following four
broad biogeographic regions: tropical subhumid, tropical semiarid, tropical
arid, subtropical humid to arid (Fig. 6.1). Within each of these Regions a
particular suite of mangrove species occurs (Table 6.1).

I Tropical Sub-humid Region

This area extends from Derby to Cape Londonderry on the north Kimberley
coast. Here the most diverse and luxuriant mangroves are found in the mouths
of the larger river systems (e.g. Drysdale, Lawley, Hunter, Roe and Prince
Regent Rivers) with seventeen species being recorded. Many of these tropical
mangroves merge with woodlands in the upper tidal areas or they may be
backed to landward by saltmarshes or salt flats.

A strongly two-season climate characterises this area. There are
approximately five months of heavy rain (November-March inclusive), five
months with exceedingly little rain (May-September inclusive) and two
transition months (April and October). During the wet season the rainfall
along the coast may exceed 1250 mm. Mean monthly temperatures range from
30°C during the wet to 40°C in the dry.

Within these more extensive mangrove communities marked zonation is
often found. The various mangrove species occur in distinct bands related to
tidal levels, soils and other factors. Thus, as one views a mangrove community
it is apparent that there are broad aggregations of species. These aggregations
commonly form belts parallel to a coastline or major creek system. Many
mangrove species have differently coloured leaves, and zonation may be
emphasised by bands of coloration. These zones are described by Macnae
(1968), who recognised a recurring pattern of mangrove species distribution
related to height above mean sea level. Macnae distinguished the following
zones from the landward to the seaward margins:

1. the landward fringe,
2. zone of *Ceriops*,
3. zone of *Bruguiera*,
4. zone of *Rhizophora*,
5. seaward *Avicennia* fringe,
6. zone of *Sonneratia*.

In zones 2-6 the species that lends its generic name to the zone occurs either in
pure stands or as the dominant mangrove.

Mangrove communities are typically zoned, with the zonation depending on
a variety of interacting factors—physical, chemical and biological—which
determine whether a species will survive in a given environment. The interplay
and balance of these factors determine whether one or several species become
established. The main factors that appear to determine the survival of
individual species, and thus zonation within a community, are:

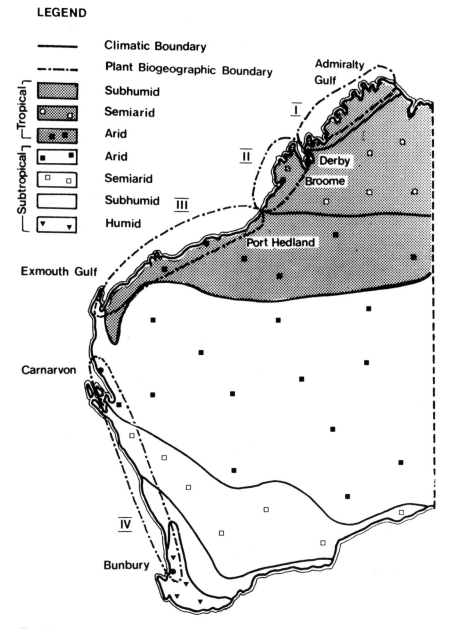

Fig. 6.1.   Map showing the four main biogeographic regions (labelled, I, II, III, IV) in
relationship to climatic boundaries. Table 6.1 lists the species that occur in
each region. Climatic boundaries are from Gentilli (1972); nomenclature of
climatic zones from Trewartha (1968). Note that mangroves occurring in
Cambridge Gulf (Thom *et al.*, 1975) have features essentially common to
those of biogeographic Region II. (From Semeniuk *et al.*, 1978).

Table 6.1   Distribution of mangrove species in biogeographic regions

Species	I	II	III	IV
Avicennia marina	X	X	X	X
Aegialitis annulata	X	X	X	X
Aegiceras corniculatum	X	X	X	
Rhizophora stylosa	X	X	X	
Ceriops tagal	X	X	X	
Osbornia octodonta	X	X	X	
Bruguiera exaristata	X	X	X	
Camptostemon schultzii	X	X		
Excoecaria agallocha	X	X		
Sonneratia alba	X	X		
Xylocarpus australasicus	X	X		
Xylocarpus granatum	X			
Pemphis acidula	X	X		
Lumnitzera racemosa	X	X		
Avicennia eucalyptifolia	X			
Bruguiera parviflora	X			
Scyphiphora hydrophyllacea	X			

1. Frequency of flooding by tidai waters. This is dependent on the tidal pattern (i.e. whether one or two tides per day, the spring tide versus neap tide ranges) and on the height of the shore above mean sea level. These factors will determine not only how often, but also to what depth, mangrove species are inundated (Macnae, 1968).

2. Soil type. This constitutes the composition, structure and other interrelated properties such as salinity, nutrient content, permeability and drainage (Macnae, 1968; Spackman *et al.*, 1964).

3. Soil salinity. This depends on evaporation, waterlogged nature of the soil, frequency of tidal inundation, and the possibility of freshwater influx. Occurrence of many mangrove species appears to be markedly controlled by soil salinity, e.g. *Ceriops* can tolerate up to 60 parts per thousand salinity and will grow in very saline soils to the exclusion of other mangrove species (Clarke and Hannon, 1970; Macnae, 1968).

4. Drainage. This is related to properties of soil, slope of surface and presence of local creeks. It is an important factor in the survival of mangroves since some species require well drained soils whereas others can flourish in poorly drained, waterlogged soils (Clarke and Hannon, 1967, 1969; Macnae, 1968).

5. Plant interactions. Interspecific competition can be an important factor in mangrove survival; for instance the *Rhizophora* canopy, by excluding light, can inhibit the establishment of other mangrove species (Jones, 1971).

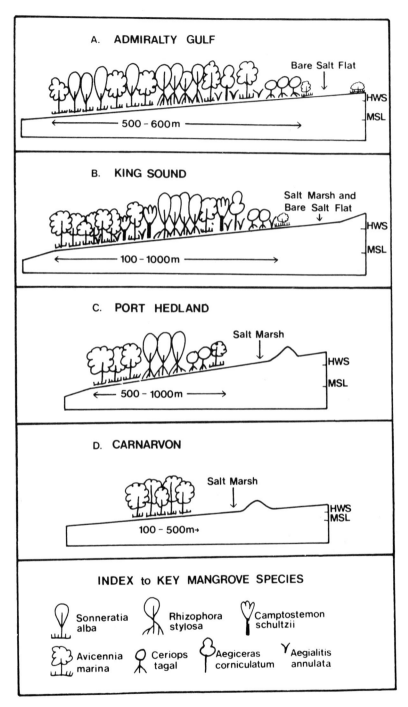

Fig. 6.2.   Diagrams illustrating zonation of mangroves in four different localities.
Each locality is representative of one biogeographic region. HWS = High
Water Spring Tide; MSL = Mean Sea Level, (From Semeniuk *et al.*, 1978).

Plate 6.1.   Mangrove fringing the base of steep sandstone cliffs at Cape Londonderry, the most northerly part of the State.

6.   Animal interactions. A host of encrusting, boring and burrowing organisms invades or inhabits mangrove communities. Some activities of animals are beneficial, such as crustacean burrowing that returns nutrients to the surface of the soil. Other activities are directly harmful, such as the boring by ship-worm (*Teredo*) and isopods into mangrove trunks and roots (Macnae, 1968; Rhem and Humm, 1973).

Some of the factors mentioned above are interrelated. For instance, with a sloping coastline, frequency of tidal flooding decreases upslope and if the climate is dry, salinity increases. Similarly, poorly drained soils tend to remain waterlogged and if subject to intense evaporation can become excessively saline. Where the environmental factors are well differentiated along a shore of gentle gradient, there will be a tendency for the development of distinct broad zones of mangroves (e.g. Figs. 6.2A and 6.2B).

The above zonation is fully developed in Region I. Here mangroves may merge with supra-tidal rain (monsoon) forest (semi-deciduous vine thicket) or more commonly with woodlands, saltmarshes or salt flats.

At Cape Londonderry, the most northern extremity of Western Australia, mangrove zonation may reach its full development in sheltered bays or fringe the bases of steep sandstone cliffs (Plate 6.1). At Admiralty Gulf, a large embayment into which the Mitchell and Lawley rivers flow, a series of well developed mangrove communities occur. Here they again reach full zonation (Fig. 6.2A) and may be backed to landward by strand species such as *Thespesia, Canavalia* and *Sporobolus*. Further south where the Prince Regent River flows into Brunswick Bay extensive mangrove communities are common. Once

Plate 6.2.   Aerial view of mangroves showing zonation of species and broad tidal salt flats adjoining low open eucalypt woodland at St George Basin, Prince Regent River. The dark band is *Rhizophora stylosa*.

Plate 6.3   Mangroves occurring in Cambridge Gulf (e. g. Wyndham) showing features similar to the mangroves of the tropical semiarid region

again they may merge with *Eucalyptus* woodlands or be backed by extensive saltmarshes or salt flats (Plate 6.2). The fern *Acrostichum speciosum* occurs in the landward fringe, but the palm *Nypa fruticans* has not been recorded for Western Australia.

The mangrove species of the Cambridge Gulf-Ord River area, east of Admiralty gulf occur in a tropical semi-arid setting which is essentially similar to Region II. Hence fewer species are recorded (Thom *et al.,* 1975) and the community is less luxuriant as, for example, at Wyndham (Plate 6.3).

The only epiphytes so far recorded in Western Australian mangroves are lichens which have been collected growing on *Ceriops tagal* and *Rhizophora stylosa*, and the Mangrove Mistletoe, *Amyema thalassium* (George and Kenneally, 1975; Hnatiuk and Kenneally, 1981). The latter species may prove to be conspecific with *Amyema gravis*, an exclusive hemiparasite of mangroves in east Java and the adjacent Kangean Islands (C.G.G.J. van Steenis, personal communication, 1979). This small number of epiphytes is unusual when compared with tropical mangroves in other parts of Australia and the world. Their absence tends to emphasise the arid setting in which Western Australian mangroves occur (van Steenis, 1962).

II Tropical Semiarid Region

This region extends from Derby south to Cape Bossut at the northern end of the Eighty Mile Beach. The most extensive mangrove communities are developed in King Sound (Fig. 6.2B) and the sheltered bays of the Dampierland Peninsula. The mangroves here may merge with woodlands in the supra-tidal area but further south extensive saltmarshes and salt flats merging with Pindan (*Acacia* thicket) are more common.

This region, like the previous one, is also subject to a two-season climate with rain falling between December and May. During the wet season rainfall may exceed 750 mm. Mean monthly temperatures range from 20°C in the wet to >30°C in the dry.

Again in the sheltered bays full zonation may be developed but some species such as *Bruguiera parviflora, Scyphiphora hydrophylacea* and *Xylocarpus granatum* are missing, being confined to Region I.

The saltmarshes and salt flats are well developed behind the coastal dunes of the Dampierland Peninsula (Plate 6.4). Here, a paperbark (*Melaleuca acacioides*) fringes broad saltmarshes which support the samphire *Halosarcia halocnemoides* and the halophytes *Sesuvium portulacastrum, Sporobolus virginicus* and *Neobassia astrocarpa*. Cattle often graze on these areas.

North of Broome at Willie Creek well developed mangroves abut a broad limestone pavement. At One Arm Point on the Dampierland Peninsula *Sonneratia* and *Avicennia* occur on a shingle beach.

III Tropical Arid Region

This region extends along the arid Pilbara coast from Cape Keraudren at the southern end of the Eighty Mile Beach to Exmouth Gulf. Mangroves are not

Plate 6.4   A salt flat bordered by saltmarsh at the landward edge of mangroves (upper left) on the Dampierland Peninsula, north of Broome. Not shown in the photograph is the paperbark (*Melaleuca acacioides*) fringe to the landward of the saltmarsh.

common along the Eighty Mile Beach presumably because of the lack of protected habitats, the exposure of the beach to strong wave and tidal activity and the lack of creeks supplying fresh water. Where they do occur at Cape Missiessy and Mandora, stands of *Avicennia marina* and *Ceriops tagal* are found fringing small creeks and adjacent saltmarshes protected from strong wave action by sand spits formed parallel to the shore. Some 30 km behind Eighty Mile Beach an inland occurrence of *Avicennia marina* has been recorded by Beard (1967), who postulated that it was a relic of estuarine conditions prevailing during a time of maximum eustatic rise in sea level in the Pleistocene. Jennings (1975) suggests that the occurrence may not be a result of Mid-Holocene emergence but could be due solely to barrier development. However, the possibility that seeds might have been transported to this locality by Aborigines should not be discounted.

In this Region seven species of mangroves have been recorded. Exmouth Gulf can be considered as the southerly cut-off point for communities embracing more than one species, as south of there only one species, *Avicennia marina*, occurs. This is also recognised by George and Davis (personal communication) in their studies of the distribution of Australian Fiddler Crabs (*Uca*). Their work shows that nine species of *Uca* are recorded from Exmouth Gulf but further south only two species occur.

Mangroves in the north of this Region are backed to landward by salt flats and saltmarshes (Fig. 6.2C) whereas in the south they often merge with hummock grasslands of *Spinifex longifolius* and *Triodia pungens*.

The climate of this Region is arid, January to June being the wettest six months. During this period an average 250 mm of rain is recorded. Temperatures may range from 17°C in the wet to 30°C in the dry season.

Plate 6.5   *Avicennia marina* fringing a shallow tidal channel at Leschenault Inlet, Bunbury. This is the southernmost occurrence of mangroves in Western Australia.

Plate 6.6.   *Avicennia marina* fringing the sheltered lagoons of Wooded Island, Houtman Abrolhos

IV Subtropical Humid to Arid

This Region extends from Shark Bay to Bunbury (Plate 6.5) in the south. It also includes a second inland occurrence of *Avicennia marina* on the shores of Lake McLeod. In this region only monotypic stands of *Avicennia* in a bushy shrub habit occur, often backed by saltmarsh (Fig. 6.2D). These are well developed in the sheltered waters of Shark Bay and the lagoons of Wooded and Pelsart Islands in the Houtman Abrolhos (Plate 6.6). Shark Bay is the southern limit for Fiddler Crabs where only two species, *Uca mjobergi* and an undescribed *Uca* occur. However, the wave-dominated sandy coastline between Shark Bay and Bunbury is devoid of mangroves, perhaps owing to the absence of sufficiently protected habitats.

The climate of this region is variable, the wettest six months being from May to October at Bunbury and March to August at Shark Bay. Average rainfall ranges from 200 mm at Carnarvon to 900 mm at Bunbury.

Fauna of Western Australian mangroves

The animals that are associated with mangroves span a wide range of invertebrate and vertebrate groups. This fauna is distributed through the community, often in distinct zones related to frequency of tidal flooding, soil type, salinity, and the type of surrounding plant community. Although many of the animals exploit mangrove communities as habitat, nursery grounds or source of food, there are some faunal groups that are directly beneficial to the community through a wide range of behavioural activities, particularly burrowing crabs and pollination by birds and insects.

Fauna in mangrove communities may be distinguished as either resident or temporary. Resident fauna includes ground-dwelling surface animals such as hermit crabs, mud whelks and other snails; burrowing organisms such as crabs, shrimps and worms; tree-dwellers such as encrusting oysters and barnacles, wandering snails, boring *Teredo* (ship-worm) and a host of insects, birds and bats which use mangrove foliage as habitat and derive food from leaves, flowers and fruit. Mangroves provide vital feeding grounds for the temporary faunas characteristic of either low or high tide conditions. At high tide the community is invaded by free-swimming animals, such as fish and crustaceans, to be replaced at low tide by terrestrial animals such as birds, reptiles and mammals.

In Western Australia the more obvious ground-dwelling animals of the mangrove community are:

Crustaceans—this group includes the brightly-coloured species of the fiddler crab *Uca*, species of *Sesarma* and *Metopograpsus* belonging to the grapsid crab family, hermit crabs, and the large edible mangrove crab *Scylla serrata*. Crustaceans are commonly distributed in distinct zones across mangal flats.

Molluscs—these include a variety of small and large snails such as *Terebralia, Telescopium* and cerithids, species of oysters, and clams.

Mudskippers—these are gobioid fish that typically reside around and in mangroves; these animals, able to survive short periods of aerial exposure, skip around on the water and mud and build the turreted (chimney-like) burrows so commonly seen in mangroves.

A search in the mangrove soil will always reveal numerous and varied burrowing organisms such as crustaceans (shrimps, amphipods and isopods in addition to the crustaceans mentioned above), worms, clams and insects. Fauna found on trunks, branches and leaves includes barnacles, oysters, the snails *Littorina* and (in some areas) *Nerita*, and a wide variety of insects; in some mangroves grapsid and xanthid crabs are found, particularly around the base of hollowed trunks.

Mangroves between Shark Bay and Cambridge Gulf provide a habitat for one of the world's richest mangrove bird faunas (G. Storr and R. Johnstone, personal communication, 1979). The broad tidal flats with their varying water depths provide food for thousands of wintering and resident wading birds like sandpipers and dotterels. Two birds, the Brown-tailed Flycatcher (*Microeca tormenti*) and the Dusky Flyeater (*Gerygone tenebrosa*), are endemic in Western Australia to the mangroves of Regions I, II and III. In all there are sixteen bird species virtually confined to mangroves in Western Australia, including the Chestnut Rail (*Eulabeornis castaneoventris*), Mangrove Kingfisher (*Halcyon chloris*) and Mangrove Golden Whistler (*Pachycephala melanura*). In other parts of Australia many of these species are not confined to the mangroves but frequent a wide range of habitats such as riverine forest, vine forest and paperbark swamps. Many other species such as the Great-billed Heron (*Ardea sumatrana*), Bar-shouldered Dove (*Geopelia humeralis*) and the Rufous Fantail (*Rhipidura rufifrons*) frequently visit mangroves to feed, nest or shelter. In Region III (the Pilbara coast) the Bar-shouldered Dove and the Shining Flycatcher (*Myiagra alecto*) are restricted to the mangroves and adjacent coastal vegetation. In this arid region the mangrove represents the major closed canopy community which appears to be an important factor for mangrove birds.

The Salt-water Crocodile (*Crocodylus porosus*) inhabits both fresh and saltwater but is concentrated in the tidal portions of large rivers where mangroves are plentiful. The mangrove environment is also used by numerous fish and crustacean species temporarily as a nursery.

Thus, in terms of plant primary production, feeding grounds, and nursery beds, mangroves are a vital resource. It has been shown elsewhere in the world that the destruction of mangroves can lead to major changes in near-shore ecology with the subsequent decline of commercial fishing. Consequent on mangrove loss is the dislocation of the food chain accompanied by the inevitable loss or severe depletion of organisms within the chain. Destruction of mangroves can also result in loss of habitats for a large range of terrestrial organisms such as insects, birds and bats. Removal of even part of a mangrove, such as a particular zone, may have detrimental effects on the ecosystem since those birds and insects that are very selective in their feeding can be lost.

Acknowledgments

The co-operation of my colleagues Vic Semeniuk and Paul Wilson during the preparation of this chapter is gratefully acknowledged. I am indebted to Glen Storr and Ron Johnstone (Ornithology and Herpetology), Ray George and Diana Davis (Carcinology), Western Australian Museum, for making available unpublished manuscripts. Alex George (Western Australian Herbarium) provided the photographs for Plates 6.3 and 6.7. John Green kindly read the paper and provided extremely helpful comments. The assistance in the field of Karl Pirkopf is greatly appreciated. The drafts and manuscript were expertly and patiently typed by Vicki Hamley and proofed by Wendy Lee-Frampton. To all of these people I extend my thanks.

The opportunity to examine historical collections in the Herbarium of the Royal Botanic Gardens, Kew, England was carried out during 1979 whilst the author was the recipient of a Churchill Fellowship.

References

Beard, J.S., 1967. An inland occurrence of mangrove. *Western Australian Naturalist* **10**, 112-15.

Burbidge, A.A., N.G. Marchant, N.L. McKenzie and P.G. Wilson, 1978. Environment. In A.A. Burbidge and N.L. McKenzie (eds.), The islands of the North-West Kimberley, Western Australia. *Wildlife Research Bulletin Western Australia* **7**, 12-21.

Clarke, L.D. and N.J. Hannon, 1967. The mangrove swamp and salt-marsh communities of the Sydney District. 1. Vegetation, soils and climate. *Journal of Ecology* **55**, 753-71.

Clarke, L.D. and N.J. Hannon, 1969. The mangrove swamp and salt-marsh communities of the Sydney District. II. The holocoenotic complex with particular reference to physiography. *Journal of Ecology* **57**, 213-34.

Clarke, L.D. and N.J. Hannon, 1970. The mangrove swamp and salt-marsh communities of the Sydney District. III. Plant growth in relation to salinity and waterlogging. *Journal of Ecology* **58**, 351-69.

Diels, L., 1906. *Die Pflanzenwelt von West-Australien südlich des Wendekreises. Mit einer Einleitung über die Pflanzenwelt Gesamt-Australiens in Grundzügen.* Leipzig, Wilhelm Engelmann. (unpubl. translation by W.J. Dakin).

Gardner, C.A., 1923. Botanical notes. Kimberley Division of Western Australia. *Western Australian Forests Department Bulletin* **32**, 1-105. Government Printer, Perth.

Gentilli, J., 1972. *Australian Climate Patterns.* Nelson, Melbourne. 285 pp.

George, A.S., 1971. The plants seen and collected in north-western Australia by William Dampier. *Western Australian Naturalist* **11**, 173-8.

George, A.S., 1978. Notes on the vegetation and flora of the Cape Londonderry Peninsula, North Kimberley, Western Australia. *Western Australian Research Notes* **1**, 1-15.

George, A.S. and K.F. Kenneally, 1975. The flora of the Prince Regent River Reserve, North-Western Kimberley, Western Australia. *Wildlife Research Bulletin Western Australia* **3**, 31-68.

Hnatiuk, R.J. and K.F. Kenneally, 1981. A survey of the vegetation and flora of the Mitchell Plateau, North-Western Australia. In *Biological Survey of Mitchell Plateau and Admiralty Gulf, Kimberley, Western Australia.* Western Australian Museum, Perth. pp. 13-93.

Jennings, J.N., 1975. Desert dunes and estuarine fill in the Fitzroy estuary (North-Western Australia). *Catena* **2**, 215-62.

Jones, W.T., 1971. The field identification and distribution of mangroves in Eastern Australia. *Queensland Naturalist* **20**, 35-51.

King, P.P., 1827. *Survey of the Intertropical Coasts of Australia.* Vol. 2. John Murray, London. 637 pp.

Miles, J.M., K.F. Kenneally and A.S. George, 1975. The Prince Regent River Reserve Environment. *Wildlife Research Bulletin Western Australia* **3**, 17-30.

Macnae, W., 1968. A general account of the fauna and flora of mangrove swamps and forests in the Indo-West-Pacific. *Advances in Marine Biology* **6**, 73-270.

Miquel, F.A.G., 1844-1845. Avicennieae. In C. Lehmann (ed.), *Plantae Preissianae,* Hamburg. 499 pp.

Mueller, F. von, 1883. *The Plants Indigenous Around Sharks Bay and Its Vicinity.* Government Printer, Perth. 24 pp.

Ostenfeld, C.H., 1918. *Contributions to West Australian Botany 11.* Dansk Botanisk Arkiv, Copenhagen. 144 pp.

Rhem, A. and H.J. Humm, 1973. *Sphaeroma terebrands:* a threat to the mangroves of south eastern Florida. *Science* **182**, 173-4.

Sauer, J., 1965. Geographic reconnaissance of Western Australian seashore vegetation. *Australian Journal of Botany* **13**, 39-69.

Semeniuk, V., K.F. Kenneally and P.G. Wilson, 1978. *Mangroves of Western Australia.* Western Australian Naturalists' Club Handbook No. 11, Perth, W.A.

Spackman, W., W.L. Riegel and C.P. Dolsen, 1964. Geological and biological interactions in the swamp-marsh complex of southern Florida. In E.D. Dapples and M.E. Hopkins (eds.) *Environments of Coal Deposition.* Geological Society of America, Special Paper 114.

Stokes, J.L., 1846. *Discoveries in Australia.* 2 volumes. T. & W. Boone, London. 1064 pp.

Thom, B.G., L.D. Wright and J.M.Coleman, 1975. Mangrove ecology and deltaic-estuarine geomorphology; Cambridge Gulf-Ord River, Western Australia. *Journal of Ecology* **63**, 203-32.

Trewartha, G.T., 1968. *An Introduction to Climate.* 4th ed. McGraw-Hill Book Co., New York 408 pp.

van Steenis, C.G.G.J., 1962. The distribution of mangrove plant genera and its significance for palaeogeography. *Proceedings of the Koninklijke Nederlandse Akademie van Wetenschappen Amsterdam,* Ser. C, 65, 164-9.

Whitlock, F.L., 1947. Animal life in mangroves. *Western Australian Naturalist* **1**, 353-6.

7

Mangrove Vegetation of the Southern and Western
Australian Coastline

P.B. Bridgewater

Introduction

Although mangrove development is most extensive north of the Tropic of Capricorn, mangrove vegetation occurs in suitable localities right around the coast of Australia. Indeed, the most poleward occurence of any mangrove in the world is found at Corner Inlet, Victoria (38°45′S, 146°30′E), where stands of *Avicennia marina* occur.

Within the coastline defined by Port Hedland (W.A.) in the north-west to Port Albert (Vic.) in the south-east, mangrove development is sporadic, and floristically simple. Over much of the coastline only one species (*A. marina*) is found, with rather more species becoming important north of Exmouth Gulf.

This chapter reviews the mangrove vegetation along this coastline, and attempts to classify the mangrove associations in the manner suggested by Chapman (1977).

Distribution

A. marina occurs in disjunct pockets along the southern Australian coastline. The major occurences are Corner Inlet (Vic.) 38°45′S, 146°19′E, Westernport Bay (Vic.) 38°22′S, 145°32′E, Spencer Gulf (S.A.) 34°30′S, 136°30′E, Gulf St Vincent (S.A.) 34°45′S, 137°57′E, Ceduna and environs (S.A.) 32°08′S, 133°41′E.

Along the Western Australian coastline *A. marina* occurs at Bunbury 33°20′S, 115°38′E, and then there is a considerable disjunction until Carnarvon 24°53′S, 113°40′E. Northward from Carnarvon the distribution of *A. marina* and other mangrove species is fairly consistent to Port Hedland 20°18′S, 118°35′E.

The distribution range from Corner Inlet to Bunbury is all within climate Type IV (transitional zone with winter rain) of Walter and Lieth (1960), and the range from Carnarvon to Port Hedland is within climate Type III (subtropical dry zone).

No other mangrove areas in Australia fall within these climatic belts. They are the most summer arid (Type IV) or totally arid (Type III) regions in Australia, and have the common feature that progression from the tidal regions to the landward regions of the mangal is associated with a salinity rise—a direct contrast to the situation in the humid tropics and subtropics.

Floristic analysis

Areas of 10 m x 5 m, of variable shape depending on the landform, were set out in respective areas of mangal. In each of these areas (relevés) a full list of mangrove and other vascular plant species present was noted, and each species assigned a value on a cover-abundance scale (Bridgewater, 1971). These data were then subjected to tabular sorting as detailed in Mueller-Dombois and Ellenberg (1974). The results are presented in Tables 7.2-7.11, and a summary of all the tables presented in Table 7.1.

A list of the relevé locations is contained in Appendix I, and the species citations used in Appendix II.

Table 7.1   Synotpic table of associations, grouped into alliances. Presence values in the table calculated as follows:

I	species present in 1-19% of the relevés
II	species present in 20-39% of the relevés
III	species present in 40-59% of the relevés
IV	species present in 60-79% of the relevés
V	species present in 80-100% of the relevés

Table number:	2	3	4	5	6	7	8	9	10	11
Number of relevés:	4	10	6	4	14	16	4	9	4	5
Alliance code (see text)	i	ii	iii	iv	iv	iv	iv	iv	v	iv
Species characteristic of higher units:										
Aegialitis annulata	V	I	—	—	I	—	—	—	I	—
Aegiceras corniculatum	—	V	—	—	—	—	—	—	—	—
Rhizophora stylosa	—	I	V	V	—	—	—	II	—	—
Avicennia marina	—	I	—	V	V	V	V	V	V	—
Bruguiera exaristata	—	—	—	—	—	—	—	—	IV	—
Ceriops tagal	—	—	—	—	—	—	—	V	V	V
Differential species of associations and sub-associations:										
Sarcocornia quinqueflora	—	—	—	—	—	V	—	—	—	—
Halosarcia halocnemoides	—	—	—	—	—	I	V	I	—	—
Osbornia octodonta	—	—	—	—	—	—	—	—	IV	—
Other species:										
Rhizophora stylosa (seedlings)	—	I	—	—	—	—	—	—	—	—
Suaeda australis	—	—	—	—	I	II	—	II	—	—
Samolus repens	—	—	—	—	—	I	—	—	—	—
Sclerostegia arbuscula	—	—	—	—	—	II	—	—	—	—
Spartina townsendii	—	—	—	—	—	I	—	—	—	—
Rhizoclonium sp.	—	—	—	—	—	I	—	—	—	—
Halosarcia indica	—	—	—	—	—	—	I	—	—	—
Limonium salicornaceum	—	—	—	—	—	—	I	II	—	—
Halosarcia pterygosperma	—	—	—	—	—	—	I	—	—	—
Hemichroa diandra	—	—	—	—	—	—	I	—	—	—

The associations

Distribution data refer solely to the section of coastline being considered and should not be taken as being indicative of the general Australian distribution of the associations.

Aegialitetum annulatae (Table 7.2). Confined to the Pilbara coastline of Western Australia, this association is found as a pure stand of *Aegialitis annulata* fringing the mangal. It typically occurs well up tidal creeks, is frequently associated with areas of sediment deposition and occurs in areas with salinity of seawater or less.

Table 7.2   Aegialitetum annulatae Association

Relevé number:	203	222	235	260
Height of dominant species (m):	1	1	1	1
Number of species:	1	1	1	2
Identifying species of association and cover-abundance:				
Aegialitis annulata	5	5	5	4

Aegiceretum corniculatae (Table 7.3); Chapman, 1977. Also usually confined to the Pilbara coastline, this association takes the form of extensive monospecific stands of *Aegiceras corniculatum*. Variants of this occur where *Avicennia marina* or *Rhizophora stylosa* occurs with *Aegicieras*. The monospecific stands are typical of low lying accreting mudbanks, whereas the variants are typical of steep sided creeks. The salinity tolerance of the association ranges from seawater to brackish water.

Table 7.3   Aegiceretum corniculatae Association

Relevé number:	245	232	237	240	236	283	234	243	254	258
Height of dominant species (m):	2	2	2	2	2	1.5	1.5	1.5	1.5	1.5
Number of species:	2	3	2	2	3	1	1	1	1	1
Differential species of variants and cover-abundance:										
Avicennia marina	3	2	—	—	—	—	—	—	—	—
Rhizophora stylosa	—	—	2	2	—	—	—	—	—	—
Aegialitis annulata	—	—	—	—	2	—	—	—	—	—
Identifying species of Association and cover-abundance:										
Aegiceras corniculatum	3	4	3	4	4	5	4	5	5	5
Other species and cover-abundance:										
Rhizophora stylosa (seedlings)	—	—	—	—	—	—	—	—	—	—

Rhizophoretum stylosae (Table 7.4); Chapman, 1977. Found on the western coast from Exmouth Gulf (22°05S, 114°15E) northward, this association represents pure stands of *R. stylosa*. It is typical of unconsolidated silts, and many form the seaward fringe of the mangal in protected zones. The salinities experienced by this association are those of seawater.

Table 7.4   Rhizophoretum stylosae Association

Relevé number:	205	219	225	246	250	280
Height of dominant species (m):	5	5	5	4	4	5
Number of species:	1	1	1	1	1	1
Identifying species of association and cover-abundance:						
Rhizophora stylosa	5	5	5	5	5	5

Avicennio-Rhizophoretum stylosae (Table 7.5). The distribution range of this association parallels that of the Rhizophoretum. It is developed where there are extensive flats of unconsolidated muds, and typically is zoned between the Rhizophoretum and Avicennietum. Where extensive flats are absent the Rhizophoretum abuts directly onto the Avicennietum, or the Ceriopo-Bruguieretum (Table 7. 10).

Avicennietum resiniferae (Table 7.6); Chapman, 1977. This is the most widespread of all the associations, occuring throughout the southern and western coastlines. The name is derived from the variety of *A. marina* var. *resinifera*. Although other works use the synonym *A. marina* var. *australasica*, as Chapman (1977) has used the var. *resinifera* it is appropriate to retain it. In many areas this represents the only mangrove association present. Two variants have been recognised — one with *Aegialitis annulata* where silt deposition is high, and one with *Suaeda australis* where consolidation is high and there is little accretion of new sediments. The height of *A. marina* ranges from 1 m in its southernmost localities to 6 m in the north-west.

Table 7.5   Avicennio-Rhizophoretum stylosae Association

Relevé number:	271	213	206	228	251
Height of dominant species (m):	3	3	3	3	3
Number of species:	3	2	2	2	2
Differential species of variant and cover-abundance:					
Aegialitis annulata	3	—	—	—	—
Identifying species of association and cover-abundance:					
Rhizophora stylosa	2	4	3	2	3
Avicennia marina	3	2	3	4	3

Table 7.6   Avicennietum resiniferae Association

Relevé number:	212	227	621	207	213	220	239	273	605	615	588	592	585	090
Height of dominant species (m):	3	6	3	2	3	5	3	2.5	5	5	4	2	4	2
Number of species:	2	3	2	1	1	1	1	1	1	1	1	1	1	1
Differential species of variants and cover-abundance:														
Aegialitis annulata	2	2	—	—	—	—	—	—	—	—	—	—	—	—
Suaeda australis	—	—	4	—	—	—	—	—	—	—	—	—	—	—
Identifying species of association and cover-abundance:														
Avicennia marina	4	5	3	4	5	4	5	3	5	5	5	5	5	5
Other species and cover-abundance:														
Rhizophora stylosa	—	+	—	—	—	—	—	—	—	—	—	—	—	—

Avicennio-Sarcocornietum quinqueflorae (Table 7.7) This accociation is confined to the coastline from Corner Inlet to Carnarvon. Apart from an outline at Carnarvon it corresponds to the occurences of mangrove in climate Type IV (Walter and Lieth 1960). It is found to the landward of the *Avicennietum resiniferae,* and frequently abuts extensive saltmarsh. Four major variants have been recognised: (i) with *Halosarcia halocnemoides—* confined to Carnarvon (W.A.) (ii) with *Samolus repens* in W.A. and S.A., (iii) with *Sclerostegia arbuscula* (S.A.) and (iv) with *Spartina townsendii* (Vic).

This last variant is of particular interest, as *S. townsendii* is an introduced species, and the plant community must therefore be regarded as 'synthetic'. Thom (personal communication, 1979) has noted an *Avicennia-Spartina* community in North America, which suggests this synthetic community may be able to achieve stability.

Table 7.7   Avicennio-Sarcocornietum quinqueflora Association

Number of relevé:	601	616	625	626	526	509	587	591	340	199	604	622	590	503	349	301
Height of dominant species (m):	1	1	1	1	1	1	1	1	1.5	1.5	1	2	1	1	0.5	1
Number of species:	3	3	3	4	4	4	4	4	2	3	2	3	2	3	2	3
Differential of variants and cover-abundance:																
Halosarcia halocnemoides	2	2	—	—	—	—	—	—	—	—	—	—	—	—	—	—
Samolus repens	—	—	3	2	3	—	—	—	—	—	—	—	—	—	—	—
Sclerostegia arbuscula	—	—	—	—	+	3	3	3	—	—	—	—	—	—	—	—
Spartina townsendii	—	—	—	—	—	—	—	—	5	3	—	—	—	—	—	—
Identifying species of association and cover-abundance:																
Avicennia marina	3	3	3	2	2	3	3	3	2	3	3	3	2	4	3	4
Sarcocornia quinqueflora	3	3	4	4	4	4	3	2	—	2	3	4	4	2	3	4
Other species and cover-abundance:																
Suaeda australis	—	—	—	1	—	—	+	+	—	—	—	2	—	3	—	1
Rhizoclonium sp.	—	—	—	—	—	3	—	—	—	—	—	—	—	—	—	—

Holosarcio-Avicennietum marinae (Table 7.8). Confined to the Pilbara coastline, this association occurs as the most landward association in the mangal, often abutting saltmarshes and dry salt pans. Soil salinities are typically hypersaline, and the association is only found on well developed and consolidated substrates. It is interesting to note that although *Halosarcia halocnemoides* occurs also at Bunbury, and widely through the distribution range of the South Australian mangal, only in climate Type III do both coexist in an association. The height of fully developed *A. marina* in this association rarely exceeds 0.75 m.

Table 7.8   Halosarcia-Avicennietum marinae Association

Number of relevé:	223	233	238	249
Height of dominant species (m):	1.5	1.0	1.0	1.0
Number of species:	3	5	2	2
Identifying species of association and cover-abundance:				
Avicennia marina	3	2	3	3
Halosarcia halocnemoides	3	2	3	3
Other species and cover-abundance:				
Halosarcia indica	+	—	—	—
Limonium salicornaceum	—	3	—	—
Halosarcia pterygosperma	—	3	—	—
Hemichroa diandra	—	+	—	—

Table 7.9   Avicennio-Ceriopetum tagalae Association

Number of relevé:	201	202	204	208	216	229	244	276	256
Height of dominant species (m):	1	2	2	2	1	2	2	2	2
Number of species:	4	3	4	2	3	2	3	2	2
Differential of variants and cover-abundance:									
Halosarcia halocnemoides	2	—	—	—	—	—	—		—
Suaeda australis	—	2	2	—	—	—	—		—
Identifying species of association and cover-abundance:									
Avicennia marina	2	2	2	2	4	2	3	3	4
Ceriops tagal	3	3	3	3	2	4	3	3	2
Other species and cover-abundance:									
Limonium salicornaceum	3	—	3	—	—	—	—		—
Rhizophora stylosa	—	—	—	—	+	—	+		—

Avicennio-Ceriopetum tagalae (Table 7.9). Again confined to the Pilbara coastline, this association is developed where there are extensive flats at the landward side of the mangal. Salinities measured in this association are well above seawater salinity, although the sediments may not be particularly consolidated. Occasionally some halophytic undershrubs can be found as variants in this association (e.g. *Suaeda australis, Halosarcia halocnemoides*).

Ceriopo-Bruguieretum (Table 7.10). Confined to well developed tidal creek systems of the Pilbara this association is probably a species-poor form of an association widely distributed across northern Australia. This is a mid-mangal association, not associated with any extremes. It is not exposed to the full force of tides, nor does it occur in areas of hypersalinity.

Table 7.10 Ceriopo-Bruguieretum Association

Number of relevé:	274	253	209	215
Height of dominant species (m):	3.0	2.0	3.0	2.5
Number of species:	3	4	4	5
Differential species of sub-association and cover-abundance:				
Rhizophora stylosa	—	—	2	2
Identifying of association and cover-abundance:				
Osbornia octodonta	—	2	2	2
Bruguiera exaristata	2	+	—	2
Ceriops tagal	2	3	3	3
Avicennia marina	3	2	2	3
Other species and cover-abundance:				
Aegialitis annulata	—	—	—	+

Table 7.11 Ceriopetum tagalae Association

Number of relevé:	221	259	231	241	278
Height of dominant species (m):	4	4	1.5	1.0	2
Number of species:	1	1	1	1	1
Identifying species of association and cover-abundance:					
Ceriops tagal	5	5	4	5	4

A *Rhizophora stylosa* variant is found along the banks of tidal creeks. Ceriopetum tagalae (Table 7.11); Chapman, 1977. This is the most landward mangal association with trees between 1-2 m in height. This form of association occurs in hypersaline regions, on well consolidated silts. This form typically adjoins Avicennio-Ceriopetum. However, a form distinguished by trees approximately 4 m high has been noted on islands and creek banks well upstream of tidal creeks. Here salinities approximate those of seawater, and this association adjoins the Ceriopo-Bruguieretum. The precise environmental factors which control these two forms are worthy of further investigation.

As Chapman (1977) has discussed, it is possible to group associations into alliances on the basis of floristic affinity. Following this approach, the following scheme can be constructed:

	Association	*Alliance*
(i)	Aegialitetum	-Aegialition
(ii)	Aegiceretum	-Aegicerion
(iii)	Rhizophoretum	-Rhizophorion
(iv)	Avicennio-Rhizophoretum	-
	Avicennietum	-
	Avicennio-Sarcocornietum	-Avicennio marinae
	Halosarcio-Avicennietum	-
	Avicennio-Ceriopetum	-
(v)	Ceriopo-Bruguieretum	-Bruguierion
(vi)	Ceriopetum	-Ceriopion

Some of these names correspond to those of Chapman's, others are newly derived from this investigation. Their value lies in making comparisons between mangrove associations in Australia and other continents.

Acknowledgments
Some of this work was supported by a grant from the Ministry for Conservation, Victoria; the West Australian work was carried out whilst the author was on study leave from Murdoch University.

Special thanks are due to Doreen Jones for typing the manuscript and tables.

Appendix I—Relevé Locations

Relevé number	Location	Latitude	Longitude
090	Hastings	38°18'	145°11'
199	Bass River	38°29'	145°28'
200-207	West Creek (W.A.)	20°19'	118°32'
208-216	Finnucane Island	20°18'	118°33'
217-222	Stingray Creek	20°20'	118°37'
223-228	Pretty Pool	20°19'	118°38'
229-237	S.E. Creek, Port Hedland	20°20'	118°35'
238-248	Honeymoon Cave	20°38'	117°10'
249-272	Cossack	20°41'	117°11'
273	Karratha	20°44'	116°50'
274-281	King Bay	20°38'	116°40'
282	Hearson Cove	20°38'	116°48'
301	French Island	38°18'	145°25'
340	Shallow Inlet	38°49'	146°09'
349	Port Albert	38°41'	146°42'
601-602	Pelican Point	24°51'	113°38'
603-609	Miaboolya Beach	24°48'	113°35'
610-612	Bush Bay	25°11'	113°48'
613-616	Oyster Creek	24°56'	113°40'
620-626	Bunbury	33°20'	115°38'
503	Port Davis	33°16'	137°51'
509	Fishermans Bay	33°34'	137°58'
526	Port Pirie	33°12'	138°00'
585	Ceduna	32°08'	133°41'
587-588	Whyalla	33°02'	137°35'
590	Port Augusta	32°30'	137°46'
591-592	Port Germein	33°01'	138°00'

Appendix II— Species and Author Citations

Aegiceras corniculatum (L.) Blanco
Aegialitis annulata R. Br.
Avicennia marina (Forsk.) Vierh.
Bruguiera exaristata Ding Hou
Ceriops tagal (Perr.) C.B. Rob.
Halosarcia halocnemoides (Nees) P.G. Wilson
H. indica (Willd.) P.G. Wilson
H. pterygosperma (J.M. Black) P.G. Wilson
Hemichroa diandra R. Br.
Limonium salicornaceum (F. Muell.) Mill.
Osbornia octodonta F. Meull.
Rhizoclonium sp.
Rhizophora stylosa Griff.
Samolus repens (Forst.) Pers.
Sarcocornia quinqueflora (Bunge ex Ung. -Sternb.) A.J. Scott
Sclerostegia arbuscula (R. Br.) P.G. Wilson
Spartina townsendii H. & J. Groves
Suaeda australis (R.Br.) Moq.

References

Bridgewater, P.B., 1971. Practical application of the Zurich-Montpellier system of phytosociology. *Proceedings Royal Society of Victoria* **84**, 255-62.

Chapman, V.J., 1977. Introduction to mangrove ecosystems. In V.J. Chapman (ed.), *Ecosystems of the World. I. Wet Coastal Ecosystems.* Elsevier, Amsterdam. 428 pp.

Mueller-Dombois, D.and H. Ellenberg, 1974. *Aims and Methods of Vegetation Ecology.* Wiley, New York. 547 pp.

Walter, H. and H. Lieth, 1960. *Klimadiagramm-Weltatlas.* Jena.

8
Mangrove-Dependent Biota

Norman E. Milward

Introduction

The term 'dependent biota' with respect to mangrove communities is difficult to define at this time, since the studies necessary to delineate it are far from complete. From our rather limited knowledge it is possible to recognise a variety of organisms that are closely dependent upon mangroves for some resource, such as food, space, and/or shelter, and to appreciate that others occurring beyond the vegetational boundaries of mangrove areas may also have varying degrees of dependence. However, the full range of dependent organisms, the extent of their dependence, and the subtleties of the interactions, both direct and indirect, between them and the mangrove vegetation are still mainly unknown.

This is particularly the case for the dependent biota in Australia. Despite the fact that many of the studies carried out in the mangroves ocurring around the coast of this continent have involved a faunal and/or floral listing, the recording and identification of all the organisms present are far from completion. Similarly, even for those components of the biota that are relatively well known, there is scant information on their interdependent relationships, and even less on the roles they individually or collectively play in the exchanges with adjacent habitats and in the dynamics of the coastal ecosystem as a whole.

Thus, while the term dependent biota (coined for discussions at the workshop) has value in evoking thought about these inadequacies in our knowledge, its use must be considered in this light and accepted as being descriptive of a level of understanding of mangrove systems to be sought rather than already achieved. This chapter has been prepared with these connotations in mind. It considers mainly the organisms which occur within, or are closely asociated with, mangrove habitats. Especial aims have been to recognise those components of the biota that are poorly known and which require further study for a fuller understanding of the ecological relationships, including dependent links with the mangrove vegetation.

As the incursions into mangrove habitats by the author have principally been for the purposes of investigating the Periophthalminae (mudskippers) and other teleosts occurring there, his acquaintance with other components of the biota, and the relevant literature, mainly derives from their position as prey, predators, or close associates of the fishes. Consequently, no comprehensive knowledge of all the groups of organisms present within mangrove communities can be claimed and in attempting as broad a treatment as possible it is hoped that no major, pertinent works have escaped attention. Thanks are due to a number of participants at the workshop for help in rectifying some initial omissions but apologies must be offered for any that remain.

In order to avoid unnecessary repetition attention is drawn to the bibliography prepared by van Tine and Snedaker (1974) and the paper by Saenger *et al.* (1977). The former (together with a compilation of references by staff in the Departments of Environmental Studies and Marine Invertebrates, Australian Museum) provides an extremely useful listing of the mangrove literature. The latter gives a valuable background for consideration of the dependent biota, the authors commenting upon the zonation and distribution of the better worked groups in Australian mangrove and coastal saltmarsh communities, and presenting species listings on the basis of previously published records and their own observations. The especial relevance of these two publications for the task in hand is acknowledged and readers are directed to them for many references that are not duplicated in this chapter.

The components of the dependent biota, in the context of the preceding preamble, are considered here under systematic headings. This treatment is primarily one of convenience, allowing easy cross-reference to the paper by Saenger *et al.* (1977) and an assessment of the state of knowledge for each group from the predominantly taxonomic literature. It is hoped that the treatment—although purposefully brief—will emphasise the need for broader, more ecologically oriented, research approaches and the necessity for much greater attention to the dependent biota as a whole and to certain groups in particular.

Components of the biota

As noted by Macnae (1968) a mangrove area, like any other intertidal area, is an area of transition from the sea to the land and hence its fauna may be derived from either. This statement may also apply to the non-mangrove plants, a point noted by Saenger *et al.* (1977) for the lichen flora which is almost identical with that commonly present in nearby terrestrial areas. However, at least for the aquatic and substrate fauna, most organisms have been derived from the sea, and as pointed out by Macnae (1968), the mangrove swamp has clearly provided one route from sea to land. As a consequence of these origins many species occurring in mangrove communities may have distributions extending over wide areas beyond them and into a variety of different habitats and environments.

Studies conducted to survey the biota within Australian mangrove communities, such as those of Macnae (1966, 1967), Hegerl and Timmins (1973), Shine *et al.* (1973), Hegerl and Tarte (1974), Hutchings and Recher (1974), and Graham *et al.* (1975) have been concerned almost exclusively with macro-organisms. Thus, of the faunal elements molluscs, larger crustaceans, insects, spiders, and vertebrates are best documented. Of the floral constituents, other than the mangrove (and adjacent saltmarsh) vegetation, lichens, macro-fungi and algae, ferns, and orchids have attracted most attention. Other groups, as noted below, have scarcely been studied and are relatively poorly known.

Bacteria

The roles of bacteria in mangroves have been considered in a number of overseas studies, for example those of Schuster (1952) and Odum and Heald (1972). Such studies have shown bacteria to be extremely important in processes of degradation of organic material, energy recycling, nitrification, etc. However, despite this, these organisms have been largely neglected within Australian mangroves.

No studies are known to the author that have aimed specifically towards evaluating the roles of bacteria in the food webs of Australian mangroves. Dall (1968), however, suggested that micro-organisms (including bacteria) are important dietary components of prawns which may occur in mangrove environments. Moriarty (1976) confirmed this, finding that bacteria were a significant component of the organic carbon in the proventriculus of the greentail or bay prawn (*Metapenaeus bennettae*) feeding on muddy estuarine sediments and, in laboratory experiments, that bacteria were digested and assimilated. He also found that bacteria formed a similar component of the organic carbon in the stomach of mullet (*Mugil cephalus*) feeding on seagrass beds. It is unquestionable that bacteria must be important as a dietary item for a variety of fishes and other organisms at the lower levels of mangrove food webs.

The pathogenic effects of certain bacteria occurring in coastal estuarine and mangrove systems have been demonstrated through the work of L. Rodgers, J. Burke, and N. Gillespie (personal communication, 1978) on 'red-spot' or 'ulcer' disease in fishes. This disease, first reported in 1972 from the Burnett River but later spreading northwards in Queensland and southwards to New South Wales, is characterised by severe lesions and ulcerations on the surface of the fish. The causative factors of the disease are considered to be several, interacting ones, involving the bacteria *Vibrio anguillarum* and *Aeromonas hydrophila* amongst others.

Studies conducted by P.A.M. Crossland (personal communication, 1979) on nitrogen fixation in mangroves near Townsville have involved the isolation and culturing of bacteria, to determine their contributions to this process in submerged, tidally inundated, and exposed muds.

Algae

Relatively few studies, at rather scattered localities, have been carried out on algae in Australian mangroves. On the basis of previous references and unpublished personal records Saenger *et al.* (1977) were able to list 16 species of Chlorophyta, one species of Phaeophyta, 25 species of Rhodophyta, 37 species of Cyanophyta, and one species of Chrysophyta. They recorded the majority as occurring on mud surfaces and slightly more than one-third (mainly the rhodophytes) as also or only present on *Avicennia* pneumatophores.

It is suggested by Saenger *et al.* (1977) that the muddy substrate beneath the mangrove cover does not provide conditions favourable for algal growth. The occurrence of algae in this habitat is mainly restricted to a few species of chlorophytes and rhodophytes, which form stunted tufts and mats attached to the pneumatophores and tree bases.

Compared with other coastal habitats the numbers and diversity of algae occurring in Australian mangroves are small. However, it appears, mainly from work overseas (e.g. Schuster, 1952; Odum and Heald, 1972), that algae are important in a number of biological processes within soils and waters of mangrove habitats and constitute a significant food resource for other organisms. Local studies demonstrating the latter are those of Beumer (1971, 1978) on four species of mangrove creek fishes and Milward (1974) on mudskippers. These have shown both filamentous and macrophytic algae to be dietary items in certain species (*Ctenogobius criniger, Anodontostoma chacunda,* and *Scartelaos histophorus*).

Little work appears to have been carried out with specific reference to diatoms in mangrove communities. However, the extensive investigations of Wood (1964) have provided considerable information on oceanic and estuarine diatoms around Australia and his findings and conspectus of species will undoubtedly be most relevant to their study on mangrove systems.

The studies of Beumer (1971, 1978) and Milward (1974) showed that diatoms are a common food component of certain mangrove inhabiting fishes and those of Moriarty (1976) indicated a similar finding for mullet (*Mugil cephalus*). Overseas studies (e.g. Odum and Heald, 1972) have shown that molluscs and crustaceans are also major consumers of diatoms and filamentous algae within mangrove communities. These trophic links and the specific organisms involved require much further study.

Other unpublished studies dealing with algae in Australian mangrove communities include an investigation of species of blue-green algae, which may be involved in nitrogen fixation in mangrove muds, by P.A.M. Crossland (personal communication, 1979), and a study of the photosynthetic activities of shade adapted macro-algae associated with exposed mangrove roots and mud surfaces by L. Borowitzka (J.S. Bunt, personal communication, 1980).

Fungi

Until recently little work appears to have been done on fungi and the roles they play in Australian mangrove communities.

In overseas studies various fungi, having both terrestrial and marine affinities, have been found associated with the mangrove vegetation, in the mud substrate, and in the waters of mangrove creeks. Several investigations have shown their importance in the breakdown of organic materials, such as those of Fell and Master (1973) who found that a wide range of fungal genera, including Phycomycetes, Deuteromycetes, and Ascomycetes, are associated with the degradation of mangrove leaves, and of Newell (1973) who suggested that fungi acted as invaders of the protective external tissues of mangrove seedlings and observed a fungal succession on both injured and uninjured seedlings from Hyphomycetes to Sphaeropsidales, Ascomycetes, and Hyphomycetes.

Fungal records from mangroves in Australia comprise only seven or eight ascomycetes, 17 basidiomycetes, and two imperfect fungi (Cribb and Cribb, 1955; George and Kenneally, 1975; Hegerl and Davie, 1977; Hegerl *et al*, 1979; and Leightley, 1979). Most forms (viz. 14 basidiomycetes) were recorded from the high rainfall areas of the north-east Queensland coast by Hegerl and Davie (1977), on the basis of Australian Littoral Society surveys of mangroves at Cairns, and as a result of identifications subsequent to the publication of their paper another 10 basidiomycetes and one ascomycete are to be noted from this region (E. Hegerl, personal communication, 1979).

From short-term tests conducted in south-east Queensland on experimental discs taken from five species of mangroves, Leightley (1979) found that a single ascomycete (*Lulworthia grandispora*) and two imperfect fungi (*Phialophora* sp. and *Phoma* sp.) were the primary decay fungi in the wood, whereas timbers in more advanced stages of decay have been observed to be colonised by several ascomycetes (Cribb and Cribb, 1955; Leightley, 1979). Further elucidation of these processes of decay and the fungi involved will be of considerable interest in relation to overseas findings.

The importance of fungi as secondary invaders of the lesions in fish suffering from 'red spot' or 'ulcer' disease in estuarine, including mangrove, systems has been recognised through the work on this problem by L. Rodgers, J. Burke, and N. Gillespie (personal communication, 1978).

Lichens
Saenger *et al*. (1977) observed that lichens found in mangroves are almost entirely common on nearby terrestrial vegetation. They noted a 'considerable' lichen flora—crustose, foliose and fruticose on mangroves of south-eastern Queensland (23 species from around Moreton Bay and 16 species from Gladstone) but markedly fewer from parts of northern Australia and apparently also southern Australia. Further collecting, though, is adding to the numbers known, at least from the northern regions. Hegerl and Tarte (1974) list 27 species from the Capricornia Coast, Graham *et al*. (1975) and Hegerl and Davie (1977) 14 species from the Cairns area, and George and Kenneally (1975) 16 species from the north-east Kimberley region.

Other plants
Saltmarsh plants, often closely associated with mangroves, have been studied by a number of workers and considered in some detail by Saenger *et al*. (1977). These authors list 55 species as being recorded from Australian saltmarshes, the number of species and complexity of the vegetation increasing greatly from the northern, tropical regions (seven species of four angiosperm families) to the southern, temperate regions (34 species of 16 angiosperm families).

Other plants are listed by Saenger *et al*. (1977) as occurring at the landward fringe of tidal saltmarsh and mangrove vegetation (see also Hegerl and Tarte, 1974). At the seaward fringe seagrasses may also be present. However, the inclusion of these plants as components of the dependent biota is questionable, although several of them may require the particular conditions to be found in the proximity of, and possibly dependent upon the presence of, the mangrove vegetation.

Some limited attention has been given to the epiphytes (other than algae and lichens) occurring in mangroves. Graham *et al.* (1975) and Hegerl and Davie (1977) list three ferns, five orchids, and two dicotyledons (including *Myrmecodia beccarii,* inhabited by ants of the genus *Pheidole*) as mangrove epiphytes from the Cairns region. The mistletoe (*Amyema mackayense*) is also found in mangroves along the northern Australian coastline (Saenger *et al.,* 1977).

Protozoa

As for other micro-organisms, the protozoans occurring within Australian mangroves have been very little studied.

Work overseas, for example that of Newell (1973), has shown that protozoans are active in the decomposition of mangrove seedlings and other detritus. Also, they are known to be important consumer links at the lower trophic levels (e.g. Odum, 1970; Odum and Heald, 1972).

Milward (1974) found foraminiferans to be significant items in the diets of *Periophthalmus* species, these protozoans being taken by mainly juvenile fish apparently from emerging mud surfaces during ebb tides. Beumer (1971, 1978) similarly noted foraminiferans in the diet of bony bream (*Anodontosoma chacunda*) from a mangrove creek. Clearly these and other protozoans are important food items for many larvae and small fishes, as well as other organisms.

Cnidaria

Little appears to have been published on the occurrence of cnidarians in mangroves.

Several species of Scyphozoa are known to occur in mangrove estuaries and creeks and on occasions vast numbers of medusae may be found densely aggregated within fairly localised areas. It is likely that at these times they may have major importance as predatory consumers of planktonic organisms within these systems.

Investigations on the box jellyfish (*Chironex fleckeri*) and other cnidarians in North Queensland are involving collections from mangrove systems (R.F. Hartwick, personal communication, 1979). A number of scyphozoan species have been obtained, of which *Catostylus mosaicus, Cytaeis tetrastylus,* and a species of *Aequorea* may be mentioned as commonly occurring in mangrove estuaries and creeks, particularly during their breeding seasons.

Platyhelminthes

There is scant knowledge of the flatworms which occur in Australian mangroves.

Decraemer and Coomans (1978) noted the presence of turbellarians in samples taken from mangroves at Lizard Island, North Queensland.

The digenean trematode, *Prototransversotrema steeri,* has been found by L. Rodgers, J. Burke, and N. Gillespie (personal communication, 1978) to be implicated in 'red spot' or 'ulcer' disease of fishes occurring in mangrove estuaries and creeks, in that it may cause the initial injury to the integument allowing entry of the pathogenic bacteria.

Other parasitic flatworms have been recorded from fishes that may inhabit mangroves but no extensive work appears to have been done on the group from this environment.

Aschelminthes

Little reference seems to have been made to aschelminth forms in Australian mangroves.

A recent paper by Decraemer and Coomans (1978) has described the nematode fauna in mangroves and adjacent habitats at Lizard Island, North Queensland. These authors recorded up to 25 species from individual sampling sites within the mangroves, noting that there were few common species between sites and that certain species, such as *Prochromadonella paramucrodonta,* could be very abundant. Decraemer and Coomans also noted Kinorhyncha in their mangrove samples.

Milward (1974) recorded nematodes as dietary items from *Periophthalmus* spp. and *Scartelaos histophorus,* and also kinorhynchs from the latter species mainly taken from mudflats fronting mangroves. Beumer (1971, 1978) also recorded nematodes as food items in four species of mangrove creek fishes (regularly in *Ctenogobius criniger,* less frequently in *Acanthopagrus berda* and *Chelonodon patoca,* and rarely in *Anodontostoma chacunda*).

In addition to free-living nematodes, parasitic forms are to be found in fish and, no doubt, other organisms inhabiting mangroves but, as yet, they have been little investigated.

Nemertinia

Weate (1975) recorded twelve species of nemertines from wetlands of the Myall River, N.S.W. Although these were mainly taken from *Zostera* beds, the areas sampled were apparently closely adjacent to mangrove vegetation. Hutchings and Recher (1974) also recorded a nemertine from *Zostera* and *Posidonia* near mangroves in Careel Bay, N.S.W., and W. McCormick (personal communication, 1979), in studies on the benthic fauna in New South Wales mangroves, collected one species from each of Currambene Creek (Jervis Bay) and Pambula Lake, two species from Wallis Lake, and three species from each of Patonga Creek and Towra Bay (Botany Bay).

Other than these records the group appears to have been neglected in Australian mangrove areas. A taxonomic revision of Australian marine nemertines, including the description of a new genus and species from teredo burrows in mangroves near Townsville, is currently being undertaken by R. Gibson (L. Winsor, personal communication, 1979).

Annelida

A few workers have looked at annelids in mangrove areas and Saenger *et al.* (1977) list a total of 27 records, comprising 25 polychaete and two oligochaete species, from mangrove habitats in Australia. Seven polychaetes and one oligochaete are recorded from far North Queensland, 14 polychaetes and one oligochaete from Moreton Bay, and 12 polychaetes from the Sydney District.

These numbers are being increased with more intensive sampling, such as that by W.A. McCormick (personal communication, 1979), which has produced up to 18 species (at Patonga Creek) and 20 species (at Towra Bay) of polychaetes in the benthic fauna of New South Wales mangroves. Nevertheless, it appears that the mangrove environment, at least in areas of the mangrove vegetation, does not support the rich annelid fauna typical of other coastal habitats. Hutchings and Recher (1974), for example, collected only five polychaete species from mangroves, compared with 28 and 37 species respectively from *Posidonia* and *Zostera* beds in Careel Bay, N.S.W.

Sipuncula and Echiura

Saenger *et al.* (1977), on the basis of information supplied by S.J. Edmonds, list three species of Sipuncula and one species of Echiura, all from Moreton Bay, The sipunculid, *Phascoloma lurco,* which was noted by Saenger *et al.* as also occurring in Malaysia, is commonly found in mangroves along the North Queensland coastline and was studied in mangroves at Townsville by Green (1969).

Mollusca

The Mollusca have been comparatively well investigated in Australian mangroves. Perhaps due to their relatively large size and often dense abundance they have attracted the attention of a number of workers, and have been especially studied with respect to their distribution and zonation within mangrove habitats. Some of the recent literature relating to Australian mangrove molluscs are the papers of Macnae (1966, 1967, 1968), Hegerl and Timmins (1973), Hutchings (1973), Shine *et al.* (1973), Hegerl and Tarte (1974), Hutchings and Recher (1974), Graham *et al.* (1975), and Hegerl *et al.* (1979)

Saenger *et al.* (1977) list one chiton, 67 gastropods (of 21 families) and 27 bivalves (of 14 families) from Australian mangroves and saltmarshes. While these records point to a quite rich and diverse mollusc fauna, it is clear that they are only a partial representation of it. Graham *et al.* (1975), for example, found, amongst a total of 57 molluscs from the Cairns area, 15 gastropod species and 10 or 11 bivalve species not listed by Saenger *et al.* Similarly, the listings are being considerably extended through other work of the Australian Littoral Society, which now has records of 215 molluscs (two chitons, 121 gastropods, three cephalopods, and 89 bivalves) from mangroves and saltmarshes along the eastern Queensland coast (Hegerl, personal communication, 1979).

Molluscs occupying mangroves show varying adaptations to the estuarine and semi-terrestrial environment. These adaptations have been the subject of a number of investigations, the main references to which are given by van Tine and Snedaker (1974). The majority of the molluscan fauna occurs on or as burrowing forms in the mud substrate. Some species live epiphytically on the roots, trunks, and/or leaves of the mangrove vegetation and may make diurnal — or tidally or seasonally influence-vertical movements on the plants. A few species of Teredinidae, the so-called ship-worms, are endophytic, boring into the mangrove tissues. As noted by Graham *et al.* (1975) these may be very abundant in frequently inundated sites and appear to be of importance not only as decomposers of mangrove wood but also as makers of tunnels and cavities for occupation by other organisms.

The commercial significance of oysters (family Ostreidae) which occur in mangroves has prompted investigations on them but most of these relate to methods of utilisation rather than to their place and role in the mangrove fauna. The paper by Thomson (1954a) describes and deals with the taxonomy of the Australian genera and species.

Other recent work on mangrove molluscs within Australia includes that of W.A. McCormick on the benthic fauna of mangroves in New South Wales (personal communication, 1979) and of P. Muggeridge on the reproductive biology and population biology of *Littorina scabra* and *Bembicium auratum* at Patonga, N.S.W. (cited by D.T. Anderson in *Australian Marine Science Bulletin* No. 59, 1977).

Crustacea

As with the molluscs the larger crustaceans occurring in mangroves have been comparatively well worked, both overseas and in Australia. In fact, this group is the most studied of all the mangrove invertebrates (see references listed by van Tine and Snedaker, 1974). This may be attributed to their apparent dominance, in terms of numbers and diversity of species and abundance of individuals, in the invertebrate fauna; their particularly interesting ecological adaptations and behavioural mechanisms; and the edible qualities and commerical significance of several forms.

The decapods are especially well represented in the crustacean fauna and Saenger *et al.* (1977) list 52 species as recorded in mangrove vegetation in Australia. Again this number is being greatly increased with more extensive and intensive collecting. Graham *et al.* (1975) added a further 19 species from the Cairns area and the Australian Littoral Society through its surveys has recorded a total of at least 102 decapods from mangroves in eastern Queensland (E. Hegerl, personal communication, 1979).

Similarly, the records of other groups as listed by Saenger *et al.* (1977) (Isopoda: five spp.; Amphipoda: two spp; Cirripedia: seven spp.; and Anomura: one sp.) are being increased. Significantly, groups such as Ostracoda and Copepoda are not listed by Saenger *et al.*, reflecting again the concentration of research effort on the larger forms and general neglect of the smaller organisms. However, Decraemer and Coomans (1978) have noted the presence of many Copepoda (mainly Harpacticoida, some Cyclopoida), as well as Tanaidacea, in samples taken from mangroves at Lizard Island. Further, these smaller crustaceans have been shown in several studies to be important links in mangrove food chains. For example, Milward (1974) found both copepods and ostracods to be important components of the diet of mudskippers and Beumer (1971, 1978) noted copepods as food in three mangrove creek fishes.

Crustaceans, especially micro forms and also as larval stages, constitute a major component of the plankton within mangrove estuaries and creeks, and require further investigation with respect to this assemblage. North Queensland studies on plankton from mangrove areas include those of Grigg (1972) on species of *Pseudodiaptomus* (Copepoda, Calanoida), Chaloupka (1978) on decapod larvae, and the current investigations by R.F. Hartwick and colleagues, which are supplemental to the work on box jellyfish (see page 126).

Much other work on crustaceans that occur in mangroves has been undertaken over recent years and is currently in progress. The researches by the Division of Fisheries and Oceanography, CSIRO, on prawns and the Queensland Fisheries Service on the mud crab, *Scylla serrate,* are to be noted and, although a comprehensive review will not be attempted, the following studies may be mentioned to indicate the broad range of investigations being pursued: Draper (1975) on environmental influences on the life cycle of barnacles; Campbell (1977) on distribution, physiology, morphology, and behaviour of Sesarminar; Warburton (1978) on behavioural isolation is *Uca* species; T. Hailstone and J. Moverley (University of Queensland) on population characteristics and biology of crabs in south-eastern Queensland mangroves; and R. Yates (University of Sydney) on distribution, density, and reproductive biology of four species of mangrove crabs.

Insecta

Due mainly to the pest characteristics and medical importance, as actual or potential vectors of disease organisms, of certain species, the insects that occur in mangroves have come under a fair amount of scrutiny.

In the main attention has been given to the biting insects but as pointed out by Macnae (1968) other species are of interest in terms of their commercial value as gatherers of honey (and obviously as pollinating agents in the mangrove and other vegetation) and their habits, such as the weaver ants, *Oecophylla* spp., and fireflies, *Pteroptyx* spp. Representatives of several orders, including Blattodea, Orthoptera, Hemiptera, Coleoptera, Diptera, Hymenoptera, Lepidoptera, Neuroptera, Homoptera, and Isoptera, are commonly present in mangroves and may be extremely abundant, either as larval or adult stages.

Mosquito species of the genera *Aedes, Anopheles,* and *Culex* are present in Australian mangroves, as also are biting, ceratopogonid midges of the genera *Culicoides* and *Laseohelea*. The papers by Marks (1974), Lee and Reye (1953, 1955 and 1962), Reye (1973, 1977), and Marks and Mabbett (1977) on these forms may be noted.

Arachnida

Spiders are commonly found in the mangrove vegetation and have been recorded from several Australian localities. These records—18 species from Careel Bay, N.S.W. (Hutchings and Recher, 1974), 26 species from Kakadu National Park, Northern Territory (Hegerl et al., 1979), and a total of 86 species from sites collected by the Australian Littoral Society in eastern Queensland (Shine et al., 1973; Graham et al., 1975; and Grimshaw, unpublished) indicate a rich diversity of spiders within Australian mangroves.

Selachii and Teleostei

It is well known to professional and amateur fishermen that many species of fishes occur in mangrove estuaries and creeks, and it has been observed many times that these systems act as nursery areas for larval and juvenile fishes.

Quite extensive studies have been carried out on fishes of Australian mangroves and Saenger et al. (1977) list some 68 species of fishes. Even so, this must be considered far from complete and significant gaps are evident in it. Thus, no records of sharks or rays are included, even though these may regularly enter mangrove systems. Several species of rays, such as *Himantura granulata* and *Amphostistius kuhlii*, are known, and have personally been observed, to feed amongst the roots of mangrove vegetation. Similarly, no listing is made of various teleost families, such as the Apogonidae, Bothidae, Chandidae, Chanidae, Dorosomidae, Elopidae, Engraulidae, Gerridae, Latidae, Leiognathidae, Megalopidae, Platycephalidae, Pseudomugilidae, Soleidae, Syngnathidae, and Toxotidae, all of which contain species occurring in mangrove systems, at least in tropical areas. Studies by the author and students (e.g. Penridge, 1971) in North Queensland have added more than 50 species to the records listed by Saenger et al.

The ichthyofauna occurring within mangrove environments may be broadly categorised into those fishes that exist there permanently, those that intermittently enter them as adults, and those that seasonally occur there as eggs, larvae, or juveniles, The components of the fauna vary geographically (see Saenger et al. 1977) and also in relation to local topographhy, tidal range, salinity variation, etc.

In addition to the survey types of studies that have been conducted (e.g. Stephenson et al., 1958; Taylor, 1964; Penridge, 1971; Shine et al., 1973; Hutchings and Recher, 1974; Allen, 1975; Graham et al., 1975), a number of investigations have been carried out on the general biology and ecology of individual or groups of species (e.g. Thomson, 1954b; Dunstan, 1959; Beumer, 1971, 1978; Milward, 1974; and Dredge, 1976). In the main these have been conducted on adult fishes and little work has been done on the early life stages.

No reliable catch statistics are available for either commercial or recreational fish production from mangroves but it is apparent that for certain species the catch has markedly declined, probably as a result of both over-exploitation and man induced environmental changes. Few studies have investigated this problem but the research program on the barramundi (*Lates calcarifer*) presently being jointly carried out by the Division of Fisheries and Oceanography, CSIRO, the Queensland Fisheries Service, and the Fisheries Branch, Northern Territory Department of Industrial Development is focusing upon it.

Amphibia

The mangrove habitat is generally not favourable for occupation by amphibians but E. Hegerl (personal communication, 1979) has pointed out that frogs are sometimes found in Australian mangrove forests. This observation is based on collections by the Australian Littoral Society of *Litoria gracilenta* from Trinity Inlet, Queensland, and *Litoria bicolor* and *Lymnodynastes convexiusculus* from Kakadu National Park, Northern Territory.

Reptilia

The saltwater crocodile, *Crocodylus porosus,* is the best known reptile occurring in the mangrove habitat but a number of snakes (both land and sea), lizards, geckos, skinks, and turtles may also be present. Although not very abundant, the reptiles found in mangroves are important by virtue of their place in the higher trophic levels. However, they have not been generally well studied and the following list derived from Worrell (1963), Cogger (1975), Swanson (1976), and records of the Australian Littoral Society (E. Hegerl, personal communication, 1979) is probably far from complete.

Fam. Crocodylidae:	*Crocodylus porosus* (Saltwater crocodile)
Fam. Gekkonidae:	*Gehyra variegata* (Tree dtella)
	Oedura ocellata (Blotched gecko)
Fam. Agamidae:	*Lophognathus temporalis* (Northern water dragon)
Fam. Varanidae:	*Varanus indicus* (Mangrove monitor)
	Varanus prasinus (Emerald monitor)
	Varanus semiremex (Rusty monitor)
Fam. Scincidae:	*Carlia fusca* (Skink)
	Carlia rhomboidalis (Rainbow skink)
	Carlia vivax (Rainbow skink)
	Cryptoblepharus boutonii (Fence skink)
	Notoscincus ornatus (Snake-eyed skink)
	Sphenomorphus tenuis (Yellow-bellied skink)

Fam. Boidae:	*Morelia spilotes variegata* (Carpet snake)
Fam. Acrochordidae:	*Acrochordus granulatus* (Little file snake)
Fam. Colubridae:	*Cerberus rhynchops australis* (Bockadam)
	Dendrelaphis punctulatus (Common tree snake)
	Fordonia leucobalia (White-bellied mangrove snake)
	Myron richardsonii (Gray's mangrove snake)
Fam. Elapidae:	*Hemiaspis signata* (Black-bellied swamp snake)
Fam. Hydrophiidae:	*Hydrelaps darwiniensis* (Sea snake)
	Laticauda colubrina (Banded sea snake)
	Laticauda laticauda (Banded sea snake)

Turtles do not appear to have been specifically recorded from Australian mangroves but both green turtle (*Chelonia midas*) and the loggerhead (*Caretta caretta*) are known to enter mangrove waterways. The utilisation by turtles of mangroves as food has been documented for some time. Parsons (1962) quoted Captain Donald McLennan of the Brig *Colonel Allen*, who visited the Galápagos in 1818, as stating 'The latter [viz., the green turtle] could be procured in any quantity, being especially fat and fine eating because they fed on the leaves of the mangroves growing on the edges of the lagoons' and James Colnett, who was at the Galápagos in 1794, as stating 'Their food, as well as that of the land tortoise, consists principally of the bark and leaves of trees, particularly the mangrove, which makes them very fat'. Pritchard (1969) also recorded green turtles as eating mangrove roots and shoots. Carr (1952) recorded that loggerhead turtles will enter coastal streams and estuaries, noting that they do not feed on the mangroves themselves but on pelagic and benthic organisms in the habitat.

The special interest of crocodiles as large predators, occasionally on man, and as commercially valuable reptiles, now showing marked signs of over-exploitation, depletion, and possible eventual extinction, has stimulated research on them. Johnson (1973) studied the behaviour of Australian crocodiles and more recently H. Messell and co-workers (G. Caughley, G.C. Grigg, G.J.W. Webb, and their students) have investigated their ecology, general biology, and physiology in Northern Australian populations (see Grigg, 1977; Messel, 1977; Webb, 1977; Webb and Messel, 1978; and Taylor, 1978). Surveys have indicated low population numbers in various rivers of the Northern Territory (Messel, 1977) and of the Kimberley Region, Western

Australia (Messel *et al.*, 1977; Burbidge and Messel, 1979), which suggest the need for stringent conservation measures. The effects of reduced numbers on trophic relationships and other members of the biota are largely unknown but, with reference to this, the finding by Taylor (1978) that small *Crocodylus porosus* (less than 180 cm in length) may in certain habitats feed predominantly on crabs and prawns, rather than fish which are a minor component of the diet, is of particular note.

Aves
The birds occurring in mangroves around the coasts of Australia have been sufficiently well studied to recognise a relatively rich avifauna. Saenger *et al.* (1977) list 229 species as being exclusive to, associated with, or visitors of Australian mangroves. Additional records by Storr (1967), Storr *et al.* (1975), and Smith *et al.* (1978) have raised the number to almost 250 species.

Few of the birds use the Australian mangrove vegetation exvlusively, Saenger *et al.* (1977) and Schodde *et al.* (this volume) each noting only 13 species as being totally dependent upon it. Smith *et al.* (1978) observed that 16 species are confined to mangroves in Western Australia. A greater number, in the order of 65-70, utilise the mangrove vegetation as an integral part of their habitat, especially for feeding purposes, and the remainder make use of it as visitors or migrants. Schodde *et al.* (this volume) further discuss the composition of the avifauna and also other aspects of its structure and origin.

Much information drawn from studies in other habitats is available on the general biology of many of the birds to be found in mangroves and this has been supplemented by the observations that have been made in the mangroves themselves. This has permitted the appraisal of the types of (e.g. feeding, nesting, sheltering, etc.) and the levels of (e.g. total, partial, continuous, seasonal, intermittent, etc.) dependence upon the mangroves for the individual species. However, few, if any, attempts have been made to relate their dependence to other components of the biota, nor to assess its overall significance within mangrove communities.

Mammalia
Studies on mammals within Australian mangroves have been mainly restricted to the fruit bats or flying foxes (*Pteropus* spp.), which are the most abundant and obvious in the habitat. They occur in dense aggregations, the so-called 'camps', of up to several hundred individuals (see Ratcliffe, 1932; Nelson, 1965). Resting in the camps by day, the flying foxes emerge at night and disperse widely, far beyond the mangroves, to feed. Their main impact on the ecosystem would be localised destruction of mangrove trees and inputs of faecal material.

Other native mammals occurring in Australian mangroves are insect-eating or little bats (*Microchiroptera*), water rats (*Hydromys* spp.), the Fawn-footed Melomys (*Melomys cervinipes*), and a small number of marsupials, such as the Agile Wallaby (*Wallabia agilis*) and the Swamp Wallaby (*W. bicolor*). However, the abundance and significance of these in the system are generally unknown.

Introduced mammals which may be found in mangroves include rats, mice, cats, pigs, and buffalo. Hegerl (personal communication, 1979) has drawn attention to the use of mangroves by feral buffalo, pigs, and cattle. He had noted (Hegerl *et al.*, 1979) trampling and grazing damage to mangroves in the Northern Territory and has also observed foraging and trampling damage to mangroves by feral pigs at Corio Bay, Central Queensland, and along creeks to the north of the Daintree River, North Queensland.

Summary comments

The dependent biota, in Australian mangrove communities is on the whole not particularly well known. A number of groups within the biota are reasonably well documented in terms of species records, although these are as yet by no means comprehensive and result from mainly limited, short-term sampling from scattered localities. The best studied components of the biota are the molluscs, crustaceans, and vertebrates, but even for these our knowledge extends little further than to faunal lists and rather fragmentary, autecological data. For several groups, particularly the micro-organisms, exceedingly little information is available.

The emphasis that has been placed in earlier studies on the larger invertebrates and vertebrates has undoubtedly occurred for a number of reasons. It may result from their size and obvious presence, often in large numbers, within the mangrove vegetation but may also be attributed simply to the fact that more researchers have been actively engaged in working on these groups of organisms. Since food chains in the mangrove ecosystem appear in the main to be relatively short, with the molluscs, larger crustaceans, and vertebrates occupying the higher trophic levels, it is important to have adequate knowledge of these components of the dependent biota. However, such knowledge is of limited value with respect to the interrelationships of the total biota and dynamics of the ecosystem, while we are largely ignorant of the components, particularly the micro-flora and -fauna, upon which they depend for food.

Thus, there is an urgent need not only for an intensification of research effort but especially for an extension of it into the components of the biota that have been until now largely neglected. Equally critical, however, is the necessity for adopting a synecological approach and conducting investigations over adequate periods of time. Only in these ways will we obtain a better assessment of the functional roles of the components of the dependent biota and a more meaningful knowledge of their significance, in part and *in toto*, within the mangrove and general coastal ecosystems.

Acknowledgments

Thanks are due to several participants in the workshop for helpful advice. In particular, I am most grateful to E. Hegerl for providing valuable information and details of records collected by the Australian Littoral Society. I must also express my gratitude to F. Olsen for his contributions prior to, at and following the workshop, and to I.R. Price for his useful comments and reading of the manuscript.

References

Allen, G.R., 1975. A preliminary check list of the fresh water fishes of the Prince Regent River Reserve, north-west Kimberley, Western Australia. In J.M. Miles and A.A. Burbidge (ed.), *A Biological survey of the Prince Regent River Reserve, North-west Kimberley, Western Australia in August 1974.* Wildlife Research Bulletin, Western Australia **3**, 89-96.

Beumer, J.P., 1971. A preliminary investigation of the trophic ecology of four fishes from a North Queensland mangrove creek. Unpubl. Hons. thesis, James Cook University of North Queensland. 94 pp.

Beumer, J.P., 1978. Feeding ecology of four fishes from a mangrove creek in north Queensland, Australia. *Journal of Fish Biology* **12**, 475-90.

Burbidge, A.A. and H. Messel, 1979. The Status of the Salt-water Crocodile in the Glenelg, Prince Regent and Ord River Systems, Kimberley, Western Australia. Department of Fisheries and Wildlife, Western Australia, *Report* **34**, 1-38.

Campbell, G.R., 1977, A comparative study of the distribution, physiology, morphology, and behaviour of five sesarminae species occurring along the Ross River Estuary, Townsville. Unpubl. M.Sc. thesis, James Cook University of North Queensland. 127 pp.

Carr, A., 1952. *Handbook of Turtles: The Turtles of United States, Canada and Baja California.* Cornell University Press, Ithaca. 542 pp.

Chaloupka, M.Y., 1978. An ecological study of the decapod crustacean larvae in a tropical estuarine embayment. Unpubl. Hons. thesis, James Cook University of North Queensland. 125 pp. + appendices.

Cogger, H.G., 1975. *Reptiles and Amphibians of Australia.* A.H. & A.W. Reed, Sydney. 584 pp.

Cribb, A.B. and J.W. Cribb, 1955. Marine fungi from Queensland — I. *University Queensland Papers, Department of Botany*, Vol. 3, 77-81.

Dall, W., 1968. Food and feeding of some Australian penaeid shrimps. F.A.O. Fisheries Report **2**, 251-8.

Decraemer, W. and A. Coomans., 1978. Scientific Report on the Belgian Expedition to the Great Barrier Reef in 1967. Nematodes XII. Ecological notes on the nematode fauna in and around mangroves on Lizard Island. *Australian Journal of Marine and Freshwater Research* **29**, 497-508.

Draper, M.R., 1975. Environmental influences on the life cycles of barnacles in Ross River Estuary. Unpubl. Ph. D. thesis, James Cook University of North Queensland. 153 pp.

Dredge, M.C.L., 1976. Aspects of the ecology of three estuarine dwelling fish in south east Queensland. Unpubl. M.Sc. thesis, University of Queensland. 121 pp. + appendixes.

Dunstan, D.J., 1959. The barramundi *Lates calcarifer* (Bloch) in Queensland waters. *Division of Fisheries and Oceanography, CSIRO, Technical Paper* **5**, 1-22.

Fell, J.W. and J.M. Master, 1973. Fungi associated with the degradation of mangrove *(Rhizophora mangle* L.) leaves in South Florida. In L.H. Stevenson and R.R. Colwell (eds.), *Estuarine Microbial Ecology.* University of South Carolina Press, Columbia, pp. 455-66.

George, A.S. and K.F. Kenneally, 1975. The flora of the Prince Regent River Reserve, north-western Kimberley, Western Australia. In J.M. Miles and A.A. Burbidge (eds.), A biological survey of the Prince Regent River Reserve, north-west Kimberley, Western Australia in August 1974. *Wildlife search Bulletin, Western Australia* **3**, 31-69.

Graham, M., J. Grimshaw, E. Hegerl, J. McNalty, and R. Timmins, 1975. Cairns Wetlands—a preliminary report. *Operculum* **4**, 117-54.

Green, W.A., 1969. Some aspects of the biology of *Phascoloma lurco* (Selenka and De Man). Unpubl. Hons. thesis, University of Queensland. 76 pp.

Grigg, G.C., 1977. Ionic and osmotic regulation in the estuary crocodile, *Crocodylus porosus*. In H. Messel and S.T. Butler (ed.), *Australian Animals and Their Environment*. Shakespeare Head Press, Sydney, pp. 333-354.

Grigg, H. 1972. The taxonomy and distribution of *Pseudodiaptomus* Copepoda, Calanoida) in the Townsville region. Unpubl. M.Sc. thesis, James Cook University of North Queensland. 150 pp.

Hegerl, E.J. and J.D.S. Davie, 1977. The mangrove forests of Cairns, northern Australia, *Marine Research in Indonesia* **18**, 23-57.

Hegerl, E.J. and D. Tarte, 1974. A reconnaissance of the Capricorn Coast tidal wetlands. *Operculum* **4**, 50-62.

Hegerl, E.J. and R.D. Timmins, 1973. The Noosa River tidal swamps: a preliminary report on the flora and fauna. *Operculum* **3**, 38-43.

Hegerl, E.J., P.J.F. Davie, G.F. Claridge and A.G. Elliott, 1979. *The Kakadu National Park Mangrove Forests and Tidal Marshes*. Vol. 1. *A Review of the Literature and Results of a Field Reconnaissance*. Australian Littoral Society, Brisbane. 90 pp.

Hutchings, P.A., 1973. The mangroves of Jervis Bay. In *Jervis Bay — The Future?* Special Publication, Australian Littoral Society, Brisbane, pp. 39-42.

Hutchings, P.A. and H.F. Recher, 1974. The fauna of Careel Bay with comments on the ecology of mangrove and sea-grass communities. *Australian Zoologist* **18**, 99-128.

Johnson, C.R., 1973. Behaviour of the Australian crocodiles, *Crocodylus johnstoni* and *C. porosus*. *Zoological Journal of the Linnaean Society* **52**, 315-36.

Lee, D.J. and E.J. Reye, 1953. Australasian Ceratopogonidae (Diptera, Nematocera). Part VI. Australian species of *Culicoides*. *Proceedings of the Linnaean Society of New South Wales* **77**, 369-94.

Lee, D.J. and E.J. Reye, 1955. Australasian Ceratopogonidae (Diptera, Nematocera). Part VII. Notes on the genera *Alluaudomyia, Ceratopogon, Culicoides* and *Lasiohelea*. *Proceedings of the Linnaean Society of New South Wales* **79**, 233-46.

Lee, D.J. and E.J. Reye, 1962. Australasian Ceratopogonidae (Diptera, Nematocera). Part X. Additional Australian species of *Culicoides*. *Proceedings of the Linnaean Society of New South Wales* **87**, 352-63.

Leightley, L., 1980. Wood decay activities of marine fungi. *Botanica Marina* **23**, 387-95

Macnae, W., 1966. Mangroves in eastern and southern Australia. *Australian Journal of Botany* **14**, 67-104.

Macnae, W., 1967. Zonation within mangroves associated with estuaries in North Queensland. In G.H. Lauff (ed.), *Estuaries*. American Association for the Advancement of Science, Washington, pp. 432-41.

Macnae, W., 1968. A general account of the fauna and flora of mangrove swamps and forests in the Indo-West Pacific Region. In F.S. Russell (ed.), *Advances in Marine Biology*. 6, pp. 73-270.

Marks, E.N., 1947. Report on a mosquito survey of Mackay and portions of Pioneer Shire, Queensland. Report, Department of Health, Brisbane.

Marks, E.N. and J.D. Mabbett, 1977. A mosquito survey and assessment of potential mosquito problems of the Brisbane airport development and environs. In *Brisbane Airport Development Project Environmental Study*. Vol. 3. Australian Government Publishing Service,.Canberra, pp. 71-5.

Messel, H., 1977. The crocodile programme in Northern Australia Population Surveys and Numbers. In H. Messel and S.T. Butler (eds.), *Australian Animals and Their Environment*. Shakespeare Head Press, Sydney, pp. 207-36.

Messel, H., A.A. Burbidge, A.G. Wells, and W.J. Green, 1977. The status of the salt-water crocodile in some river systems of the north-west Kimberley, Western Australia. *Department of Fisheries and Wildlife, Western Australia, Report* **24**, 1-50.

Milward, N.E., 1974. Studies on the taxonomy, ecology, and physiology of Queensland Mudskippers. Unpubl. Ph. D. thesis, University of Queensland. 276 pp.

Moriarty, D.J.W., 1976. Quantitative studies on bacteria and algae in the food of mullet *Mugil cephalus L.* and the prawn *Metapenaeus bennettae* (Racek and Dall). *Journal of Experimental Marine Biology and Ecology* **22**, 131-43.

Nelson, J.E., 1965. Behaviour of Australian Pteropodidae (Megachiroptera). *Animal Behaviour* **13**, 544-57.

Newell, S.Y., 1973. Succession and role of fungi in the degradation of red mangrove seedlings. In L.H. Stevenson and R.R. Colwell (ed.), *Estuarine Microbiology and Ecology.* University of South Carolina Press, Columbia, pp. 467-80.

Odum W.E., 1970. Utilization of the direct grazing and plant detritus food chains by the striped mullet *Mugil cephalus.* In J. Steele (ed.), *Marine Food Chains.* Oliver and Boyd, Edinburgh, pp. 222-40.

Odum, W.E. and E.J. Heald, 1972. Trophic analyses of an estuarine mangrove community. *Bulletin of Marine Science* **22**, 671-738.

Parsons, J.J., 1962. *The Green Turtle and Man.* University of Florida Press, Gainesville. 126 pp.

Penridge, L.K., 1971. A study of the fish community of a North Queensland mangrove creek. Unpubl. Hons. thesis, James Cook University of North Queensland. 114 pp.

Pritchard, P.C.H., 1969. The survival and status of Ridley sea turtles in American waters, *Biological Conservation* **2**, 13-17.

Ratcliffe, F., 1932. Notes on the fruit bats *(Pteropus* spp.) of Australia. *Animal Ecology* **32**, 32-57.

Reye, E.J., 1973. Midges and mangroves. *Operculum* **3**, 31-4.

Reye, E.J., 1977. Biting midges—the problem as at October, 1972. In *Brisbane Airport Development Project Environmental Study.* Vol. 3. Australian Government Publishing Service, Canberra, pp. 71-5.

Saenger, P., M.M. Specht, R.L. Specht and V.J. Chapman, 1977. Mangal and coastal salt-marsh communities in Australasia. In V.J. Chapman (ed.), *Ecosystems of the World.* I. *Wet Coastal Ecosystems.* Elsevier, Amsterdam, pp. 293-345.

Schuster, W.H., 1952. Fish culture in brackish water ponds of Java. *Indo-Pacific Fisheries Council, Special Publication* **1**, 1-143.

Shine, R., C.P. Ellway and E.J. Hegerl, 1973. A biological survey of the Tallebudgera Creek estuary. *Operculum* **3**, 59-94.

Smith, L.A., R.E. Johnstone and J. Dell, 1978. Birds. In A.A. Burbidge and N.L. McKenzie (eds.), *The islands of the north-west Kimberley. Wildlife Research Bulletin, Western Australia,* **7**, 29-41.

Stephenson. W., R. Endean and I. Bennett, 1958. An ecological survey of the marine fauna of Low Isles, Queensland. *Australian Journal of Marine and Freshwater Research* **9**, 261-318.

Storr, G.M., 1967. List of Northern Territory birds. *Western Australian Museum Special Publication* **4**, 1-90.

Storr, G.M., R.E. Johnstone, J. Dell and L.A. Smith, 1975. Birds of the Prince Regent River Reserve, north-west Kimberley, Western Australia. In J.M. Miles and A.A. Burbidge (eds.), A biological survey of the Prince Regent River Reserve, north-west Kimberley, Western Australia in August 1974. *Wildlife Research Bulletin, Western Australia,* **3**, 75-83.

Swanson, S., 1976, *Lizards of Australia.* Angus and Robertson, Sydney. 80 pp.

Taylor, J., 1978. The foods and feeding habits of sub-adult *Crocodylus porosus,* Schneider, in northern Australia. Unpubl. M.Sc. thesis, University of Sydney.

Taylor, W.R., 1964. Fishes of Arnhem Land. In R.Specht (ed.), *Records of the American-Australian Scientific Expedition to Arnhem Land. 4. Zoology.* Melbourne University Press, pp. 45-307.

Thomson, J.M., 1954a. The genera of oysters and the Australian species. *Australian Journal of Marine and Freshwater Research* **5**, 132-68.

Thomson, J.M., 1954b. The organs of freeding and the food of some Australian mullet. *Australian Journal of Marine and Freshwater Research* **5**, 469-85.

van Tine, M. and S.C. Snedaker, 1974. *A Bibliography of the Mangrove Literature.* Prepared for the International Symposium on Biology and Management of Mangroves, Oct. 1974. Hawaii. University of Florida, Gainesville, Florida.

Warburton, N.J., 1978. Field observations on behavioural isolation in the *Uca* species of Ross River estuary. Unpubl. Hons. thesis, James Cook University of North Queensland. 99 pp.

Weate, P., 1975. A study of the wetlands of the Myall River. *Operculum* 4, 105-13.

Webb, G.J.W. 1977. The natural history of *Crocodylus porosus.* In H. Messel and S.T. Butler (eds.), *Australian Animals and Their Environment.* Shakespeare Head Press, Sydney, pp. 239-312.

Webb. G.J.W. and H. Messel, 1978. Morphometric analysis of *Crocodylus porosus* from the north coast of Arnhem Land, Northern Australia. *Australian Journal of Zoology* 26, 1-28.

Wood, E.J. 1964. Studies in microbial ecology of the Australiasian region. *Nova Hedwigia* 3, 5-568.

Worrell, E. 1963. *Reptiles of Australia.* Angus and Robertson, Sydney. 207 pp.

9

The Avifauna of the Australian Mangroves
A Brief Review of Composition, Structure and Origin

Richard Schodde, I.J. Mason
and H.B. Gill

Faunistic composition and origin

Of the two hundred or so species of birds that have been recorded from Australian mangrove vegetation (Saenger *et al.*, 1977), fourteen are virtually confined to it (Table 9.1), another twelve are limited by it for at least part of their range (Table 9.1) and a further sixty or so use it regularly throughout the year or in certain seasons. This is a rich avifauna by world standards (cf. Macnae, 1968, pp. 153-6; Chapman, 1976, Table 35), surprisingly so because mangroves are not a typical environment for Australian land and freshwater birds. Mangroves occur in thin, patchy, isolated stands which limit the numbers of viable populations that can be supported; they are comparatively uniform in structure so that diversity in foraging surfaces is rather restricted; and the twice-daily tidal flooding denies food to ground foragers for up to half a day and requires that they be adapted to feeding in mud.

Probably because of this, the greater proportion of bird species occurring in mangroves are not tied to them, living in other habitats as well and feeding, sheltering and breeding in the mangrove community opportunistically because of unique features that it offers. Many honeyeaters and lorikeets, for example, visit it seasonally when the mangroves are flowering and attracting insects, or at times when other habitats nearby are less productive. The Torresian Imperial Pigeon (*Ducula spilorrhoa*) and Pied Cormorant (*Phalacrocorax varius*) are present respectively in stands off-shore in north-eastern Queensland (Crome, 1975) and along tidal creeks in the South Australian gulfs when breeding, taking advantage of the trees and isolation for their nesting. Species of egrets, herons, the Sacred Ibis (*Threskiornis aethiopicus*) and Little Pied Cormorant (*Phalacrocorax melanoleucos*) also nest together in rookeries in mangroves in northern Australia (e.g. White, 1917; Seton, 1971). Still others occupy mangroves during migration, for example, the south-eastern Australian populations of the Rufous and Grey Fantails (*Rhipidura rufifrons, R. fuliginosa*).

What seems noteworthy is that (1) so many species live only in mangroves or are restricted to them to a large extent and (2) their collective ecological and zoogeographical attributes have not been described before now. A number of these species are confined to mangroves in parts of north-western Australia but occur widely through adjacent rain and gallery forests elsewhere in eastern Australia. Examples are the Great-billed Heron (*Ardea sumatrana*), Brahminy Kite (*Milvus indus*), Bar-shouldered Dove (*Geopelia humeralis*), Azure Kingfisher (*Alcedo azurea*), Little Shrike-thrush (*Colluricincla megarhyncha*), Shining Flycatcher (*Myiagra alecto*), Large-billed Gerygone (*Gerygone*

Table 9.1
List and distribution of mangrove-dependent birds (obligate and primary facultative
species) in Australia.

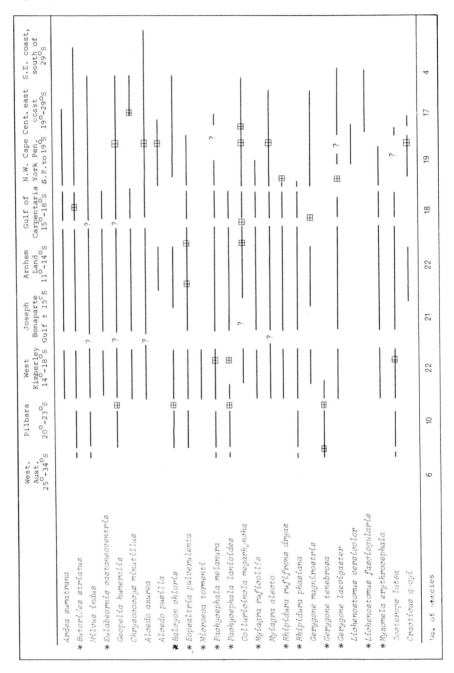

Solid lines indicate more-or-less continuous range, breaks in lines indicate major breaks
in range (> 50 km), and boxed symbols indicate subspecific change i.e. populations on
either side belong to different subspecies. Distributional data are drawn from Storr
(1973, 1977) and our own records. Species asterisked are obligate mangrove species i.e.
virtually confined to it; the remainder are primary facultative species, i.e. restricted to it
for at least part of their range.

magnirostris) and Black Butcherbird (*Cracticus quoyi*). For these, mangroves, with their closed, evergreen canopy and rather leafless, many-stemmed interior, offer a rainforest-like environment.

The species dependent on mangrove wholly or partly comprise two herons and one kite of palaeotropical or pan-tropical distribution, one white-eye of uncertain origin, and one rail, one dove, one cuckoo, three kingfishers, five pachycephaline flycatchers, four myiagrine flycatchers, three acanthizine warblers, three honeyeaters and one butcher-bird of Australo-Papuan origin (Schodde, in prep.). These are listed in Table 9.1. Only ten of them are endemic to mangroves in the region, and there is only one endemic genus, the monotypic Chestnut Rail (*Eulabeornis*), which has near-relatives in the swamp forests of lowland New Guinea and the Moluccas (Olson, 1973). In all cases except the acanthizine warblers *Gerygone magnirostris—G. tenebrosa* and the honeyeaters *Lichenostomus versicolor—L. fasciogularis* which are closest to each other, the nearest relatives of each occur in habitats outside mangrove, mainly rainforest and wet sclerophyll forest in Australia and New Guinea. Moreover, although close congeners of *Eopsaltria pulverulenta, Microeca tormenti, Pachycephala lanioides, Rhipidura phasiana* and *Gerygone laevigaster* live in sclerophyllous forests and woodland in Australia, they are also linked with rainforest-inhabiting forms, respectively *Peneothello*, the Papuan species of *Microeca*, the *Pachycephala monacha* group, the *Rhipidura albolimbata —R. castaneiventris* group and Papuan *Gerygone ruficollis*, and appear to have been derived from such sources.

The affinities of all these taxa, the dearth of old (generic) endemics, and the poor representation of Australia's two largest families, Meliphagidae and Psittacidae, suggest that the avifauna of the Australian mangroves has been built quite recently, in piecemeal fashion, mainly from rainforest sources in Australo-Papua.

Adaptations
None of the endemics have extensive morphological adaptations for life in mangroves, although there are incipient developments in the Mangrove Robin (*Eopsaltria pulverulenta*), White-breasted Whistler (*Pachycephala lanioides*) Mangrove Fantail (*Rhipidura phasiana*), Dusky Gerygone (*Gerygone tenebrosa*), Mangrove Gerygone (*Gerygone laevigaster*) and Red-headed Honeyeater (*Myzomela erythrocephala*). Like the Mangrove Golden Whistler, all have bills that are longer than those of their allospecific congeners, which probably developed in response to mode of feeding and to avoid clogging rictal bristles and muddying faces when they pick food off the forest floor and from damp, tidally inundated trunks and branches. Australian mangrove-inhabiting birds in general seem to develop long bills, even in subspecies, those of the Little Shrike-thrush (*Colluricincla megarhyncha aelptes*), Shining Flycatcher (*Myiagra alecto melvillensis*) and Black Butcherbird (*Cracticus quoyi spaldingi*) having disproportionally longer bills than rainforest-inhabiting subspecies in north-eastern Australia and New Guinea. The comparatively heavy and strongly hooked bill of the White-breasted Whistler

may also be adapted to handling crustacea and shell-fish, which appear to form a staple part of its diet. The Mangrove Robin has, furthermore, a more rounded wing and tail than other species of *Eopsaltria*. This confers greater aerial manoevrability and slower stalling speeds and may be adapted to the greater amount of hawking and flutter-sallying that it seems to do over and on its miry foraging substrate.

There appear to be no significant phenological or other biological adaptations among mangrove-dependent species. In northern Australia, many of them breed in the months of the wet monsoon (October-April) with a hiatus during late November-January when there are spring tides. This is at variance with most breeding in adjacent eucalypt woodlands but more coincident with that in rainforests, as might be expected from their ancestry (Schodde and Mason, in prep.). The Chestnut Rail (*Eulabeornis castaneoventris*) constructs a larger-than-usual nesting platform of sticks in the crotches of trunks of mangroves above high tide mark, a situation unusual in Rallidae. The Large-billed Gerygone (*Gerygone magnirostris*) also builds a long, coarse, straggly tailed nest that, slung from a low branch near or over a tidal creek, mimics flood debris; this, however, seems to be more an adaptation to a stream-side environment. Other mangrove-inhabiting gerygones build normal, compactly domed nests.

Coexistence of congeners

There are several groups of birds where more than one member of a particular genus has been attracted to mangroves, namely kingfishers of *Alcedo* and *Halcyon*, whistlers (*Pachycephala*), flycatchers (*Myiagra*), fantails (*Rhipidura*) and canthizid warblers (*Gerygone*). All except the kingfishers are insectivorous passerines that forage arboreally, or have been derived from such forms, e.g. White-breasted Whistler.

The two species of *Alcedo* (*A. azurea, A. pusilla*) and two of *Halcyon* (*H. chloris, H. sancta*) coexist in several parts of northern Australia. The first pair, both diving fishers, differ greatly in size (*A. azurea* 28-35g; *A. pusilla* 10-13g), and probably take prey of differing size and identity; data, however, are lacking. The second pair, which feed by perch-pouncing on to a more substantial littoral substrate, also differ in size but to a lesser extent. Along coastal Arnhem Land they seem to be partitioned more by foraging zone, *H. chloris* feeding in the seaward *Sonneratia alba* fringe and following the front of the tide in and out, and the versatile *H. sancta* keeping more to the drier, lower mangroves inland along estuaries and on the landward side of the *Rhizophora* zone.

Three whistlers are sympatric along much of the north-western Australian coast, namely the mangrove Golden, White-breased and Rufous (*P. rufiventris*), and a fourth, the Brown Whistler (*P. simplex*), overlaps them in Arnhem Land. The last two are normally separated from the first two by habitat; the Rufous Whistler, a bird of eucalypt woodland, usually keeps to the landward fringe of *Avicennia-Ceriops* woodland where the canopy is open, and the Brown, essentially a rainforest-inhabiting species, frequents the upper stages of taller, closed mangrove forest > 10 m high, usually in the *Rhizophora-Bruguiera* zone. Both White-breasted and Mangrove Golden Whistlers coexist in low, dense brakes in all zones but appear to avoid competition by usually taking different food (*q.v.* Adaptations). Both differ in size (*P. lanioides* 35-45 g; *P. melanura* 18-26 g) and forage prevailingly at different levels, the Mangrove Golden gleaning mainly for insects and their larvae through the upper branches and the White-breasted keeping to the lower stages, often diving on to and foraging about on mud.

The three myiagrine flycatchers and three fantails are partitioned similarly. Of these, the woodland-inhabiting Leaden Flycatcher (*Myiagra rubecula*) and Northern Fantail (*Rhipidura rufiventris*) keep mainly to the landward fringe where the canopy is patchy. The other four flycatchers and fantails occur within regularly flooded, closed mangroves and are there partitioned more by foraging technique and vertical strata in the vegetation. The Broad-billed Flycatcher (*Myiagra ruficollis*) captures food on the wing by short sallies among the middle stages and seaward edge of the forest; the Shining (*M. alecto*) flutters about the substage and stilt-roots usually within a metre of the mud, hover- and perch-gleaning from the surface of twigs, leaves, trunks and mud with their slender bills; the Mangrove Fantail (*Rhipidura phasiana*)[1] flutterhawks rapidly with flicking wings and jerking of fanned tail along trunks among all stages of the forest; and the mangrove-inhabiting subspecies of the Rufous Fantail (*R. rufifrons dryas*) uses similar foraging techniques but with more sedate sallying and less tail fanning in the lower stages.

All gerygonine warblers forage in much the same way, by perch-and hover-gleaning among outer foliage, and are zoned primarily by habitat. Five species of gerygones enter mangrove vegetation in north-western Australia, where two are virtually confined to that habitat, viz. the Dusky Gerygone (*G. tenebrosa*) and Mangrove Gerygone (*G. laevigaster*)[2]. The White-throated (*G. olivacea*) and Green-backed (*G. chloronota*) Gerygones, of eucalypt woodland and rainforest respectively, visit mangroves locally and temporarily, the former foraging into the landward fringe where it is open and abuts on eucalypt woodland and the latter entering the taller, denser forests of *Rhizophora-Bruguiera* along tidal creeks where they connect and become inter-mixed with galleries of coastal rainforest. The Large-billed Gerygone (*G. magnirostris*) occurs in the same tall, dense forests as the Green-backed but is more widespread throughout coastal mangroves and breeds there. The Dusky Gerygone (*G. tenebrosa*), which replaces it in Western Australia north to the south-west Kimberley Division (cf. Johnstone, 1975), prefers similar habitat but, perhaps because the mangroves of that region are stunted and floristically depauperate, it copes with the *Avicennia* fringes as well. The Mangrove Gerygone (*G. laevigaster*) is usually segregated from them because it keeps to

---

[1] Often treated as a subspecies of *R. Fulginosa* (eg. Keart, 1958; Ford, 1971) but differs in rounded, shorter rectrices, larger bill, pallid colour, distinct territorial song and habitat requirements.

[2] Includes *G. cantator* Weatherill.

the low shrubberies and brakes of *Avicennia* and associated mangroves on the landward fringe and along tidal creeks and estuaries, penetrating paperbark (*Melaleuca*) lined streams well inland in the Kimberley Division (Johnstone, 1975). Overlap with the Dusky Gerygone nevertheless occurs between York Sound and Collier Bay, and further study is needed to clarify their strategies for coexistence or integration.

Patterns of geographical variation and derivation
Three particular generalisations can be drawn from Table 9.1 for mangrove-dependent birds in Australia. Included in the category 'mangrove dependent' are species confined to mangrove (obligate species) and thosethat are completely dependent on it for part (but not all) of their geographical range (primary facultative species).

(1) Number (and diversity) of species increases with increasing number (and structural diversity) of tree species, but has been limited at least in part by historical factors. Six and four species occupy the floristically poor, *Avicennia*-dominated mangroves at high latitudes on the western and eastern coasts respectively, and none occur in the isolated pockets of *Avicennia* on the southern coast. This compares with 22 and 19 species in the floristically rich, humid mangroves in north-western and north-eastern Australia, respectively, north of 19°S. There is a significant anomaly here in that the floristically richest and tallest mangroves—with 26+ tree species—in north-eastern Queensland have fewer mangal-dependent species of birds than the floristically poorer and more stunted mangroves in north-western Australia with only 16-20 tree species. The anomaly is magnified by the even higher proportion of birds confined to mangroves (obligate species) in north-western Australia, 12 as against 8 in north-eastern Australia north of 19°S. Only two species of mangrove-dependent birds are restricted to the eastern seaboard—the essentially allopatric honeyeaters, *Lichenostomus versicolor* and *L. fasciogularis*—whereas six, including *Rhipidura rufifrons dryas,* do not reach it.[3] Because there appear to be no environmental limitations in north-eastern Australia, it seems likely that these distributional anomalies reflect disparate geographical origins (see below).

(2) Disjunctions in the distribution of the dependent birds, and therefore in the mangroves themselves, have been many and various, historic breaks being not always coincident with contemporary ones. Today the major disjunctions (> 50 km) between the more complex floras and avifaunas north of the Tropic of Capricorn are, west to east, the Eighty Mile Beach, the north-east coast of the Kimberleys between Cape Londonderry and Cambridge Gulf, the central Gulf of Carpentaria between the MacArthur River and Settlement Creek, and the mid-west coast of Cape York Peninsula. These breaks are indicated on Table 9.1. Historic disjunctions are revealed by subspecific and specific change or terminations on Table 9.1, the populations on either side having

---

[3]Records of *Myiagra ruficollis* from Cape Tribulation (Cowan, 1977) and of *Pachycephala lanioides* from Yandazan (Tucker, 1977) on the east coast need confirmation.

subspeciated or speciated in former isolation. Few coincide with contemporary breaks and many have now been closed up, for example the former barrier between Cairns and Cooktown which has contributed to subspeciation in *Geopelia humeralis*, *Alcedo azurea*, *A. pusilla*, *Colluricinela megarhyncha*, *Myiagra alecto* and *Cracticus quoyi* (the Torresian Barrier of Schodde and Mason, 1980).

The dearth of subspeciation on either side of contemporary breaks testifies to their recency, those around the Gulf of Carpentaria being no older than the foundering of the Gulf, *c.* 10,000 years BP (Phipps, 1970), and that on the steep north-east coast of the Kimberleys probably forming after the last eustatic rise in sea level, at the height of the present inter-glacial period, from 6000 years BP (Galloway and Löffler, 1972). Two current breaks, however, appear to have had a longer history. One is the Eighty Mile Beach which marks subspecific change in four species and the westernmost limits of another ten; the other is along the western coast of Cape York Peninsula which marks a subspecific change in two species and the eastern limits of another four (including *Rhipidura rufifrons dryas*).

The disparities and congruences in these past and present disruptions can probably be ascribed to the cyclical eustatic changes in sea-level during the Pleistocene (cf. Jongsma, 1970a). At times of fall, the various populations were probably spread along flat shores and estuarine meanders stretching north from Australia to New Guinea; and at times of rise they were split by sections of hilly, sandy and non-estuarine coast as today, each successive rise nevertheless creating breaks at new points and local extinctions in these populations because of the rapidity of transgression (cf. Galloway and Löffler, 1972).

(3) The terminations of species and subspecies on Cape York Peninsula identify that area as a former land bridge between Australia and New Guinea (Galloway and Löffler, 1972) that prevented interchange between mangrove-inhabiting birds on western and eastern coasts during most of the Pleistocene, perhaps until very recently (Jennings, 1972; cf. Schodde *et al.*, 1980). This in turn suggests that the richer avifauna in north-western Australia east to Cape York Peninsula was drawn from Arafura Land. This stable plain between Australia and New Guinea supported extensive, if patchy, stands of mangroves along the southern Arafura estuaries and Fly-Digoel trough when they were exposed at times of low sea-level (cf. Tjia, 1966; Jongsma, 1970b). In effect, it seems to have served as the cradle of evolution for most endemic elements of Australo-Papuan mangrove avifauna. Nine forms may have reached the eastern coast of Cape York Peninsula from Arafura Land only within the last 8000 years after the final breaching of the land bridge by Torres Strait (Jennings, 1971, 1972), viz. *Alcedo azurea ruficollaris*, *Alcedo pusilla ramsayi*, *Eopsaltria pulverulenta*, *Pachycephala melanura spinicauda*, *Myiagra ruficollis*, *Myiagra alecto melvillensis*, *Myzomela erythrocephala*, *Zosterops lutea* and *Cracticus quoyi spaldingi* (Schodde *et. al.*, in prep.)

The former mangrove-dependent avifauna of the eastern seaboard appears to have been much poorer and, because of steeper and sandier coasts, mangrove vegetation there may have been little more extensive at times of low sea level than it is today. The only birds autochthonous to it in Australia are *Butorides striatus macrorhynchus, Chrysococcyx minutillus barnardi, Alcedo a. azurea, Alcedo pusilla halli, Myiagra alecto wardelli, Gerygone magnirostris cairnsensis, Gerygone laevigaster cantator, Lichenostomus versicolor, L. fasciogularis* and *Cracticus quoyi rufescens,* some of which are equally frequent in rainforest. Only two, *Butorides* striatus macrorhynchus and *Gerygone magnirostris cairnsensis,* have reached the western coast of Cape York Peninsula.

The eastern seaboard, however, was probably not at all devoid of birds in the recent past, judged by the number of rainforest-inhabiting species that enter it as part of their range today. Among many are the Rose-crowned Fruit-Dove (*Ptilinopus regina*), Torresian Imperial Pigeon (*Ducula spilorrhoa*), Common Koel (*Eudynamis scolopacea*), Varied Triller (*Lalage leucomela*), Helmeted Friar-bird (*Philemon buceroides*), Yellow-spotted and Graceful Honeyeaters (*Meliphaga notata, M. gracilis*), Spangled Drongo (*Dicrurus hottentottus*) and Yellow Oriole (*Oriolus flavocinctus*).

Such adventitious use of mangroves provides a further clue to the evolution of disparate avifaunas east and west of Cape York Peninsula. We mentioned above that most, if not all, mangrove-dependent species autochthonous to the Australo-Papuan region (23 out of 26) had arisen from rainforest-inhabiting ancestors (cf. Schodde and Calaby, 1972). As Australia cooled and dried through the later Cainozoic (e.g. Kemp, 1978), the eastern scarps of the Great Dividing Range and the rising New Guinean cordillera, with their regional effects on climate, appear to have served as refuges for the dwindling stocks of a formerly widespread rainforest-adapted avifauna in Australia. The proximity of the rainforest to mangroves on the eastern seaboard throughout this period probably facilitated continual interchange among avian populations there, effectively cutting down isolation between those in the mangroves, and thereby evolution and speciation within them.

The situation on the Arafura Land plain seems to have been just the reverse. Nix and Kalma (1972), among others, have pointed out that a much drier climate prevailed west of the Great Dividing Range in northern Australia during the late Pleistocene and probably earlier, supporting woodlands and open forests at best. There the rainforest source forms were undoubtedly much more restricted to mangroves, and the mangroves themselves patchier and locally more isolated around a drier coastline, than in the east. These circumstances, offering greater opportunities for speciation and divergent evolution, make the development of a more varied mangrove-dependent avifauna in Arafura Land easier to imagine. They also appear to explain the greater number of endemics (subspecies and the species *Pachycephala lanioides* and *Gerygone tenebrosa*) on the dry Australian than wet New Guinean shores of the Arafura Sea today.

Epilogue

The foregoing review, written in 1979, is only as accurate and complete as available data allow. Much of the information has come from our own studies of the mangrove avifauna at King Sound (Western Australia), Van Diemen Gulf (Arnhem Land), the delta of the McArthur River (Gulf of Carpentaria) and north-eastern Queensland between Cairns and Townsville, augmented by examination of material in all Australian State and national museums to determine subspecific limits. These are the subject of a much more detailed explanatory paper in preparation (Schodde *et. al.*, in prep.).

Many gaps nevertheless still remain. Both east and west coasts of Cape York Peninsula, critical to understanding the avifaunistic interrelationships of mangrove-dependent birds, are still among the least explored ornithologically in the whole of Australia. Only recently have the Mangrove Golden Whistler (Galbraith, 1967) and Yellow Silvereye (Lavery and Grimes, 1974) been reported on its mid north-east coast and, in 1978, Ford (1978) described the first hybrids between the Varied and Mangrove Honeyeaters (*Lichenostomus versicolor, L. fasciogularis*) from that area. The state of knowledge is such that more detailed exploration of the mangroves of the Peninsula may unearth distributions that could amend some of the conclusions of this chapter.

Acknowledgments

We wish to record our debt to Mr R.E. Johnstone, Western Australian Museum, Perth, for information of value in compiling this paper.

References

Chapman, V.J., 1976. *Mangrove Vegetation*. J. Cramer, Vaduz. 447 pp.

Cowan, I, 1977. Bird notes. *Qld Orn. Soc Newsletter* **8**(6), 2.

Crome, F.H.J., 1975. Breeding, feeding and status of the Torres Strait Pigeon at Low Isles, north-eastern Queensland. *Emu* **75**, 189-98.

Ford, J.R., 1971. Distribution, ecology and taxonomy of some Western Australian Passerine birds. *Emu* **71**, 103-20.

Ford, J.R., 1978. Intergradation between the Varied and Mangrove Honeyeaters. *Emu* **78**, 71-4.

Galbraith, I.C.S., 1967. The Black-tailed and Robust Whistlers *Pachycephala melanura* as a species distinct from the Golden Whistler *P. pectoralis*. *Emu* **66**, 289-94.

Galloway, R.W. and E. Löffler, 1972. Aspects of geomorphology and soils in the Torres Strait Region. In D. Walker (ed.), *Bridge and Barrier, The Natural and Cultural History of Torres Strait*. Publication BG/3, Australian National University, Canberra, pp. 11-28.

Jennings, J.N., 1971. Sea level changes and land links. In D.J. Mulvaney and J. Golson (eds.), *Aboriginal Man and Environment in Australia*. Australian National University Press, Canberra, pp. 1-13.

Jennings, J.N., 1972. Some attributes of Torres Strait. In D. Walker (ed.), *Bridge and Barrier: the Natural and Cultural History of Torres Strait*. Publication BG/3, Australian National University, Canberra, pp. 29-38.

Johnstone, R.E., 1975. Distribution and taxonomic status of the Dusky Warbler *Gerygone tenebrosa*. *Emu* **75**, 185-8.

Jongsma, D., 1970a. Eustatic sea level changes in the Arafura Sea. *Nature (Lond.)* **228**, 150-1.

Jongsma, D., 1970b. Texture of sediments of the Arafura Sea. *Bureau of Mineral Resources Australia Recs.* 1970/59 (unpubl.).

Keast, A., 1958. Variation and speciation in the Australian Flycatchers. (Aves: Muscicapinae). *Aust. Mus. Rec.* **24**, 73-108.

Kemp, E.M., 1978. Tertiary climatic evolution and vegetation history in the south-east Indian Ocean Region. *Palaeogeogr., Palaeoclim., Palaeoecol.* **24**, 169-208.

Lavery, H.J. and R.J. Grimes, 1974. The Yellow Silvereye in north-east Queensland. *Sunbird* **5**, 42-3.

Macnae, W., 1968. A general account of the fauna and flora of mangrove swamps and forests in the Indo-West-Pacific Region. *Advances in Marine Biology* **6**, 73-270.

Nix, H.A and J.D. Kalma, 1972. Climate as a dominant control in the biogeography of northern Australia and New Guinea. In D. Walker (ed.), *Bridge and Barrrier: The Natural and Cultural History of Torres Strait.* Publication BG/3, Australian National University Canberra, pp. 60-91.

Olson, S.L., 1973. A classification of the Rallidae. *Wilson Bull.* **85**, 381-416.

Phipps, C.V.G., 1970. Dating of eustatic events from cores taken in the Gulf of Carpentaria and samples from the New South Wales continental shelf. *Aust. J. Sci.* **32**, 329-30.

Saenger, P., M.M. Specht, R.L. Specht and V.J. Chapman, 1977. Mangal and coastal salt-marsh communities in Australasia. In V.J. Chapman (ed.), *Ecosystems of the World.* I, *Wet Coastal Ecosystems,* Elsevier, Amsterdam, pp. 293-345.

Schodde, R. and I.J. Mason (in prep.). Zoogeography of the avifauna of the Australian mangroves.

Schodde, R., M.L. Dudzinski, I.J. Mason and J.L. McKean, 1980. Variation in the Striated Heron (*Butorides striatus*) in Australasia. *Emu* **80**, 203-12

Schodde, R. and I.J. Mason, 1980. *Nocturnal Birds of Australia.* Landsdowne, Melbourne. 136 pp.

Schodde, R. and I.J. Mason (in prep.). Birds. In *A Survey of the Vertebrate Land Fauna of the Alligator Rivers Region.* CSIRO Division of Wildlife Research Tech. Paper series.

Seton, D.H.C., 1971. Mangrove rookery near Ayr, Queensland. *Aust. Birdwatcher* **4**, 96-7

Tjia, H.D., 1966. Arafura Sea. In R.W. Fairbridge (ed.), *The Encyclopaedia of Oceanography.* Reinhold, New York, pp. 44-7.

White, H.L., 1917. Northern Australian birds. *Emu* **16**, 117-58.

Part III
BIOLOGICAL ADAPTATIONS
Introduction

A.M. Gill

'Adaptation' is selective change. From one particular set of characteristics in one particular environment, the species has changed (or adapted) its characteristics to suit the new environment. As time has passed, the species has adapted to changed environments or has colonised new ones. Just how this has happened is difficult to determine. Most observers have been content to imply adaptation-as-change by attempting to explain how well a species is suited to its present environment. This has been done by comparing the characteristics of the species in question with those of other species in other environments, and is the method adopted by the authors of the two reviews which follow.

Mangroves are particularly interesting subjects for the student of adaptation. They live, often as trees, rooted in a saline, anaerobic substrate: abundant salt is usually toxic to trees and oxygen is necessary for root respiration, so how do these plants persist, let alone grow and reproduce successfully? The answer to this question, and others like it, may be found in the morphology, physiology or ecology of the species. The salt glands on the leaves and the remarkable aerial morphologies of the roots may be visible expressions of coping with salt and oxygen-free substrates but not all mangroves are structured like this and physiological studies may be essential to elucidate mechanisms. Adaptational questions may be elicited by observation of the environment (how does this plant cope with salt?) or of specific characteristics of the plants (what is the significance of the aerial root?). In any event, all answers are ultimatley concerned with the *interrelationships* between the organisms and their environment.

The topics which attract the student of adaptation will depend on his training, his interests, the current state of knowledge and the tractability of the problems he perceives. To one, the high tannin concentrations often found in mangrove tissues may excite his interest; to another the function and importance of the rhizosphere in saline, anaerobic substrates may seem to be most pertinent; while, to a third person, the most significant question may be how large-fruited mangroves protect their investment in propagules from herbivorous crabs and other predators. These topics suggest the scope of the subject of adaptation and the many new directions which are possible for future research.

Mangroves have excited interest for a long time and the literature goes back to the fourth century B.C. During the last decade, however, there has been a tremendous growth in the literature of mangroves which now includes books, proceedings of international conferences, and regional and topical reviews. Themes of interest through this literature have been the ability of mangroves to cope with the saline, anaerobic substrate induced by tidal flooding, and the unusual anatomical and morphological features of the plants themselves. Both reviews of the present segment of this book consider complementary aspects of these great themes with Saenger majoring on anatomy and morphology and Clough, Andrews and Cowan emphasising physiology.

Australia's shores are host to most of the world's genera of mangroves. Australia lies in the 'eastern' realm of mangrove distribution but includes the major genera of the floristically-poor, but species-distinct, mangrove flora of the 'western' realm (the Americas and the western coast of Africa). Because of this, much of the research conducted in North America is relevant to Australian mangroves and is included in the present reviews. These chapters, then tend to have a world-wide perspective on mangrove adaptations, rather than the strictly regional and narrower view suggested by the title of this treatise.

10

Morphological, Anatomical and Reproductive Adaptations of Australian Mangroves

P. Saenger

Introduction

On the basis of a review of fossil evidence and the modern distribution of mangrove genera, Specht (1981) concluded that the origin of the mangrove flora was centred on south-west and northern Australia to New Guinea. It would follow from this that the mangrove flora of the Australasian region should give an indication of the full range of adaptations—physiological, morphological and reproductive — that has allowed this flora to surivive in what must always have been a most difficult environment.

Descriptive accounts of many of the morphological adaptations are available but little or no quantitative data on the efficacy and competitive significance of these adaptations have been collected, particularly for Australian conditions. Consequently this review of the morphological, anatomical and reproductive adaptations draws heavily on studies largely undertaken outside the Australasian region, some of which have been reviewed by Chapman (1976).

The mangrove environment is indeed a harsh one due to the combination of periodic fluctuations and extremes in various of its physicochemical parameters. Despite this harshness, however, the flora has successfully occupied this niche, and the morphological and reproductive manifestations of this occupancy are reviewed below.

Morphological anatomical adaptations

Xeromorphy

Leaves of most mangroves exhibit a range of xeromorphic features (Stace, 1966) although this is disputed by some (Uphof, 1941) and there are few experimental studies in support of their water-conserving functions (Miller *et al.*, 1975).

All genera of mangroves have a thick-walled epidermis (Plate 10.1) which, at least on the upper surface of the leaf, is covered by a thick, waxy cuticle (Artz, 1936; Stace, 1966; Sidhu, 1975a) or by a tomentum of variously shaped hairs. Examples of the latter include tricellular peltate hairs in *Avicennia* (Baker, 1915; Fahn and Shimony, 1977; Plate 10.2), stellate hairs in *Hibiscus tiliaceus* (Plate 10.3), stellate scales in *Heritiera* (Plate 10.4) and glandular scales in *Camptostemon* (Jones, 1971). Where present, this tomentum covers salt glands and stomata, presumably reducing water loss via these apertures.

With the known exception of species with isobilateral leaves, stomata are restricted to the lower leaf epidermis (Sidhu, 1975a; Joshi *et al.*, 1975a; Table 10.1) despite comments to the contrary in Mullan (1931a) and Walter and

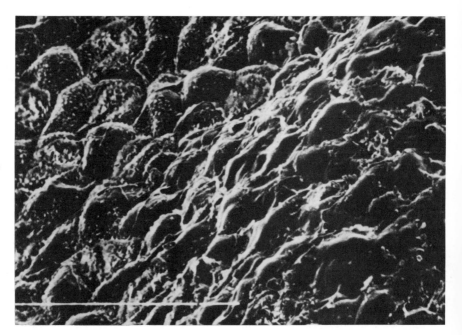

Plate 10.1   Scanning electron micrograph of the lower leaf surface of *Cynometra ramiflora*, showing undifferentiated epidermis with thick, somewhat pitted cuticle.

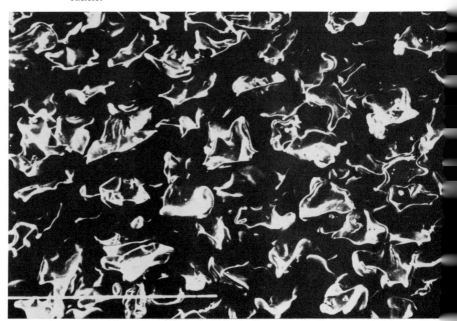

Plate 10.2.   Scanning electron micrograph of the lower leaf surface of *Avicennia marina*, showing dense covering of peltate hairs.

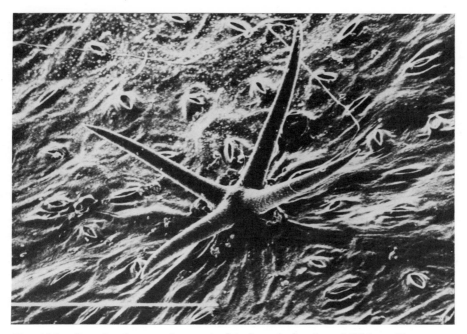

Plate 10.3.   Scanning electron micrograph of the lower leaf surface of *Hibiscus tiliaceus*, showing stellate hairs and slightly raised stomata.

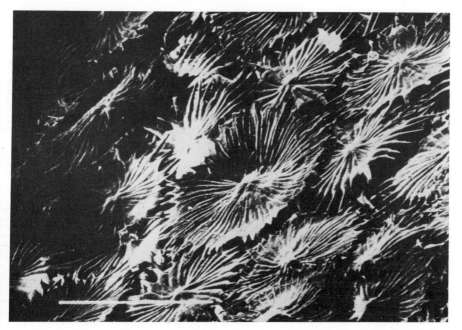

Plate 10.4.   Scanning electron micrograph of the lower leaf suface of *Heritiera littoralis*, showing interlocking stellate hairs.

Steiner (1936). In terms of frequency (Table 10.1) and dimension, mangrove stomata are similar to plants of other habitats but many genera (*Avicennia, Aegiceras, Bruguiera, Ceriops, Lumnitzera, Rhizophora*) show stomata sunk beneath the level of the epidermis (Mullan, 1932; Stace, 1966). While substomatal chambers are present in many genera (*Avicennia, Ceriops, Rhizophora*), these are lacking in *Xylocarpus* and *Excoecaria* (Sidhu, 1975a).

Three stomatal types (Caryophyllaceous, Ranunculaceous, Rubiaceous) have been reported from mangroves but Sidhu (1975a) was unable to attach any ecological significance to them. The stomata of mangroves show considerable variation in behaviour. Joshi *et al.* (1975a) report that in a number of species in India the stomata are wide open between 4 am and 10 am, closed in the early afternoon, and again slightly open in the evening. On the other hand, photosynthetic studies with *Avicennia* and *Rhizophora* in Australia have shown the stomata to remain open throughout the day (B. Clough, personal communication, 1979). A response to high temperature is probably involved (Zelitch, 1971) and this behaviour is reflected in the transpiration rates (Lewis and Naidoo, 1970; Lugo *et al.*, 1975).

Table 10.1 Stomatal frequencies on the upper and lower leaf surfaces of Australian mangroves. Salt gland frequencies are given in parentheses

	No. per mm^{-2}	
Species	Upper epidermis	Lower epidermis
Acanthus ilicifolius	0 (8)	210-317 (8)
Acrostichum speciosum	0	200-210
Aegialitis annulata	0 (10-15)	60-70 (0)
Aegiceras corniculatum	0 (4-5)	72 (10-12)
Amyema mackayense	70-75	70-75
Avicennia marina	4 (8-18)	80-180 (80)
Bruguiera gymnorhiza	0	110-135
Bruguiera exaristata	0	95-135
Ceriops tagal	0	50-85
Cynometra ramiflora	0	330-430
Excoecaria agallocha	0	150
Heritiera littoralis	0	835-1060
Hibiscus tiliaceus	0	75-85
Lumnitzera racemosa	65-95	65-95
Osbornia octodonta	130	170
Rhizophora stylosa	0	135
Scyphiphora hydrophyllacea	0	150-170
Sonneratia caseolaris	75-100	90-110
Xylocarpus australasicus	0	600

Note: Based on material collected at Port Curtis and Princes Charlotte Bay, Queensland, except for *Scyphiphora hydrophyllacea* where the frequencies are from Sidhu, 1975a.

Both Stace (1966) and Sidhu (1975a) concluded that the presence of a thick cuticle, wax coatings, sunken stomata and the distribution of cutinised and sclerenchymatous cells throughout the leaf, including the epidermis, are xeric characters which had probably developed in response to the physiological dryness of the mangrove environment.

Succulence is a feature common in mangrove leaves (Mullan, 1931b) and it is generally associated with xeromorphy (Shields; 1950; Wylie, 1954). Based on studies of *Rhizophora* (Bowman, 1921) and *Sonneratia* (Walter and Steiner, 1936) growing in saline and freshwater conditions, it appears that succulence is a response to the presence of chloride. Anatomical factors contributing to succulence in leaves include the presence of a well developed large-celled water-storing hypodermis, a strongly developed palisade mesophyll and generally small intercellular space volumes (Fig. 10.1). Hypodermal aqueous tissue is present in most mangroves (Mullan, 1931a; Stace, 1966) and it consists of two to several cell layers in *Avicennia* (Baylis, 1940), *Aegiceras, Hibiscus, Ceriops, Acrostichum, Heritiera* and *Rhizophora* (Stace, 1966; Gessner, 1967). It consists of a single cell layer in *Bruguiera, Xylocarpus, Acanthus, Cynometra* and *Excoecaria* (Stace, 1966). Both *Ceriops* and *Bruguiera* possess both an upper and a lower hypodermal layer. With the exception of *Ceriops,* those species with isobilateral leaves do not possess a hypodermis but in several of these species (*Sonneratia, Osbornia, Lumnitzera, Amyema*), large undifferentiated mesophyll cells form a central aqueous tissue. The leaves of *Aegialitis* appear to be unique amongst the mangroves in that they possess neither a mesophyllous nor a hypodermal aqueous tissue. Chloroplasts are absent from hypodermal cells and they are also generally absent or greatly reduced in number in the enlarged mesophyll cells.

Spongy mesophyll is absent from species with isobilateral leaves with the exception of *Ceriops,* and it generally forms less than 40 per cent of the cross-sectional area of those species with dorsiventral leaves (Baylis, 1940; Stace, 1966). The distribution and generally strong development of palisade mesophyll in mangroves is shown in Fig. 10.1.

In several genera (*Avicennia, Bruguiera, Ceriops*) the ends of the vascular bundles are surrounded by irregular groups of tracheids which are much larger than the conducting elements (Baker, 1915; Watson, 1928; Rao and Sharma, 1968; Breen and Jones, 1969). Their walls bear spiral, reticulated or pitted thickenings, and since they possess a flange-like connection to the hypodermis, a water-storage function has been attributed to them (Baylis, 1940). Stace (1966) found that in all genera except *Avicennia* and the western *Conocarpus,* no lateral and lesser epidermal veins were present, a condition associated with the development of an aqueous tissue.

In addition to storage tracheids, various other structures have been reported from the leaves of some species. For instance stone cells have been reported from *Avicennia, Rhizophora, Sonneratia* and *Xylocarpus* (Bowman, 1921; Watson, 1928; Malaviya, 1963); sclereids from *Rhizophora* (Rao, 1957; Shah and Sundarraj, 1965), *Scyphiphora* (Rao and Wan, 1969) and *Bruguiera* (Rao and Sharma, 1968) and mucilage cells from *Sonneratia* and *Rhizophora*

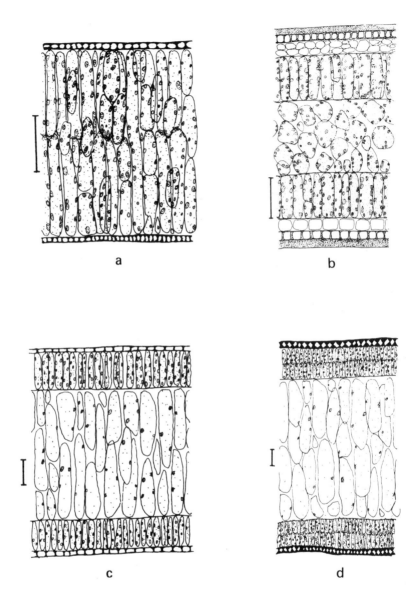

Fig. 10.1.   Transverse sections of leaves of Australian mangroves wth isobilateral leaves, based on material collected along the Queensland coastline. The calibration bar is 100 μm in all sections. The sections have been somewhat simplified through the omission of leaf vasculature.

(a) *Aegialitis annulata*—note absence of hypodermis and spongy mesophyll; (b) *Ceriops tagal*—note upper and lower hypodermis and enlarged spongy mesophyll cells; (c) *Amyema mackayense*; (d) *Sonneratia caseolaris, Lumnitzera racemosa, Osbornia octodonta*—note enlarged water-storing cells.

(Watson, 1928). These cells undoubtedly give toughness and rigidity to the leaf, reduce damage from wilting and may be involved in conserving water (Malaviya, 1963).

Other features possibly related to the physiological dryness of their environment include the thick cuticles covering the leaf-bearing stems and the presence of hypodermal aqueous tissue in petioles, as in *Avicennia* (Baylis, 1940), higher chromosome numbers than other species of the same genera from mesic habitats (Sidhu, 1962, 1968), and a modified wood anatomy (Panshin, 1932). According to Janssonius (1950), the mangroves possess more vessels per square millimetre, with a larger total cross-sectional area, while the pores are mostly distinctly smaller than in the nearest related inland species. This trend has been confirmed by others for the majority of mangroves (e.g. for Sonneratiaceae by Venkatiswarlu and Rao, 1964) but *Heritiera littoralis* appears to be exceptional in not differing markedly from other genera of the Sterculiaceae (Reinders-Gouwentak, 1953). While the role of this anatomical modification remains obscure, it is possibly related to increasing the resistance to water movement in the conducting tissue (Janssonius, 1950) or the reduced likelihood of rupturing the water column in narrow vessels (Reinders-Gouwentak, 1953). The mangroves of the Rhizophoraceae are similarly distinguishable from non-mangrove genera on the basis of wood anatomy (Marco, 1935; Carlquist, 1975). The wood of the rhizophoraceous mangroves is characterised by heavily barred, exclusively scalariform perforation plates, characteristic scalariform intervascular pitting, little vasicentric parenchyma, numerous fine-celled multiseriate rays and very few uniseriate rays, libriform fibres with inconspicuous pits, and unilaterally or bilaterally compound pitting between rays and vessels. Marco (1935) was unable to determine whether or not these were significant adaptive features although Carlquist (1975, p. 156) noted that the perforation plate arrangement seemed 'ideal to resist collapse in vessels under tension'.

Salt regulation
Mangroves growing in saline environments absorb sodium and chloride ions. Various physiological strategies are apparent to control uptake and concentration of these ions in metabolic tissues although the various mechanisms are incompletely known (Walter, 1973; Walsh, 1974).

Various authors have suggested that mangroves regulate salt by three mechanisms: exclusion, extrusion and accumulation. Scholander *et al.* (1962) classified mangroves into salt-secretors and salt-excluders. Jennings (1968) reviewed the mechanisms of salt-extrusion, exclusion and succulence in mangroves, and it appears that all three of these mechanisms are to be found. It is not proposed to review the physiological aspects of salt regulation here but rather to describe the morphological and anatomical features involved in each of these mechanisms.

Salt-excluders possess an effective selective-absorption mechanism, presumably an ultra-filter in the roots (Rains and Epstein, 1967; Scholander, 1968), whereby water is taken up and salt is largely filtered out. Genera found

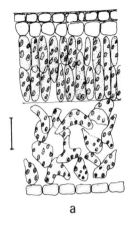

a

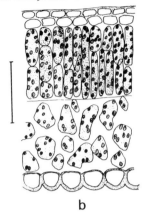

b

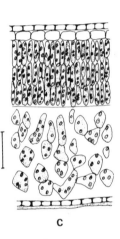

c

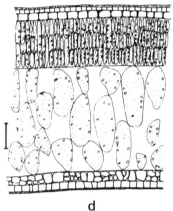

d

Fig. 10.2. Transverse sections of leaves of Australian mangroves with dorsiventral leaves having a single-layered upper hypodermis, based on material collected along the Queensland coastline. The calibration bar is 100 μm in all sections. The sections have been somewhat simplified through the omission of leaf vasculature.

(a) *Acanthus ilicifolius*—note absence of lower cuticle; (b) *Cynometra ramiflora*—note lower epidermal structure; (c) *Bruguiera exaristata*; (d) *Bruguiera gymnorhiza* — note several-layered lower hypodermis; (e) *Excoecaria agallocha, Xylocarpus australasicus* — note elongated upper hypodermis.

e

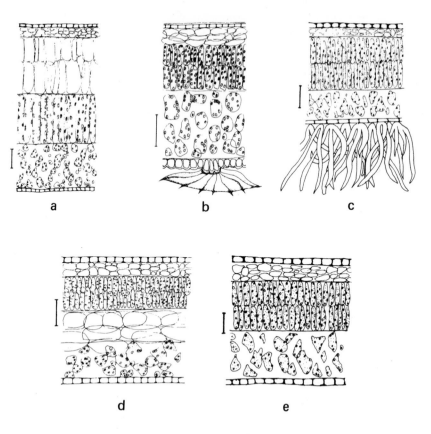

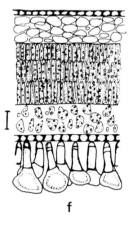

Fig. 10.3. Transverse sections of leaves of Australian mangroves with dorsiventral leaves having a several-layered upper hypodermis, based on material collected along the Queensland coastline. The calibration bar is 100 μm in all sections. The sections have been somewhat simplified through the omission of leaf vasculature. (a) *Rhizophora stylosa* — note differentiation of hypodermis into small tannin cells and large, colourless water-storing cells; (b) *Heritiera littoralis* — note stellate scales on lower epidermis; (c) *Hibiscus tiliaceus* — note stellate hairs on lower epidermis; (d) *Acrostichum speciosum* — note central accessory transfusion tissue; (e) *Aegiceras corniculatum*; (f) *Avicennia marina* — note hairs on lower epidermis.

to be able to exclude salt were *Rhizophora, Ceriops, Sonneratia, Avicennia, Osbornia, Bruguiera, Excoecaria, Aegiceras, Aegialitis* and *Acrostichum*.

Salt-extrusion occurs by means of salt glands in the leaves of *Avicennia marina* (Baylis, 1940), *A. nitida* (Trochain and Dulau, 1942), *Sonneratia alba* (Walter and Steiner, 1936), *Aegiceras* (Cardale and Field, 1971), *Aegialitis* (Atkinson *et al.*, 1967), *Acanthus* (Mullan, 1931a), *Laguncularia* (Biebl and Kinzel, 1965) and the saltmarsh plant *Limonium* C. (Ziegler and Lüttge, 1966).

Ultrastructural studies of the salt glands of *Aegiceras* (Cardale and Field, 1971; Bostrom and Field, 1973) have shown that the gland consists of 24-40 secretory cells situated over a single, large basal cell. The secretory cells are densely packed with mitochondria and other organelles, suggesting some metabolically active function. The basal cells appear to be more vacuolated. The junction between the basal cell and the secretory cells contains plasmodesmata. On the other hand, the junction between the basal cell and the sub-basal cells, which form a layer above the palisade mesophyll, seems to be a partially cutinised area continuous with the leaf cuticle. The mesophyll cells contain two types of vacuoles; one contained large amounts of an organic solute and little or no chloride while the other was free of organic solute but rich in chloride (Van Steveninck *et al.*, 1976). The radio-isotope fluxes of Na^+, K^+ and Cl^- have been measured (Cardale and Field, 1975) and all of these ions are actively transported out of the parenchyma by the gland cells.

In *Avicennia*, salt glands are formed only under saline conditions (Mullan, 1931a; Macnae, 1968a), whereas in *Aegiceras* they appear to be formed whether or not salt is present in the medium (Cardale and Field, 1971). They are entirely absent from *Acanthus* grown in freshwater (Mullan, 1931a). Joshi *et al.* (1975b) conclude that among salt-extruding species, *Avicennia* is the most efficient and consequently able to grow in highly saline conditions whereas the less efficient *Acanthus* and *Aegiceras* are restricted to less saline habitats.

Salt accumulating mangroves (*Excoecaria, Lumnitzera, Osbornia, Sonneratia, Xylocarpus*) often deposit sodium and chloride in the stem and pneumatophore barks and in older leaves (Joshi *et al.*, 1975b). Leaf storage of salt is generally accompanied by succulence (Bowman, 1921; Mullan, 1931b; Jennings, 1968). Joshi *et al.* (1975b) have shown that in old senescent leaves of *Sonneratia, Excoecaria* and *Lumnitzera,* sodium and chloride were deposited, and potassium and phosphorus were simultaneously withdawn prior to leaf fall. In this way excess salt was removed from metabolic tissue. For deciduous species like *Xylocarpus,* annual leaf fall may be a mechanism for the removal of excess salt prior to the onset of a new growing and fruiting season.

An interesting interaction worthy of detailed study is the salt regulation of mangrove mistletoes when growing on salt-extruders (*Avicennia*), salt-excluders (*Rhizophora*) and salt-accumulators (*Lumnitzera*). Preliminary observations at Port Curtis on *Amyema mackayense* suggest that the degree of succulence of this species, a xylem sap parasite, appears to be highest whilst on *Lumnitzera* and *Avicennia,* and least developed on *Rhizophora*.

Movement of salt into viviparous and cryptoviviparous seedlings while still attached to the parent tree appears to be regulated in *R. mangle* (Loetschert and Liemann, 1967), *R. racemosa* (Chin and Fang, 1958), *R. mucronata* (Joshi *et al.*, 1972), *Avicennia* (Chin and Fang, 1958; Joshi et al., 1972), *Ceriops, Bruguiera, Aegiceras* and *Acanthus* (Joshi *et al.*, 1972; 1975b).

Loetschert and Liemann (1967) found that changes in the contents of Cl, Na, K, Ca and N in *R. mangle* seedlings indicated that there is a barrier between the cotyledonary body and the peripheral tissues. The outer layer of the cotyledonary body consists of small, nearly spherical cells (Loetschert and Liemann, 1967) which, according to Pannier (1962), are characterised by an increased phosphatase activity, a condition generally indicative of secretory tissue. Loetschert and Liemann (1967) conclude that the reduced salt uptake by seedlings of *R. mangle* is accomplished by the active exclusion of salt by this gland tissue. Preliminary observations showed that a similar gland tissue is present on the outside of the cotyledonary body in *R. stylosa,* and this tissue may be identical to the papillose layer described from *Rhizophora* and *Ceriops* by Carey (1934).

Soil interactions

Most adaptations which aid mangroves in overcoming the problems of anaerobic soils and in anchoring the plant in the often semi-fluid soils, are obvious and widely known. These include the root systems with their diversity of form and function, and the almost ubiquitous presence of aerenchyma and lenticels.

Table 10.2 Root/shoot biomass ratios of mangrove communities compared with non-mangrove vegetation types

Mature mangroves	Root/shoot ratio	Reference
Panama	0.68	Data from Golley *et al.*, 1974, cited by Lugo and Snedaker, 1974.
Puerto Rico	0.80	Golley *et al,*, 1962
Australia (N.S.W.)	1.02	Briggs, 1977
Non-mature mangroves		
Florida	1.73	Data from Snedaker and Lugo, 1973, cited by Lugo and Snedaker, 1974
Australia (N.S.W.)	1.41	Briggs, 1977
Dwarfed mangroves		
Australia (Vic.)	1.70	Clough and Attiwill, 1975
Non-mangroves		
Mean of six communities	0.20 ± 0.04	Data from Ulrich *et al.*, 1974, cited by Clough and Attiwill, 1975

Below the substrate surface, all mangroves possess a system of laterally-spreading cable roots with smaller, vertically-descending anchor roots; the latter bear the fine nutritive roots (Attims and Cremers, 1967; Gill and Tomlinson, 1977). The root system is shallow (generally less than 2 metres) in most species and tap roots have not been reported (Walsh, 1974). Despite the shallowness of the root system, the ratio of below- to above-ground biomass is higher for mangroves than for other vegetation types (Table 10.2), particularly during early seral stages. This high biomass ratio may be an adaptation to the unstable substrate.

Some species of mangroves do not possess a specialised root system (e.g. *Aegialitis, Excoecaria*) and their cable root system lies near or on the substrate surface. Since in these species only relatively small surface areas are available for the assimilation of oxygen, these species tend to be found on less waterlogged (*Excoecaria*) or coarser, more aerobic sediments (*Aegialitis*). In the other extreme however, *Nypa*, which grows from an underground rhizome and has no specialised aerial root system (Tomlinson, 1971), is found in areas of frequent inundation.

Other species (Table 10.3) possess an array of above-ground root types (Percival and Womersley, 1975; Gill and Tomlinson, 1975-1977). These include: 1. Pneumatophores: negatively-geotropic unbranched (*Avicennia, Xylocarpus*) or branched (*Sonneratia*) roots arising from the cable root system. 2. Knee-roots: modified sections of the cable roots with a period of negatively-geotropic followed by a period of positively-geotropic growth. 3. Stilt roots: positively-geotropic arching (*Rhizophora*) or straight (*Ceriops*) generally branched roots arising from the trunk and growing into the substrate. 4. Buttress roots: similar to stilt roots in origin but expanding into flattened, blade-like structures. 5. Aerial roots: positively-geotropic, generally unbranched (unless injured or penetrating the substrate; Gill and Tomlinson, 1971, 1977) roots arising from the trunk (*Avicennia*) or lower branches (*Avicennia, Rhizophora*) and generally remaining free of the substrate.

Evidence that these root structures are adaptations to subterranean root aeration and to physical anchoring of the plant comes from a variety of sources. The most apparent is that those mangroves growing at lower tide levels and consequently more frequently inundated, tend to possess the greatest array of above-ground root types, e.g. *Avicennia, Rhizophora, Bruguiera* and *Sonneratia*. Considered together with the presence of aerenchymatous tissue (Brenner, 1902; Chapman, 1944; Gill and Tomlinson, 1971) and numerous lenticels in most of the above-ground roots (Chapman, 1947; Lugo and Snedaker, 1975), this strongly suggests a role in aeration. The mechanisms of air uptake through the development of a negative gas pressure have been investigated by Scholander *et al*. (1955) in *R. mangle* and *Avicennia germinans*. Mangroves presumably rely on this mechanism only in situations where poor soil aeration occurs, for Gessner (1967) showed that for *Avicennia nitida*, growing on coarse coral sand (presumably with reasonable drainage and aeration), experimental removal of pneumatophores had no effect on the tree. On the other hand, in situations where soil aeration is poor, continued covering

Table 10.3 Occurrence of different root types in Australian mangroves*. (+ Present; +/— Present in some species; in monotypic genera sometimes present).

Genus	Surface cable roots	Pneumato-phores	Knee roots	Stilt roots	Buttress roots	Aerial roots
Acanthus	+			+		
Aegilaitis	+					
Aegiceras	+					
Avicennia		+	+/—			+
Bruguiera		+/—	+	+/—	+/—	+/—
Camptostemon	+				+	
Ceriops			+	+	+	
Cynometra					+/—	
Excoecaria	+					
Heritiera					+	
Lumnitzera		+/—	+	+/—		
Nypa	+?					
Osbornia	+	+/—				
Rhizophora				+		+
Scyphiphora	+?					
Sonneratia	+/—	+/—			+/—	
Xylocarpus	+/—	+			+	

*Compiled from: Goebbel, 1886; Liebau, 1914; Ernould, 1921; Watson, 1928; Troll and Dragendorff 1931; Marco, 1935; Attims and Cremers, 1967; McCusker, 1971; Jones, 1971; Percival and Womersley, 1975; Gill and Tomlinson, 1971, 1975, 1977; and personal observations.

of the above-ground roots either by water (Breen and Hill, 1969; Bacon, 1975) or by flood-deposited sediments (Watson, 1928; Hegerl, 1975) will cause widespread mortality and rapid degradation of root tissue (Albright, 1976).

More direct evidence of the aeration function of stilt roots in *Rhizophora* was obtained by Canoy (1975) who noted an increase in the number of stilt roots produced per square metre (Fig. 10.4) with increased temperature—and consequently reduced dissolved oxygen concentrations in a thermally polluted environment.

Under quiet sedimentary conditions, mud may accumulate at up to 1.5 cm per year (Bird, 1971; Bird and Barson, 1977) and the root system must be able to respond in order to meet root aeration requirements. Negatively-geotropic pneumatophores are one obvious adaptation found in *Avicennia*, *Xylocarpus australasicus* and *Sonneratia* (Troll and Dragendorff, 1931; Metcalf, 1931; Chapman, 1944; Gill, 1975). Other species cope with sediment accumulation by forming extra arches of the stilt roots (*Rhizophora*), additional knee-roots in *Bruguiera* and *Ceriops*, or the upward secondary thickening of the roots (*Xylocarpus granatum*) or buttresses (*Heritiera*).

Biological Adaptations

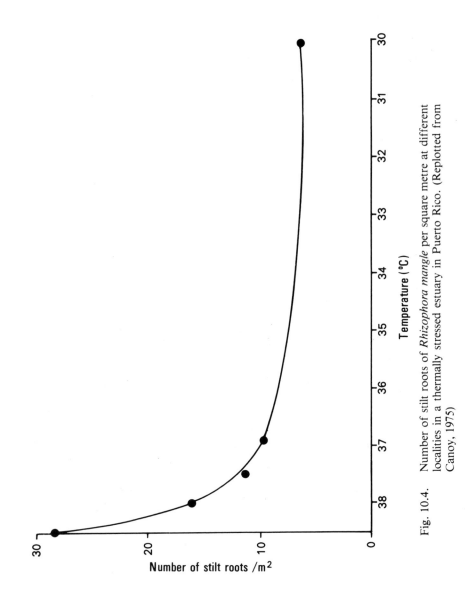

Fig. 10.4. Number of stilt roots of *Rhizophora mangle* per square metre at different localities in a thermally stressed estuary in Puerto Rico. (Replotted from Canoy, 1975)

In exposed erosional situations, anchorage of the plant must be maintained in order to survive. Massive development of the various above-ground roots may serve to reduce water movement around the plant while an extensive cable root system (as in *Avicennia* and *Osbornia*), may effectively anchor the plant despite its shallow roots. For example, Thom *et al.* (1975) have described the successful colonisation of tidal sand flats in the Joseph Bonaparte Gulf by *Avicennia* despite the rigorous conditions induced by the passage of long-period waves.

The effect of water movement and inundation on the above-ground root development in *Kandelia candel* has been described by Hosokawa *et al.* (1977). In this rhizophoraceous species, the basal part of the stem is buttress-like on plants near creeks with flowing water, but with comparatively still water, typical stilt roots are formed. Individuals growing on river terraces where inundation is reduced possess no specialised root structures.

The anatomical changes appearing in the aerial and stilt roots of *Rhizophora* on penetrating the substrate have been described by Bowman (1921), Gill and Tomlinson (1971, 1975, 1977) and Karstedt and Parameswaran (1976); the external colour of the root changes from tan to white as the thin surface layers lose their chlorophyll and thickened walls, trichosclereids are no longer formed and the ground parenchyma becomes lacunose—the aerial root normally has only approximately 5 per cent gas space before penetration into the substrate compared with about 50 per cent after penetration.

Lenticels are common in the periderm of stems and roots of most mangroves (Chapman, 1947; Roth, 1965; Lugo and Snedaker, 1975). Outwardly, a lenticel often appears as a vertically or horizontally elongated mass of loose cells that protrudes above the surface through a fissure in the periderm. Dimension and frequency of lenticels vary between species and with the height above the water surface (Lugo and Snedaker, 1975).

Baker (1915 p. 265) describes the lenticels occurring on the pneumatophores of *Avicennia marina* as 'raised black spots scattered over the surface ... a section showing these layers of cells to be raised over what is a vacant cavity or air space in direct communication with the ventilating system', and he concludes they may be secondary organs of ventilation. Baker (1915) notes their occurrence on the stem up to 3 m above high water mark. On the other hand, the leaf-bearing stems of this species are devoid of lenticels (Baylis, 1940) and these must be aerated through the foliage. Baylis (1940) suggests that the aerenchyma in the petiole is an adaptation for this purpose.

Light
Wylie (1949) has shown that the leaves developing in high light intensity show a higher degree of xeromorphy than those protected from it. Thus it is possible that some of the features discussed under xeromorphy may in fact be responses to high light intensities. Isobilateral leaf anatomy is generally regarded as a xeromorphic character but when it is combined with a mechanism for orienting the leaf towards the sun, as occurs for example in *Ceriops,* then it seems reasonable to assume a light response is involved. Leaf characteristics

associated with high light intensities (Wylie, 1949) include various xeromorphic features but particularly a high ratio of volume to surface area and a well developed, highly differentiated, often isobilateral palisade mesophyll. These features are present in many mangrove species (Fig 10.1) and they presumably form the basis of the adaptability of the different species to varying conditions of light and shade.

Different light and shade requirements have been noted in the mangroves and these are summarised in Table 10.4. Clearly there are inconsistencies in the data, probably largely due to variation from one geographic locality to another and whether adults, seedlings or saplings were being considered. However, two groups seem to emerge: those genera which are shade tolerant, both as seedlings and as adults—*Aegiceras, Ceriops, Bruguiera* and *Avicennia*(?)—and those which are shade intolerant—*Avicennia* (?), *Acrostichum, Acanthus, Aegialitis, Rhizophora, Lumnitzera, Scyphiphora* and *Sonneratia*. From observations made at Port Curtis, *Osbornia, Xylocarpus* and *Excoecaria* can be added to the shade-tolerant list.

Isobilateral leaves are found in both of these groups. Three genera possess leaves that point upwards and are oriented towards the sun (*Ceriops, Lumnitzera* and *Osbornia*) and these genera are distributed in each of the above groups. Uphof (1941) has suggested that since a water storage tissue is present between the epidermis and palisade mesophyll of most mangroves, its function is to protect the mesophyll from excessive heat or infra-red radiation. Tannin cells on the upper surface of the leaf of *Rhizophora* and *Ceriops* for example, may protect the leaf from intense visible or ultra-violet radiation. However, the role of tannins both in leaves and bark is not clear (Walsh, 1974) and it has been suggested that they are involved in preventing fungal infestations (Swain, 1965) or in the removal of excess salt (Bowman, 1921; Macnae, 1968b). Macnae (1968a) maintains that the presence of a mesophyllous rather than a hypodermal water storage tissue in some species (e.g. *Sonneratia*) seems to dispel its role in protecting underlying palisade tissue as Uphof (1941) has postulated.

The canopy shape of mangroves is largely determined by endogenous growth patterns which lend themselves to a plant architectural analysis (Hallé *et al.*, 1978). However, the canopy seems to assume certain shapes under specific environmental conditions. For example, Macnae (1968a, p. 115) figures an *Avicennia* which he maintains has the shape it characteristically assumes when growing under the influence of strong winds on the shallow soil of coral islands. Wester (1967) has described similar specimens—'umbrella types'—from sandy areas in South Australia, while Saenger and Hopkins (1975) have reported identically shaped specimens growing on deep alluvial soils in the Gulf of Carpentaria. It thus seems unlikely that shallow soils or high winds or coral sands determine this canopy shape. Baker (1915) maintains that the pneumatophores of *A. marina* must remain shaded in order to continue to function and that when growing as an isolated specimen, the plant assumes a flattened canopy to protect its pneumatophores. More work is required on this possible light response.

Table 10.4 Shade tolerance of Australian mangroves

Genus	Shade tolerant	Shade intolerant
Acanthus		Macnae, 1966, 1968a
Acrostichum		Macnae, 1966
Aegialitis		Macnae, 1966, 1968a
Aegiceras	Clarke and Hannon, 1971 Thom *et al.*, 1975	Macnae, 1966, 1968a
Avicennia	Clarke and Hannon, 1971	Macnae, 1963, 1966, 1968a Thom *et al.*, 1975
Bruguiera	Macnae, 1966 Macnae and Kalk, 1962 Watson, 1928	
Ceriops	Macnae and Kalk, 1962 Thom *et al.*, 1975	Macnae, 1966, 1968a
Lumnitzera		Macnae, 1966, 1968a
Rhizophora	Macnae, 1966	Macnae, 1968a
Sonneratia		Macnae, 1968a
Scyphiphora		Macnae, 1966

Table 10.5 Comparison of morphology and anatomy of sun and shade leaves of *Ceriops tagal* from Port Curtis, Central Queensland

Parameter	Sun leaves	Shade leaves
Leaf Length (mm)	24.0 ± 1.9	29.9 ± 10.3
Leaf Width (mm)	48.7 ± 2.1	62.4 ± 8.3
Leaf Area (mm^2)	818 ± 83	1402 ± 447
Length/width ratio	2.03 ± 0.09	1.97 ± 0.18
Leaf Thickness (μm)	164 ± 21	780 ± 165
Leaf Volume (mm^3)	134.2 ± 5.3	1094 ± 43.1
Leaf Surface Area (mm^2)	1636	2804
Volume/Surface area ratio	8.20 × 10^{-2}	39.02 × 10^{-2}
Number of Stomata mm^{-2}	78 - 85	50 - 55
Thickness in section (μm)		
upper cuticle	2.8	12.0
upper epidermis	3.3	12.7
Tannin cells/hypodermis	8.5	84.8
upper palisade mesophyll	30.5	116.4
spongy mesophyll	84.6	402.0
lower palisade mesophyll	21.6	90.0
lower tannin cells/hypodermis	3.4	39.3
lower epidermis	3.6	12.4
lower cuticle	5.2	9.7

Plate 10.5.   (a)   'Sun' leaves of *Ceriops tagal*, showing their vertical position and
                    orientation towards the sun.
              (b)   'Shade' leaves of *Ceriops tagal*, showing their rosette-like, horizontal
                    arrangement.

Since leaves developing in intense light show a higher degree of xeromorphy (Wylie, 1949), a differentiation into sun and shade leaves can be expected. Several species show a marked morphological differentiation (e.g. *Lumnitzera, Ceriops, Aegiceras*) and a detailed comparison between sun and shade leaves of *Ceriops* (Plate 10.5) is presented in Table 10.5. These data show that the shade leaves when compared with sun leaves are: (1) larger but more variable, (2) thicker but more variable, (3) have a higher volume to surface area ratio, (4) possess fewer stomata per square millimetre on the lower leaf surface, and (5) possess a proportionally thicker tannin-filled hypodermis on both upper and lower surface, and a proportionately thinner upper palisade mesophyll, lower epidermis and lower cuticle. These findings are in agreement with the general concept of xeromorphy except that xeromorphic leaves generally possess a higher volume to surface area ratio than shade leaves (Shields, 1950). Of interest is that the hypodermis is relatively reduced in the sun leaves compared with the shade leaves. This suggests that a tannin-filled hypodermis plays little part in protecting the palisade mesophyll from high visible or ultra-violet radiation.

Wind, wave and frost damage
Different species of mangroves have adapted differently to these naturally occurring types of damage. Whilst the factor causing the damage is of low to moderate intensity, different species show varying degrees of tolerance. At high to catastrophic intensities, most species are killed or damaged severely, and various recovery patterns can be observed.

Most mangroves are susceptible to frosts although the degree of susceptibility varies with species and geographic location. McMillan (1975) has shown that both *Avicennia germinans* and *A. marina,* collected from a range of localities and subjected to frost (2-4°C) under identical experimental conditions, have populations selectively adapted to a latitudinal range of habitats, including ones with recurrent low winter temperatures. Leaf scorch seems to be the predominant symptom (McMillan, 1975; Chapman and Ronaldson, 1958), often followed by a reduction in the leaf area index (Lugo and Zucca, 1977).

Wind damage caused by cyclone Tracy has been classified into four types (Stocker, 1976): windthrow, where the tree is felled; crown damage, where leaves and twigs are removed and/or branches are torn off; bole damage, where the bole is broken, severely fractured or leaning; and death, where the tree remains standing. Because each of these damage types can equally be caused by wave action, damage caused by wind and/or water is not differentiated in the following discussion.

Windthrow is the severest form of damage and Stocker (1976) found several species particularly susceptible, including *Camptostemon schultzii, Ceriops tagal, Rhizophora stylosa, Bruguiera parviflora* and *Excoecaria agallocha.* Other mangroves including *Xylocarpus australasicus, Aegiceras, Aegialitis* and *Lumnitzera racemosa,* showed little or no windthrow and rapidly developed new crowns. It seems likely that windthrow-susceptible species are those with weakly developed cable root systems, or where the root system is weakened through erosion or bank-slumping (Thom *et al.*, 1975) or through some biological agency (e.g. isopod infestations—Rehm, 1976). For most species, windthrow results in death although for *Sonneratia* and *Avicennia*, epicormic shoots ('proleptic' shoots of Gill, 1971b) will rapidly develop while some root connection remains.

Bole damage susceptibility varies considerably between genera. The anomalous wood structure of *Avicennia*, with its non-concentric, non-annual growth rings of alternating bands of xylem and phloem (Baker, 1915; Panshin, 1932; Studholme and Philipson, 1966; Gill, 1971b) give the wood some unusual qualities; it is extremely strong for its weight; it is extremely difficult to split radially yet it is easy to do so tangentially (hence used as shield trees by the Aborigines); the unusual ring structure ensures that if any part of the trunk is damaged, sufficient intact conductive tissue remains to supply the crown and epicormic shoots. As a consequence of this distribution of xylem and phloem tissue, *Avicennia* cannot be killed by ring-barking, an apparently useful adaptation in minimising damage from water-borne objects.

From what little information is available on the secondary wood anatomy of other species (Panshin, 1932; Heiden, 1893; Marco, 1935; Chattaway, 1932, 1938; Venkatiswarlu and Rao, 1964), adaptations of various sorts can be expected. In *Ceriops* thick-walled bast fibres form a mechanical tissue cylinder giving strength and rigidity to the stem (Rao and Sharma, 1968). In *Rhizophora* abundant sclereids occur in non-functional phloem tissue (Karstedt and Parameswaran, 1976) while stone cells and fibres occur throughout the plant (Bowman, 1921). The wood of *Bruguiera* has been described as extremely strong (Banerji, 1958) as has that of *Heritiera*, *Rhizophora apiculata* and *Lumnitzera littorea* (Panshin, 1932).

In the case of a broken bole, *Bruguiera* and *Ceriops* generally do not regrow from the stumps (Ding Hou, 1958), although this has been observed in occasional specimens of *B. gymnorhiza* along the Mooloolah River in Queensland. On the other hand, *Avicennia, Sonneratia, Xylocarpus, Excoecaria* and the western hemisphere *Laguncularia* coppice readily (Watson, 1928; Alexander, 1967; Teas and Kelly, 1975; Stocker, 1976).

Crown damage is the most common type of damage, with the plant being defoliated in extreme cases. Leaves of most mangroves are coriaceous and strengthened by various sclerenchymatous cells (Malaviya, 1963; Shah and Sundarraj, 1965; Stace, 1966; Rao and Sharma, 1968) and in strong winds, leaf-bearing twigs appear to be shed rather than individual leaves despite the presence of abscission layers at the base of the petiole in several species (Kenneally *et al.*, 1978). Recovery from twig and leaf damage is usually rapid (Stocker, 1976). *Avicennia, Excoecaria* and *Sonneratia* have abundant reserve buds in the stem; in *Rhizophora* reserve buds may be present in the stem of saplings (Ding Hou, 1958), but they become restricted to the thin terminal branches as the trees mature (Gill and Tomlinson, 1969; Teas and Kelly, 1975). Conditions severe enough to remove or kill all branches possessing viable reserve buds (i.e. branches less than 2 cm in diameter), will kill *Rhizophora* (Gill, 1971a).

Where the tree is dead but remains standing, a number of causative factors appear to be involved, including changes in the substrate (Breen and Hill, 1969; Hegerl, 1975; Stocker, 1976), fatal root or bole damage caused by wind sway (Stocker, 1976), or stress consequent upon the near-total loss of leaves (Lugo and Snedaker, 1975).

Reproductive adaptations
Flowering onset and pollination
No detailed information is available on the initiation of flowering. Flower primordia develop on young plants when little more than three (Gill and Tomlinson, 1969) or four (Noakes, 1955) years old. Flowering was first observed in *R. mangle* in plants about 1 m high (Gill and Tomlinson 1969), in *B. gymnorhiza* at 0.8 m (Steinke and Ward, 1973), in *L. racemosa* at 0.41 m, in *Aegiceras* at 0.27 m, in *Aegialitis* at 0.31 m, and in *Avicennia marina* at 0.38 m.

Most species commence flowering in the summer months (Jones, 1971; Graham *et al.*, 1975; Specht *et al.*, 1977; Byrnes *et al.*, 1977); the predominance of summer flowering periods in Central Queensland species is shown in Fig. 10.5. Gill and Tomlinson (1969) have reported *R. mangle* as ever-flowering, i.e. flowers and fruits in all stages of development can be found throughout the year. In Australian species of *Rhizophora,* however, as in most Australian mangroves, flowering roughly coincides with summer although some geographic and specific variation occurs.

Pollination in most mangroves occurs through the agency of winds, insects and birds (Clifford and Specht, 1979) and most species possess small, non-sticky pollen grains (Wright, 1977) which may be distinctive for each species (Muller and Caratini, 1977). In *Nypa* the pollen is sticky and pollination probably occurs via the many insects that visit the inflorescence (Uhl, 1972), particularly drosophilid flies (Essig, 1973). The vasculature, histology and growth patterns of the flowers of *Nypa* appear to be directly related to this type of pollination (Uhl and Moore, 1977). *Aegiceras, Cynometra* and probably *Avicennia,* with their scented flowers, are predominantly bee-pollinated (Blake and Roff, 1972; Chanda, 1977; Clifford and Specht, 1979); the western mangrove *Avicennia germinans* appears to be exclusively pollinated by the bee *Apis mellifera* (Percival, 1974). *Excoecaria* is dioecious, bears flowers in catkins and possesses 2-celled pollen grains (Venkateswarlu and Rao, 1975) and it can be presumed that it is wind-pollinated (Clifford and Specht, 1979). *Sonneratia* releases copious amounts of dry or slightly sticky pollen at dusk when the flower opens (Muller, 1969), and it is dispersed by bats (Faegri and van der Pijl, 1971) and moths (N. Duke, workshop discussion). In South Africa, *Bruguiera gymnorhiza* is pollinated by insects and sunbirds, and the petals of this species are peculiarly adapted to aid in this dispersal (Davey, 1975) in that they possess a heavily cutinised epidermal region, which on the application of gentle pressure, causes the petal lobes to spring apart, thereby releasing the stamens together with a puff of pollen. Tomlinson (unpublished observations) has observed that large flowered species of *Bruguiera* are bird-pollinated while small flowered species are pollinated by butterflies. He further

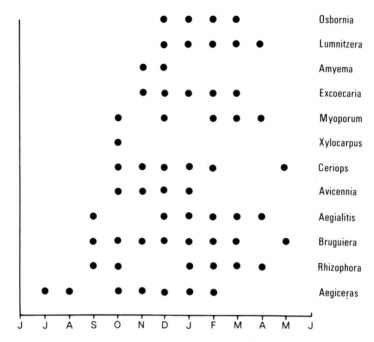

Fig. 10.5.   Monthly occurrence of flowering in Port Curtis mangrove vegetation, as observed during 1975-1979.

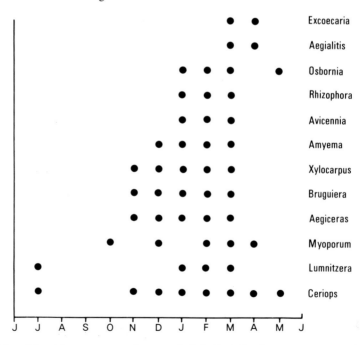

Fig. 10.6.   Monthly occurrence of mature fruit in Port Curtis mangrove vegetation, as observed during 1975-1979.

reports that *Ceriops* is pollinated by moths and *Rhizophora* appears to be wind-pollinated. Tomlinson *et al.* (1978) found that while *Lumnitzera racemosa* was insect-pollinated, *L. littorea,* with its red flowers, was largely pollinated by honeyeaters, particularly *Meliphaga gracilis.*

The occurrence of propagules in mangroves at Port Curtis (Fig. 10.6) showed a maximum in the summer months (February-March) when all species bore mature propagules. These fruiting periods generally agree with the east coast fruiting times given by Jones (1971) and Graham *et al.* (1975), and are similar to the mangroves in the Townsville region (N. Duke, workshop discussion). On the Natal coast of South Africa, *A. marina* also has its main fruiting period in March-April (Steinke, 1975). In some species the time from flower to mature propagule is considerable—3 years from flower primordia to mature propagule in *R. apiculata* (Christensen and Wium-Andersen, 1977); 6 months from open flower to mature propagule in *R. mangle* (Guppy, 1906); 12 months from flower buds to mature propagule in *Kandelia candel* (Nishihira and Urasaki, 1976), in *R. mangle* (Gill and Tomlinson, 1971), and in *Aegiceras* (Carey and Fraser, 1932). This suggests that the coincidence between flowering and fruiting in the summer months may be related to some environmental parameter. Since leaf production in *Rhizophora* is also seasonal with maxima during summer (Christensen and Wium-Andersen, 1977; Gill and Tomlinson, 1971; N. Duke, workshop discussion), it seems that fruiting, like flowering, is timed for the period most favourable for growth.

Various types of fruits are found amongst the mangroves and those of Australian genera are listed in Table 10.6. Also included in that table are references to detailed embryological or developmental accounts of mangrove fruits.

In several genera, the fruits contain seeds which develop precociously; the seed germinates while still attached to the parent tree. In these species, the embryo develops into a seedling without any dormant period (Macnae, 1968a; Gill and Tomlinson, 1969), although a form of seedling dormancy, induced by a low water content, may occur as in *R. mangle* (Sussex, 1975). *Bruguiera, Ceriops, Rhizophora, Kandelia* (Macnae, 1968a; Carey, 1934) and *Nypa* (Tomlinson, 1971) are viviparous in that the embryo ruptures the pericarp and grows beyond it, sometimes to considerable lengths. In *Aegialitis, Acanthus* (Sidhu, 1975b), *Avicennia* (Chapman, 1944), *Aegiceras* (Carey and Fraser, 1932), *Laguncularia* (Rabinowitz, 1978) and *Pelliciera* (Howe, 1911; Rabinowitz, 1978), the embryo, while developing within the fruit, does not enlarge sufficiently to rupture the pericarp. These genera are termed crypto-viviparous. In *Excoecaria* (Venkateswarlu and Rao, 1975), *Heritiera* and *Xylocarpus* (Sidhu, 1975b) the seeds, like those of most plants, pass through a resting stage prior to germination.

Vivipary has frequently been cited as an adaptation to some aspect of the mangrove environment. Its adaptive significance could include rapid rooting (Macnae, 1968a), salt regulation (Joshi, 1933), ionic balance (Joshi *et al.,* 1972), development of buoyancy (Gill, 1975) and nutritional parasitism (Pannier and Pannier, 1975). In the viviparous seagrasses, *Amphibolus* and

Table 10.6 Fruit types of Australian mangrove genera, together with references to detailed descriptions of their embryology and/or seedling development

Genus	Fruit	Description of embryology and/or seedling development
Acanthus	Capsule with several flat seeds	
Aegialitis	Indehiscent nut	
Aegiceras	Fleshy capsule, shed with calyx attached	Haberlandt, 1896; Carey and Fraser, 1932; Collins, 1921
Amyema	Baccate, with viscous seeds	
Avicennia	Fleshy capsule with single seed	Treub, 1883; Collins, 1921; Padmanabhan, 1960, 1962a, 1962b
Bruguiera	Fleshy single-seeded berry, shed with calyx attached	
Camptostemon	Capsule with two to several woolly seeds	
Ceriops	Fleshy berry, usually single-seeded, shed with calyx attached	Carey, 1934
Cynometra	Wrinkled one-seeded pod	
Excoecaria	Trilobed exploding capsule, each lobe one-seeded	Venkateswarlu and Rao, 1975
Heritiera	Clusters of woody, keeled carpels	
Lumnitzera	Indehiscent woody fruit thin outer fleshy layer	Clifford and Specht, 1979
Nypa	Aggregate head of one-seeded fruits	Tomlinson, 1971
Osbornia	Capsule	
Rhizophora	Ovoid fleshy berry, with single seed	Carey, 1934; Cook, 1907; Gill and Tomlinson, 1969
Scyphiphora	Axillary clusters of ribbed fruits, surmounted by calyx	
Sonneratia	Many-celled, many-seeded capsule	Venkateswarlu, 1935
Xylocarpus	Several-seeded capsule	Percival and Womersley, 1975

Thalassodendron (Den Hartog, 1970), vivipary appears to be an adaptation to assist in rapid root attachment of the plant (Ducker and Knox, 1976; Ducker, personal communication, 1979). However, the occurrence of apparently successful mangroves without viviparous fruits (e.g. *Osbornia, Sonneratia, Lumnitzera, Xylocarpus, Excoecaria*), makes it doubtful whether the possession of vivipary *per se* is of any real adaptive advantage. Tidal buffeting and wave-borne objects pose a threat to establishing seedlings, and it could be expected that the smaller the seedling, the larger the threat. Because of this, vivipary in the mangroves may simply be a means of producing a large seedling which is less likely to be damaged by water movements. It is interesting to note in this respect that many of the non-viviparous genera also possess large seeds (e.g. *Xylocarpus, Heritiera, Cynometra*), which may similarly be a means of alleviating damage by water movements.

Considerable mortality has been reported while the developing seedling is still attached to the tree. Gill and Tomlinson (1971) showed that for *R. mangle* between 0 and 7.2 per cent of flower buds produced mature seedlings, although the number of flowers produced may be markedly increased by an increase in nutrients (Onuf *et al.*, 1977). Lugo and Snedaker (1975) followed the development of selected seedlings of *R. mangle* while still attached to the parent tree and found a mortality of 0 per cent, 13.4 per cent and 20.9 per cent for the months of January, April and May respectively. Similar figures were noted in *R. apiculata* where Christensen and Wium-Andersen (1977) report that only 7 per cent of flower buds formed flowers, and only 1-3 per cent formed fruits. In *Kandelia candel* less than 30 per cent of flower buds ultimately developed into mature propagules (Nishihira and Urasaki, 1976). Much of this pre-dispersal mortality can be attributed to fungal and insect attacks on the fruit and to such inherent factors as albinism, as in *Rhizophora* and *Avicennia* (H.J. Teas, personal communication, 1977), and other morphogenetic malfunctions.

Propagule dispersal and establishment
The propagules of all mangroves are buoyant (Tomlinson, 1971; Gill, 1975; Steinke, 1975; Rabinowitz, 1975, 1978) and are adapted to dispersal by water. The seeds of the mangrove mistletoes are dispersed by the mistletoe bird, *Dicaeum hirundinaceum,* and they are capable of withstanding passage through the alimentary canal of this species (Barlow, 1967). The spores of *Acrostichum* appear to be wind-dispersed since they do not float; the prothalli of this species, however, float in seawater but mostly sink in freshwater. The dispersal unit of mangroves may be a single seed (*Excoecaria*), a one-seeded fruit (*Cynometra*), a several-seeded fruit (*Sonneratia, Xylocarpus*), a multiple fruit (*Heritiera*), an aggregated fruit (*Nypa*) or a precociously developed seedling (*Avicennia, Aegiceras, Rhizophora, Ceriops, Bruguiera*).

Few data are available on the periodicity of propagule dispersal but Clarke and Hannon (1969) found that dispersal of *Aegiceras* coincided with unusually high tides while that of *Avicennia* coincided with low tides.

Buoyancy in the propagules may be due to the radicle as in *Rhizophora*

(Banus and Kolehmainen, 1975), the pericarp as in *Avicennia* (Steinke, 1975), the endosperm (e.g. *Xylocarpus*) or the cotyledon as in *Pelliciera* (Rabinowitz, 1978), and it becomes possible for changes in any of these features to alter the buoyancy. For example, Steinke (1975) showed that propagules of *Avicennia marina* sink after losing their pericarp, generally within four days. Subsequent investigation of the rate of pericarp shedding showed that high (35%) and low (0%) salinities decreased the rate at which they are shed when compared with the rate at medium (17.5%) salinities. Consequently propagules in brackish water will disperse less than those in water of high or low salinity. Similarly, high temperatures increased the rate of pericarp shedding; high water temperatures consequently shorten the potential dispersal distance.

Propagules of *R. mangle* initially float horizontally but rapidly assume a vertical position in sunlight (Banus and Kolehmainen, 1975). Roots appear within 10-17 days whether or not the propagule was floating or stranded, in light or in the shade, and floating horizontally or vertically, despite claims that contact with the substrate was important prior to root formation (Teas and Montgomery, 1968). The first leaves appeared after approximately 40-50 days regardless of whether or not the propagule had become stranded (Banus and Kolehmainen, 1975).

A buoyant propagule appears to be an efficient means of widespread, water-based dispersal. Amongst the seagrasses, however, only few genera (*Posidonia, Thalassodendron, Enhalus*) have buoyant fruits, and paradoxically, these species have restricted distributions (Den Hartog, 1970). It would seem that other dispersal parameters are involved.

Rabinowitz (1978) has investigated the dispersal parameters of six Panamanian mangroves, including longevity and vigour, period of floating, period required for establishment and the period of obligate dispersal. Two contrasting dispersal patterns were observed, one for small and another for large propagules.

In contrast to those of *A. marina* (Steinke, 1975), the propagules of *A. geminans* always float and this species seems to have an absolute requirement for a stranding period in order to establish. So as to be free of tidal disturbance, this species is restricted to higher ground where inundation is less frequent (Rabinowitz, 1978). The time required for this species to root is approximately seven days while *A. marina,* whose propagules sink after approximately four days, becomes firmly rooted in five days (Clarke and Hannon, 1969). *Laguncularia,* whose propagules sink after approximately 20 days, also requires a period of stranding of five days or more in order to become firmly rooted (Rabinowitz, 1978).

The two genera that have larger propagules (*Rhizophora, Pelliciera*), have a lesser requirement for freedom from tidal disturbance than do either *Avicennia* or *Laguncularia*; their propagules are capable of taking root in both deep and shallow water because their weight affords a resistance to tidal buffeting, and growth continues under water (Rabinowitz, 1978). The longevity of the propagules ranged from 35 days in *Laguncularia* to a year or more in *R. mangle.*

Table 10.7 Production, establishment and mortality rates for propagules of Central Queensland mangroves. Data from permanent plots, 1975-1979.

Genus	No. of propagules establishing per 30 m of shoreline during 4 years	No. of established propagules per adult of same species	% Mortality of established propagules during first year	Mean mortality (%) of adults during one year
Rhizophora	276	1.64	71.7	2.98
Aegialitis	3	1.50	0	0
Avicennia	199	1.47	22.1	5.97
Lumnitzera	9	1.00	0	2.78
Aegiceras	27	0.18	14.8	1.51
Ceriops	52	0.13	36.5	1.01
Osbornia	0	—	—	—
Bruguiera	0	—	—	0
Xylocarpus	0	—	—	0

The number of mangrove propagules establishing along 30 m of intertidal zone in permanent plots (Saenger and Robson, 1977) at Port Curtis, a semi-enclosed bay, is given in Table 10.7. The number of propagules establishing per adult of the same species is also given. In an area of vigorous regrowth after flooding, Breen and Hill (1969) found a mean of 2.32 propagules per adult *Bruguiera,* a figure comparable to those from Central Queensland. These figures are low in view of the apparently high numbers of propagules borne by most species. However, considerable mortality occurs prior to dispersal, while crabs (particularly species of *Sesarma*) and insects (Rabinowitz, 1977) damage considerable numbers of propagules when fallen. Further mortality occurs during dispersal, including stranding on unfavourable substrates, injury through boring or decomposing marine organisms, and sinking through the attachment of fouling organisms such as barnacles and tubeworms. Once the propagules are stranded, physical damage by wave-borne objects has frequently been observed. Amongst those that establish successfully—that is become firmly rooted and possess at least one leaf—mortality rates in Central Queensland are variable, ranging in their first year from 72 per cent in *R. stylosa* to 0 per cent in *Lumnitzera* and *Aegialitis* (Table 10.7). Involved in this post-establishment mortality are physical factors (e.g. wave-borne objects), biological factors (e.g. crab damage) and physiological factors (e.g. high soil salinities).

While investigating the factors involved in zonation, Rabinowitz (1975) transplanted seedlings of each species into the various mangrove zones and she observed that after one year, no difference in growth in the various zones had occurred. She concluded that the mangroves were not optimally adapted to the

Table 10.8 Association between newly-established seedlings with adults of same species at time of establishment and one year later. Data from permanent plots, 1975-1979.

Genus	X^2 at time of establishment	Association	X^2 after one year	Association
Avicennia	10.3	** positive	15.8	*** positive
Aegialitis	22.2	*** positive	22.2	*** positive
Aegiceras	7.4	** positive	12.0	*** positive
Ceriops	7.9	** positive	6.5	** positive
Lumnitzera	9.2	** positive	9.2	** positive
Rhizophora	0.8	— none	0.8	— none

*** significant at 1% level
** significant at 5% level
— no significance

Table 10.9 Summary of morphological and reproductive features in Australian mangrove genera

Genus	Aqueous tissue	Root modifica- tions	Salt glands	Coppicing ability or vegetative prolifera- tion	Pollinating agent	Vivipary	High propagule production	High propagule mortality	High propagule dispersal
Acanthus	+	+	+	+	?	+ +	?	?	?
Aegialitis	—	—	+	—	I,B	+ +	+ + +	—	—
Aegiceras	+ + +	—	+ +	—	I,B	+ +	+ +	+	+ +
Avicennia	+ + +	+ + +	+ + +	+	I,B	+ + +	+ + +	+ +	+
Bruguiera	+	+ + +	—	+ / —	I,B	+ + +	+ +	?	?
Camptostemon	?	+ +	—	?	?	—	?	?	?
Ceriops	+ + +	+ +	—	—	I	+ + +	+ +	+ +	+ +
Cynometra	+	+	—	?	?	—	?	?	?
Excoecaria	+	—	—	+	W	—	+	?	?
Heritiera	+ +	+	—	?	?	—	?	?	?
Lumnitzera	+ + +	+ +	—	—	I,B	—	+ + +	—	+
Osbornia	+ + +	+	—	—	I,B	—	+	?	?
Rhizophora	+ + +	+ +	—	—	W	+ + +	+ + +	+ + +	+ + +
Scyphiphora	?	?	?	?	?	—	?	?	?
Sonneratia	+ + +	+ + +	—	+	Bt,I	+	?	?	?
Xylocarpus	. +	+ + +	—	—	I,B	+	+	?	?
Nypa	?	+	?	?	I	+ + +	?	?	?
Hibiscus	+ +	—	—	?	I,B	—	?	?	?
Amyema	+ +	+ + +	—	—	I,B	—	?	?	?
Myoporum	?	—	—	?	I,B	—	+ +	?	?

Table 10.9 Explanation of symbols used.

Aqueous tissue and root modifications:	+ + + conspicuous + + well-developed + present — absent
Salt glands:	+ + + dense + + less dense + present — absent
Coppicing ability:	+ present — absent
Pollinating agent:	I insects B birds W wind Bt bats
Vivipary:	+ + + viviparous + + cryptoviviparous + large seeds — small, non-viviparous seeds
Propagule production, mortality and dispersal:	+ + + high + + medium + low — very low

sites where they normally grew and that habitat division amongst the four species was not controlled by physiological preferences.

As an alternative, a tidal sorting mechanism was proposed (Rabinowitz, 1975). This mechanism assumes that large propagules cannot invade higher ground since the water depth is insufficient, and that small propagules are widely dispersed but unable to root except in shallow areas (Rabinowitz, 1975, 1978), and that zonation patterns are simply related to propagule sizes. In eliminating physiological control of mangrove zonation, Rabinowitz (1975) assumed that seedlings have similar tolerances to adults of the same species, and that one year is sufficient to express average physiological conditions at any point in the intertidal zone. As Barbour (1970) has stated in relation to defining criteria of salt tolerance, it is the ability to reproduce rather than short-term growth that should be studied in the field, and it seems that vegetative growth over one year may be insufficient to allow subtle physiological preferences to express themselves.

The possibility of tidal sorting of propagules in relation to the tide height has been investigated in the permanent plots at Port Curtis. For analyses, the plots were divided into 4 m^2 quadrats and the distribution of adults and established propagules (seedlings) of each species were mapped, and their mutual distributions calculated (χ^2 tests, Table 10.8). Propagules of all species occurred throughout the plots although with the exception of *R. stylosa*, they were significantly positively-associated with the adults of the same species. *Rhizophora* seedlings occurred randomly throughout all plots, and as the propagules of this species are the heaviest amongst the Port Curtis mangroves, this suggests that tidal sorting may not be as important as Rabinowitz (1975) has suggested. In fact, evidence for the physiological control comes from a recalculation of the association after one year, when some mortalities had occurred (Table 10.7). With the exception of *Ceriops,* all species showed identical or increased χ^2 values, suggesting that physiological selection had increased the spatial association between the seedlings and their adults.

Overview

Whilst the morphological adaptations of mangroves have been relatively well studied, Gill (1975, p. 140) recently stated that 'there is little known of the general reproduction strategies of mangroves as a group'. The main types of morphological features of mangroves are summarised in Table 10.9 along with some reproductive features that appear to be significant. It is difficult to compare mangroves as a group with non-mangroves, particularly in terms of reproductive potential. Differences in growth rates and seed production seem to reflect the general lack of competition in the mangrove environment, and the distinction between mangroves and non-mangroves is in many instances blurred. Hence it seems more profitable for comparisons amongst species recognised as mangroves to be made.

Gill (1975) has suggested that because of the continually changing mangrove environment, successional sequences should be short and colonising features should be pronounced. Successional sequences are indeed short in terms of species although they appear to be long in terms of time, and most species can be readily classified into colonising, seral and 'climax' species on the basis of morphological (and perhaps reproductive) features.

Colonising species could be expected to show the following features: (1) diverse morphological adaptations; (2) long flowering/fruiting periods; (3) unspecialised pollination mechanisms; (4) abundant, long-lived propagules; (5) either widespread dispersal with high initial post-establishment mortalities (e.g. *R. stylosa*) or less widely dispersed propagules with somewhat reduced initial mortality rates (e.g. *A. marina*) *r*-strategists; and (6) short juvenile periods with high growth rates.

'Climax' species, on the other hand, could be expected to show some or all of the following features: (1) fewer morphological adaptations; (2) short flowering/fruiting periods; (3) more specialised pollination mechanisms; (4) few, short-lived propagules; (5) propagules positively associated with adults and with low initial mortalities *k*-strategists; and (6) long juvenile periods with variable to low growth rates.

The seral species would be expected to show features between the two categories above. On this basis, using the limited reproductive data from Port Curtis (Table 10.9), it would appear that *Rhizophora* and *Avicennia* can be classified as colonisers, *Ceriops* and *Aegiceras* as seral species, and *Lumnitzera, Aegialitis, Osbornia* and possibly *Xylocarpus,* as 'climax' species. This scheme is similar to the more intuitive classification of these genera into the above categories by Macnae (1966, 1968a) and supports the premise that considerable ecological insight can be gained from an examination of the various adaptations found in the mangroves: it is hoped that review will stimulate further analytical studies into their this efficacy and significance.

Acknowledgments

I thank the Queensland Electricity Generating Board for allowing me to use data from the Gladstone Environmental Survey for this review. I also thank Dr J. Jessop, Adelaide Herbarium, South Australia, for his comments on the first draft; Mr J. Moverley of the Q.E.G.B., for his unfailing assistance in the field; Prof. R.L. Specht, Botany Department, Queensland University, for allowing me to read his unpublished manuscripts; Mr N. Duke, Australian Institute of Marine Science, for his constructive commentary at the workshop; and to the Queensland Museum for giving me access to their scanning electron microscope and in particular to Mr R. Raven, for taking the s.e.m. photographs.

References

Albright, L.J., 1976. In situ degradation of mangrove tissue. *New Zealand Journal of Marine and Freshwater Research* **10**, 385-9.

Alexander, T.R., 1967. Effect of hurricane Betsy on the south-eastern everglades. *Quarterly Journal of the Florida Academy of Science* **30**, 10-24.

Artz, T., 1936. Die Kutikula einiger Afrikanischen Mangrove Pflanzen. *Berichte der Deutschen Botanischen Gesellschaft* **54**, 247-60.

Atkinson, M.R., G.P. Findley, A.B. Hope, M.G. Pitman, H.D.W. Saddler and K.R. West, 1967. Salt regulation in the mangroves *Rhizophora mucronata* Lam. and *Aegialitis annulata* R. Br. *Australian Journal of Biological Sciences* **20**, 589-99.

Attims, Y. and G. Cremers, 1967, Les radicelles capillaires des palétuviers dans une mangrove de Côte d'Ivoire. *Adansonia (Sér. 2)* **7**, 547-51.

Bacon, P.R., 1975. Recovery of a Trinidadian mangrove swamp from attempted reclamation. In G.E. Walsh, S.C. Snedaker and H.J. Teas (eds.), *Proceedings of the International Symposium on Biology and Management of Mangroves.* Institute of Food and Agricultural Sciences, University of Florida, Gainesville, Florida, Vol. II, pp. 805-15.

Baker, R.T., 1915. The Australian 'Grey Mangrove', (*Avicennia officinalis,* Linn.). *Journal and Proceedings of the Royal Society of New South Wales* **49**, 257-88.

Banerji, J., 1958. The mangrove forests of the Andamans, *Tropical Silviculture* **20**, 319-24.

Banus, M.D. and S.E. Kolehmainen, 1975. Floating, rooting and growth of red mangrove (*Rhizophora mangle* L.) seedlings: effect on expansion of mangroves in south-western Puerto Rico. In G.E. Walsh, S.C. Snedaker and H.J. Teas (eds.), *Proceedings of the International Symposium on Biology and Management of Mangroves.* Institute of Food and Agricultural Sciences, University of Florida, Gainesville, Florida, Vol. I, pp. 370-84.

Barbour, M.G., 1970. Is any angiosperm an obligate halophyte? *American Midland Naturalist* **84**, 105-20.

Barlow, B.A., 1967. Parasitic flowering plants. *Australian Natural History Magazine* **15**, 365-8.

Baylis, G.T.S., 1940. Leaf anatomy of the New Zealand mangrove. *Transactions of the Royal Society of New Zealand* **70**, 164-70.

Biebl, R. and H. Kinzel, 1965. Blattbau und Salzhaushalt von *Laguncularia racemosa* (L.) Gaertn. f. und anderer Mangrovenbäume auf Puerto Rico. *Österreichische Botanische Zeitung* **112**, 56-93.

Bird, E.C.F., 1971. Mangroves as land-builders. *Victorian Naturalist* **88**, 189-97.

Bird, E.C.F. and M.M. Barson, 1977. Measurement of physiographic changes on mangrove-fringed estuaries and coastlines. *Marine Research in Indonesia* **18**, 73-80.

Blake, S.T. and C. Roff, 1972. *The Honey Flora of Queensland.* Government Printer, Brisbane. 234 pp.

Bostrom, T.E. and C.D. Field, 1973. Electrical potentials in the salt gland of *Aegiceras.* In W.P. Anderson (ed.), *Ion Transport in Plants.* Academic Press, London, pp. 385-92.

Bowman, H.H.M., 1921. Histological variations in *Rhizophora mangle* L. *Papers of the Michigan Academy of Science* **22**, 129-34.

Breen, C.M. and B.J. Hill, 1969. A mass mortality of mangroves in Kosi Estuary. *Transactions of the Royal Society of South Africa* **38**, 285-303.

Breen, C.M. and I.D. Jones, 1969. Observations on the anatomy of foliar nodes of young *Bruguiera gymnorrhiza. Journal of South African Botany* **35**, 211-18.

Brenner, W., 1902. Uber die Luftwurzeln von *Avicennia tomentosa. Berichte der Deutschen Botanischen Gesellschaft* **20**, 175-89.

Briggs, S.V., 1977. Estimates of biomass in a temperate mangrove community. *Australian Journal of Ecology* **2**, 369-73.

Byrnes, N.B., S.L. Everist, S.T. Reynolds, A. Specht and R.L. Specht, 1977. The vegetation of Lizard Island, North Queensland. *Proceedings of the Royal Society of Queensland* **88**, 1-15.

Canoy, M.J., 1975. Diversity and stability in a Puerto Rican *Rhizophora mangle* L. forest. In G.E. Walsh, S.C. Snedaker and H.J. Teas (eds.), *Proceedings of the International Symposium on Biology and Management of Mangroves.* Institute of Food and Agricultural Sciences, University of Florida, Gainesville, Florida, Vol. I, pp. 344-56.

Cardale, S. and C.D. Field, 1971. The structure of the salt gland of *Aegiceras corniculatum. Planta* **99**, 183-91.

Cardale, S. and C.D. Field, 1975. Ion transport in the salt gland of *Aegiceras.* In G.E. Walsh, S.C. Snedaker and H.J. Teas (eds.), *Proceedings of the International Symposium on Biology and Management of Mangroves.* Institute of Food and Agricultural Sciences, University of Florida, Gainesville, Florida, Vol. II, pp. 608-14.

Carey, G., 1934. Further investigations on the embryology of viviparous seeds. *Proceedings of the Linnaean Society of New South Wales* **59**, 392-410.

Carey, G. and L. Fraser, 1932. The embryology and seedling development of *Aegiceras majus* Gaertn. *Proceedings of the Linnaean Society of New South Wales* **57**, 341-60.

Carlquist, S., 1975. *Ecological Strategies of Xylem Evolution.* University of California Press, Berkeley. 259 pp.

Chanda, S., 1977. An eco-floristic survey of mangroves of Sundarbans, West Bengal, India. *Transactions of the Bose Research Institute (Calcutta)* **40**, 5-14.

Chapman, V.J., 1944. The 1939 Cambridge University Expedition to Jamaica. III. The morphology of *Avicennia nitida* Jacq. and the function of its pneumatophores. *Journal of the Linnaean Society of London, Botanical Series* **52**, 487-533.

Chapman, V.J., 1947. Secondary thickening and lenticels in *Avicennia nitida* Jacq. *Proceedings of the Linnaean Society of London* **158**, 2-6.

Chapman, V.J., 1976. *Mangrove Végetation.* J. Cramer, Vaduz. 447 pp.

Chapman, V.J. and J.W. Ronaldson, 1958. The mangrove and salt-marsh flats of the Auckland Isthmus. *New Zealand Department of Scientific and Industrial Research Bulletin* **125**, 1-79.

Chattaway, M.M., 1932. The wood of the Sterculiaceae. I. Specialisation of the vertical wood parenchyma within the subfamily Sterculieae. *New Phytologist* **31**, 119-32.

Chattaway, M.M., 1938. The wood anatomy of the family Sterculiaceae. *Philosophical Transactions of the Royal Society of London* **228**, 313-65.

Chin, C.H. and I.H. Fang, 1958. The biological significance of mangrove vivipary. *Acta Botanica Sinica* **7**, 51-8.

Christensen, B. and S. Wium-Andersen, 1977. Seasonal growth of mangrove trees in Southern Thailand. I. The phenology of *Rhizophora apiculata* B1. *Aquatic Botany* **3**, 281-6.

Clarke, L.D. and N.J. Hannon, 1969. The mangrove swamp and salt-marsh communities of the Sydney District. II. The holocoenotic complex with particular reference to physiography. *Journal of Ecology* **57**, 213-34.

Clarke, L.D. and N.J. Hannon, 1971. The mangrove swamp and salt-marsh communities of the Sydney District. IV. The significance of species interaction. *Journal of Ecology* **59**, 535-53.

Clifford, H.T. and R.L. Specht, 1979. *The Vegetation of North Stradbroke Island, Queensland (With notes on the fauna of mangrove and marine meadow ecosystems by M.M. Specht).* University of Queensland Press, St Lucia. 141 pp.

Clough, B.F. and P.M. Attiwill, 1975. Nutrient cycling in a community of *Avicennia marina* in a temperate region of Australia. In G.E. Walsh, S.C. Snedaker and H.J.

Teas (eds.), *Proceedings of the International Symposium on Biology and Management of Mangroves*. Institute of Food and Agricultural Sciences, University of Florida, Gainesville, Florida, Vol. I, pp. 137-46.

Collins, M.I., 1921. On the mangrove and salt-marsh vegetation near Sydney, N.S.W., with special reference to Cabbage Creek, Port Hacking. *Proceedings of the Linnaean Society of New South Wales* **46**, 376-92.

Cook, M.T., 1907. The embryology of *Rhizophora mangle*. *Bulletin of the Torrey Botanical Club* **34**, 271-7.

Davey, J.E., 1975. Note on the mechanism of pollen release in *Bruguiera gymnorhiza*. *Journal of South African Botany* **41**, 269-72.

Ding Hou, 1958. Rhizophoraceae. *Flora Malesiana, Series I,* **5**, 429-93.

Ducker, S.C. and R.B. Knox, 1976. Submarine pollination in seagrasses. *Nature (Lond.)* **263**, 705-6.

Ernould, M., 1921. Recherches anatomiques et physiologiques sur les racines respiratoires. *Mémoires de l'Acádemie Royale des Sciences, Lettres et Beaux Arts de Belgique* **6**, 1-52.

Essig, F.B., 1973. Pollination in some New Guinea palms. *Principes* **17**, 75-83.

Faegri, K. and L. van der Pijl, 1971. *The Principles of Pollination Ecology*. Pergamon Press, New York. 291 pp.

Fahn, A. and C. Shimony, 1977. Development of the glandular and non-glandular hairs of *Avicennia marina* (Forskal) Vierh. *Journal of the Linnaean Society of London, Botanical Series* **74**, 37-46.

Gessner, F., 1967. Untersuchungen an der Mangrove in Ost-Venezuela. *Internationale Revue der gesamten Hydrobiologie* **52**, 769-81.

Gill, A.M., 1971a. Mangroves: Is the tide of opinion turning? *Bulletin of the Fairchild Tropical Garden* **26**, 5-9.

Gill, A.M., 1971b. Endogenous control of growth-ring development in *Avicennia*. *Forest Science* **17**, 462-5.

Gill, A.M., 1975. Australia's mangrove enclaves: A coastal resource. *Proceedings of the Ecological Society of Australia* **8**, 129-46.

Gill, A.M. and P.B. Tomlinson, 1969. Studies on the growth of red mangrove (*Rhizophora mangle* L.). I. Habit and general morphology. *Biotropica* **1**, 1-9.

Gill, A.M. and P.B. Tomlinson, 1971a. Studies on the growth of red mangrove (*Rhizophora mangle* L.). II. Growth and differentiation of aerial roots. *Biotropica* **3**, 63-77.

Gill, A.M. and P.B. Tomlinson, 1971b. Studies on the growth of red mangrove (*Rhizophora mangle* L.). III. Phenology of the shoot. *Biotropica* **3**, 109-24.

Gill, A.M. and P.B. Tomlinson, 1975. Aerial roots: An array of forms and functions. In J.G. Torrey and D.T. Clarkson (eds.), *The Development and Function of Roots*. Academic Press, London, pp. 237-60.

Gill, A.M. and P.B. Tomlinson, 1977. Studies on the growth of red mangrove (*Rhizophora mangle* L.). IV. The adult root system. *Biotropica* **9**, 145-55.

Goebbel, K., 1886. Über die Luftwurzeln von *Sonneratia*. *Bericht der Deutschen Botanischen Gesellschaft* **4**, 249-55.

Golley, F., H.T. Odum and R.F. Wilson, 1962. The structure and metabolism of a Puerto Rican red mangrove forest in May. *Ecology* **43**, 9-19.

Graham, M., J. Grimshaw, E. Hegerl, J. McNalty and R. Timmins, 1975. Cairns wetlands—a preliminary report. *Operculum* **4**, 117-48.

Guppy, H.B., 1906. *Observations of a Naturalist in the Pacific between 1896 and 1899*. Vol. 2, *Plant Dispersal*. Macmillan, London. 627 pp.

Haberlandt, G., 1914. *Physiological Plant Anatomy*. Macmillan, London. 777 pp.

Hallé, F., R.A.A. Oldeman and P.B. Tomlinson, 1978. *Tropical Trees and Forests: An Architectural Analysis*. Springer Verlag, Berlin. 441 pp.

Hartog, C. den, 1970. *The Sea Grasses of the World*. North-Holland Publishing Co., Amsterdam. 275 pp.

Hegerl, E.J., 1975. The effects of flooding on Brisbane River mangroves. *Operculum* 4, 156-7.

Heiden, H., 1893. Anatomische Charakteristik der Combretaceen. *Botanisches Zentralblatt* 55, 353-91.

Hosokawa, T., H. Tagawa and V.J. Chapman, 1977. Mangals of Micronesia, Taiwan, Japan, the Philippines and Oceania. In V.J. Chapman (ed.), *Ecosystems of the World. I. Wet Coastal Ecosystems.* Elsevier, Amsterdam, pp. 271-92.

Howe, M.A., 1911. A little-known mangrove of Panama. *Journal of the New York Botanic Garden* 12, 61-72.

Janssonius, H.H., 1950. The vessels in the wood of Javan mangrove trees. *Blumea* 6, 465-9.

Jennings, D.H., 1968. Halophytes, succulence, and sodium—a unified theory. *New Phytologist* 67, 899-911.

Jones, W.T., 1971. The field identification and distribution of mangroves in eastern Australia. *Queensland Naturalist* 20, 35-51.

Joshi, A.C., 1933. A suggested explanation of the prevalence of vivipary on the seashore. *Journal of Ecology* 21, 209-12.

Joshi, G.V., L. Bhosale, B.B. Jamale and B.A. Karadge, 1975a. Photosynthetic carbon metabolism in mangroves. In G.E. Walsh, S.C. Snedaker and H.J. Teas (eds.), *Proceedings of the International Symposium on Biology and Management of Mangroves,* Institute of Food and Agricultural Sciences, University of Florida, Gainesville, Florida, Vol. II, pp. 579-94.

Joshi, G.V., B.B. Jamale and L. Bhosale, 1975b. Ion regulation in mangroves. In G.E. Walsh, S.C. Snedaker and H.J. Teas (eds.), *Proceedings of the International Symposium on Biology and Management of Mangroves.* Institute of Food and Agricultural Sciences, University of Florida, Gainesville, Florida, Vol. II, pp. 595-607.

Karstedt, P. and N. Parameswaran, 1976. Anatomy and systematics of *Rhizophora. Botanische Jahrbücher für Systematik, Pflanzengeschichte und Pflanzengeographie* 97, 317-38.

Kenneally, K.F., P.G. Wilson and V. Semeniuk, 1978. A new character for distinguishing vegetative material of the mangrove genera *Bruguiera* and *Rhizophora. Nuytsia* 2, 178-80.

Lear, R. and T. Turner, 1977. *Mangroves of Australia.* University of Queensland Press, St Lucia. 84 pp.

Lewis, O.A.M. and G. Naidoo, 1970. Tidal influence on the apparent transpirational rhythms of the white mangrove. *South African Journal of Science* 66, 268-70.

Liebau, O., 1914. Beiträge zur Anatomie und Morphologie der Mangrove-Pflanzen, insbesondere ihres Wurzelsystems. *Beiträge zur Biologie der Pflanzen* 12, 181-213.

Loetschert, W. and F. Liemann, 1967. Die Salzspeicherung im Keimling von *Rhizophora mangle* L. während der Entwicklung auf der Mutterpflanze. *Planta* 72, 142-56.

Lugo, A.E. and S.C. Snedaker, 1974. The ecology of mangroves. *Annual Review of Ecology and Systematics* 5, 39-64.

Lugo, A.E. and S.C. Snedaker, 1975. Properties of a mangrove forest in southern Florida. In G.E. Walsh, S.C. Snedaker and H.J. Teas (eds.), *Proceedings of the International Symposium on Biology and Management of Mangroves.* Institute of Food and Agricultural Sciences, University of Florida, Gainesville, Florida, Vol. I, pp. 170-212.

Lugo, A.E., G. Evink, M.M. Brinson, A. Broce and S.C. Snedaker, 1975. Diurnal rates of photosynthesis, respiration, and transpiration in mangrove forests of South Florida. In F.B. Golley and E. Medina (eds.), *Tropical Ecological Systems.* Springer-Verlag, New York, pp. 335-50.

Lugo, A.E. and C.P. Zucca, 1977. The impact of low temperature stress on mangrove structure and growth. *Tropical Ecology* 18, 149-61.

Macnae, W., 1963. Mangrove swamps in South Africa. *Journal of Ecology* **51**, 1-25.

Macnae, W., 1966. Mangroves of eastern and southern Australia. *Australian Journal of Botany* **14**, 67-104.

Macnae, W., 1968a. A general account of the fauna and flora of mangrove swamps and forests in the Indo-West-Pacific region. *Advances in Marine Biology* **6**, 73-270.

Macnae, W., 1968b. Mangroves and their fauna. *Australian Natural History Magazine* **16**, 17-21.

Macnae, W. and M. Kalk, 1962. The ecology of the mangrove swamps of Inhaca Island, Mozambique. *Journal of Ecology* **50**, 19-34.

Malaviya, C.V., 1963. On the distribution, structure and ontogeny of stone cells in *Avicennia officinalis* L. *Proceedings of the Indian Academy of Science* **58**, 45-50.

Marco, H.F., 1935. Systematic anatomy of the woods of the Rhizophoraceae. *Tropical Woods (Yale University)* **44**, 1-26.

McCusker, A., 1971. Knee roots in *Avicennia marina* (Forsk.) Vierh. *Annals of Botany* **35**, 707-12.

McMillan, C., 1975. Adaptive differentiation to chilling in mangrove populations. In G.E. Walsh, S.C. Snedaker and H.J. Teas (eds.), *Proceedings of the International Symposium on Biology and Management of Mangroves*. Institute of Food and Agricultural Sciences, University of Florida, Gainesville, Florida, Vol. I, pp. 62-70.

Metcalf, C.R., 1931. The breathing roots of *Sonneratia* and *Bruguiera,* a review of recent work by Troll and Dragendorff. *Kew Bulletin* **11**, 465-7.

Miller, P.C., J. Hom and D.K. Poole, 1975. Water relations of three mangrove species in south Florida. *Oecologia Plantarum* **10**, 355-67.

Mullan, D.P., 1931a. Observations on the water storing devices in the leaves of some Indian halophytes. *Journal of the Indian Botanical Society* **10**, 126-33.

Mullan, D.P., 1931b. On the occurrence of glandular hairs (salt glands) on the leaves of some Indian halophytes. *Journal of the Indian Botanical Society* **10**, 184-9.

Mullan, D.P., 1932. Observations on the biology and physiological anatomy of some Indian halophytes. I. *Journal of the Indian Botanical Society* **11**, 103-18.

Muller, J., 1969. A palynological study of the genus *Sonneratia* (Sonneratiaceae). *Pollen et Spores* **11**, 223-98.

Muller, J. and C. Caratini, 1977. Pollen of *Rhizophora* (Rhizophoraceae) as a guide fossil. *Pollen et Spores* **19**, 361-90.

Nishihira, M. and M. Urasaki, 1976. Production, settlement and mortality of seedlings of a mangrove, *Kandelia candel* (L.) Druce in Okinawa. *Abstracts of Symposia and Contributed Papers, International Symposium on the Ecology and Management of Some Tropical Shallow Water Communities*. Jakarta, July 1976. 15 pp.

Noakes, D.S.P., 1955. Methods of increasing growth and obtaining natural regeneration of the mangrove type in Malaya. *Malayan Forester* **18**, 23-30.

Onuf, C.P., J.M. Teal and I. Valiela, 1977. Interactions of nutrients, plant growth and herbivory in a mangrove ecosystem. *Ecology* **58**, 514-26.

Padmanabhan, D., 1960. The embryology of *Avicennia officinalis* L. I. Floral morphology and gametophytes. *Proceedings of the Indian Academy of Science* **52**, 131-45.

Padmanabhan, D., 1962a. The embryology of *Avicennia officinalis* L. III. The embryo. *Journal of Madras University* **32**, 1-19.

Padmanabhan, D., 1962b. The embryology of *Avicennia officinalis* L. IV. The seedling. *Proceedings of the Indian Academy of Science* **56**, 114-22.

Pannier, P., 1962. Estudio fisiológico sobre la viviparia de *Rhizophora mangle* L. *Acta Científica Venezolana (Botanical Series)* **13**, 184-97.

Pannier, P. and R.F. Pannier, 1975. Physiology of vivipary in *Rhizophora mangle*. In G.E. Walsh, S.C. Snedaker and H.J. Teas (eds.), *Proceedings of the International Symposium on Biology and Management of Mangroves*. Institute of Food and Agricultural Sciences, University of Florida, Gainesville, Florida, Vol. II, pp. 632-42.

Panshin, A.J., 1932. An anatomical study of the woods of the Philippine mangrove swamps. *Philippine Journal of Science* **48**, 143-208.

Percival, M., 1974. Floral ecology of coastal scrub in south-east Jamaica. *Biotropica* **6**, 104-29.

Percival, M. and J.S. Womersley, 1975. *Floristics and Ecology of the Mangrove Vegetation of Papua New Guinea.* Department of Forests, Lae. 96 pp.

Rabinowitz, D., 1975. Planting experiments in mangrove swamps of Panama. In G.E. Walsh, S.G. Snedaker and H.J. Teas (eds.), *Proceedings of the International Symposium on Biology and Management of Mangroves.* Institute of Food and Agricultural Sciences, University of Florida, Gainesville, Florida, Vol. I, pp. 385-93.

Rabinowitz, D., 1977. Effects of a mangrove borer, *Poecilips rhizophorae* on propagules of *Rhizophora harrisonii* in Panama. *Florida Entomologist* **60**, 129-34.

Rabinowitz, D., 1978. Dispersal properties of mangrove propagules. *Biotropica* **10**, 47-57.

Rains, D.W. and E. Epstein, 1967. Preferential absorption of potassium by leaf tissue of the mangrove *Avicennia marina:* an aspect of halophytic competence in coping with salt. *Australian Journal of Biological Science* **20**, 847-57.

Rao, T.A., 1957. Comparative morphology and ontogeny of foliar sclereids in seed plants. *Proceedings of the National Institute of Science, India, Series B (Biological Science)* **23**, 143-51.

Rao, A.R. and M. Sharma, 1968. The terminal sclereids and tracheids of *Bruguiera gymnorhiza* Blume and the cauline sclereids of *Ceriops roxburghiana* Arn. *Proceedings of the National Institute of Science, India, Series B (Biological Science)* **34**, 267-75.

Rao, A.R. and L.C. Wan, 1969. A new record of foliar sclereids in *Scyphiphora hydrophyllacea. Current Science* **38**, 594-5.

Rehm, A.E., 1976. The effects of the wood-boring isopod *Sphaeroma terebrans* on the mangrove communities of Florida. *Environmental Conservation* **3**, 47-57.

Reinders-Gouwentak, C.A., 1953. Sonneratiaceae and other mangrove-swamp families, anatomical structure and water relations. *Flora Malesiana* **4**, 513-15.

Roth, I., 1965. Histogenese der Lentizellen am Hypocotyl von *Rhizophora mangle* L. *Österreichische Botanische Zeitung* **112**, 640-53.

Saenger, P. and M.S. Hopkins, 1975. Observations on the mangroves of the south-eastern Gulf of Carpentaria, Australia. In G.E. Walsh, S.C. Snedaker and H.J. Teas (eds.), *Proceedings of the International Symposium on Biology and Management of Mangroves.* Institute of Food and Agricultural Sciences, University of Florida, Gainesville, Florida, Vol. I, pp. 126-36.

Saenger, P. and J. Robson, 1977. Structural analysis of mangrove communities on the Central Queensland coastline. *Marine Research in Indonesia* **18**, 101-18.

Scholander, P.F., 1968. How mangroves desalinate seawater. *Physiologia Plantarum* **21**, 258-68.

Scholander, P.F., H.T. Hammel, E. Hemmingsen and W. Carey, 1962. Salt balance in mangroves. *Plant Physiology* **37**, 722-9.

Scholander, P.F., L. van Dam and S.I. Scholander, 1955. Gas exchange in the roots of mangroves. *American Journal of Botany* **42**, 92-8.

Shah, J.J. and K.P. Sundarraj, 1965. Stipular sclereids in *Rhizophora mucronata* L. *Current Science* **34**, 155-6.

Shields, L.M. 1950. Leaf xeromorphy as related to physiological and structural influences. *Botanical Review* **16**, 399-447.

Sidhu, S.S., 1962. Chromosomal studies on some mangrove species. *Indian Forester* **88**, 585-92.

Sidhu, S.S., 1968. Further studies on the cytology of mangrove species in India. *Caryologia* **21**, 353-7.

Sidhu, S.S., 1975a. Structure of epidermis and stomatal apparatus of some mangrove species. In G.E. Walsh, S.C. Snedaker and H.J. Teas (eds.), *Proceedings of the International Symposium on Biology and Management of Mangroves*. Institute of Food and Agricultural Sciences, University of Florida, Gainesville, Florida, Vol. II, pp. 569-78.

Sidhu, S.S., 1975b. Culture and growth of some mangrove species. In G.E. Walsh, S.C. Snedaker and H.J. Teas (eds.), *Proceedings of the International Symposium on Biology and Management of Mangroves*. Institute of Food and Agricultural Sciences, University of Florida, Gainesville, Florida, Vol. I, pp. 394-401.

Specht, R.L., 1981. Biogeography of halophytic angiosperms (salt-marsh, mangroves and sea-grass). In A. Keast (ed.), *Ecological Biogeography of Australia*. Junk, The Hague. pp. 575-90.

Specht, R.L., R.B. Salt and S.T. Reynolds, 1977. Vegetation in the vicinity of Weipa, North Queensland. *Proceedings of the Royal Society of Queensland* **88**, 17-38.

Stace, C.A., 1966. The use of epidermal characters in phylogenetic considerations. *New Phytologist* **65**, 304-18.

Steinke, T.D., 1975. Some factors affecting dispersal and establishment of propagules of *Avicennia marina* (Forsk.) Vierh. In G.E. Walsh, S.C. Snedaker and H.J. Teas, (eds.), *Proceedings of the International Symposium on Biology and Management of Mangroves*. Institute of Food and Agricultural Sciences, University of Florida, Gainesville, Florida, Vol. II, pp. 402-14.

Steinke, T.D. and C.J. Ward, 1973. *Ceriops tagal* (Perr.) C.B. Robinson at Kosi Bay. *Journal of South African Botany* **39**, 245-7.

Stocker, G.C., 1976. Report on cyclone damage to natural vegetation in the Darwin area after cyclone Tracey 25 December 1974. *Forestry and Timber Bureau, Leaflet No.* **127**. 40pp.

Studholme, W.P. and W.R. Philipson, 1966. A comparison of the cambium in two woods with included phloem: *Heimerliodendron brunoianum* and *Avicennia resinifera*. *New Zealand Journal of Botany* **4**, 332-41.

Sussex, I., 1975. Growth and metabolism of the embryo and attached seedling of the viviparous mangrove *Rhizophora mangle*. *American Journal of Botany* **62**, 948-53.

Swain, T., 1965. The tannins. In J. Bonner and J.E. Varner (eds.), *Plant Biochemistry*. Academic Press, New York. 1054 pp.

Teas, H.J. and J. Kelly, 1975. Effects of herbicides on mangroves of South Vietnam and Florida. In G.E. Walsh, S.C. Snedaker and H.J. Teas (eds.), *Proceedings of the International Symposium on the Biology and Management of Mangroves*. Institute of Food and Agricultural Sciences, University of Florida, Gainesville, Florida, Vol. II, pp. 719-28.

Teas, H.J. and F. Montgomery, 1968. Ecology of red mangrove seedling establishment. *Bulletin, Association of Southeastern Biologists* **15**, 56-7.

Thom, B.G., L.D. Wright and J.M. Coleman, 1975. Mangrove ecology and deltaic-estuarine geomorphology; Cambridge Gulf-Ord River, Western Australia. *Journal of Ecology* **63**,203-32.

Tomlinson, P.B., 1971. The shoot apex and its dichotomous branching in the *Nypa* palm. *Annals of Botany* **35**, 865-79.

Tomlinson, P.B. and A.M. Gill, 1973. Growth habits of tropical trees; some guiding principles. In B.J. Meggers, E.S. Ayensu and W.D. Duckworth (eds.), *Tropical Forest Ecosystems in Africa and South America: A Comparative Review*. Smithsonian Institution Press, Washington, D.C., pp. 129-43.

Tomlinson, P.B., J.S. Bunt, R.B. Primack and N.C. Duke, 1978. *Lumnitzera rosea* (Combretaceae)—its status and floral morphology. *Journal of the Arnold Arboretum* **59**, 342-51.

Treub, M., 1883. Notes sur l'embryon, le sac embryonaire et l'ovule de *Avicennia officinalis*. *Annales du Jardin Botanique de Buitenzorg* **3**, 79-87.

Trochain, J. and L. Dulau, 1942. Quelques particularites anatomiques d'*Avicennia nitida* (Verbenaceae) de la mangrove ouest-africaine. *Bulletin de la Société d'Histoire Naturelle de Toulouse* **77**, 271-81.

Troll, W. and O. Dragendorff, 1931. Uber die Luftwurzeln von *Sonneratia* Linn. und ihre biologische Bedeutung. *Planta* **13**, 311-473.

Uhl, N.W., 1972, Inflorescence and flower structure in *Nypa fruticans* (Palmae). *American Journal of Botany* **59**, 729-43.

Uhl, N.W. and H.E. Moore, 1977. Correlations of inflorescence, flower structure, and floral anatomy with pollination in some palms. *Biotropica* **9**, 170-90.

Uphof, J.C.T., 1941. Halophytes. *Botanical Review* **7**, 1-58.

Van Steveninck, R.F.M., W.D. Armstrong, P.D. Peters and T.A. Hall, 1976. Ultrastructural localization of ions. III. Distribution of chloride in mesophyll cells of mangrove (*Aegiceras corniculatum* Blanco). *Australian Journal of Plant Physiology* **3**, 367-76.

Venkateswarlu, J., 1935. A contribution to the embryology of the Sonneratiaceae. *Proceedings of the Indian Academy of Science* **5**, 23-9.

Venkateswarlu, J. and R.S.P. Rao, 1964. The wood anatomy and taxonomic position of Sonneratiaceae. *Current Science* **33**, 6-9.

Venkateswarlu, J. and P.N. Rao, 1975. A contribution to the embryology of the tribe Hippomaneae of the Euphorbiaceae. *Journal of the Indian Botanical Society* **54**, 98-103.

Walsh, G.E., 1974. Mangroves: A review. In R. Reimold and W. Queen (eds.), *Ecology of Halophytes*. Academic Press, New York, pp. 51-174.

Walter, H., 1973. *Die Vegetation der Erde*. 3rd ed. I. Fischer, Stuttgart. 743 pp.

Walter, H. and M. Steiner, 1936. Die Ökologie der Ost-Afrikanischen Mangroven. *Zeitschrift für Botanik* **30**, 65-193.

Watson, C.J.J., 1928. Notes on the growth of the grey mangrove (*Avicennia*) in the upper Brisbane River. *Queensland Naturalist* **6**, 83-4.

Watson, J.G., 1928. Mangrove forests of the Malay Peninsula. *Malayan Forest Records* No. 6. 275 pp.

Wester, L.L., 1967. The distribution of the mangrove in South Australia. Unpublished Honours thesis, University of Adelaide.

Wright, D., 1977. Pollen morphology of Australian mangroves. Unpublished thesis, James Cock University of North Queensland.

Wylie, R.B., 1949. Differences in foliar organization among leaves from four locations in the crown of an isolated tree (*Acer plantanoides*). *Proceedings of the Iowa Academy of Science* **56**, 189-98.

Wylie, R.B., 1954. Leaf organization of some woody dicotyledons from New Zealand. *American Journal of Botany* **41**, 186-91.

Zelitch, I., 1971. *Photosynthesis, Photorespiration and Plant Productivity*. Academic Press, New York. 347 pp.

Ziegler, H. and U. Lüttge, 1966. Die Salzdrüsen von *Limonium vulgare*. I. Die Feinstruktur. *Planta* **70**, 193-206.

11

Physiological Processes in Mangroves

B.F. Clough, T.J. Andrews
and
I.R. Cowan

Introduction

The question may be asked: 'What is interesting about the physiology of mangroves which sets them apart from other trees as particular objects of study by plant physiologists?' This seems to be a useful approach in our attempt to assess what is known and to delineate outstanding gaps in our knowledge where future research effort may be directed profitably.

One answer is suggested by the common feature which characterises all mangrove species; namely, their ability to thrive in the intertidal zone, using saline water for growth and transpiration. This leads us to the first major topic of this chapter—the osmoregulatory mechanisms of mangroves and their water relations. Related to this is the fact that the intertidal zone is not only saline but usually also waterlogged and therefore deficient in the oxygen required by the respiratory processes which underlie root growth, nutrient uptake and perhaps also salt exclusion. Thus the physiology of the roots of mangroves is of particular interest, especially as it relates to adaptations to the anoxic environment.

Another answer to our initial question is suggested by the prime role of mangroves as primary producers in inshore marine food webs. Other chapters in this volume will deal with more ecological approaches. Our purpose here is to assess the physiology which underlies and sets constraints upon this very important productivity. Thus the other main sub-division of this chapter will be concerned with photosynthesis in mangroves and its response to variation in environmental conditions. Lastly we shall indicate the way in which the salt balance and growth physiology of mangroves may be interrelated through the coupling of water loss and carbon fixation.

Clearly, reproduction is another interesting aspect of mangrove physiology, particularly the physiology of vivipary which is a characteristic of so many important mangrove species. Aspects of this topic are considered in an accompanying chapter in this volume.

Osmoregulation and salt balance

Seawater contains about 35 grams solute per litre, mostly as NaCl, and has an osmotic potential of about -2.5 MPa (1 MPa = 10 atm). Mangroves are the only trees to grow on such a saline substrate, though a number of succulent and herbaceous saltmarsh plants also grow on substrates which often have salinities equal to or greater than that of seawater.

As a group mangroves do not appear to be obligate halophytes, as many species grow well in freshwater (McMillan, 1974). However, most species seem to grow best at salinities which lie somewhere in the range between freshwater and seawater (Stern and Voigt, 1959; Connor, 1969; Ministry for Conservation, Victoria, 1975), suggesting that growth is stimulated by the presence of NaCl in the substrate. The beneficial effect of NaCl on the growth of other plants has been attributed to Na^+ (Jennings, 1968).

While moderate levels of NaCl in the substrate may well be beneficial to growth, high concentrations of salt in the cytoplasm of cells inhibits metabolism (Flowers et al., 1977). The question which concerns us here is 'how do man-groves maintain a salt balance which is acceptable physiologically while growing on substrates with very high salinities?' Based on what we currently know, it seems likely that the mechanisms by which mangroves regulate internal salt levels will be similar to those in other halophytes. Recent reviews of various aspects of osmoregulation and salt tolerance in halophytes can be found in Jennings (1968), Waisel (1972), Rains (1972), Poljakoff-Mayber and Gale (1975), Hellebust (1976), and Flowers et. al. (1977).

Adaptations thought to be important in the maintenance of a salt balance by mangroves include the capacity of the roots to discriminate against NaCl, the possession by some species of specialised salt-secreting glands in their leaves, the accumulation of salt in leaves and bark, and the loss of salt when leaves and other organs are shed. Apart from the possession of salt-secreting glands by a few species, all these adaptations are found to varying degrees in all species of mangrove, despite their wide generic origins. It therefore seems unwise to classify particular species as 'salt excluders', or 'salt accumulators', until the quantitative significance of these adaptations has been established clearly.

Salt uptake by roots
Detailed descriptions of the structure of root systems in many species of mangroves can be found in Chapman (1976). It is generally accepted that uptake of water and nutrients occurs via a complex system of fibrous roots which are attached to the lateral root system and, in those species which possess them, to pneumatophores and prop roots. This fibrous root system is most dense in the upper 50-100 cm of the substrate. By analogy with root systems in other woody plant species it seems likely that the lateral root system serves only to support the tree and to provide the vascular connection between the absorbing roots and aerial parts of the tree. In those species with prop roots the vascular system of the prop root probably provides the 'plumbing' between the absorbing roots at its base and the rest of the tree. However, none of these generalisations appear to have been examined experimentally.

The roots of higher plants characteristically display a high degree of selec-tivity in ion uptake and transport to the xylem. Measurements of the NaCl concentration and osmotic potential of the xylem sap of mangroves indicate that NaCl is largely excluded from the xylem (Scholander et al., 1962, 1966; Atkinson et al., 1967; Scholander, 1968). Species with salt-secreting glands in their leaves have the capacity to exclude 80-85 per cent of the NaCl in sea-water; those species without salt-secreting glands are more efficient, excluding 95-98 per cent of the NaCl in seawater (Scholander et al., 1962, 1966; Atkinson *et al.*, 1967). Evidence reviewed later suggests that the low concentration of NaCl in the xylem sap of mangroves is due to discrimination against Na^+. It is unlikely that Cl^- *per se* is directly excluded from the xylem; it is more probable that uptake of Cl^- is regulated by the necessity to maintain a balance between cations and anions in the xylem sap following exclusion of Na^+.

Few data are available for the concentrations of other ions in the xylem sap of mangroves. Atkinson *et al.* (1967) and Field (C.D. Field, workshop discussion) found the concentration of K^+ in the xylem sap to be greater than its concentration in seawater (about 12mM K^+). The concentration of other ions in the xylem of mangroves is not known. The results of Scholander *et al.* (1962) suggest that the concentrations of Na^+, K^+ and Cl^- together are sufficient to account for most of the osmotic potential of the xylem sap in species possessing salt-secreting glands; the relative contribution of NaCl to the total osmotic potential of the xylem sap is probably less in other species which show greater discrimination against NaCl uptake.

A number of comprehensive reviews of various aspects of ion transport across plant roots have been published in recent years (e.g. Laties, 1969; Rains, 1972; Läuchli, 1976; Pitman, 1976, 1977). It seems to be generally accepted that two parallel pathways are available for ion transport across the root to the xylem. One involves uptake across the plasmalemma of cortical or endodermal cells in the root, and subsequent transport to the stele via the intracellular symplasm. The other involves direct flow to the stele in association with the flow of water through cell walls and liquid-filled intercellular spaces (the apoplast) of the root. These pathways are not operationally isolated from each other, however, because ions and water exchange readily between the apoplast and symplast over most of the distance between the cortex and stele.

Kinetic evidence obtained from studies with crop plants suggests that two mechanisms are involved in ion transport across the plasmalemma to the symplasm. The best evidence for these comes from studies of uptake of Na^+ and K^+, which appear to compete for similar uptake sites. At low external concentrations (< 1 mM K^+), K^+ uptake appears to be mediated by a carrier with a high specific affinity for K^+ and a low affinity for Na^+. At high external concentrations (> 2-5 mM), uptake of Na^+ is favoured relative to K^+ (Laties, 1969; Rains, 1972), but it is uncertain whether uptake at high concentrations is carrier mediated or simply a diffusive flux (Glass, 1976). Rains and Epstein (1967) have shown that these two mechanisms also exist in the leaf tissue of *Avicennia marina*, but their presence in the roots of mangroves has not yet been demonstrated.

No direct measurements have been made of cytoplasmic Na^+ concentrations. However, indirect evidence (see Flowers *et al.*, 1977) suggests that the concentration of Na^+ in the cytoplasm of plant cells is low, even in the presence of high external concentrations where transport processes favour the uptake of Na^+ relative to K^+ (see earlier discussion). The presence of an outwardly directed Na^+ pump at the plasmalemma (Pitman and Saddler, 1967) and an inwardly directed pump at the tonoplast (Pitman *et al.*, 1968; Pierce and

Higinbotham, 1970) could account for low cytoplasmic concentrations of Na^+ in halophytes (Jennings, 1968; Rains, 1972).

Direct flow of ions and water to the stele via the apoplast is prevented over most of the length of the root by the deposition of suberin in the walls of the endodermis to form the casparian strip (Läuchli, 1976). In some plants this process begins at a distance of a few millimetres from the root tip (Pitman, 1977), and therefore passive transport of solute to the xylem is likely to be restricted to a relatively small region of the root. However, we have no information on the development of a casparian strip in mangrove roots. Moreover, Pitman (1977) has pointed out that at high external solute concentrations even a small direct flow of water to the stele via the apoplast could result in a significant influx of salt. This could be an important component of salt uptake by mangroves. In *Rhizophora*, for example, the concentration of Cl^- in the xylem sap is about 3 per cent of seawater (Atkinson *et al.*, 1967). Most of this could be supplied directly via the apoplast if we assume that 1-5 per cent of the total water uptake to the shoot occurs across the apoplast (see Pitman, 1977). Any shortfall in K^+ and other essential ions might be provided by carrier-mediated transport via the symplasm.

This explanation is consistent with the observation of Scholander (1968) that exposure of mangrove roots to low temperatures (about 2°C) and to the inhibitors carbon monoxide and dinitrophenol had no effect on the concentration of NaCl in the xylem sap of mangroves. It is also consistent with the apparent absence of a diurnal variation in the salt concentration of xylem sap (Scholander *et al.*, 1966), which could be interpreted as an indication that salt uptake was tied closely to water uptake. At this stage the evidence for a major role for the apoplast in salt uptake by mangroves is circumstantial and alternative explanations are possible. Nevertheless, it forms a useful working hypothesis which warrants further investigation. In this connection, it is interesting to speculate whether the degree of development of the endodermis has any bearing on the observed differences in the capacity of mangroves with and without salt-secreting glands to discriminate against NaCl.

Another interesting aspect of mangrove physiology is the role of pneumatophores and prop roots. A number of studies (reviewed by Chapman, 1976) have demonstrated the occurrence of gas exchange via pneumatophores, and suggest that they could be an important pathway for gas exchange between subterranean roots and air. However, quantitative data on the kinetics of gas exchange are lacking. We have no information at all on the degree of anaerobiosis of the root rhizosphere and on its effect on either the physiology of the roots or on the overall growth of mangroves. This is an important aspect because the degree of anaerobiosis may well have a profound influence on nutrient availability, and on nutrient and salt uptake.

Salt glands
Only a few genera of mangroves (*Avicennia, Aegiceras, Aegialitis, Acanthus, Laguncularia ?, Sonneratia ?*) appear to possess salt-secreting glands in their leaves (see Saenger, this volume). The structure and function of these glands

has been studied by a number of investigators (Scholander *et al.*, 1962; Atkinson *et al.*, 1967; Cardale and Field, 1971; Billard and Field, 1973; Cardale and Field, 1975). The structural aspects have been summarised by Saenger (this volume).

Atkinson *et al.* (1967) have demonstrated that the salt glands of *Aegialitis* secrete mainly NaCl. Secretion was particularly active in the light (about 90 p-equiv Cl⁻ Cm⁻² S⁻¹) and was reduced by more than 90 per cent in the dark (Aitkinson *et al.*, 1967), but diurnal variations in the rate of secretion may be less marked in other species (Scholander *et al.*, 1962). Evidence from electron micrographs and tracer experiments using[36] Cl⁻ suggest that in *Aegialitis* the salt passes directly to the glands from leaf veins, via the palisade layer, without complete equilibration with intracellular pools of Cl⁻ in the palisade and epidermis (Atkinson *et al.*, 1967). More recently, Van Steveninck *et al.* (1976), working with *Aegiceras* leaves, observed that in some mesophyll cells the vacuoles contained large amounts of organic solutes but little Cl⁻, whereas in others the vacuoles contained large amounts of Cl⁻. It was suggested that the latter cells might be involved in salt transport to the salt-secreting glands via the symplast (Van Stevenick *et al.*, 1976). Irrespective of the pathway of salt transport to the secretory glands it appears that salt secretion is an active process (Atkinson *et al.*, 1967). Thus respiration has particular significance in the leaves of salt-secreting mangroves because of the likelihood that the energy required by the salt-secreting mechanism of the salt glands is derived from respiratory processes. Moore *et al.* (1972, 1973) observed that dark respiration in *A. germinans* leaves was almost twice as active in summer as in winter and suggested that this might be correlated with increased salt loading of the leaves as a result of higher transpirational throughput in summer. On the other hand, dark respiration in leaves of the non-salt-secreting mangroves *R. mangle* and *L. racemosa* was similar in summer and winter (Moore *et al.* 1972, 1973).

Salt accumulation

Leaf succulence in mangroves is associated with the enlargement of cells in the leaf, principally in the hypodermal and mesophyll tissues (Chapman, 1976; Saenger, this volume). This is apparently a response to elevated levels of Na^+ in the leaf (Jennings, 1968). Mangrove leaves characteristically contain high levels of NaCl (Atkinson *et al.*, 1967; Walsh, 1974; Joshi, 1975; Spain and Holt, 1980), most of which is probably located in cell vacuoles. Osmotic potentials obtained from measurements of the freezing point depression of sap extracted from crushed leaves (see Chapman, 1976) agree well with those obtained using the pressure bomb technique (Scholander, 1968), both yielding values in the range —2.5 to —6.0 MPa. These osmotic potentials are somewhat lower than one would predict from the observed concentrations of 200-600 mM Na^+ and 300-600 mM Cl^- on a leaf water basis (Atkinson *et al.*, 1967; Ball and Cowan, unpublished results), suggesting that other solutes play an important role in the osmotic balance of mangrove leaves.

It is widely accepted that leaf succulence in mangroves is an adaptation which allows salt that cannot be excluded by the roots to be accumulated in tissues within the leaf where it can cause little physiological damage. It is easy to conceive how, in the short term, salt left behind at the evaporating surfaces within the leaf is accumulated in the vacuoles of surrounding cells. In the longer term, however, continued accumulation of salt in the leaf would necessitate an increasing degree of succulence as the leaf aged. This is not supported by the data presently available. The results of Atkinson *et al.* (1967) show that the dry weight and water content of leaves remain nearly constant for all but the most recently unfolded, and perhaps the oldest, leaves on a shoot. Similar results for a number of species in North Queensland were obtained by Ball and Cowan (unpublished data). These results argue against the development of increasing succulence as the leaf ages. Some implications of this for the overall salt balance of mangroves will be considered later.

Leaf shedding
What little evidence there is does not support the notion that leaf shedding in mangroves is an important means of disposing of accumulated salt, in the sense that it does not appear to decrease the average salt content per unit dry weight of the plant. Ball and Cowan (unpublished) examined five species of Rhizophoraceae growing on Hinchinbrook Island, and found no tendency for Cl⁻ per unit dry weight to increase with age amongst mature green leaves within a given leaf rosette. Chloride concentrations seemed to be only marginally greater in senescing leaves. Working with *Avicennia*, Clough and Attiwill (1975) found slightly higher levels of sodium per unit dry weight in leaves which had just fallen relative to those remaining on the tree. Both of these findings could have been due to retranslocation of other soluble compounds out of leaves during senescence.

Intuitively, it seems reasonable to suggest that both the rate of salt accumulation by a leaf and its salt content could influence its lifespan. This should be most evident in species without salt-secreting glands. It is possible, for example, that if the photosynthetic capacity of a mangrove leaf decreases with age, as it does in leaves of many other plants, there may come a time in the life of the leaf where the metabolic cost of maintaining a salt balance outstrips its assimilative capacity. This might not be the case in mangroves if a declining photosynthetic potential is associated with a reduction in stomatal conductance, since this would result in a concomitant reduction in transpiration and presumably salt loading to the leaf as it aged.

Whatever the relationship between salt loading, assimilative capacity, and the lifespan of a leaf, the threshold beyond which a leaf can no longer effectively maintain a salt balance is likely to vary appreciably with metabolic events in nearby leaves, with the degree of exposure, with soil salinity and with other edaphic factors. For example, Duke (N. Duke, personal communicaiton, 1980) has observed that higher than normal rates of litter fall in some communities in North Queensland are associated with periods of above average salinity. The most extreme example of this occurs in genera like *Excoecaria, Barringtonia* and *Xylocarpus* which are either deciduous or lose most of their leaves prior to the initiation of new leaves. Although there is now a large body of data on leaf litter fall for Australian mangroves (see Bunt, this volume; Clough and Attiwill, this volume) simple comparisons of litter fall unfortunately will not necessarily reveal a relationship between salt loading and the lifespan of leaves, unless measurements of total leaf biomass, rates of leaf initiation and the degree of leaf exposure are also made simultaneously.

Osmoregulation and metabolism

The activity of enzymes in higher plant cells is generally inhibited by high levels of salt. It appears that in this respect the enzymes of halophytes are similar to those of other plants (Flowers et al., 1977). Whereas inorganic ions, especially Na^+ and Cl^-, seem to be responsible for osmoregulation in the cell vacuoles of mangroves and other halophytes, osmotic adjustment in the cytoplasm appears to be maintained by accumulation of the amino acid proline and the quarternary ammonium compounds choline and betaine (Flowers et al., 1977). Comparable work on mangroves is sparse. Benson (A. Benson, personal communication, 1980) has found choline sulphate in mangroves and Pannier (F. Pannier, personal communication, 1980) has noted a positive correlation between substrate salinity and the levels of choline and betaine in the leaves of some species of mangrove. There is considerable scope for further work on this aspect, particularly in relation to osmotic adaptation to fluctuations in salinity.

Water relations

In order to maintain a positive water balance mangroves must have tissue water potentials which are lower than the osmotic potential of the substrate. Since the osmotic potential is the main component of water potential in the protoplast the minimum requirement is that the intracellular osmotic potential must be more negative than the osmotic potential of the substrate. Data which indicate that this condition is met have been reviewed earlier in this chapter.

It should be emphasised that the osmotic potential in leaves and other tissues is probably influenced substantially by substrate salinity. Thus, while most of the data presently available indicate that intracellular osmotic potentials are lower (more negative) than the osmotic potential of seawater, mangroves growing in less saline substrates may well have intracellular osmotic potentials somewhat higher than the osmotic potential of seawater. On the other hand, some species of mangroves (e.g. Avicennia) are often found growing on saltpans and on claypans which dry out between wet seasons. The water potential of these substrates may be substantially lower than that of seawater, and mangroves growing in such habitats must have very low intracellular osmotic potentials in order to survive. Chapman (1976) cites several examples where osmotic potentials in the leaves appear to have been influenced by the osmotic potential of the substrate. These considerations serve to emphasise that measurements of water status in mangroves have limited ecological significance unless accompanied by measurements of the water status of the substrate on which they are growing. Such measurements need to be made with caution, however, because the salinity of the immediate rhizosphere may be much higher than that of the bulk soil solution due to accumulation of salt which is excluded during uptake of water by the roots.

Scholander (1968) measured the hydrostatic pressure potential in the xylem of a number of mangrove species, using a pressure bomb. He found values ranging from —2.7 to —5.7 MPa. Values at the lower end of the range tended to be recorded at night, and the larger values during the day-time when evaporative loss from leaves generally exceeds water intake by the roots. Similar results were obtained by Attiwill and Clough (1980) in *Avicennia* in Westernport Bay. There the hydrostatic pressure potential in the xylem ranged from —2.5 to —2.9 MPa at night, and averaged —3.5 MPa during the day-time. The hydrostatic pressure potential in the xylem is an order of magnitude lower than the osmotic potential and is thus the major component of the water potential in the xylem.

It is clear, both from theoretical considerations and from the discussion above, that the highest water potential that can be attained in the leaves of mangroves is dictated by the prevailing osmotic potential of the substrate, and that leaf water potentials commonly lie in the range —2.5 to —4.0 MPa. Few, if any, glycophytes could survive such low water potentials. There is good reason to believe that the integrity of metabolic processes in leaves depends on the state of hydrature of the cytoplasm and cell membranes rather than on the water potential *per se*. Studies of the equilibrium water relations of mangroves (Scholander *et al.*, 1965; Scholander, 1968) indicate that a large drop in water potential results in a relatively small loss of intracellular water. This condition could arise from the relative inelasticity of the cell walls, coupled with low intracellular osmotic potential for relatively small changes in cell volume. In this respect the equilibrium water relations of mangrove leaves resemble those of conifers and xerophytic trees (Scholander *et al.*, 1965; Connor and Tunstall, 1968) and are quite unlike those of glycophytes (e.g. Gardner and Ehlig, 1965; Wenkert *et al.*, 1978; Acevedo *et al.*, 1979). This is clearly an important adaptation for survival on substrates with low water potentials.

Thus, while there is no doubt that mangroves suffer a severe and consistent water deficit, it is by no means certain that this constitutes a 'water stress'. Further work needs to be carried out on the relationship between leaf water status and physiological processes, particularly in relation to substrate salinity and in relation to diurnal variations in leaf water status.

Photosynthesis and gas exchange

The environment around a mangrove leaf

Before beginning an assessment of our knowledge of the photosynthetic physiology of mangrove leaves, it may be useful to consider the unique environment in which they exist and to which they presumably have become adapted.

Mangroves grow characteristically in the lower latitudes where solar radiation and air temperatures are commonly high. These factors combine to ensure that leaves subject to direct sunlight often experience temperatures which are supra-optimal for C_3 photosynthesis and give rise to large water vapour pressure deficits. Casual observation of North Queensland mangroves, particularly of the Rhizophoraceae family, reveals that leaf angle has an important role in adaptation to these environmental realities. Leaves at the top of the canopy which receive the highest irradiances are steeply inclined, often nearly vertical, while the shade leaves are nearly horizontal. The effectiveness of this strategy for maximising photosynthetic production has long been recognised by modellers (Monsi and Saeki, 1953). The incident radiation, which often would be more intense than that required to saturate C_3 photosynthesis if intercepted in the horizontal plane, is shared over a larger photosynthetic surface, thus maximising its utility while at the same time reducing the thermal input per unit leaf area and therefore reducing leaf temperature. Measurements of leaf temperature high in the canopy of *Rhizophora stylosa* at Hinchinbrook Island in full sunlight in summer showed that leaves at their natural inclination were often over 5° cooler than leaves artificially held horizontal and had concomitantly lower rates of water loss and higher photosynthetic rates (Andrews and Cowan, unpublished).

Another characteristic of the mangrove environment is the constraints that it sets on the plant's water relations. Not only is the water supplied to the leaf at a considerable negative hydrostatic pressure potential but the demand for water, as specified by the vapour pressure difference between the evaporating surfaces inside the leaf and the surrounding air, may be high, despite the humid nature of the mangrove environment. Leaves which are exposed to solar radiation are hotter than the surrounding air; hence the internal vapour pressure is greater than that of the ambient air and transpiration occurs if the stomata are open. As in all plants, the rate of transpiration is limited by the number and aperture of the stomata. However, the smaller the 'leaf conductance' to vapour transfer, the greater the temperature of the leaf. Thus, diminution of conductance does not produce an equivalent relative decrease in rate of transpiration. Moreover, limitation of transpiration in this way by an extensive community of plants causes the temperature to increase and therefore the vapour deficit of the air in the upper parts of the canopy to increase. In other words, the combined effect of physiological limitation of transpiration in all of the leaves exposed to radiation is to make the environment of each individual leaf somewhat harsher. These factors, together with leaf temperature which may be up to 5°C higher than ambient temperature may lead to substantial vapour pressure deficits between the leaves and their environment.

Leaves lower in the canopy may lose as much water relative to the amount to carbon fixed as those in the upper part. Typically leaves in full shade receive only 6 per cent of full sunlight and can thus contribute only slightly to carbon fixation of the whole canopy. When, however, they are illuminated by a sun-fleck, leaf temperature may be up to 15°C greater than ambient air temperature, due to the very small rates of ventilation. Rates of transpiration from such leaves may then actually be greater than those higher in the canopy.

It becomes clear from the foregoing that temperature is one key variable which governs the photosynthetic physiology of mangrove leaves. While in no way detracting from the importance of the physiological studies of mangroves undertaken to date, it is perhaps a little unfortunate that so often the study area has been right at one or other latitudinal extreme of the distribution of mangroves where the importance of adaptations which minimise leaf temperature is less noticeable.

Leaf anatomy

The anatomy of leaves of most mangroves has many features in common with that of xerophytes. These features, which include thick cuticles, wax coatings, sunken or otherwise hindered stomata and the presence of various types of water storage tissue, have been reviewed by Macnae (1968) and Walsh (1974), and studied more recently by Sidhu (1975).

For most mangroves, stomata are restricted to the lower leaf epidermis. Exceptions include the genera *Sonneratia* and *Osbornia* and the family Combretaceae (*Lunmitzera, Languncularia*, etc).

These stomatal and other epidermal characters would be expected to result in low rates of gaseous exchange with the leaf's environment and, as will be discussed later, the maximum leaf conductances for water vapour exchange that have been reported for mangroves are low. These adaptations are presumably responses to the 'physiological dryness' of the mangrove habitat. They may be taken as evidence that the supply of water to the mangrove leaf is indeed limiting.

The function of the water storage tissue found in leaves of most mangroves is less obvious. Jennings (1968) suggested that the high content of water might serve to dilute the salt entering the leaf with the transpirational stream, thus minimising the concentrations of possibly toxic ions. Bowman (1921) observed a positive correlation between the content of water storage tissue in *R. mangle* leaves and the salinity of the water in which they grew.

Biochemical pathway of CO_2 fixation

It seems clear that, in common with the great majority of trees, mangroves employ C_3 photosynthetic biochemistry. This may be deduced from the leaf anatomy of mangroves, their discrimination against carbon-13 and their gas exchange properties. In no case does the leaf anatomy of a mangrove show any suggestion of the cellular dimorphism which is fundamental to the C_4 intercellular transport system. Furthermore, the $^{13}C/^{12}C$ carbon isotope ratios of leaf material of 16 species from 14 genera of mangroves from a wide range of habitats in the Hinchinbrook Island area of North Queensland showed a range of $\delta^{13}C$ values from $-24.6°/oo$ to $-32.2°/oo$ (Andrews, unpublished). These values are typical of C_3 plants and clearly more negative than the range of C_4 plants (Smith and Epstein, 1971). Since it reflects discrimination against ^{13}C by the initial carboxylation reaction of photosynthesis, the $\delta^{13}C$ value has proved to be a most reliable character for distinguishing between C_3 and C_4 photosynthesis, at least for terrestrial higher plants. The gas exchange properties of mangroves will be discussed in the next section. It suffices here to state that the data obtained for the relatively few species studied to date seem more consistent with the operation of the C_3 pathway than with other photosynthetic mechanisms. Mangrove photosynthesis typically is saturated at moderate light intensities and has a temperature optimum below 35°C. Additionally, several species have been shown to have easily measurable CO_2-compensation points (Moore *et al.*, 1972; Cowan, 1978; Ball and Cowan, unpublished; Andrews and Clough, unpublished). These are clearly C_3 characters.

These conclusions are at variance with those of Joshi and co-workers (1974, 1976). This group observed that aspartate and alanine were heavily labelled after a few seconds exposure of leaf material of some Indian mangroves to carbon-14 and concluded that the C_4 pathway operated. However, it is difficult to determine whether conditions of steady-state photosynthesis prevailed during these labelling experiments since the tissue was floated on a buffer solution, with the label being supplied via this solution as $NaH^{14}CO_3$. Results of ^{14}C labelling experiments become difficult to interpret under non-steady-state conditions. Furthermore, since no 'pulse-chase' experiments were performed, it cannot be determined whether the labelled aspartate behaved as an intermediate in the photosynthetic sequence, as is required for the operation of the C_4 pathway.

Despite the apparent 'succulence' of some mangrove leaves due to the presence of water storage tissue, there have been no reports of Crassulacean acid metabolism in mangroves. Here again, the C_3-like $\delta^{13}C$ values would seem to indicate that this extreme xerophytic adaptation does not occur in mangroves.

Gas exchange properties

As discussed earlier, the stomata of mangroves are adapted so that gaseous exchange between the air spaces inside the leaves and external air is considerably hindered. Maximum values for leaf conductances for water vapour, i.e. the conductances when the stomata are widest open, are typically less than 0.13 mol m^{-2} s^{-1}, or, in terms of resistances, greater than 3 s cm^{-1} (Moore *et al.*, 1972, 1973; Attiwill and Clough, 1980; Ball and Cowan, unpublished; Andrews, unpublished), and maximum conductances considerably smaller than this value have been reported for the Florida species (Moore *et al.*, 1973). Maximum rates of CO^2 assimilation are also moderately low. Highest observed values appear to be about 12 μmol m^{-2} s^{-1} for *A. marina* and *R. stylosa* (Ball and Cowan, unpublished; Andrews, unpublished), while the Florida species appear to have lower assimilation rates (Moore *et al.*, 1972, 1973; Lugo *et al.*, 1975). Assimilation rates of mangrove leaves therefore appear to be roughly comparable to most trees but low compared to herbaceous plants (Larcher, 1963).

Assimilation in *A. marina* becomes light saturated at a radiation level about one-third of full sunlight (Attiwill and Clough, 1980; Ball and Cowan, unpublished). The species from Florida were observed to saturate at higher intensities. *Laguncularia racemosa*, in particular, became light saturated only at intensities approaching full sunlight (Moore, *et al.*, 1972, 1973). Differences in the response to light between sun-adapted and shade-adapted leaves of a particular species might be expected but so far no thorough analysis of this aspect has been reported. Contrary to expectations, one study which used the diurnal variation in natural sunlight as the variable light source appeared to show that the light compensation point was higher for shade leaves than for sun leaves (Attiwill and Clough, 1980).

The effect of CO_2 partial pressure on assimilation has so far been studied only in leaves of *Avicennia* (Cowan, 1978; Ball and Cowan, unpublished) and of *Rhizophora apiculata* (Andrews and Clough, unpublished). A typical C_3 type of CO_2 response was observed, with a CO_2 compensation point in both species of around 60 μl l^{-1} at 25° and a virtually linear response of assimilation to internal CO_2 partial pressure until well above the normal atmospheric level. Moore *et al.* (1972) studied the effect of temperature on the CO_2 compensation point for the three Florida species and found that it increased with temperature, ranging from about 75 μl l^{-1} at 20° to 110-140 μl l^{-1} at 35°. Andrews and Clough (unpublished) have obtained qualitatively similar results for *Rhizophora apiculata* in North Queensland.

The optimum temperature for photosynthesis by Florida mangroves was subject to seasonal variation (Moore *et al.*, 1972, 1973). *R. mangle*, in particular, showed quite marked adaptation to the seasonal growth temperature. In all cases the optimum temperatures were below 35°C, with very little or no photosynthesis occurring at 40°. A sharp decline in assimilation at temperatures above 35° has also been observed with *A. marina* (Ball and Cowan, unpublished), *R. stylosa* (Andrews, unpublished) and *R. apiculata* (Andrews and Clough, unpublished).

Inadequacies in present knowledge about mangrove photosynthetic productivity
It is clear from the foregoing that existing data, particularly gas exchange data, are restricted to a few species and from a fairly narrow range of habitats. There is an obvious necessity to broaden the data base from which our ideas about mangrove photosynthesis and respiration are derived. One very clear instance of this general deficiency is the lack of data which relate leaf gas exchange properties to position of the leaf within the canopy. For many species, both leaf angle and general leaf morphology vary according to the leaf's position in the canopy. It is reasonable to assume that aspects of the physiology of the leaf, such as its light and temperature responses, will also reflect its environment. Another clear deficiency is the lack of data relating gas exchange parameters to salinity of the substrate during growth. For instance, it would be useful to know if mangroves are able to tolerate a greater rate of water loss from their leaves if that bathing their roots is of lower salinity.

It is also desirable that there be more detailed physiological input into the models used to extrapolate from data obtained with single leaves, or small groups of leaves, to obtain estimates of photosynthesis and respiration for a whole canopy or community. The uncertainty associated with such extrapolations currently must be so great as to render their usefulness questionable. Possible refinements which might be incorporated include the likely differences in light and temperature responses of sun and shade leaves just mentioned, seasonal differences in assimilatory potential relating to changing environment and reproductive status, and effects of differences in substrate salinity on assimilatory potential.

Salt balance in relation to gas exchange
The obvious success with which mangroves grow under saline conditions

depends to a large degree on their ability to maintain a physiologically acceptable salt balance in the foliage. Salt balance in other organs is maintained at
the cellular level by regulation of ion uptake and extrusion across cell membranes. By contrast, the leaves are particularly vulnerable to salt loading
because they are the repository for salt carried upwards in the xylem as a
consequence of the inevitable evaporative loss of water from the leaves.

The flux of water and therefore of salt is an inevitable concomitant of the
uptake of CO_2 associated with photosynthesis. As photosynthate provides both
metabolic energy required for active salt transport and substrate for growth of
tissues in which salt is accumulated, it follows that some aspects of the salt
balance in mangroves involve the relationship between the flux of salt and
assimilation of CO_2 in leaves. We shall examine the significance of this relationship first in mangroves with salt glands, and secondly in those without.

For a vapour pressure difference between leaf and ambient air of 20 mb at a
leaf temperature of 30°C on a clear sunny day in North Queensland the ratio of
water transpired to carbon dioxide fixed in mangrove leaves is about 200 mmol
mol^{-1}. The concentration of chloride in xylem sap in *Aegialitis* is about 2 mmol
mol^{-1} (Atkinson *et al.*, 1967). Therefore, under the conditions specified,
approximately 0.4 mol chloride enters a leaf per mol CO_2 assimilated. If all
the chloride and photosynthate were retained in the leaf then the concentration
of chloride would become, assuming that one mol CO_2 provides substrate for
24 gm dry matter, about 17 mmol gm^{-1} dry weight. In fact the concentration of
chloride in leaves of *Aegialitis* is more than an order of magnitude smaller.
Thus it is plain that most of the salt taken up is expelled through the salt-
secreting glands, as has been confirmed from measurements of rates of secretion
by Atkinson *et al.* (1967).

It is possible to make a tentative estimate of the 'cost' of salt secretion in
terms relating to carbon fixation. We assume that secretion involves active
transfer of the chloride ion (or the associated cation) across one membrane
only, that the energy of one ATP molecule is required (see Penning de Vries,
1975), and that approximately six ATP molecules derive from the respiratory
release of one CO_2 molecule. Therefore, for our example with *Aegialitis*, the
rate of respiration associated with salt secretion is $0.4/6 = 7$ per cent of the rate
of photosynthetic carbon fixation. Clearly this calculation is highly speculative.
However, it seems more likely that the energy requirement of secretion is an
underestimate than an overestimate. Thus the figure serves to indicate that the
cost of secretion is not negligible, and might be very substantial in conditions
of high salinity and large atmospheric humidity deficits.

The salt balance in species without salt-secreting glands presents an interesting
problem of a different kind. In these species the concentration of chloride in
the xylem sap is thought to be about 0.4 mmol per mol water. Though much
less than in salt-secreting species, it is nevertheless significant in terms of
progressive salt accumulation. For example, mature exposed leaves of *Rhizophora
stylosa* were estimated, on the basis of measurements of leaf conductance,
leaf temperature, and ambient humidity, to transpire some 60 mol H_2O m^{-2}
day^{-1}. The superficial density of the leaves was about 170 g m^{-2}. Thus, if all of

the salt entered the leaves freely with the transpiration stream, and remained there, then the concentration would increase by 0.14 mmol g^{-1} day^{-1}. Within 100 days it would reach 14 mmol g^{-1}. Yet measurements revealed that the concentration was only 0.9 to 1.4 mmol g^{-1}, amongst the leaves of a given rosette (Ball and Cowan, unpublished). Similar observations were made by Atkinson et al. 1967. These seem to be inconsistent with the nearly constant dry weight of leaves with increasing age (Atkinson et al., 1967; Ball and Cowan, unpublished), with the apparent absence of increasing succulence with age of leaves on the same rosette (Ball and Cowan, unpublished) and with the lifespan of leaves in the Rhizophoraceae (6-18 months; Gill and Tomlinson, 1971; N.C. Duke, personal communication, 1980). It should be emphasised that photo-synthesis and transpiration may vary appreciably, and not necessarily in parallel, between leaves on the same shoot, depending on stomatal conductance, leaf age, angle and degree of exposure to direct sunlight. In consequence, simple comparisons between transpiration, salt loading, succulence and growth can be misleading, unless the factors outlined above are taken into considera-tion. Nevertheless, on balance it is questionable whether salt accumulation can account for all the salt reaching the leaves of species without salt-secreting glands, unless the salt concentration in the xylem is substantially lower than that reported in the literature.

Salt balance in mangrove leaves could also be maintained if salt was with-drawn from the xylem before reaching the leaves. Joshi et al. (1975) have reported relatively high salt concentrations in the stem and bark of some species of mangroves. In the roots of some plants there is evidence that Na^+ is reabsorbed from the xylem vessels by structurally-modified xylem parenchyma cells (Läuchli, 1976). However, this phenomenon has not yet been demonstrated in stems, and the possibility of such a mechanism in mangroves is therefore hypothetical at this stage.

Finally, it is possible that salt is indeed carried into the leaves at roughly the rate calculated, but that it is subsequently retranslocated along with the export of photosynthate to other tissues within the plant. Some evidence suggests that NaCl accumulated in plant leaves is immobile and not readily translocated to other organs (Flowers et al., 1977). However, it relates to a few species only, and no relevant study has been made with mangroves. Assuming, as in the previous calculations with Aegialitis, that 200 mol H_2O are transpired per mol CO_2 assimilated, and that one mol CO_2 provides substrate for 24 g plant dry matter, then it follows, with 0.4 mmol chloride per mol water taken up by the roots, that the average chloride concentration within the plant would be 3 mmol g^{-1}. In view of the uncertainties in measurements of xylem sap concentration and estimates of transpiration ratio, this figure is probably not significantly different from the chloride concentrations found in the leaves of Rhizophoraceae. It is at least possible, therefore, that these species cope with salt by distributing it more or less uniformly throughout the plant. Further comment is not justified at present; it must await a thorough study of distribution, and changes in distribution of salt amongst all the plant tissues.

Future directions

There is very little that we currently know about the physiology of mangroves that helps to explain their climatic distribution, particularly their absence from colder coastlines. Mangroves employ C_3 photosynthesis with its characteristically moderate temperature optimum and known ability to adapt to cold conditions. Furthermore, the transpirational demands on mangroves would be expected to be lower in colder maritime conditions. Thus a lower rate of sea-water desalination and/or salt secretion would be required. From what we know of their water relations, this would be beneficial to mangroves. The sensitivity of mangroves to frost may restrict the distribution of some species (Lugo and Zucca, 1977). However, this merely poses the question: 'How is it that mangroves have not been able to exploit the avenues of adaptation to frost resistance which have been available to other tree species?' Furthermore, the species diversity of mangroves seems to correlate negatively with latitude and many species disappear at quite low latitudes where frost is unknown.

Since it does not seem likely that the particular geomorphological and substrate characteristics required by mangroves are totally absent at higher latitudes, an at least partly physiological explanation for mangroves' rather unusual climatic range seems indicated. Clearly, a considerable research effort could be channelled profitably in this direction. One possibility might lie in an unusual respiratory requirement of mangrove roots. This current lack of knowledge about the physiology and metabolism of mangrove roots has been highlighted earlier. If respiration is involved in the salt-excluding mechanism, either directly in providing energy for the process or indirectly in the synthesis and maintenance of a salt-excluding membrane, the respiratory requirements of the roots may be higher than those of glycophytic trees. Since respiration in most tissues is strongly temperature dependent, mangroves may be more intolerant than glycophytes of low temperature in the root zone.

Future research also might be directed towards bringing the concept of 'physiological drought' more clearly into focus. Obviously most mangroves have an abundant supply of water at all times. The concept of 'drought' concerns the 'physiological cost' of this water. The xerophytic adaptations of the epidermis of mangrove leaves and the observed low leaf conductances attest to this cost. Research needs to be directed towards understanding its physiological basis. Is metabolic energy required by the salt-excluding and/or salt-secreting mechanisms? Alternatively, if metabolic energy is not obligatorily required in this way, is the maintenance of a large salt-excluding surface in the root tissue a major expenditure in the mangrove's energy budget? Or is the necessity to avoid a deleterious accumulation of salt in the leaves the main reason for mangroves' sparing use of water? Even in salt-excluding mangroves, the excluding mechanism does not reduce the salt concentration in the xylem sap to levels quite as low as those found in glycophytes (Scholander *et al.*, 1962) and this residual salt might accumulate in the leaves at a rate dependent on the transpiration rate.

These are just some of the more obviously outstanding problems in mangrove research awaiting the attention of physiologists. Others include the biochemistry and energy requirements of salt glands in salt-secreting species and the nature of propagule reserves and mechanisms involved in their synthesis and mobilisation.

Acknowledgments

We acknowledge the valuable contribution of workshop discussion to this paper. We are also grateful to Professor M.G. Pitman and Dr C.D. Field for critically reading the manuscript and suggesting alternative points of view.

References

Acevedo, E., E. Fereres, T.C. Hsiao and D.W. Henderson, 1979. Diurnal growth trends, water potential, and osmotic adjustment of maize and sorghum leaves in the field. *Plant Physiology* **64**, 476-80.

Atkinson, M.R., G.P. Findlay, A.B. Hope, M.G. Pitman, H.D.W. Saddler and K.R. West, 1967. Salt regulation in the mangroves *Rhizophora mucronata* Lam. and *Aegialitis annulata* R. Br. *Australian Journal Biological Sciences* **20**, 589-99.

Attiwill, P.M. and B.F. Clough, 1980. Carbon dioxide and water vapour exchange in the white mangrove. *Photosynthetica* **14**, 40-7.

Billard, B. and C.D. Field, 1973. Electrical properties of the salt gland of *Aegiceras*. *Planta* **115**, 285-96.

Bowman, H.H.M., 1921. Histological variations in *Rhizophora mangle. Pap. Michigan Acad. Sci.* **22**, 129-34.

Cardale, S. and C.D. Field, 1971. The structure of the salt gland of *Aegiceras corniculatum. Planta* **99**, 183-91.

Cardale, S. and C.D. Field, 1975. Ion transport in the salt gland of *Aegiceras*. In G.E. Walsh, S.C. Snedaker and H.J. Teas (eds.), *Proceedings of the International Symposium on Biology and Management of Mangroves*. Institute of Food and Agricultural Sciences, University of Florida, Gainsville, Florida, Vol. II, pp. 608-14.

Chapman, V.J., 1976. *Mangrove Vegetation*. J. Cramer, Vaduz, 447 pp.

Clough, B.F. and P.M. Attiwill, 1975. Nutrient cycling in a community of *Avicennia marina* in a temperate region of Australia. In G.E. Walsh, S.C. Snedaker and H.J. Teas (eds.), *Proceedings of the International Symposium on Biology and Management of Mangroves*. Institute of Food and Agricultural Sciences, University of Florida, Gainsville, Florida, Vol. I, pp. 137-46.

Connor, D.J., 1969. Growth of the grey mangrove *(Avicennia marina)* in nutrient culture. *Biotropica* **1**, 36-40.

Connor, D.J. and B.R. Tunstall, 1968. Tissue water relations for brigalow and mulga. *Australian Journal Botany* **16**, 487-90.

Cowan, I.R., 1978. Stomatal responses in mangroves. Paper presented at the Nineteenth General Meeting Australian Society Plant Physiologists, Sydney, Australia.

Cram, W.J., 1976. The regulation of nutrient uptake by cells and roots. In I.F. Wardlaw and J.B. Passioura (eds.), *Transport and Transfer Processes in Plants*. Academic Press, New York, pp. 113-24.

Flowers, T.J., P.F. Troke and A.R. Yeo, 1977. The mechanism of salt tolerance in halophytes. *Annual Review Plant Physiology* **28**, 89-121.

Gardner, W.R. and C.F. Ehlig, 1965. Physical aspects of the internal water relations of plant leaves. *Plant Physiology* **40**, 705-10.

Gill, A.M. and P.B. Tomlinson, 1971. Studies on the growth of red mangrove *(Rhizophora mangle* L.) 3. Phenology of the shoot. *Biotropica* **3**, 109-24.

Glass, A.D.M., 1976. The regulation of potassium influx into barley roots: an allosteric model. In I.F. Wardlaw and J.B. Passioura (eds.), *Transport and Transfer Processes in Plants*. Academic Press, New York, pp. 137-43.

Hellebust, J.A., 1976. Osmoregulation. *Annual Review Plant Physiology* **27**, 485-505.

Jennings, D.H., 1968. Halophytes, succulence and sodium—a unified theory. New *Phytologist* **67**, 889-911.

Joshi, G.V. 1976. *Studies in Photosynthesis in Saline Conditions.* Shivaji University Press, Kolhapur, India. 195 pp.

Joshi, G.V., M.D. Karekar, C.A. Jowda and L. Bhosale, 1974. Photosynthetic carbon metabolism and carboxlating enzymes in algae and mangrove under saline conditions. *Photosynthetica* **8**, 51-2.

Larcher, W., 1963. Die Leistungsfaigkeit der CO_2-Assimilation hoherer Pflazen unter Laboratoriumsbedingungen und am naturlich Standort. *Mitt. Floristch-soziology. Arbeitsgemeinsch,* N.F. **10**, 20-33.

Laties, G.G., 1969. Dual mechanisms of salt uptake in relation to compartmentation and long-distance transport. *Annual Review Plant Physiology* **20**, 89-116.

Lauchli, A., 1976. Symplasmic transport and ion release to the xylem. In I.F. Wardlaw and J.B. Passioura (eds), *Transport and Transfer Processes in Plants.* Academic Press New York, 101-12.

Lugo, A.E., G. Evink, M.M. Brinsan, A. Broce and S.C. Snedaker, 1975. Diurnal rates of photosynthesis, respiration and transpiration in mangrove forest of South Florida. In F.B. Golley and E. Medina (eds.), *Ecological Studies 11. Tropical Ecological Systems.* Springer-Verlag, New York, pp. 335-50.

Lugo, A.E. and C.P. Zucca, 1977. The impact of low temperature stress on mangrove structure and growth. *Tropical Ecology* **18**, 149-61.

Macnae, W., 1968. A general account of the flora of mangrove swamps and forests in the Indo-West-Pacific region. *Advances in Marine Biology* **6**, 73-270.

McMillan, C., 1974. Salt tolerance of mangroves and submerged aquatic plants. In R.J. Reimold and W.H. Queen (eds.), *Ecology of Halophytes.* Academic Press, New York, pp. 379-90.

Ministry of Conservation, Victoria, 1975. Environmental factors affecting the growth and establishment of *Avicennia marina* in Westernport Bay. In *Westernport Bay Environmental Study, 1973-1974.* Ministry for Conservation, Victoria, Australia, pp. 361-5.

Monsi, M. and T. Saeki, 1953. Über den Lichtfaktor in den Pflanzengesellschaften und seine Bedentung für Stoffproduction. *Japanese Journal Botany* **14**, 22-52.

Moore, R.T., P.C. Miller, D. Albright and L.L. Tieszen, 1972. Comparative gas exchange characteristics of three mangrove species in winter. *Photosynthetica* **6**, 387-93.

Moore, R.T., P.C. Miller, J. Ehleringer and W. Lawrence, 1973. Seasonal trends in gas exchange characteristics of three mangrove species. *Photosynthetica* **7**, 387-94.

Penning de Vries, F.W.T., 1975. The cost of maintenance processes in plant cells. *Annals of Botany* **39**, 77-92.

Pierce, W.S. and N. Higinbotham, 1970. Compartments of K^+ Na^+ and Cl^+ in *Avena* coleoptile cells. *Plant Physiology* **46**, 666-73.

Pitman, M.G., 1976. Nutrient uptake by roots and transport to the xylem: Uptake processes. In I.F. Wardlaw and J.B. Passioura (eds.), *Transport and Transfer Processes in Plants.* Academic Press, New York, pp. 85-99.

Pitman, M.G., 1977. Ion transport into the xylem. *Annual Review Plant Physiology* **28**, 71-88.

Pitman, M.G., A.C. Courtice and B. Lee, 1969. Comparison of potassium and sodium uptake by barley roots at high and low salt status. *Australian Journal Biological Sciences* **21**, 871-81.

Pitman, M.G., H.D. Pitman and W. Saddler, 1967. Active sodium and potassium transport in cells of barley roots. *Proceedings National Academy Science* **57**, 44-9.

Poljakoff-Mayber, A. and J. Gale (eds.), 1975. *Plants in Saline Environments.* Springer-Verlag, Heidelberg. 213 pp.

Rains, D.W., 1972. Salt transport by plants in relation to salinity. *Annual Review Plant Physiology* **23**, 367-88.

Rains, D.W. and E. Epstein, 1967. Preferential absorption of potassium by leaf tissue of the mangrove, *Avicennia marina:* An aspect of halophytic competence in coping with salt. *Australian Journal Biological Sciences* **20**, 847-57.

Scholander, P.F., 1968. How mangroves desalinate seawater. *Physiologia Plantarum* **21**, 251-61.

Scholander, P.F., E.D. Bradstreet, H.T. Hammel and E.A. Hemmingsen, 1966. Sap concentrations in halophytes and some other plants. *Plant Physiology* **41**, 529-32.

Scholander, P.F., H.T. Hammel, E.A. Hemmingsen, and E.D. Bradstreet, 1964. Hydrostatic pressure and osmotic potential in leaves of mangroves and some other plants. *Proceedings National Academy Science* **52**, 119-25.

Scholander, P.F., H.T. Hammel, E.A. Hemmingsen and W. Garey, 1962. Salt balance in mangroves. *Plant Physiology* **37**, 722-9.

Sidhu, S.S., 1975. Structure of epidermis and stomatal apparatus of some mangrove species. In G.E. Walsh, S.C. Snedaker and H.J. Teas (eds.), *Proceedings of the International Symposium on Biology and Management of Mangroves.* Institute of Food and Agricultural Sciences, University of Florida, Gainesville, Florida, Vol. II, pp. 569-78.

Smith, B.N. and S. Epstein, 1971. Two categories of $^{13}C/^{12}C$ raitos for higher plants. *Plant Physiology* **47**, 380-4.

Spain, A.V. and J.A. Holt, 1980. The elemental status of the foliage and branchwood of seven mangrove species from northern Queensland. CSIRO (Aust.) Division of Soils, Divisional Report No. 49.

Stern, W.L. and G.K. Voigt, 1959. Effect of salt concentration on growth of red mangrove in culture. *Botanical Gazette* **121**, 36-9.

Van Steveninck, R.F.M., W.D. Armstrong, P.D. Peters and T.A. Hall, 1976. Ultrastructural localization of ions. III. Distribution of chloride in mesophyll cells of mangrove (*Aegiceras corniculatum* Blanco). *Australian Journal Plant Physiology* **3**, 367-76.

Waisel, Y., 1972. *Biology of Halophytes.* Academic Press, New York, 395 pp.

Walsh, G.E., 1974. Mangroves: A review. In R.J. Reimold and W.H. Queen (eds.), *Ecology of Halophytes.* Academic Press, New York, pp. 51-174.

Wenkert, W., E.R. Lemon and T.R. Sinclair, 1978. Water content-potential relationships in soya bean: Changes in component potentials for mature and immature leaves under field conditions. *Annals of Botany* **42**, 195-307.

Part IV
PRIMARY PRODUCTIVITY AND TROPHIC DYNAMICS

Introduction

J.A. Redfield

Productivity, both primary and secondary, and trophic dynamics are critical areas in need of intensive research if we are to understand the functioning of mangrove ecosystems. The job is difficult because the environment is harsh, but the rewards will undoubtedly repay the effort. Some information suggests that the functioning of this interface community may be critical to the development of other nearby offshore communities. With such a potentially important ecosystem so common throughout northern Australia, it is perhaps surprising that so little is known about the ecosystems development and functioning. Research activity and results in this area are covered by the four chapters in this section.

The chapter by Clough and Attiwill discusses biomass and primary productivity as measured by leaf growth and turnover, and production of wood and roots. The summary clearly indicates many of the problems as well as exciting avenues for future research in the area. In particular, there is an almost total lack of information available from Australian mangrove forests, a situation that is being rectified. Their chapter clearly indicates the limited nature of the information available and the areas we need to investigate to understand primary production in mangrove communities. Three areas of future research are outlined: 1) How do physical and chemical factors affect primary productivity?; 2) How do seasonal variables affect the pattern of production and the allocation of photosynthetically-fixed materials for growth and turnover?; and 3) What is the relationship between canopy structure and primary production? They end with a plea for integrated research on a mangrove community concentrated at a single site.

In the second chapter in this section, Dr Bunt summarises information on litter fall in mangrove forests, concentrating on information collection in tropical north Queensland. It is, perhaps, the most satisfying chapter in this section because the work has been done primarily in Australian mangrove forests, particularly at Hinchinbrook Island. Bunt's chapter also significantly broadens our understanding of litter fall in mangrove forests in Australia. Previous studies in the Caribbean region were concentrated in a single vegetational type. Bunt's study includes 18 of 30 mangrove vegetation associations. One message coming from this chapter is the apparent similarity of litter fall figures from north Australia and southern Florida. But Bunt cautions that studies of litter production may be less than 50 per cent of the total primary production of a mangrove forest. One final exciting conclusion is that nutritional quality of litter may be related to the time and place of origin of the litter. Further work will help clarify this relationship.

Boto reviews studies on nutrient and organic fluxes in mangroves with particular reference to areas which may be contributing to such fluxes. Boto's chapter then takes us into the world of the speculative. It is perhaps surprising that so little is known about nutrient fluxes in mangrove communities, especially since they may be so important to the productivity of our shallow-water tropical estuaries. It is clear from his discussion that more work needs to be done on nutrient and organic fluxes and that the information available is of limited use in the construction of predictive models of mangrove communities. Many of the possible input/output modules have not even been investigated in any great detail, especially in tropical mangrove systems.

Finally, Redfield introduces the little that is known about trophic relationships in animals living in mangroves. This is, perhaps, the area where the least amount of information is available, especially in Australia. Yet this information is potentially vitally important to our understanding of the ecological and trophic dynamics of a wide range of communities in and near mangrove forests. Most of the information needed is still unavailable, not the least of which is a simple description of the animal species present. Redfield summarises information collected in subtropical Florida, where it appears that mangroves are detritally based systems with mangrove leaves as perhaps one of the more important food sources.

Clearly, a concentrated, persistent research program is needed to fill the gaps in our knowledge. Of the areas discussed in this section all are in need of further description and experimentation. Primary productivity, nutrient and organic dynamics remain poorly understood. The call for research to be concentrated at a single site is important as is the need for experimental work. Simultaneous with the development of research objectives and priorities, an ever mindful eye needs to be kept on the development of simulation models of these complex systems.

12

Primary Productivity of Mangroves
B.F. Clough
and
P.M. Attiwill

Introduction

Net primary production by mangroves is the difference between their gross photosynthetic carbon fixation and their respiration. It includes organic matter incorporated into tree biomass during growth, and that subsequently lost as litter or consumed by heterotrophs.

As primary producers mangroves are now thought to make a significant contribution to estuarine and inshore productivity via an energy flow pathway based on detritus (Heald, 1969; Odum, 1971). Relevant aspects of the trophic dynamics of mangrove ecosystems are considered later in this volume (Redfield). The purpose of this chapter is to assess what is known about the primary productivity of mangroves and, in an ecological context, the factors which influence that productivity. Some more general comments will also be made on methods of estimating primary production.

In the past five years a number of studies have been initiated in Australia to investigate the primary productivity of mangroves. Data has only just begun to emerge from these studies and much of the present chapter is therefore based on work carried out overseas, particularly in southern Florida. While acknowledging the contribution of this work to our knowledge of mangrove productivity it must be recognised that climatic, floristic, and other environmental and biological differences may restrict the usefulness of overseas data in assessing the productivity of Australian mangroves. Indeed, environmental and biological variation within the Australian mangroves may well be so great as to limit the extent to which data on primary production from one location in Australia can be extrapolated meaningfully to another location.

Biomass

While not itself a direct measure of the rate of primary production, biomass or standing stock is often used as the basis for making comparisons of potential productivity. Lugo and Snedaker (1974) have summarised and tabulated estimates of biomass from a range of mangrove stands in Florida, Panama, Puerto Rico and the Philippines, and Christensen (1978) has estimated biomass in a stand of *Rhizophora* in southern Thailand; these estimates are summarised here in Table 12.1. The only data available for Australian mangroves are for monospecific stands of *Avicennia* in southern Australia (Clough and Attiwill, 1975 and unpublished; Briggs, 1977); these are summarised in Table 12.2.

With the exception of the data from Panama and from the Florida Succession and Scrub communities, the spread in the published figures for above-ground and leaf biomass is not very great (Tables 12.1 and 12.2), despite

Table 12.1 Estimates of biomass for mangroves outside Australia.

Locality/type	Leaf	Above-ground	Below-ground
Panama	0.4	27.9	19.0
Puerto Rico	0.8	6.3	5.0
Philippines	1.3	4.6	—
Florida Overwash	0.7	13.0	—
	0.7	12.0	
Florida Riverine	0.4	9.8	—
	1.0	17.4	—
Florida Fringe	0.6	8.6	—
	0.6	11.8	—
	0.7	15.3	—
Florida Scrub	0.1	0.8	—
Florida Island	0.5	4.9	0.8
Florida Succession	0.2	0.8	1.4
Thailand	0.7	15.9	—

Source: The data from Panama, Puerto Rico, Philippines and Florida are taken from Lugo and Snedaker (1974) who cite the original sources; data from Thailand are from Christensen (1978). Estimates are expressed as kg m^{-2}.

Table 12.2 Estimates of biomass for mangroves in Southern Australia. Data are expressed as kg m^{-2}.

	Lane Cove[1]		Westernport Bay[2]
	Site A	Site B	
Leaves	1.5	1.2	0.6
Branchwood	(	)	6.4
	(13.0	10.0)	
Trunk	(	)	2.0
Roots	14.7	16.0	14.6
Total	29.2	27.2	23.6

1. Briggs (1977)
2. Clough and Attiwill (1975 unpublished)

the diversity of locality, climate, community structure, age and past history which the data represent. This could partly be a reflection of the more general observation that, in well-developed mangrove communities, tree size and tree density often tend to vary inversely, with consequent variations in canopy structure. On the other hand, large differences can occur in the rate of accumulation of mangrove biomass as a consequence of relatively small differences in gross photosynthesis, respiration, or the amount of carbon incorporated into durable woody materials relative to that allocated to expendable organs like leaves and propagules which account for most of the litter. Current studies in northern Queensland indicate that many of these processes are particularly responsive to regional and local variations in climate and other environmental variables.

Unlike temperate forest species where roots seldom make up more than about 20 per cent of the total biomass (see data tabulated by Ulrich *et al.*, 1974), mangroves commonly have high root/shoot ratios (Tables 12.1 and 12.2). Unfortunately, good data for root biomass in mangroves are rare, largely because of the difficulty of sampling subsurface roots quantitatively. The very considerable root biomass in mangroves suggests that they could be important in cycling organic and inorganic materials. This aspect requires detailed investigation.

Net primary production

Net primary production has been defined by Whittaker *et al.* (1975) as 'that part of the total or gross primary productivity of photosynthetic plants that remains after some of this material is used in the respiration of those plants'. The respiratory component of net primary production is thus that of the whole plant. This is r ot what is measured in gas exchange studies with leaves, and net primary produ tion does not equal gross photosynthesis minus respiration (of leaves). This po nt would not need labouring here were it not for the fact that many estimates of net primary production derived from gas exchange measurements on mangroves neglect the respiratory loss from stems and roots. These may be appreciable.

With a few exceptions (e.g. Christensen, 1978; Bunt *et al.*, 1979) net primary production in mangroves has been estimated from measurements of photosynthesis and respiration by individual leaves or small branches (e.g. Golley *et al.*, 1962; Carter *et al.*, 1973; Lugo *et al.*, 1975). A general feature of these estimates is that they are all plausible, generally falling within the range that might be expected for the majority of woody plants with the C_3-pathway of carbon fixation. However, as pointed out above, studies which include measurements of respiration of parts other than leaves are the exception rather than the rule. The data given by Lugo *et al.* (1975) for mangroves in southern Florida suggest that 4-10 per cent of gross primary production might be lost via respiration by stems or surface roots. However, it is by no means certain that gas exchange by surface roots (prop roots and pneumatophores) fully reflects the respiratory activity of the whole root system. Furthermore, account also needs to be taken of the respiratory losses by branchwood (as distinct from the trunk). Respiratory losses from the woody parts of mangroves thus might be somewhat larger than suggested by the data of Lugo *et al.* (1975).

Periphyton attached to surface roots and stems may make a small but measurable contribution to net primary production in mangrove communities. Lugo *et al.* (1975), for example, reported rates of 0.1-0.2 g C m^{-2}hr^{-1} for net photosynthesis of periphyton growing on the prop roots of *Rhizophora*.

Assimilation of carbon in photosynthesis is influenced by many factors, some of which have not been explored fully in studies of mangrove productivity. The physiology of photosynthesis in mangroves and the factors which affect it are considered elsewhere in this volume and will not be dealt with here. On a broader scale, however, characteristics of the canopy such as leaf area index, leaf inclination and the distribution of leaves within the canopy have a dominating influence on primary productivity by modifying light interception, leaf temperature and boundary layers. The model developed by Miller (1972) suggested that a leaf area index of about 2.5 was optimum for canopy photosynthesis in *Rhizophora* in southern Florida. The model also predicted higher rates of photosynthesis in canopies with steeply inclined leaves, both because of a reduction in leaf temperature and because of more efficient light interception; this prediction agrees well with the observations of Andrews and Cowan (unpublished) at Hinchinbrook Island. These kinds of interactions between net primary production and canopy ch racteristics are unlikely to be fully revealed by studies of leaf photosynthesis a one; they seem likely to be resolved only by alternative approaches such as structural modelling (e.g. Monsi, 1968).

Tidal flushing, salinity, nutrient status and perhaps other substrate characteristics also appear to influence primary production. Carter *et al.* (1973) observed marked differences in rates of photosynthesis and respiration by *Rhizophora, Avicennia* and *Laguncularia* growing in different tidal regimes and attributed this effect to differences in the salinity of surface water. They noted that the ratio gross photosynthesis/24-hour respiration initially increased with increasing surface water salinity, reaching a maximum at chloride levels of 1-13 per cent, thereafter falling with increasing salinity. These observations also appeared to be related to differences in nutrient inflows.

Direct evidence for an effect of nutrients on mangrove productivity was obtained by Onuf *et al.* (1977) who compared nutrient levels and growth on two adjacent islands near Fort Pierce in Florida, one a control island and the other which had been enriched by guano from a colony of birds. They found a significant enhancement of growth of above-ground elements of *Rhizophora* in response to enrichment. On the other hand, Clough and Attiwill (unpublished) found no evidence of an effect of long-term enrichment by sewage on tree size or canopy structure in mangroves around Darwin, despite the fact that levels of nitrogen and phosphorus in the solid and interstitial phases of the sediment and in the leaves at enriched sites were twice those at unenriched sites.

These studies are far from definitive and they raise important questions concerning the role of the physical and chemical characteristics of the substrate and of tidal flushing as determinants of both productivity and zonation in mangroves. Some of the more general aspects of these questions have been considered by Lugo and Snedaker (1974) and Lugo et al. (1975), but there is a need for more detailed studies.

There are difficulties inherent in all methods currently in use for estimating primary production in mangroves. Gas exchange measurements carried out on individual leaves or branches and on woody components cannot account for variations in canopy characteristics unless combined with detailed structural models (e.g. Monsi, 1968). Even these do not account fully for variations in boundary conditions for CO_2 exchange within the canopy. The measurement of exchange properties of whole canopies using flux-profile (Monteith, 1968) or eddy-flux-correlation (Inoue, 1968) techniques overcome many of these problems, but these are expensive and technically difficult. On the other hand, the procedure adopted by Bunt et al. (1979) of relating leaf pigments to light attenuation through the canopy offers a simple and convenient method for obtaining survey estimates of potential primary production, but may not resolve more subtle differences in production resulting from biological and environmental variation.

A major difficulty with gas exchange measurements is the uncertainty associated with extrapolating from measurements taken generally over short periods to the longer time scale needed for comparisons to be made between annual net primary production, growth and turnover. Seasonal differences in gas exchange characteristics (e.g. Moore et al., 1973) and marked seasonal variations in leaf growth and litter fall (discussed later) both imply that rates of net primary production may vary appreciably over the course of a full year. Clough and Attiwill (unpublished) attempted to account for this seasonal variation by relating photosynthesis and respiration to seasonal trends in solar radiation and temperature. They found that 67 per cent of annual net photosynthetic production occurred in spring and summer, and only 15 per cent in winter. This approach, however, might be less useful in northern Australia where seasonal variation in solar radiation and temperature is less pronounced and where rainfall follows a marked seasonal cycle.

Changes in biomass have been used extensively for estimating primary production in temperate forest systems (e.g. Madgwick, 1973; Whittaker and Marks, 1975; Attiwill, 1979). These techniques have not been widely applied to mangroves.

One of the limitations inherent in the use of such techniques is that accurate estimates of primary production require long-term studies of at least 5-10 years. Repeated destructive harvesting of the forest can be avoided by using allometric relationships between the biomass of individual components of the vegetation and some easily measured parameter like stem diameter (e.g. Attiwill, 1966). This technique was used by Clough and Attiwill (unpublished) to obtain estimates of growth of *Avicennia* in Westernport Bay.

Leaf growth and turnover
Both leaf production and leaf loss as litter have special relevance to studies of primary production by mangroves. The importance of leaf litter lies in its

contribution as a primary source of energy for consumer organisms, whereas leaf production maintains and expands photosynthetic potential and provides the basis for a continuing supply of leaf litter.

Rates of litter fall for a wide range of mangroves in southern Florida and in Puerto Rico appear to be remarkably uniform at a rate of about 700 g m^{-2} year^{-1} (Golley et al., 1962; Pool et al., 1975). At least comparable and often significantly higher rates of litter fall in northern Australia are reported elsewhere in this volume (Bunt), while Goulter and Allaway (1979) reported a rate of about 580 g m^{-2} year^{-1} for Avicennia at Sydney. A much lower rate of leaf litter fall (162 g m^{-2} year^{-1}) was recorded by Clough and Attiwill (unpublished) for Avicennia in Westernport Bay. A strongly seasonal pattern of litter fall with a peak in summer has been observed in most studies.

The higher rates of litter fall typical of better developed mangroves in warmer climates imply high rates of leaf production. Gill and Tomlinson (1971), working with Rhizophora in southern Florida, found rates of leaf production of about 1.8 leaves per shoot per month during the summer, falling to about 0.25 leaves per shoot per month over winter. Each shoot maintained a more or less constant number of 8-10 leaves (4-5 pairs), suggesting that net increments in leaf biomass within the canopy arise from the development of new shoots rather than from an increase in leaf number on existing shoots. The average leaf life was estimated to be 6-12 months. These observations are in general accord with those of Christensen and Wium-Andersen (1977) for Rhizophora in southern Thailand.

More recently, Christensen (1978) estimated total leaf production to be 556 leaves m^{-2}year^{-1}. Based on his estimated of an average ash-free dry weight of 0.69 g per leaf, we calculate annual gross leaf production to be 383 g ash-free dry weight per m^2 or, in terms of total dry weight, about 437 g m^{-2} year^{-1}. However, leaf loss as litter was calculated to be about 530 g m^{-2} year^{-1} (ash-free and excluding bud scales), indicating substantial net loss of leaf biomass from the community. By contrast, Clough and Attiwill (unpublished), working with Avicennia in Westernport Bay, estimated gross leaf production to be 324 g m^{-2} year^{-1} of which 50 per cent was lost as litter.

The strong correlation between peaks in litter fall and peaks in leaf production (Gill and Tomlinson, 1971; Clough and Attiwill, unpublished) suggest a common internal control mechanism. Gill and Tomlinson (1971) concluded that endogenous control of leaf production was expressed simply through changes in the rate of production of primordia. This is an interesting physiological problem which might be pursued profitably with species from within and outside the family Rhizophoraceae.

Production of wood and roots

Interest in wood production has generally centered on the use of mangroves in silviculture. Walsh (1974) cites a number of estimates for wood production in units of cubic feet per acre which we have not attempted to convert to more useful units. Other estimates include: 307 g m^{-2} year^{-1} for Rhizophora in Puerto Rico (Golley et al., 1962); 2000 g m^{-2} year^{-1} for Rhizophora in Thailand

(Christensen, 1978); $14g\,C\,m^{-2}\,day^{-1} \approx 10\,kg\,dry\,matter\,m^{-2}\,year^{-1}$ for *Rhizophora* in Malaysia (Noakes, cited by Walsh, 1974); $356\ g\ m^{-2}\ year^{-1}$ for *Avicennia* in Westernport Bay (Clough and Attiwill, unpublished).

We have been unable to find any estimates of root production in the literature. This is hardly surprising considering the difficulties associated with sampling and with distinguishing between living and dead roots. However, as pointed out earlier, mangrove roots would appear to have considerable potential for cycling organic and inorganic materials, and reliable methods are urgently needed for estimating growth and turnover.

Primary production budgets

Relatively few attempts have been made to construct overall budgets for primary production in which net gains and losses of biomass in different compartments (e.g. leaves, wood, roots and propagules) are balanced against net primary production. This was first attempted by Golley *et al.* (1962) who measured net photosynthesis, respiration, wood growth and export of particulate organic materials from a stand of *Rhizophora* in Puerto Rico. They found a net loss of carbon from the community. Their results, however, are difficult to interpret because the restricted time scale of the measurements (a few weeks) does not account for seasonal variations in production which, as discussed earlier, are so characteristic of mangrove productivity.

More recently, Lugo *et al.* (1975) and Lugo and Snedaker (1975) have presented more detailed data for some components of net primary production by mangroves in Rookery Bay, Florida. They found considerable variation between different mangrove communities in net photosynthesis, night-time respiration and net carbon accumulation in various parts of the forest. Respiration of above-ground components in some cases accounted for losses of up to 50 per cent of the carbon fixed in photosynthesis.

A similar approach was used by Clough and Attiwill (unpublished) to derive a preliminary carbon budget for a community of *Avicennia marina* in Westernport Bay, Victoria, where it is close to its southernmost limit. At this latitude (38°21′S) propagules are formed only every 2-3 years. The results of the study suggested a cyclic pattern of growth in which vegetative growth took place in some years and reproduction predominated in others. This cyclic pattern of growth over a period of 2-3 years appears to be related to unfavourable climatic conditions in southern Australia since *Avicennia marina* and other species of mangroves reproduce annually in northern Australia.

These studies clearly indicate the limitations of 1-2 year investigations of primary production and growth in mangroves. Longer term studies of at least 5-10 years in duration, like that of Attiwill (1979) for a eucalypt forest, are necessary to obtain reliable estimates of the overall budget for organic matter in mangroves.

One of the benefits of such studies is that they may provide initial estimates of gross root production. Based on estimates of annual net photosynthetic carbon fixation, and the growth and turnover of above-ground biomass, Clough and Attiwill (unpublished) estimated that about 15 per cent of the annual net photosynthetic production was allocated for root growth by *Avicennia marina* in Westernport Bay. This relatively small allocation to the roots suggests a very slow turnover of roots. It should be noted, however, that the reliability of such estimates depends on the accuracy with which other elements in the budget are estimated.

Another benefit of long-term studies of carbon budgets of the kind described for temperate terrestrial forests by Whittaker and Likens (1973) and Attiwill (1979) is that they may give an indication of the stage of development of mangrove forests. Whittaker (1966) has suggested that the 'biomass accumulation ratio' (BAR = the ratio of biomass to net primary production; Whittaker, 1961) can be used as an index of the stage of forest maturity. Using such an analysis, Attiwill (1977) has proposed that the growth of a forest may be regarded as a sequence of three definable stages—(i) growth of living biomass, (ii) heartwood formation, (iii) maintenance stage—and that this sequence regulates both the growth of biomass and net primary production. An analysis of mangrove biomass and productivity using a similar approach could add considerably to our knowledge of the way mangrove forests develop and of their role as primary producers in coastal regions.

Current status and future directions
We currently have very little information on the magnitude or variation in net primary production by mangroves at a national level. This kind of information is necessary, in the first instance, to put mangroves in the perspective of national patterns of productivity. It is also needed for the formulation of broad policies for management of coastal and fisheries resources. A simple technique which could provide such estimates of gross primary production has been described by Bunt *et al.* (1979), but the reliability of the technique needs to be checked against more detailed measurements at a number of sites. Combined with other simple measurements like litter fall, this technique may provide the sort of information needed to meet the objectives outlined above.

It is clear from the body of this chapter that we need a better understanding of the factors regulating primary production. Three broad areas where research is needed can be delineated. The first concerns the effect of the physical and chemical qualities of both the substrate and the water on primary production; here there are questions concerning the effect of salinity, tidal flushing, and nutrients on primary production. The second relates to the effect of temperature and other seasonal variables on the pattern of production and the allocation of photosynthetically-fixed materials for growth and turnover, particularly of leaves and roots. Thirdly, research could be directed profitably towards exploring the relationship between canopy structure and net primary production.

Our final comment concerns the need to integrate future research activities. The most useful and productive contributions to our knowledge of primary production by mangroves are likely to be those where studies of the kind suggested above are all carried out at the same site. The potential benefits of this approach have been demonstrated by the studies carried out in southern Florida. For purposes of comparison it might be desirable to establish a limited number of such sites at strategic locations along the coast.

References

Attiwill, P.M., 1966. A method of estimating crown weight in *Eucalyptus*, and some implications of relationships between crown weight and stem diameter. *Ecology* **47**, 795-804.

Attiwill, P.M., 1979. Nutrient cycling in a *Eucalyptus obliqua* (L'Herit.) forest. III. Growth, biomass, and net primary production. *Australian Journal Botany* **27**, 439-58.

Briggs, S.V., 1977. Estimates of biomass in a temperate mangrove community. *Australian Journal Ecology* **2**, 369-73.

Bunt, J.S., K.G. Boto and G. Boto, 1979. A survey method for estimating potential levels of mangrove forest primary production. *Marine Biology* **52**, 123-8.

Carter, M.R., L.A. Burns, T.R. Cavinder, K.R. Dugger, P.L. Fore, D.B. Hicks, H.L. Revells, T.W. Schmidt and R. Farley, 1973. *Ecosystems Analysis of the Big Cypress Swamp and Estuaries.* United States Environmental Protection Authority, South Florida Ecological Study, Atlanta, Georgia.

Christensen, B., 1978. Biomass and primary production of *Rhizophora apiculata* Bl. in a mangrove in southern Thailand. *Aquatic Botany* **4**, 43-52.

Christensen, B. and S. Wium-Andersen, 1977. Seasonal growth of mangrove trees in southern Thailand. I. The phenology of *Rhizophora apiculata* Bl. *Aquatic Botany* **3**, 281-6.

Clough, B.F. and P.M. Attiwill, 1975. Nutrient cycling in a community of *Avicennia marina* in a temperate region of Australia. In G.E. Walsh, S.C. Snedaker and H.J. Teas (eds.). *Proceedings of the International Symposium on Biology and Management of Mangroves.* Institute of Food and Agricultural Sciences, University of Florida, Gainesville, Florida, Vol. I, pp. 137-46.

Gill, A.M. and P.B. Tomlinson, 1971. Studies on the growth of red mangrove (*Rhizophora mangle* L.). 3. Phenology of the shoot. *Biotropica* **3**, 109-24.

Golley, F., H.T. Odum and R.F. Wilson, 1962. The structure and metabolism of a Puerto Rican red mangrove forest in May. *Ecology* **43**, 9-19.

Goulter, P.F.E. and W.G. Allaway, 1979. Litter fall and decomposition in a mangrove stand (*Avicennia marina* Forsk. (Vierh.)) in Middle Harbour, Sydney. *Australian Journal Marine and Freshwater Research* **30**, 541-6.

Heald, E.J., 1969. Production of organic detritus in a South Florida estuary. Ph.D. thesis, University of Miami.

Inoue, E., 1968. The CO_2-concentration profile within crop canopies and its significance for the productivity of plant communities. In F.E. Eckardt (ed.), *Functioning of Terrestrial Ecosystems at the Primary Production Level.* Proceedings Copenhagen Symposium. UNESCO, Paris, pp. 359-66.

Lugo, A.E. and S.C. Snedaker, 1974. The ecology of mangroves. *Annual Review Ecology and Systematics* **5**, 39-64.

Lugo, A.E. and S.C. Snedaker, 1975. Properties of a mangrove forest in southern Florida. In G.E. Walsh, S.C. Snedaker and H.J. Teas (eds.), *Proceedings of the International Symposium on Biology and Management of Mangroves.* Institute of Food and Agricultural Sciences, University of Florida, Gainesville, Florida,Vol. I, pp. 170-212.

Lugo, A.E., G. Evink, M.M. Brinson, A. Broce and S.C. Snedaker, 1975. Diurnal rates of photosynthesis, respiration and transpiration in mangrove forests in South Florida. In F.B. Golley and E. Medina (eds.), *Tropical Ecological Systems.* Springer-Verlag, New York, pp. 335-50.

Madgwick, H.A.I., 1973. Biomass and productivity models of forest canopies. In D.E. Reichle (ed.), *Analysis of Temperate Forest Ecosystems.* Springer-Verlag, New York, pp. 47-54.

Miller, P.C., 1972. Bioclimate, leaf temperature, and primary production in red mangrove canopies in South Florida. *Ecology* **53**, 22-45.

Monsi, M., 1968. Mathematical models of plant communities. In F.E. Eckardt (ed.), *Functioning of Terrestrial Ecosystems at the Primary Production Level*. Proceedings Copenhagen Symposium, UNESCO, Paris, pp. 131-49.

Monteith, J.L., 1968. Analysis of the photosynthesis and respiration of field crops from vertical fluxes of carbon dioxide. In F.E. Eckardt (ed.), *Functioning of Terrestrial Ecosystems at the Primary Production Level*. Proceedings Copenhagen Symposium, UNESCO, Paris, pp. 349-58.

Moore, R.T., P.C. Miller, J. Ehleringer and W. Lawrence, 1973. Seasonal trends in gas exchange characteristics of three mangrove species. *Photosynthetica* 7, 387-94.

Odum, W.E., 1971. Pathways of energy flow in a South Florida estuary. *University of Miami Sea Grant Technical Bulletin* 7, 162 pp.

Onuf, C.P., J.M. Teal and I. Valiela, 1977. Interactions of nutrients, plant growth and herbivory in a mangrove ecosystem. *Ecology* 58, 514-26.

Pool, D.J., A.E. Lugo and S.C. Snedaker, 1975. Litter production in mangrove forests of southern Florida and Puerto Rico. In G.E. Walsh, S.C. Snedaker, and H.T. Teas (eds.), *Proceedings of the International Symposium on Biology and Management of Mangroves*. Institute of Food and Agricultural Sciences, University of Florida, Gainesville, Florida, Vol. I, pp. 213-37.

Ulrich, B., R. Mayer and H. Heller (eds.), 1974. *Data Analysis and Data Synthesis of Forest Ecosystems. Göttinger Bodenkundliche Berichte* 30, 459 pp.

Walsh, G.E., 1974. Mangroves: A review. In R.J. Reimold and W.H. Queen (eds.), *Ecology of Halophytes*. Academic Press, New York, pp. 51-174.

Whittaker, R.H., 1961. Estimation of net primary production of forest and shrub communities. *Ecology* 42, 177-80.

Whittaker, R.H., 1966. Forest dimensions and production in the Great Smoky Mountains. *Ecology* 47, 103-21.

Whittaker, R.H. and G.E. Likens, 1973. Carbon in the biota. In G.M. Woodwell and E.V. Pecan (eds.), *Carbon in the Biosphere*. U.S. Atomic Energy Commission, Springfield, Virginia, pp. 281-302.

Whittaker, R.H. and P.L. Marks, 1975. Methods of assessing terrestrial productivity. In H. Lieth and R.H. Whittaker (eds.), *Primary Productivity of the Biosphere*. Springer-Verlag, New York, pp. 55-118.

Whittaker, R.H., G.E. Likens and H. Lieth, 1975. Scope and purpose of this volume. In H. Lieth and R.H. Whittaker (eds.), *Primary Productivity of the Biosphere*. Springer-Verlag, New York, pp. 3-5.

13
Studies of Mangrove Litter Fall in Tropical Australia
J.S. Bunt

Introduction

Mangrove forests are adapted for and restricted to the intertidal zone. They are most luxuriant and extensive along, although not limited to, tropical and subtropical coastlines. Recognition of their ecological significance and productivity, (e.g. Golley, Odum and Wilson, 1962; Odum, 1970; Heald, 1971; Pool, Lugo and Snedaker, 1974), has followed belatedly a long history of interest by natural historians and scientific specialists (Lugo and Snedaker, 1974), and stems largely from work in Florida and Puerto Rico. The communities of that region, however, are of a particular kind and of very restricted diversity. Information on the productivity of the mangroves of South-east Asia with their far greater species diversity and range of character is largely lacking. A study by Christensen (1978) in Thailand, albeit with the single species *Rhizophora apiculata*, is a notable exception.

This account pays attention to the major features of mangrove litter fall recorded at a number of sites in tropical Queensland, north-east Australia (Bunt, *et al.*, 1980). The study forms part of a long-term program aimed at developing a comprehensive understanding of mangrove ecology in this region.

Location and character of the study area

Observations were centred on Hinchinbrook Island, a heavily forested and mountainous wilderness preserve of granite character at 18°20'S and 146°10'E, close by the Australian mainland and approximately 100 km north-west of the city of Townsville (Fig. 13.1). The entire western boundary of the island is fringed with mangrove forest as is Missionary Bay at the north and certain sheltered locations on the eastern coast. Within Missionary Bay, where observations were concentrated, the mangroves are extensive and occupy a total area of approximately 50 km². Of at least 40 species of mangrove now known to occur in north-east Queensland, 27 are to be found commonly on Hinchinbrook. Because of environmental variability, there exists considerable diversity of forest character, both floristically and structurally, ranging from *Rhizophora* stands attaining heights above 20 m near the water's edge to stunted *Ceriops* thickets fringing extensive areas of uncolonised bare mud in parts of the upper intertidal zone. Other sections of the inner zone mangroves form dense canopies closely adjacent to well developed rainforest. More detailed accounts of the vegetation will be published separately.

Hinchinbrook Island lies on a sharp climatic gradient. While Townsville receives an average annual rainfall of around 1000 mm yr⁻¹, the coast immediately to the north of Hinchinbrook normally registers over 6000 mm yr⁻¹.

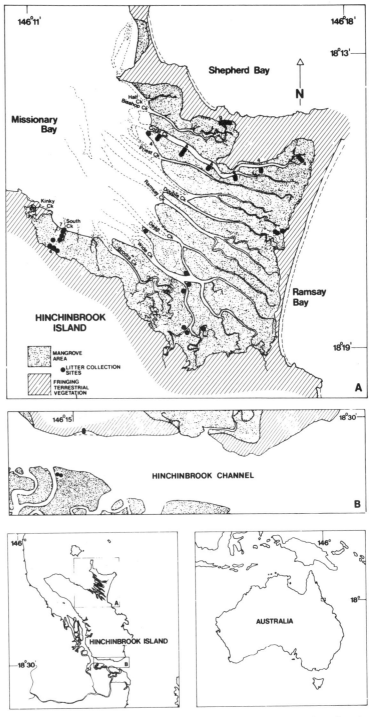

Fig. 13.1.   The location of Hinchinbrook Island and of the litter catcher sites in Missionary Bay and Hinchinbrook Channel

Incidence throughout the region is strongly biased to the summer monsoon season. Within Missionary Bay, present data records indicate that yearly figures probably range mostly between 2000 and 3000 mm yr^{-1}. On the western sectors of the embayment there exists a substantial additional freshwater influence through runoff from high island watersheds. The tidal range on this part of the coast averages around 2 m with spring tides exceeding 3 m.

Methods

Altogether, 84 litter catchers were installed, mostly at locations in Missionary Bay as shown in Fig. 13.1. Several additional catchers were placed towards the southern end of the Hinchinbrook Channel within forest types not otherwise accessible. Some catchers were attended over a period of 3 years while others were maintained for either one year or two. Observations extended over the period 1975-1978.

Each catcher was suspended above the tidal limit by cords attached to convenient trees and consisted of a stiff plastic tubing hoop 2 m^2 in area supporting an inverted cone of Sarlon mesh, the diameter of the mesh apertures being approximately 2 mm. The use of mesh provided for the ready drainage of rainwater and retained all but relatively trivial amounts of finely divided debris delivered from the canopy above. For logistic reasons, intercepted litter was recovered at monthly intervals and returned to the laboratory in plastic bags. With this procedure, some leaching losses were inevitable, especially in the wet season. The extent of loss, which must have varied from catcher to catcher, is not known but has been assumed to be relatively small. It should be recognised, however, that litter yield rates so obtained are conservative.

In the laboratory, the contents of each litter bag were sorted manually into the categories of leaves, stipules, twigs and bark, reproductive materials and remaining debris. Where possible, these categories were further separated into components by species and type, e.g. flower buds, propagules etc. The separated materials were then transferred to glacine or brown paper bags and dried to constant weight at 70°C. Representative samples were ground in a Wiley mill for subsequent elemental analysis, using a Perkin Elmer analyser for C, H and N and wet digestion for P.

Results

Of the 27 species known to be present around Hinchinbrook Island, litter data are now available for 15, either in pure stands or in mixed association. These species have been listed in Table 13.1, together with the codings used for convenience elsewhere in the chapter. The genera *Melaleuca* and *Pandanus* cannot be considered mangroves but are among a number of mangrove associates found at the tidal limit. For those more typically mangrove species not included in this account, a brief comment is necessary. *Acanthus ilicifolius* and the fern *Acrostichum* sp., although not uncommon, are ground forms and would require special techniques to be investigated as litter producers. *Aegialitis annulata, Aegiceras corniculatum* and *Osbornia octodonta* occur in the study area but are normally stunted in development and locally unimportant.

Table 13.1 Species of mangroves represented within the set of catcher sites. Coded abbreviations at right.

Avicennia marina	AVI
Bruguiera gymnorhiza	BG
B. parviflora	BP
Ceriops tagal var. *tagal* and *australis*	CT
Excoecaria agallocha	EA
Heritiera littoralis	HL
Lumnitzera littorea	LL
L. racemosa	LR
Rhizophora apiculata	RA
R. lamarckii	RL
R. stylosa	RS
Sonneratia alba	SA
Xylocarpus granatum	XG
X. australasicus	XM
Also	
Melaleuca sp.	MEL
Pandanus sp.	PAN

Bruguiera sexangula, Cynometra ramiflora var. *bijuga* and *Lumnitzera rosea*, although reasonably well developed when found, are relatively rare on Hinchinbrook. *Scyphiphora hydrophyllacea, Bruguiera exaristata* and *Rhizophora mucronata* lend themselves readily to litter recovery and are not uncommon in the study area but remain to be investigated.

The essential features of all catcher sites, including also several remote locations on Cape York, have been listed in Table 13.2.

Rates of total annual litter fall on a daily basis ranged from slightly less than 1.0-7.7 g.d.w. m^{-2}. The grand mean of litter production, based on all available data, was 2.28 g.d.w.m^{-2}d^{-1}. Such a value cannot be used reliably as a regional or even as a local guide for litter production because the numbers of catchers were not proportionally distributed according to the relative dominance of various forest types. In fact, concurrent and more extensive studies (Bunt and Williams, 1980) have indicated that a minimum of 30 mangrove vegetational types (species association groups) may be identified in the mangroves of north-east Queensland. Of these 30 groups, it emerges that litter fall data to date have been accumulated for only 18, some with better representation in the data base than others. Production figures for these vegetational types have been summarised in Table 13.3.

Notice that the set of mean production figures constitutes a rather smooth continuum and, in particular, that the ranges of values for individual vegetational associations, especially those more extensively sampled, span a good part of the total range between vegetational types. Year to year variations in litter fall (Table 13.4) appear relatively limited, at least in this time span.

	Site No.	Species	Height (m)	Topographic height (m)	Collection period
Coral Creek	1	RL	20+	0.5	20.3.75-21.5.77
	2	RS	15	0.1	17.3.75-19.6.78
	3	RS,RA,RL,CT,BG	10	1.0	"
	4	RS,RL	10	1.4	"
	5	RS,RA	15	1.0	"
	6	RS	15	0.4	18.3.75-21.5.77
	7	RL	10-15	0.9	"
	8	RL	5-10	1.2	"
	9	RL,CT	5	1.3	18.3.75-22.2.77
	10	RA	15	0.2	18.3.75-21.5.77
	11	RA,BG	10-15	0.6	"
	12	RS,RA	10-15	0.2	"
	13	RS	10-15	0.1	"
	14	RA	10-15	0.3	19.3.75-21.5.77
	15	RS,RA	10-15	0.5	"
	16	RS,RA	10-15	0.6	"
	17	RA	10-15	0.6	"
	18	RS	10-15	0.1	17.3.75-21.5.77
	19	RS	10-15	0.3	19.3.75-21.5.77
	20	RS,RA	10-15	0.6	19.3.75-21.5.77
	21	RL	10-15	1.0	"
	22	RS	10	0.2	17.3.75-18.1.77
	23	RA	10	0.3	19.3.75-19.4.77
	24	RA	10	0.6	19.3.75-21.5.77
	25	RL	10	0.9	"
Coral Creek Walkway	65	BG,RA	10-15	0.1	19.6.77-19.6.78
	66	RS,RA	10-15	0.1	"
	67	RS,RA,BG	10-15	0.1	"
	68	RS,RA,RL,BG	10-15	0.8	"
	69	RS,RA,BG,CT	10-15	0.7	"
	70	RS,BG	10-15	0.7	"
	71	RS,RA,BG	10-15	0.9	"
	72	RS,RA,BG,CT	10-15	0.8	"
	73	RS,RA,RL,CT	10-15	0.9	"
	74	RS,RA,RL,BG	10	1.0	"
	75	RA	10	1.0	"
	76	RS,RA,BG	10	1.1	"
	77	RL	5-10	1.3	"
	78	RS,RL	5-10	1.3	"
	79	RS,RL	5-10	1.3	"
	80	RS,RA	5-10	1.2	"
	81	RS,RA,RL,CT	5-10	1.2	19.6.77-19.6.78
	82	RS,RA,RL	5-10	1.2	"
Coral Creek Walkway	83	RS,RA	10-15	1.0	"
	84	RS,RA	10-15	1.0	"
	85	RS,RA,RL	10-15	1.0	"
	86	RS,RA	15	0.6	19.6.77-19.6.78
	87	RS,RA	15	0.6	"
	88	RS	15	0.6	"
Double Creek	26	BG,MEL	10-20		
	27	CT,AVI	8		
	28	CT,LR	8		
South Creek	29	BG,EA	5	2.0	16.4.75-27.3.76
	30	PAN,MEL	5-20	2.1	"
	31	LR,AVI	5	2.0	"
	32	AVI	5	2.0	"
	33	CT	5-7	1.7	16.4.75-27.5.76
	34	CT	5-7	1.6	"
	35	RS,CT	3-5	1.4	"
	36	RS,CT	3-5	1.4	"
	37	RS,BG	10	1.2	18.4.75-27.5.76
	38	RA	10-15	1.0	"
	39	RA	10-15	0.3	19.4.75-29.5.76
	40	AVI	3	0.0	16.4.75-27.5.76
Bisshop Creek	41	BG,XG,HL,MEL	5-10		20.3.75-26.5.76
	42	BG,XG,HL,MEL	5-10		"
	43	BG,XG,MEL	5-10		"
	44	LL,EA,MEL	2-3		"
	45	LL,EA,BG,MEL	2-3		20.3.75-26.5.76
	46	HL,BG,MEL	5-10		18.3.75-26.5.76
	47	XG,HL,EA,MEL	5-10		"
	48	EA,MEL	5		"
	49	EA,MEL	5		"
Hinchinbrook Channel	50	BG	10-15		17.4.75-25.5.76
	51	SA	5-10		"
	52	BP	20+		"
	53	BP,XM	20+		"
Deep Creek	54	RS	10		Oct.75-19.6.78
	55	BG,RL	10-15		"
	56	RS,RL	10		"
	57	RA	10-15		"
	58	RS	5		"
	59	RS	5		"
	60	RA	10		"
Cape York	61	RS	10-15		17.9.76-15.10.76
	62	RS,BP	10-15		"
	63	RS,BP,BG	10-15		"
	64	RA	10-15		"

Table 13.2 Details of litter catcher sites

Table 13.3 Annual means of litter fall by vegetational association arranged in order of production

Association No.	Identify- ing spp.	Main spp. in litter	No. of sites	Litter fall (g.d.w.m⁻².d⁻¹) Mean	Litter fall (g.d.w.m⁻².d⁻¹) Range
27	RA	RA	10	3.05	1.68-7.70
29	Residual grp	SA,BP, PAN*	4		2.33-3.48
11	BP,RS	BG,RS	1	2.83	
12	BG,CT	BG,RL	1	2.6i	
23	RS	RS	10	2.56	1.68-4.30
13	BG	BG	4	2.36	1.08-3.21
22	RS,RA	RS,RA	16	2.29	1.78-2.95
20	CT,AVI	CT	2	2.28	2.18-2.38
8	BG,XG	XG	4	2.21	1.46-2.94
10	BG,RA	RA	2	2.13	2.06-2.19
21	CT	CT	2	2.06	1.92-2.20
9	BR,RA,RS	RS,RA	14	2.02	1.35-3.08
25	EA,AVI	AVI	3	2.00	1.71-2.55
24	RL	RL	11	1.98	1.25-2.72
15	LL,CT,EA	LL	2	1.82	1.74-1.90
17	RL,CT	RL,CT	2	1.60	1.54-1.66
18	RS,CT	RS,CT	2	1.57	1.41-1.73
26	EA	EA(Mela- leuca†)	2	1.42	0.98-1.90

* Single sp. sites
† Adjacent forest

Table 13.4 Year to year variation in litter production for selected sites and vegetational associations

Association No.	Main spp. in litter	No. of sites	Ranges in mean daily production (g.d.w.m.⁻².d⁻¹) 1975-76	Ranges in mean daily production (g.d.w.m.⁻².d⁻¹) 1976-77
22	RS,RA	3	2.90-3.33	2.41-3.23
23	RS	4	2.36-2.42	2.45-3.34
24	RL	3	2.72-3.38	2.47-2.87
27	RA	3	2.11-7.89	2.11-6.38
17	RL,CT	1	1.36	1.40

Returning to Table 13.3; it is worth drawing attention to a trend in litter yields indicating that, in relatively pure stands of the more prominent mangrove RA>RS>BG>CT>AVI and RL. For the first four species in the sequence, the trend holds as well for maximum recorded yields as for means. It is also worth noting that, among these species, mean litter fall in mixed stands with RA as an identifying species was lower than at sites where RA was strongly dominant. On the other hand, the reverse situation held for BG whereas, with RS, CT and RL, both higher and lower mean values of litter production were recorded in mixed stands than in those where these species were predominant. It should be explained that the 'residual' vegetation group in Table 13.3 is diverse in character and, in this study, was represented by catchers in pure stands of either SA, BP or PAN, the reason why a mean litter fall figure has not been listed.

In addition to species influences, it might be expected that levels of litter fall could also respond to the effects of site location. Figure 13.2 is a regression between yields of litter over the same 12 month period from a number of sites situated at various positions above mean sea level. Notwithstanding a degree of scatter in the data, the negative influence associated with increasing topographic height in the intertidal zone is clear and significant at the $P < 0.001$ level. Further, at least for sites in Coral Creek, effectively a tidal channel, there was a clear indication that litter yields tended to increase with distance upstream from the mouth. This trend was not evident, however, in Deep Creek, a more complex waterway receiving drainage from island watersheds.

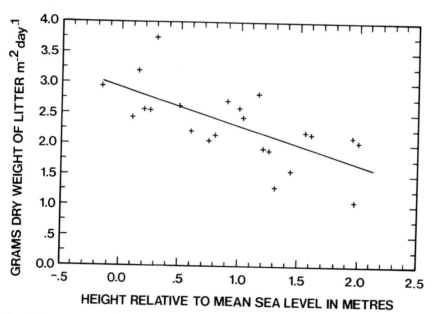

Fig. 13.2.   Relationship between total litter production and topographical height. The linear regression is given by the equation y = 2.914-0.623 x, which is significant at the P <0.001 level.

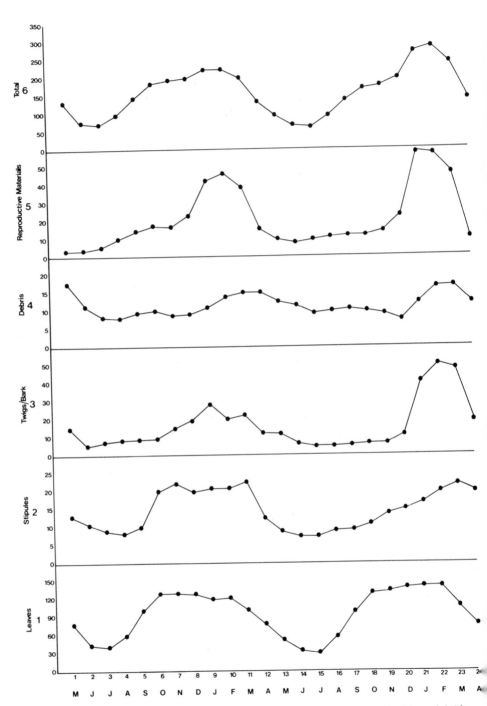

Fig. 13.3.   Three-monthly running means of litter production per catcher (dry weight) in several categories

Daily means of total litter fall based on annual yields provide no indication of possible seasonality in production or of the contribution of major litter components. To this end, Figure 13.3 displays 3-monthly running means of total litter fall and litter fall by component/catcher based on 24 sites over the period May 1975 to April 1977. The existence of pronounced seasonal patterns in production are obvious. Leaf fall reached peaks over the summer period between October and February and declined to lowest levels during June and July. Stipule fall followed a similar trend. Note, however, that the drop in this component in 1975/76 was more sharply defined than in 1976/77. The reverse was true of twig drop, the more substantial yields in 1976/77 being associated with periods of strong cyclonic weather. On the other hand, yields of residual debris were less markedly patterned in time. Reproductive materials, dominated by the propagules of *Rhizophora* and for which the term 'litter' is used for convenience, were recovered in strong peaks over the period January to March. Considered in aggregate, it will be seen that a roughly 5-fold variation in total litter fall occurred over the 24 month period of data collection with a clear and consistent summer bias.

Against this background, it is worth paying some attention now to differences in gross character of litter fall between the types of mangrove vegetation represented in the study. Data for mean annual totals (d.w.m^{-2}) by component in each of 18 vegetational associations have been set out in Table 13.5. To

Table 13.5 Total annual dry weight yield of litter by component in the vegetational associations listed

Vegetational association	Leaves	Stipules	Twigs	Debris	Reproductive tissue	Totals
8	453.66	10.68	148.83	101.51	92.01	806.69
9	465.88	65.87	43.83	52.28	110.61	738.48
10	483.27	74.61	56.66	65.22	96.37	776.15
11	511.95	71.30	114.35	69.75	265.65	1033.00
12	568.90	85.10	43.85	102.95	152.10	952.90
13	467.63	21.18	119.01	87.86	165.43	861.10
15	604.40	0.00	34.60	17.15	6.60	662.75
17	346.13	50.85	103.40	49.58	33.85	583.80
18	335.35	65.30	79.05	40.83	53.00	573.53
20	473.20	0.00	71.95	198.75	89.10	833.00
21	419.13	1.75	55.63	244.83	31.18	752.50
22	522.34	86.30	56.16	52.81	119.43	837.03
23	558.86	82.78	87.14	74.48	131.53	934.79
24	427.95	67.32	87.61	71.64	68.83	723.35
25	556.48	0.00	57.63	101.50	16.43	732.05
26	330.08	0.00	124.35	62.23	.68	517.33
27	600.39	98.52	88.82	76.15	250.89	1114.77
29	556.58	31.21	111.35	130.33	207.65	1037.11

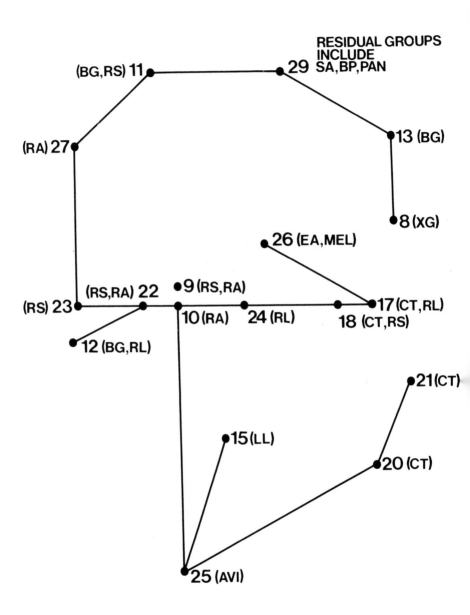

Fig. 13.4.   Minimum spanning tree showing affinities between vegetational associations based on litter yield and character. The major species in the catchers are shown in brackets. The form of the figure is explained in the text.

permit consideration of this complex data set, it has been found expedient to use classificatory techniques analogous to those described by Bunt and Williams (1980). Briefly, similarity measures were employed in generating a conventional minimum spanning 'tree' (see e.g. Burt and Williams, 1979). This 'tree' was further rearranged (Bunt and Williams, 1980) by attention to the results of the monothetic divisive strategy, DIVINF (Lance and Williams, 1968) to display as effectively as possible patterns of affinity in the data. The result is shown in Figure 13.4 in which the nodes have been identified by each of the vegetational associations connected by lines whose length is inversely proportional to affinities in litter composition and total yield. The structure of the figure is generally indicative of grouping affinities. Several features of this display deserve comment.

With sites representative of vegetational associations 9, 10 and 22 known to be closely similar and with the scale of their affinities in terms of litter yield and composition displayed in Figure 13.4, the diversity among sites from the remaining vegetational associations is readily recognisable. Note, in particular, that sites characterised by each of the major species, e.g. associations 27, 23, 24, 21 and 13, are generally well distributed on the similarity 'tree'. At the same time, anticipated affinities are reflected in the groupings shown, although species combinations, e.g. association 12, introduce unexpected relationships. The basis of the linkages and separations may be traced through careful inspection of Table 13.5. Note, for example, that sites in associations 11, 27 and 29 were highest in total litter yield but distinctive in one or other of the components stipules, twigs and bark, and residual debris. A wide spectrum of comparisons is available for exploration.

More detailed distinctions may be based on consideration of elemental composition. Representative data by species and litter component have been assembled in Tables 13.6, 13.7 and 13.8. It will be clear from Tables 13.6 and

Table 13.6 Data on the elemental composition (% dry wt.) of *Rhizophora* spp. litter components.

	No. of* samples	C mean	C range	N mean	N range	P mean	P range
Leaves							
RA	7, 10	45.72	43.90-47.84	0.49	0.37-0.59	0.036	0.020-0.058
RS	9, 8	45.72	42.43-48.60	0.34	0.20-0.60	0.046	0.032-0.057
RL	15, 12	45.02	40.33-47.87	0.36	0.25-0.58	0.028	0.024-0.033
Stipules	28	44.28	38.57-45.33	0.22	0.15-0.57		
Debris[†]	35	46.94	39.53-51.13	0.64	0.20-1.33		
Twigs	35	47.50	34.91-51.43	0.44	0.22-0.86		
Flower buds	6,124	47.40	46,68-48.20	0.56	0.34-0.74	0.033	0.007-0.103

* Samples for (C, N) and (P) respectively.
[†] Mainly flower parts.

13.7 that the nitrogen content of the litter was found to be generally low. Among the Rhizophoras, rather higher levels of nitrogen were found in flower buds and debris than in other components. Leaf stipules were poorest in nitrogen. The leaves of RA were rather richer in nitrogen than RS and RL although the nitrogen levels in individual samples in all categories showed considerable variation. Variations, by species, in the nitrogen content of leaves, nonetheless, were evident, with XA, for example, yielding approximately three times as much nitrogen/unit dry weight as the commoner species. Among the components for which data have been accumulated to date, highest levels of phosphorus were found in reproductive tissues. Note, in particular, the value for a single sample of *Avicennia* fruit (Table 13.8). As with nitrogen, however, the range of phosphorus levels in extensively sampled components was substantial. With a single exception, the leaves of BP, carbon levels were generally less than 50 per cent dry weight but generally higher than 44 per cent.

Table 13.7 Data on the C and N content (% dry wet.) of the leaves of various mangroves species

	No. of samples	C mean	C range	N mean	N range
CT	17	43.92	41.01-47.47	0.38	0.13-0.77
BG	11	46.91	42.54-53.77	0.42	0.27-0.74
LL	9	44.54	34.76-49.61	0.48	0.22-0.68
SA	12	46.10	43.37-50.57	1.04	0.77-1.37
AVI	9	47.42	45.38-50.83	0.83	0.32-1.25
BP	12	53.51	43.60-56.72	0.53	0.37-0.71
HL	10	48.74	46.01-51.33	0.80	0.58-1.10
XA	5	44.73	44.00-48.19	1.13	0.88-1.36
XG	10	45.40	42.09-48.03	0.80	0.48-1.27
EA	19	47.40	41.65-52.76	0.97	0.65-1.55

Table 13.8 Data on the content of P (% dry wt.) in reproductive tissues of various mangrove species

	No. of* samples	Flower buds	Fruit	Hypocotyls
RA	13, 2, 0	0.037 (0.007-0.103)	0.023 (0.016-0.030)	
RS	100, 0, 2	0.035 (0.008-0.073)		0.069 (0.063-0.074)
RL	11, 1, 0	0.028 (0.014-0.036)	0.067	
BG	27, 1, 3	0.024 (0.008-0.049)	0.029	0.043 (0.030-0.063)
CT	4, 3, 2	0.011 (0.007-0.017)	0.021 (0.006-0.030)	0.057 (0.048-0.067)
AVI	4, 1, 0	0.024 (0.021-0.028)	0.168	
BP	2, 2, 4	0.042 (0.036-0.047)	0.053 (0.027-0.080)	0.048 (0.027-0.060)
LL	2, 3, 0	0.007 (0.004-0.010)	0.023 (0.014-0.038)	

* Flower buds, fruit and hypocotyls respectively.

Discussion

Studies of mangrove litter production in the Caribbean region, e.g. Pool, Lugo and Snedaker (1975) cover the species *Rhizophora mangle, Avicennia germinans* and *Laguncularia racemosa*. An isolated study in South-east Asia (Thailand) by Christensen (1978) was based on the single species *Rhizophora apiculata*. The present investigations embrace 11 major species and several which are less common in 18 vegetational associations, a substantial expansion on the available data base.

Mean daily values for total litter production obtained at sites in north-east Queensland are comparable with those reported by Pool, Lugo and Snedaker (1975) for Florida and Puerto Rico. Christensen's (1978) estimate of 6.9 $g.d.w.m^{-2}d^{-1}$ net production by *R. apiculata* is compatible with litter fall in the same species in this study ranging to 7.7 $g.d.w.m^{-2}d^{-1}$. While it is encouraging and useful to find these agreements and to offer data from a wider range of species, the continuing inadequacy of the information in the South-east Asian region must be recognised. Of 30 principal vegetational associations in north-east Queensland alone, we offer data for only 18, some at least poorly represented by catcher sites.

In particular, attention has been drawn to the range of yields in those associations which were relatively well sampled. This is a reflection of the environmental range through which any single vegetational association may exist. It would be desirable to have clear indications of the spread of litter yields possible in every major association, particularly to establish whether the potential maximum yields differ between associations, an indication of possibly inherent biological and/or environmental constraints. Data on distributions, reliable means and deviations in litter yield by association, furthermore, are prerequisite for dependable resource assessment in specified areas. With present knowledge allowing more appropriate site selection, opportunities exist to clarify effectively the primary influences of vegetational type, location and associated environmental influences on rates and levels of litter fall.

The seasonal patterns of litter production observed in the mangroves of Hinchinbrook Island have been noted already in the Caribbean. It is of some interest, however, that peaks of production coincide with the warmer, wetter summer periods in each hemisphere. In this account, only the broadest attention has been paid to seasonal trends in the production of litter components or to differences in litter character between vegetational associations. In fact, more detailed treatment is warranted for the insights offered for an understanding of the autecological characteristics of individual species. This information is under consideration at the present time and will be offered for publication independently. In wider ecological perspective, it seems reasonable to expect that diversity in the physical character of the mangrove litter with differences in overall vegetational character from estuary to estuary, may well exert a substantial influence on the character of dependent food webs and on trophic dynamics. These possibilities remain to be explored.

Beyond the diversity already identified, it is necessary to recognise the potential ecological significance of differences in elemental composition between components of the litter between species, and, not least, between individual samples.

It is clear from the data presented that substantial variation in nutritional quality might be expected to be associated with litter entering detrital food chains according to time and place of origin. However, more extensive sampling and more comprehensive chemical analyses will be needed to establish the extent to which edaphic and genetic factors influence litter composition, especially among the more commonly occurring species. The data now presented justifies such an endeavour. Information of this description is needed not only for its relevance to trophic studies but also as a basis for establishing the character and extent of nutrient fluxes influencing primary production. This is particularly true for North Queensland where active tidal flushing largely prevents *in situ* recycling of primary nutrients from litter materials.

It would be unrealistic to complete this account without acknowledging that measurements of litter fall, however useful they may be, reflect only one of several components of net primary production. In this regard, Bunt *et al.,* (1979) have presented evidence which indicates that litter products may account for no more than 50 per cent of mangrove primary production. Similar conclusions have been reached for terrestrial forests (e.g. Whittaker and Woodwell, 1971). *In situ* gas exchange studies from these laboratories (Andrews and Clough, personal communication, 1979) are expected to provide more reliable estimates of the full extent of photosynthetic production in the Queensland mangrove communities. It will remain then to determine how much of that production is invested in long-lived supportive structures and how much in fine roots and root exudates. These materials may be expected to be as important, trophically, as above ground litter.

References

Bunt, J.S., K.G. Boto and G. Boto, 1979. A survey method for estimating potential levels of mangrove forest primary production. *Marine Biology* **52**, 123-28.

Bunt, J.S., N.C. Duke, K.G. Boto, R. Sim and P. Edwards, 1981. *Data on Litter Fall in Some Australian Mangroves.* AIMS Data Report (in prep.).

Bunt, J.S. and W.T. Williams, 1980. Studies in the analysis of data from Australian tidal forests (Mangroves). I. Vegetational sequences and their graphic representation. *Aust. J. Ecol.* **5**, 385-90.

Burt, R.L. and W.T. Williams, 1979. Strategy of evaluation of a collection of tropical herbaceous legumes from Brazil and Venezuela. III. The use of ordination techniques in evaluation. *Agro-Ecosystems* **5**, 135-46.

Christensen, B., 1978. Biomass and primary production of *Rhizophora apiculata* Bl. in a mangrove in southern Thailand. *Aquat. Bot.* **4**, 43-52.

Golley, F.B., H.T. Odum and R.F. Wilson, 1962. The structure and metabolism of a Puerto Rican red mangrove forest in May. *Ecology* **43**, 9-19.

Head, E.J., 1971. The production of organic detritus in a south Florida estuary. *Sea Grant Technical Bulletin* No. 6, University of Miami. 110 pp.

Lance, G.N. and W.T. Williams, 1968. Note on a new information-statistic classificatory program. *Comput. J.* **11**, 195.

Odum, W.E., 1970. Pathways of energy flow in a south Florida estuary. Ph.D. Dissert. University of Miami, Coral Gables, Fla.

Pool, D.J., A.E. Lugo and S.C. Snedaker, 1974. Litter production in mangrove forests of southern Florida and Puerto Rico. In G.E. Walsh, S.C. Snedaker and H.J. Teas (eds.), *Proceedings of the International Symposium on Biology and Management of Mangroves.* Institute of Food and Agricultural Sciences, University of Florida, Gainesville, Florida, Vol. I, pp. 213-37.

14
Nutrient and Organic Fluxes in Mangroves
K.G. Boto

Introduction

The amount of organic carbon and nitrogen exported from mangrove forests is a very important parameter of the productivity of these systems. In fact, the accumulation of such data is an essential first step in any attempt to describe the importance of mangroves in inshore ecosystems. Studies of nutrient input/output are, in turn, essential in defining factors limiting production not only of the macrophytes but also of the plankton in the waters associated with the mangroves. For example, are the mangroves an important source of inorganic nutrients supporting near-shore plankton production?

Despite the probable importance of mangroves in coastal ecosystems, especially in an area such as North Queensland, there have been few studies of either of these aspects of mangrove productivity. Some reasons for this lack of data are obvious. Mangroves are essentially tropical or subtropical plants with a marked inability to withstand cold winters. Hence, most of the developed countries with the capacity to support marine research have little or no mangrove forests on their coastlines. For example, the mangroves in the U.S.A. are virtually confined to Florida. Further north, marsh grasslands are dominant. Therefore, a great deal of research in many Northern Hemisphere countries has been devoted to studies of marsh grassland productivity, and associated factors. The small amount of research that has been carried out on mangroves is probably of limited value because of the much lower species diversity and probable lower productivity in these areas compared with the situation in Northern Australia and Papua New Guinea.

The object of this chapter, therefore, is not so much to review previous mangrove studies but more to define aspects that need attention. Results from previous studies, both on mangrove and grassland systems, will be examined as to their relevance in studies of tropical mangroves. The vast amount of research that has been done on subtropical and temperate marsh grasslands can in many cases be usefully extrapolated or at least provide a good basis for similar studies in our area of interest.

Nutrient fluxes

It is convenient to arbitrarily define and examine the various sources of nutrient inputs and outputs and to attempt estimates of the quantitative importance of each. As some of these sources are static (e.g. nitrogen fixation) and others dynamic (tidal transport) it is obvious that there will be a good deal of interaction between many of them. However, these arbitrarily chosen 'compartments' are useful as an initial approach.

Inorganic nutrients (nitrate, ammonia, phosphate, metals etc.) can enter the mangrove system via:

(a) Rainfall
(b) Freshwater runoff from surrounding land forests—including both dissolved and particulate-bound nutrients
(c) Nitrogen fixation
(d) Mineralisation (decomposition—heterotrophic conversion of organic N,P to inorganic form)
(e) Tidal borne dissolved or particulate-bound nutrients
(f) Chemical release from fixed states in soil, i.e. by changes in soil Eh and pH conditions
(g) Man-made influences, e.g. agricultural land drainage, sewage, clearing of mangrove areas etc.

The relative importance of each of these sources will now be discussed. Nutrient outputs (see later) will be treated similarly.

Rainfall
Probably the most important nutrient in rainfall is nitrogen, converted to oxides during electrical storms. Falling rain can also absorb nutrients from dust particles in the atmosphere. However, this source of nitrogen input is most likely very minor.

De Laune *et al.* (1976) have estimated that nitrogen input via rainfall into a Louisiana coastal marsh system accounts for about 8-10 kg ha^{-1}year^{-1} or 13-16 per cent of the total annual input of inorganic nitrogen through various sources. In a less heavily industrialised area, such as North Queensland, rainfall would probably account for a substantially smaller percentage of the total. In addition, estimates of the nitrate concentration in rainfall are difficult and subject to gross overestimation because of contamination. Valiela *et al.* (1978) have concluded that rain-borne particulate matter has a high C:N ratio and contributes little to nutrient enrichment of marsh areas.

Eriksson (1952) has reviewed results of nitrogen content of rainwater all over the world and computes an average input of 1-20 kg N ha^{-1}year^{-1}. The higher values were recorded for areas in close proximity to urban and agricultural activity. These results and results from many other workers (see Valiela *et al.*, 1978; Lugo and Snedaker, 1973) indicate that nutrient input into tropical mangroves via rainfall is likely to be minor, although this prediction still requires confirmation.

Freshwater input
Freshwater (excluding direct rainfall) entering marshes or mangrove forests is a potentially important source of inorganic nutrients. The nutrients may be either dissolved or adsorbed on sediments (in the case of ammonia and phosphate, for example).

Despite the probable importance of this source, little quantitative work appears to have been done. This is probably because of the difficulty in defining or measuring the total amount of freshwater input. For example Valiela *et al.* (1978) found that freshwater entered the marsh through a variety of springs and channels. The only way they could estimate the amount of freshwater input was by calculation of the amount required to reduce the salinity of the marsh water to the value as measured at low tide. However, even approximate estimates such as theirs can be very useful, as demonstrated by their results. They found that dissolved nutrient input via freshwater was seasonally dependent and that the annual totals for input of inorganic N and P were sufficient to account for the amounts required for plant growth.

We have begun a program of freshwater nutrient sampling in mangrove systems. The first major sampling trip was made at selected rivers along the Cape York coast between Thursday Island and Cooktown. These samples were taken just before the beginning of the wet season when freshwater flows were minimal.

Nutrient levels in these waters were, in general, low, and comparable with the concentrations found in the tidal waters, i.e. with total inorganic N being about 2 μg-at l^{-1} and P < 1.0 μg-at l^{-1}. These may be compared with the results of Valiela *el al.* (1978) who found inorganic N levels of generally > 50 μg-at l^{-1} and P > 5 μg-at l^{-1}. This would suggest that, at least at this time of the year, the freshwater flows into these mangrove systems are not a major supplier of dissolved nutrients. As far as nutrient input by freshwater-borne sediments is concerned, one would expect the sediments to be rich in phosphate but that most of the nitrogen would be in the nitrate form and hence be mainly dissolved. Further sampling at different times of the year will be necessary to establish fully the extent of nutrient input via freshwater flow into these systems.

Nitrogen fixation

Many marsh systems (De Laune *et al.*, 1976) and probably mangroves, are nitrogen limited. Therefore most studies of nutrient fluxes are devoted to defining sources of nitrogen input into these systems. The ability of some organisms to convert molecular nitrogen to forms available for plant growth (NH_4, NO_3), i.e. nitrogen fixation, is an obvious source and consequently has been widely studied in many ecosystems. A review of the very extensive literature on nitrogen fixation studies that have been carried out in marsh systems is quite obviously beyond the scope of this chapter. The work described by Haines *et al.* (1977) is typical of the types of studies attempted. In this study, fixation was found to occur on the marsh surface, in the soil profile to a depth of *c.* 15 cm (mainly in the dense root zone) and in *Spartina* culms. Most N fixation was attributed to blue-green algae and photosynthetic bacteria. Fixation rates showed a high seasonal dependence and typical rates measured were:

(i)   Marsh surface   30 to 600 μg N_2 m^{-2} hr^{-1}.
(ii) Soil profile   0.940 to 705 μg N_2 m^{-2} hr^{-1}.
(iii) Culms   35 to 75 μg N_2 m^{-2} hr^{-1}.

The total annual estimated input of nitrogen was about 5.8 μg N m^{-2} year^{-1}, a very significant input.

It is the author's view that many studies of nitrogen fixation yield questionable results due to the experimental methods used (i.e. acetylene reduction, and not nitrogen reduction, is usually measured) and the highly questionable extrapolations from small scale measurements to large scale land areas. These studies are more useful in defining areas of potentially high fixation. The algae and/or bacteria involved in N$_2$ fixation are unlikely to be homogeneously distributed throughout the whole of the marsh area.

Studies of nitrogen fixation in mangroves have been limited. A recent publication by Zuberer and Silver (1978) describes the relative nitrogen fixing activity of various components in mangrove communities of the Tampa Bay region (Florida, U.S.A.). Plant-free sediments gave rise to low rates of acetylene reduction (0.01 to 1.84 n mole C_2H_4 g^{-1} wet weight hr^{-1}) while plant-associated sediments gave slightly higher rates. Higher rates of acetylene reduction were associated with washed excised roots of *Rhizophora mangle, Avicennia germinans* and *Laguncularia racemosa* (15-53 n mole g^{-1} hr^{-1}).

These authors did not attempt to arrive at a precise figure for the overall contribution by nitrogen fixation but comment that 'the rates of root-associated N$_2$ fixation observed in this study are sufficient to supply much of the nitrogen requirement for plant growth in South Florida communities'. Zuberer and Silver also briefly review the limited amount of previous mangrove N-fixation studies and the reader is referred to their article for the appropriate references.

Because of the reasons outlined above, and as recognised by Zuberer and Silver (1978), it is very difficult to make quantitative predictions concerning the overall contribution by nitrogen fixation in mangroves. However, preliminary studies of North Queensland mangroves have not revealed any potential areas of high N-fixing activity (Floodgate, unpublished data; Borowitzka, unpublished data), although more intensive studies are required before we can properly evaluate the relative importance of this source of nitrogen input.

Mineralisation
In many ways, this aspect of nutrient input is more relevant to nutrient recycling, rather than an overall input/output scheme. However, the decomposition of imported organic material must be considered as a possible source of nutrient input.

In any case, there have been very few studies of rates of decomposition of organic matter in mangrove swamps (Albright, 1976). Decomposition processes have been more widely studied in marsh grasslands (Odum and Heywood, 1978; Channie and Richardson, 1978). However, these studies are of limited value as far as extrapolation to the mangrove situation is concerned. This is mainly because of the probable difference in chemical constituents and in the types of organisms involved, temperature effects etc.

Rates of decomposition of mangrove plant material (Albright, 1976) were low when the material was buried in the sediment. After a fairly rapid initial loss of weight, the decomposition slowed markedly after the first two months. Decomposition was much faster at the aerobic sediment-water interface. Tusneem and Patrick (1971) also discuss the slow nature of anaerobic decomposition in waterlogged soils. Our observations of apparently unaffected fibrous root material (in large quantities) in soil cores taken from areas that have been devoid of mangrove for years is a further indication of very slow below-ground decomposition. These results imply that the anaerobic decomposition processes are very slow and probably contribute little to nutrient recycling. Although the aerobic decomposition of leaves was quite rapid, in most mangrove situations the dynamic tidal effects cause the leaves to be exported from the system very quickly. Hence, aerobic decomposition would also be expected to contribute little to nutrient enrichment.

Tide-borne nutrients
An obvious source of nutrient input to the mangroves is the tidal water. Again, we have the situation that the nutrients may be dissolved or bound to sediment particles. Dissolved nutrients in incoming tidal waters, especially in tropical areas unaffected by agricultural or industrial activity, are generally quite low and one would expect that the water would tend to leach nutrients from the soil, rather than add them, leading to a probable net export of dissolved nutrients. This was, in fact, observed in a saltmarsh (Valiela *et al.*, 1978) where tidal dissolved nutrient export was quite large (see later). Our studies, although as yet far from complete, show low and generally constant concentrations of dissolved nutrients in mangrove creek waters throughout a tidal cycle and little or no net input or export is indicated. Figure 14.1 shows the variation of dissolved inorganic nitrogen ($NO_3 + NO_2 + NH_4$-N) during a spring tide and a neap tide. Preliminary calculations of the inorganic nitrogen exchanges for these tides show a small net export for the spring tide and a similar degree of import for the neap. If the results for each are extrapolated over a full year an annual import/export of about 17 kg N ha^{-1} year^{-1} is obtained. Although we cannot at this stage estimate whether a net input or loss occurs, even these extremes represent a very small fraction of the total nitrogen budget. From previous productivity estimates (Bunt *et al.* 1979) an annual nitrogen requirement to support plant growth of some 90-150 kg N ha^{-1} year^{-1} can be calculated. Further work needs to be done in order to evaluate any possible seasonal effect, but it seems quite reasonable at this stage to rule out dissolved nutrient input or loss via tidal exchange as a major source. Particulate-bound nutrient input, on the other hand, could be a possible major source of nitrogen (as ammonia) and phosphate. De Laune *et al.* (private communication, 1979) have recently studied this effect in a Louisiana saltmarsh system. Using a novel method to determine recent sedimentation rates (De Laune *et al.*, 1978) and from nutrient analyses of the recently deposited sediments, they estimate annual inputs of nitrogen and phosphorus to be as high as 210 kg N ha^{-1} and 16.5 kg P ha^{-1}. These are very significant rates of input and point to a similarly rich source of nutrient input in mangrove ecosystems.

This subject requires urgent study and a project is planned to begin this year.

It is anticipated that this study will contribute significantly to our understanding of nutrient cycling in mangroves.

Chemical release from soils
This mechanism of nutrient input may be of some importance in areas where tidal inundation is infrequent, i.e., where the soil will undergo considerable changes in redox potential. During periods of low tidal amplitude these soils

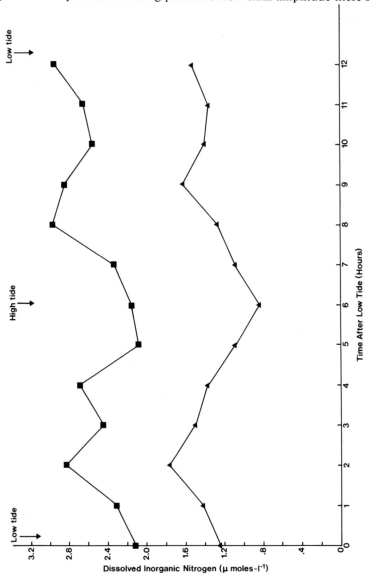

Fig. 14.1.   Variation of the concentrations of dissolved inorganic nitrogen ($NO_3 + NO_2 + NH_3$-N) with time during a spring tide (■) and a neap tide (▲) in Coral Creek, Hinchinbrook Island.

revert from a flooded, anaerobic to a partially aerobic state and consequently many nutrients, particularly manganese, iron, zinc, phosphorus and sulphur can undergo drastic chemical changes. Large changes in pH can occur due to changes in the sulphur oxidation states (Van Breemen, 1976) and the strongly acidic conditions, as well as high redox potentials, both contribute to extensive chemical mobilisation of certain nutrients. Patrick and Gotoh (1972) have studied the conversion of soil manganese under different Eh and pH conditions and showed that, in strongly acidic soils (pH <5) almost all of the soil manganese is converted to the water soluble form, even at Eh levels of $+500$ mV. At lower Eh, dissolution can occur at pH 6-8. Engler and Patrick (1975) and Sims and Patrick (1978) have studied the distribution of chemical states of micronutrient cations (Fe, Mn, Zn, Cu) under conditions of varying redox potential and pH. The metals were shown to exist in potentially water soluble forms at low redox potentials (anaerobic) but the presence of sulphide and apparently greater degree of organic chelation tended to immobilise the metals. At higher Eh levels and especially in acid conditions, the metals were much more water soluble and hence subject to leaching losses. This could result in severe losses of micro-nutrient cations from infrequently flooded areas with the cations being transported via groundwater or above ground flow (rainfall etc.) to more permanently anaerobic areas where they will be again immobilised (in exchangeable states to a large extent). The extent of nutrient mobilisation will depend on the time lag between the flooded and dry conditions. Measurements of redox potential, pH and nutrient status of such areas over extended time periods ($>$ 1 year) would be necessary before any quantitative evaluations could be made.

Man-made influences

In many areas along the North Queensland coast, the coastal rivers drain extensive sugar-cane growing areas. It is highly likely that a significant proportion of the extensive quantities of nitrogenous fertilisers used in these areas are transported, via the rivers, into the nearby mangroves. The extent to which the mangrove growth is affected by this source of nutrient input has yet to be determined, although the lush growth observed in some nearby coastal areas indicates that the effect may be significant. This artificial enhancement is probably beneficial in many ways but, from the scientific viewpoint, tends to interfere with studies of natural nutrient cycling effects. There are consequently only a few convenient study areas which could be considered to be unaffected and hence suitable for our studies.

Nutrient outputs

Nutrients can leave mangrove systems via a number of possible modes:

(a) Tidal transport of dissolved and particulate-bound nutrients and plant litter
(b) Leaching of nutrients from plants (followed by tidal export)
(c) Denitrification and volatilisation
(d) Immobilisation of inorganic nitrogen in the soil
(e) Leaching of soils by freshwater

Tidal transport

This aspect of nutrient input/output was discussed above. Valiela *et al.* (1978) have calculated the extent of dissolved nutrient export from a marsh. The amounts of nutrient exported in that particular system are highly significant, the estimated annual net outputs being 1757 kg ($NO_3 + NO_2 + NH_4$) and 136 kg PO_4-P. Unfortunately, these authors did not state the area of marshland drained by the tides so it is impossible to quote the export figures on a more significant area basis; however, the amounts involved point to large net losses of dissolved N and P via tidal transport. Most of the dissolved nutrients in tidal waters would arise from the leaching of soil nutrients, although in some cases, the nutrients leached from plants may also be significant (see below).

Leaching of nutrients, especially ammonia or nitrate, would be controlled by the degree of soil permeability. In areas where sandy soils predominate, the high permeability of the soil would allow a free exchange between the interstitial and the tidal waters and severe losses of inorganic nitrogen would occur. Conversely, in areas where the soil is impermeable, the tidal water would be far less efficient in leaching nutrients. Preliminary studies of the soils at one of our Hinchinbrook Island sites indicate that very little exchange between the tidal water an soil interstitial water takes place. This is evidence by the observation that the water tables are invariably high even at low tide and also the interstitial water salinity is significantly higher than the tidal water salinity (e.g. 45 *vs* 35 parts per thousand). This lack of free exchange of the tidal and soil water must be an important factor in nutrient conservation.

As stated above, the amount of nutrients bound to sediment particles may also be significant and the degree of net import or export will obviously be dependent on the degree of sediment accretion or erosion within the marsh/mangrove system.

Leaching of plants

Rain and dew can be responsible for large amounts of nutrient losses from plants by leaching. Tukey (1971) has extensively reviewed the qualitative and quantitative aspects of macrophyte leachates. Losses vary according to seasonal effects and plant type, but all plants are subject to some degree of leaching. Arens (1934) (quoted in Tukey, 1971) calculated that 62 kg of ash constituents, 39 kg of phosphoric acid equivalents and 5 kg CaO could be lost per hectare from sugar beet crops during 18-24 hr of rainfall. Losses of up to 80 per cent of K can also be sustained by apple trees during a similar period. The waxy nature of some mangrove leaves probably helps to protect against leaching losses to some extent, although no studies of this mechanism of nutrient loss appear to have been made. Mangroves which are salt excretors may be vulnerable to large losses. The leached nutrients may be readsorbed to some extent by soil particles but a great deal would also undergo tidal transport out of the system. In their study of nutrient fluxes in the Great Sippewissett saltmarsh, Valiela *et al.* (1978) speculate that the high NH_4^+-N output in August is due to maximum leaching removal from the marsh plants at that time. Tidal waters in contact with mangrove or marsh plants would also be expected to contribute to leaching losses. Reimold (1972) has pointed out that significant losses of phosphorus can occur in marsh grasslands via a nutrient 'pump'-leaching mechanism. *Spartina alterniflora* (cordgrass), a dominant species in many subtropical marshlands, can translocate measurable quantities of phosphorus from the sediment to the leaves. Then, with tidal inundation, an average of 9.8 mg-at P m^{-2} is released into the marsh waters. Seasonal data also indicate that the flux of phosphorus is closely linked to periods of high plant productivity.

This aspect of nutrient loss from mangrove systems does not appear to have been studied at all. In the high rainfall areas of North Queensland, for example, leaching losses may be very large unless the mangrove plants have special physiological adaptations to prevent such losses. Lugo and Snedaker (1973) reported high concentrations of various inorganics in rain percolating through a mangrove canopy. Their study appears to be the only published work on the subject of plant leachates in mangrove systems.

Denitrification and volatilisation
Losses of nitrogen from flooded, anaerobic soils can be very severe (Tusneem and Patrick, 1971) because of the process of denitrification, i.e., the microbially catalysed reactions[1]. Here, ammonia located in the anaerobic zone of the soil diffuses towards the aerobic layer, which is usually very thin. Here it can be oxidised to nitrate and diffuse back down into the anaerobic zone where it is reduced, not to ammonia, but to nitrous oxide and/or nitrogen gas which can rapidly escape from the system by diffusion.

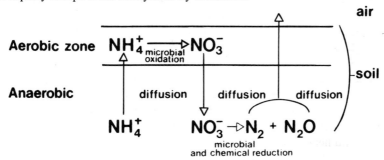

This process has been so widely studied and reviewed previously (Tusneem and Patrick, 1971) that only a few general observations will be discussed here, especially regarding the relevance of previous findings towards predicting the possible extent of this loss in mangrove systems. The process of denitrification has received a lot of attention mainly because of its agricultural implication, e.g. in rice growing. Unfortunately, while this earlier work has been useful in outlining the possible magnitude of denitrification losses (e.g. up to 60 per cent of applied ammonia can be lost), the results are of limited value because of the large amounts of applied nitrogen used in these studies. 'Swamping' the system with nitrogen to give levels many orders of magnitude greater than found in natural soils is very likely to disturb the microbial balance normally found and give rise to quite different rates of denitrification than would be found in an unamended soil. Also, most of the earlier work was in fact related to estimation of the degree of fertiliser efficiency in rice growing and only relatively recently have Patrick and co-workers made significant studies of the more fundamental aspects of denitrification. Kinetic studies (Reddy *et al.*, 1978; Phillips *et al.*, 1978) and investigations of the effects of placement and concentration of applied ammonium (Reddy and Patrick, 1977) have contributed greatly to our basic knowledge of this effect. In addition, the importance of such factors as the thickness of the aerobic layer (Patrick and Gotoh, 1974) and the effects of fluctuating anaerobic-aerobic conditions, such as occur in tidal flooding, serve as very useful bases for similar projected studies in mangrove soils.

However, even these studies have involved the addition of appreciable quantities of nitrogen. More recent studies of marsh soils where small increments of ^{15}N labelled nitrate and ammonium were added over longer time periods, i.e., more closely approximating the natural conditions in the marsh, have indicated that denitrification losses may not be nearly so severe as when relatively large additions are made over short time periods (R. Buresh and W. Patrick, personal communication, 1978). Another factor which may significantly reduce nitrogen losses in mangrove soils is the presence of considerable quantities of tannins exuded from the roots in the soil. It has been shown that tannins and other phenolic root exudates in soils can greatly inhibit nitrification, i.e. the $NH_4 \rightarrow NO_3$ conversion (Munro, 1966; Rice and Pancholy, 1973). This of course would greatly inhibit the overall denitrification reactions occurring in anaerobic systems. Recent developments in the use of ^{15}N tracers (Hauck and Bremner, 1976) have greatly facilitated studies of nitrogen conversion in soils research. We plan to carry out studies of denitrification rates in mangrove soils in the near future, with special reference to the possible effect of tannins in the conservation of nitrogen.

The burrowing activity of various mangrove fauna may significantly increase soil aeration and denitrification (M. Ball, workshop discussion). Unfortunately, this aspect of nutrient fluxes and indeed many factors related to mangrove faunal activity have received little or no attention (Milward, this volume) and hence it is impossible at this stage to give any sort of estimate of such effects. Because of this and other possible complicating effects, the reliability of extrapolation from laboratory experiments is perhaps questionable. It would appear that *in situ* measurements of denitrification rates by direct measurement of nitrogen and nitrous oxide fluxes from marsh or mangrove soils are preferable. Such measurements are logistically difficult and can be expensive as large quantities of highly enriched ^{15}N compounds would be necessary in many cases. However, interest in these types of measurements is increasing not only because of the importance of obtaining accurate nitrogen budgets in nitrogen-limited ecosystems but also due to a growing interest in natural nitrogen oxide emissions by atmospheric physicists (Galbally and Roy, 1978).

Another mechanism of nitrogen loss, ammonia volatilisation, requires brief discussion. Volatilisation can lead to severe losses in fertilised paddy fields (Vlek and Stumpe, 1978, and references therein). However, with the generally lower pH of mangrove soils (pH 6-7) and the much lower initial ammonia concentrations (1-10 ppm), one can safely predict that volatilisation losses would be insignificant.

Immobilisation in soil

Just as the decomposition or mineralisation of organic nitrogen-containing compounds is a source of inorganic nitrogen input, the immobilisation process contributes to losses of useable nitrogen, although not necessarily permanent losses. The inorganic nitrogen (NH_4^+, NO_3^-, NO_2^-) is assimilated by micro-organisms and metabolised into nitrogenous constituents of their cells. A complicating feature is that mineralisation is always necessarily accompanied by immobilisation and the two processes tend to counteract each other so far as the production of inorganic nitrogen is concerned (Tusneem and Patrick, 1971). The extent to which these processes balance each other is highly dependent on the C:N ratio of the organic material undergoing decomposition. As a general rule, those substances rich in nitrogen favour net mineralisation (net input) and those poor in nitrogen favour net immobilisation (net output).

This aspect of nitrogen fluxes in mangrove systems does not appear to have been investigated. In fact, this subject has received scant attention in anaerobic soils in general (Tusneem and Patrick, 1971).

Leaching of soils by freshwater

Rainwater or freshwater flow over mangrove soils could be expected to leach nutrients from the soils. Ammonia is the major inorganic nitrogen form in anaerobic soils and, being fixed on cation exchange sites, would not be subject to leaching by freshwater. However, partial aeration of the soils by oxygen rich water could result in some conversion to nitrate which would be subject to severe leaching losses. Phosphate is somewhat more mobile in anaerobic than in aerobic soils and could also be subject to some leaching losses (Patrick *et al.*, 1973). In high rainfall areas, these losses may be measurable, although minor, as only the surface soil is likely to be affected to any extent. This aspect of nutrient output has not been studied and should be investigated as the extent of such losses is very difficult to predict.

It is obvious that most aspects of nutrient fluxes in mangroves have received little or no attention. In the discussion above I have attempted to point out the many possible modes of nutrient input/output and to make some tentative predictions on the relative importance of each. A great deal of research is required before a realistic quantitative discussion of nutrient fluxes can be attempted.

Organic fluxes

There is a real need for reliable, quantitative data on organic fluxes from tropical mangrove systems. Again we have a situation where most studies have been devoted to subtropical marsh grasslands and, to a lesser extent, mangroves, with little or no data available for the more productive tropical

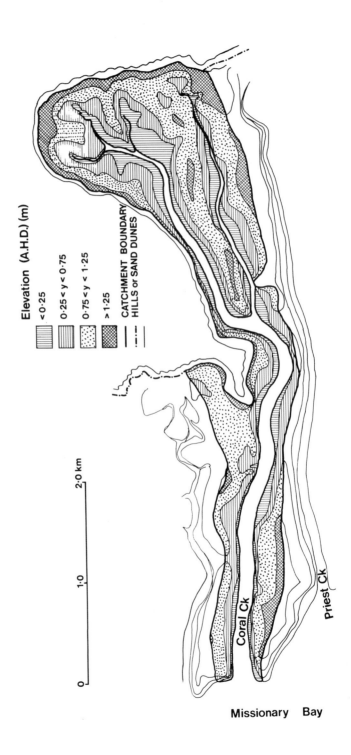

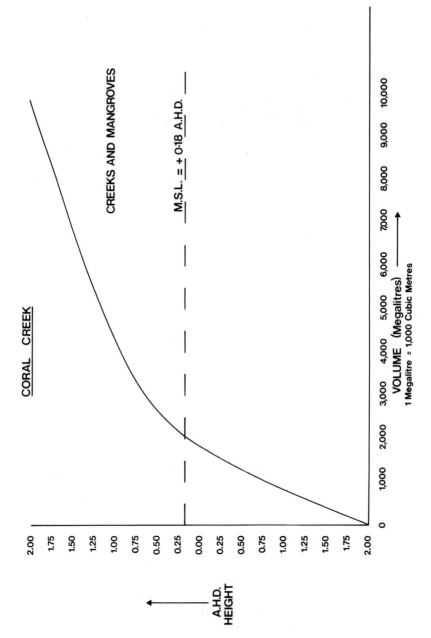

Fig. 14.2. (a) Map of Coral Creek showing topographic contours. The number shown on each contour line is the height above Australian High Datum (A.H.D.). The scale is shown on the map.

(b) The variation of water volume contained in the Coral Creek basin as a function of tide height.

The survey and volume data shown in Figure 14.2 are by courtesy of the Department of Administrative Services, Australian Government.

mangroves. Organic detritus (Odum and Heald, 1972) and dissolved organic matter (Prakash *et al*.; 1973) from mangroves are known to be important contributors to inshore food webs. In their recent evaluation of the fisheries value of tropical wetlands, Turner and May (1977) point out that shrimp productivity of wetlands generally follows the relationship $y = 159e^{-0.07x}$, where y is the shrimp yield ha^{-1} of wetlands and x is degrees latitude. In addition, the types of shrimp caught reflect the vegetational characteristics of the area. Both of these observations indicate that data obtained on organic fluxes in subtropical systems are of limited value in assessing the extent and importance of organic export in tropical mangroves. The greater species diversity in the tropics and closer proximity to the equator will affect both the total amounts and the potential food value of exported organic matter. Apart from these considerations, the amount of data available on organic fluxes in mangroves, even in the simpler subtropical systems, is limited.

Carbon is exported in the form of litter, particulate carbon and dissolved carbon. Our observations and measurements carried out over a 2 year period in a tidal creek have indicated that litter export is the most important of these. The creek drains an area of 400 ha on an average tide. From litter collection data and taking into account the observation that the new litter fall is almost totally 'flushed' from the system during each tidal cycle, we estimate that the total annual export of litter is about 3600 tonnes (dry wt) or approximately 1800 tonnes of carbon. This is equivalent to an average rate of 25 kg (dry wt) $ha^{-1}day^{-1}$. The results are slightly overestimated due to no allowance for decomposition in some infrequently flooded areas. Lugo and Snedaker (1973) have calculated the litter export rate for a mangrove forest in South Florida to be about 5 kg (dry wt) $ha^{-1}day^{-1}$. This is compared to a litter fall rate of about 14 kg (dry wt) $ha^{-1}day^{-1}$. The difference between the two values is due to their calculated decomposition rate. This estimated loss due to decomposition would be much higher than in our system in view of the fact that the litter normally resides on the soil surface for much longer periods in their case.

Our studies of particulate carbon fluxes have been carried out over thirteen tidal cycles in a 2 year period. Coral Creek, actually a tidal channel, has been extensively surveyed (by Department of Administrative Services personnel) and the topographic data (see map in Figure 14.2a) was used to calculate the basin volume-tide height relationship shown in Figure 14.2b. In this way, volume fluxes during a tidal cycle could be computed from tide height-time data, thus simplifying the logistics of the sampling exercises. By sampling over a whole tidal cycle at the mouth of the creek, the net import or export during the cycle was determined. The results are highly variable, ranging from a net export of about 10 tonnes C per cycle to a net import of about the same magnitude. This means that calculation of an average exchange per cycle is subject to large errors. However, a simple average of all the results indicates that there is a net export of 1 tonne per cycle or a rate of 5 kg C $ha^{-1}day^{-1}$. This means that the annual net export is ≤ 800 tonnes carbon. This POC export estimate is probably overestimated as the majority of tidal runs studied were greater than the annual average. Figure 14.3 shows the variation of POC fluxes

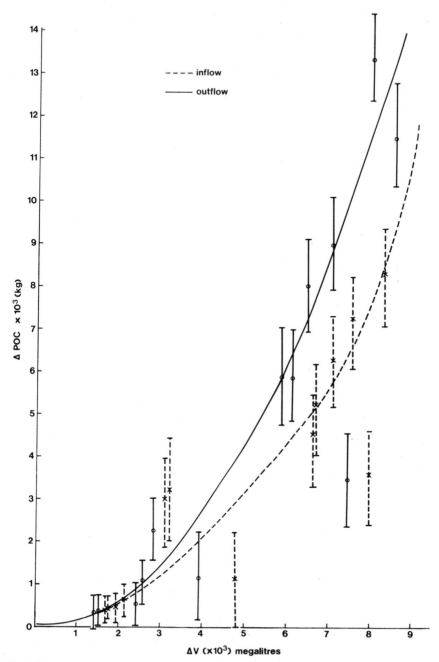

Fig. 14.3.   Quantity of particulate organic carbon imported or exported as a function of
the volume changes in the Coral Creek basin for inflow and outflow cycles of
the tides studied. The circles show the **outflow** cycle, the crosses the inflow
cycle

for the inflow and outflow periods of the tides as a function of the water volume exchange during each half-cycle. From these results, the POC exchange for an average tidal run could be determined and the annual export estimate was calculated to be 300 (± 300) tonnes. The large errors are the result of errors involved in both the water flux calculations and the difficulties in obtaining representative POC analyses because of the heterogeneity of the distribution of particulate matter. Imberger (J. Imberger, workshop discussion) has questioned the accuracy of integration techniques such as this and the present data tend to support his conclusions. In fact, the above data has been presented in some detail to illustrate this important point as many workers have used and are still using similar methods to estimate annual imports/export of carbon nutrients etc. in marsh systems (for example, see Valiela and Teal, 1979). In summary, the POC export figure of 300 tonnes per annum for our system can only be considered as a rough estimate; however, it is of some value in that it does show that litter export (1800 tonnes per annum) is the major form of particulate carbon output in the system.

Our POC export estimates can be compared with the results of Lugo and Snedaker (1973) who quote particulate carbon export rates equivalent to 12-450 kg C ha^{-1}day^{-1}. As this data is derived from only three sampling periods and is highly variable, an annual average cannot be estimated. Golley *et al.* (1962) have also reported several parameters related to a *Rhizophora mangle* forest. These authors report a particulate carbon (presumably including litter) export of 11 kg C ha^{-1}day^{-1}. Again, the uncertainty in this figure must be stressed as only two samples were used to obtain this estimate. Odum and Heald (1972) have estimated detrital export from a Florida mangrove community to be in excess of 18 kg dry wt ha^{-1}day^{-1}. or about 9 kg C ha^{-1}day^{-1}.

A comparison of our tentative estimates for a tropical mangrove system and the results obtained from the Florida and Puerto Rican mangroves indicates that the total particulate carbon export rate (including litter and small particulate matter) from the tropical system is about 1.5 to 2 times higher than from the subtropical systems. This would appear to be a very reasonable result considering the potentially higher productivity of tropical mangroves (Bunt *et al.*, 1979). It also agrees with the observations of Turner and May (1977) that the productivity of shrimp increases with decreasing latitude, if one can directly equate detritus export with shrimp productivity. There is, however, a lack of data on the food value and utilisation of detritus from mangrove systems (D. Moriarty, workshop discussion). The study by Odum and Heald (1972) on such trophic relationships is a start in this direction but, as discussed by Redfield (this volume), there are many detailed questions still to be answered before the importance of mangroves in coastal ecosystems can be properly evaluated. The C:N ratio of detrital material is an important factor influencing its value as a primary food source.

Dissolved organic (DOC) export from mangrove systems has received very little attention. Plant exudates and leachates, as well as soil-derived humic and fulvic acids, must be considered as a potentially large source of carbon export. Turner (1978) has pointed out the possible importance of macrophyte leachates as an energy source for plankton in a saltmarsh estuary, while Prakash *et al.* (1973) have demonstrated the influence of humic substances on the growth of marine phytoplankton diatoms in mangrove-influenced coastal waters. Both of these studies indicate the possible significance of dissolved carbon in inshore food webs and quantitative estimates of DOC export should receive more attention in wetlands research.

Some very preliminary data of ours have indicated the presence of fairly high dissolved carbon concentrations in a mangrove tidal channel and this appears to have a pronounced effect on the dissolved oxygen concentration and pH of the water (perhaps indirectly via enhanced bacterial activity). No attempts have been made to estimate the amount of DOC export as yet.

Summary and conclusions

Quantitative data for nutrient and organic fluxes in mangrove systems is sparse and limited in scope. As outlined above, there are many possible major mechanisms of nutrient input and output that have not been investigated at all. Lugo *et al.* (1973) have attempted to construct a predictive model of a simple mangrove community. While this appears to be a very reasonable first attempt, the amount of data available to test such a model is sparse and derived from a very limited number of samples over relatively short time periods. Also, the data available refers mainly to substantially less productive subtropical systems with little species diversity. Unfortunately, at the present state of our knowledge, we can only attempt to outline the problem and indicate those aspects which may be of greatest importance.

References

Albright, L.J., 1976. In situ degradation of mangrove tissues. *New Zealand Journal Marine Freshwater Research* **10**, 385-9.

Bunt, J.S., K.G. Boto and G. Boto, 1979. A survey method for estimating potential levels of mangrove forest primary production. *Marine Biology* **52**, 123-8.

Channie, J.P.M. and C.J. Richardson, 1978. Decomposition in northern wetlands. In R.E. Good, D.F. Whigham and R.L. Simpson (eds.), *Freshwater Wetlands. Ecological Processes and Management Potential.* Academic Press, New York, pp. 115-30.

De Laune, R.D., W.H. Patrick Jr and J.M. Brannon, 1976. *Nutrient Transformations in Louisiana Salt Marsh Soils.* Sea Grant Publication No. LSU-T-76-009. Centre for Wetlands Resources, Louisiana State University, U.S.A. 38 pp.

De Laune, R.D., W.H. Patrick Jr and R.J. Buresh, 1978. Sedimentation rates determined by $137C_s$ dating in a rapidly accreting salt marsh. *Nature (Lond.)* **275**, 532-5.

Engler, R.M. and W.H. Patrick Jr, 1975. Stability of sulfides of manganese, iron, zinc, copper and mercury in flooded and non-flooded soil. *Soil Science* **119**, 217-21.

Erikkson, E., 1952. Composition of atmospheric precipitation. 1. Nitrogen compounds. *Tellus* **4**, 215-32.

Galbally, I.E. and C.R. Roy, 1978. Loss of fixed nitrogen from soils by nitric oxide exhalation. *Nature (Lond.)* **275**, 734-5.

Golley, F., H.T. Odum and R.F. Wilson, 1962. The structure and metabolism of a Puerto Rican red mangrove forest in May. *Ecology* **43**, 9-19.

Gotoh, S. and W.H. Patrick Jr, 1972. Transformation of manganese in a waterlogged soil as affected by redox potential and pH. *Soil Science Society America Proceedings,* **36**, 738-41.

Haines, E., A. Chalmers, R. Hanson and B. Sherr, 1977. Nitrogen pools and fluxes in a Georgia salt marsh. In M. Wiley (ed.), *Estuarine Processes. Volume II. Circulation, Sediments and Transfer of Materials in the Estuary.* Academic Press, New York, pp. 241-54.

Hauck, R.D. and J.M. Bremner, 1976. Use of tracers for soil and fertiliser nitrogen research. *Advances in Agronomy* **28**, 219-66.

Lugo, A.E., M. Sell and S.C. Snedaker, 1973. *The Role of Mangrove Ecosystems: Mangrove Ecosystem Analysis.* Resource Management Systems Program, University of Florida (Gainesville), U.S.A. Report No. DI-SFEP-74-37. 62 pp.

Lugo, A.E. and S.C. Snedaker, 1973. *The Role of Mangrove Ecosystems: Properties of a Mangrove Forest in South Florida.* Resource Management Systems Program, University of Florida (Gainesville), U.S.A. Report No. DI-SFEP-74-34. 62 pp.

Munro, P.E., 1966. Inhibition of nitrite oxidisers by roots of grass. *Journal Applied Ecology* **3**, 227-9.

Odum, W.E. and E.J. Heald, 1972. Trophic analysis of an estuarine mangrove community. *Bulletin Marine Science* **22**, 671-738.

Odum, W.E. and M.A. Heywood. 1978. Decomposition of intertidal freshwater marsh plants. In R.E. Good, D.F. Whigham and R.L. Simpson (eds.), *Freshwater Wetlands. Ecological Processes and Management Potential.* Academic Press, New York, San Francisco, London, pp. 89-97.

Patrick, W.H. Jr and S. Gotoh, 1974. The role of oxygen in nitrogen loss from flooded soils. *Soil Science* **118**, 78-81.

Patrick, W.H. Jr, S. Gotoh and B.G. Williams, 1973. Strengite dissolution in flooded soils and sediments. *Science* **179**, 564-5.

Phillips, R.E., K.R. Reddy and W.H. Patrick Jr, 1978. The role of nitrate diffusion in determining the order and rate of denitrification in flooded soil. II. Theoretical analysis and interpretation. *Soil Science Society America Proceedings* **42**, 272-8.

Prakash, A., M.A. Rashid, A. Jensen and D.V. Subba Rao. 1973. Influence of humic substances on the growth of marine phytoplankton: Diatoms. *Limnology Oceanography* **18**, 516-24.

Reddy, K.R. and W.H. Patrick Jr, 1977. Effect of placement and concentration of applied NH_4^+-N on nitrogen loss from flooded soils. *Soil Science* **123**, 142-8.

Reddy, K.R., W.H. Patrick Jr and R.E. Phillips, 1978. The role of nitrate diffusion in determining the order and rate of denitrification in flooded soil. I. Experimental results. *Soil Science Society America Proceedings* **42**, 268-72.

Reimold, R.J., 1972. The movement of phosphorus through the salt marsh cordgrass, *Spartina alterniflora* Loisel. *Limnology Oceanography* **17**, 606-11.

Rice, E.L. and S.K. Pancholy, 1973. Inhibition of nitrification by climax ecosystems. II. Additional evidence and possible role of tannins. *American Journal Botany* **60**, 691-702.

Sims, J.L. and W.H. Patrick Jr, 1978. The distribution of micro-nutrient cations under conditions of varying redox potential and pH. *Soil Science Society America Proceedings* **42**, 258-62.

Tukey, H.B. Jr, 1971. Leaching of substances from plants. In T.F. Preece and C.H. Dickinson (eds.), *Ecology of Leaf Surface Micro-organisms.* Academic Press, New York, pp. 68-80.

Turner, R.E., 1978. Community plankton respiration in a salt marsh estuary and the importance of macrophyte leachates. *Limnology Oceanography* **23**, 442-51.

Turner, R.E. and L.N. May, 1981. An alternative evaluation of the fisheries potential of tropical and subtropical wetlands. *Cectas del IV Simposium Internacional de Ecologic Tropical.* University of Panama, Panama City. Tomo III, pp 836-52.

Tusneem, M.E. and W.H. Patrick Jr, 1971. *Nitrogen Transformation in Waterlogged Soil.* Bulletin No. 657. Department of Agronomy, Louisiana State Univ., U.S.A. 75 pp.

Valiela, I., J.M. Teal, S. Volkmann, D. Shafer and E.J. Carpenter, 1978. Nutrient and particulate fluxes in a salt marsh ecosystem: Tidal exchanges and inputs by precipitation and groundwater. *Limnology Oceanography.* **23**, 798-812.

Valiela, I. and J.M. Teal, 1979. The nitrogen budget of salt marsh ecosystem. *Nature (Lond.)* **280**, 652-6.

Van Breeman, N., 1976. Genesis and solution chemistry of acid sulfate soils in Thailand. *Verslagen van Landbouwkundige Onderzoekingen* (Agric. Res. Rep.), **848**, 1-263.

Vlek, P.L.G. and J.M. Stumpe, 1978. Effects of solution chemistry and environmental conditions on ammonia volatilisation from aqueous systems. *Soil Science Society America Proceedings* **42**, 416-21.

Zuberer, D.A. and W.S. Silver, 1978. Biological dinitrogen fixation (acetylene reduction) associated with Florida mangroves. *Applied Environmental Microbiology* **35**, 567-75.

15

Trophic Relationships in Mangrove Communities

J.A. Redfield

Mangrove communities function as a solar-powered, tidal-subsidised, pulse stabilised ecosystem (Odum, 1974). Production is high with the 'cost-of-adaptation' to the 'harsh' environment outweighed by the tidal payment. Translation of the high production of mangroves into the energy economy of the system has not often been examined and our understanding of the trophic structure and food webs in mangrove ecosystems is poor (Lugo and Snedaker, 1974), especially in Australia. This lack of information should not be taken as a lack of importance of mangrove communities in coastal dynamics. Decisions are made daily which potentially affect mangrove ecosystem energy dynamics and which could have far-reaching implications for the future viability not only of mangroves but also of offshore fisheries and fringing ecosystems as well. Because trophic relationships in mangroves are important to a large number of fisheries and fringing ecosystems, because of the paucity of information available, and considering the potential differences between the species-rich Australian mangrove forest fauna and the relatively simple subtropical American mangrove systems previously studied (Malley, 1978), a thorough understanding of trophic relationships in Australian mangrove communities is essential for the proper management of this system.

As a first step in understanding trophic dynamics of mangrove ecosystems, we must gain an appreciation for their faunal species composition. The species present, their spatial and temporal abundances and productivity must be understood on both the macro- and micro-scale. As well, information on the short-term and seasonal shifts in abundance, utilisation by the various life history stages, and the infauna and pelagic components of the community should lead to an evaluation of the dependence of each species on the community, whether that dependence be direct or indirect.

Mangrove forests, like other intertidal vegetation types, offer a unique intertidal habitat for community development. The complex habitat structure results in Australian mangroves harbouring an enormous variety of marine and terrestrial animals (Macnae, 1968). Although some progress in defining the animal species present in mangrove communities in the Indo-West Pacific has already been made, and some rather impressive lists can be compiled which show an active utilisation of mangroves (Liem and Haines, 1977; Milward, this volume), little is known of seasonal or spatial distribution and abundance. In Australia we have an additional particularly perplexing problem: the system is species rich yet our understanding of the taxonomic structure is particularly poor. Clearly, studies on the systematics of the system are in need of dedicated, long-term research at all levels.

Trophic dynamics studies also require an understanding of the food and feeding roles of each species in the community. Analyses of these relationships involve an examination of gut contents (e.g. Beumer, 1978; Malley, 1978; Odum and Heald, 1972), direct observation of feeding *in situ,* and a study of utilisation by different life-history stages. In aquatic communities it is common for species to have mixed-mode feeding, i.e. the diet of many species changes seasonally, tidally, or with age of the individual. Variations, in both space and time, in feeding habits of mangrove species complicate trophic studies and make it necessary to allocate an enormous amount of effort to this work. For example, Livingstone (pers. comm.) found it necessary to analyse over 100,000 individual fish from a Florida estuary over an 8-year period before he was able to comprehend the trophic relationships of that system.

Odum and Heald (1975) examined the food webs in an estuarine mangrove community (*Rhizophora mangle*) in south Florida, U.S.A. Their study is one of the few detailed accounts of food webs available for mangroves. The mangrove community they studied was characterised by a large vascular plant production and a low algal production. Most of the mangrove leaf and stem production was not directly consumed but became part of the decaying matter in the forest floor, similar to a young terrestrial forest. Detritus formed the basic component in the primary marine consumers' diet. Among the herbivore and mixed-herbivore species recognised by Odum and Heald (1975), 20 per cent material in the gut was classed as detritus of vascular plant origin. They concluded that mangrove leaf detritus was one of the most important elements in the food web.

Research needed in trophic studies also includes a descriptive-experimental study of the functional components of the mangrove ecosystem, not only the food webs in mangroves and the major links involved but also adaptability of the species within the food web. Competitive relationships, physiological tolerances and flexibilities, productivity, energy and nutrient transfers between compartments, and an understanding of the variability of the species studied, are all in critical need of attention. As well, the controlling links within the community will need to be determined. Is the trophic structure of mangrove communities controlled by physical factors, primary production, competition, predation, or other factors? What are the consequences of restructuring the trophic components within the community? Are relationships in the mangrove communities fixed by evolutionary processes? This study of the control points and keystone species (Krebs, 1978) in community and trophic dynamics is likely to prove of great theoretical and practical interest and will undoubtedly aid in the management of these communities. Experiments needed in this phase of research should be field exclosures and enclosures (Davies *et al.*, 1975), selective removals (Paine, 1966), and other manipulations of relationships within the feeding community.

As an example of one type of experiment, Onuf *et al.* (1977) studied the effects of nutrient enrichment on plant growth and utilisation in a mangrove community (*Rhizophora mangle*) in southern Florida, U.S.A. A high-nutrient site was in an area where guano was deposited by a large bird rookery and a control, low-nutrient site was located nearby outside the rookery. The mangroves of the high-nutrient area produced more flowers, leaves, and branches, at least for some of the year, than on the control area. In addition, the leaves produced on the high-nutrient site had a higher level of nitrogen and presumably were of a higher nutritional quality than those on the low-nutrient site.

The primary response of plants to the addition of nutrients was accompanied by an apparent population increase on the high-nutrient area by four species of resident herbivorous insects (three larval lepidopterans and one coleopteran) and two species (both larval lepidopterans) of invaders from the surrounding forest. These insects cropped the mangrove leaves and seedlings and, owing to their feeding in the high-nutrient area, caused the final standing crop of leaves to be no higher than in the low-nutrient area nearby. More than 25 per cent of potential leaf production was consumed by herbivorous insects in the high-nutrient site as compared with less than 10 per cent in the low-nutrient area. Additionally, seedlings on the nutrient enriched area were more severely attacked by a scolytid beetle than on the low-nutrient area. Higher order responses in the food web were not investigated but it seems reasonable that there may have been some. For example, increased cropping by insects may have increased the detrital load in the sediments and thereby increased bacterial density, or the density of predatory insects or birds may have increased.

In another study, de Silva (1975) reported on the structure of food webs in mangrove communities in Vietnam. As a result of the war in Vietnam in the late 1960s and early 1970s, large tracts of mangroves were defoliated and destroyed. These disturbances were not suitably controlled experiments, but the results of the food web analysis in defoliated and non-defoliated communities suggests that for nektonic fish at least, the major effect of defoliation was to simplify the food web.

Another important area needing attention in the study of trophic dynamics in mangrove communities is an experimental-theoretical assessment of the stability and resilience (Holling, 1973) of feeding relationships in mangroves. The stability of mangrove feeding relationships must be known if we are to predict the potential impact of foreshore development. The study of the trophic aspects of mangrove communities should lead to an evaluation of the relationship between mangroves, important fisheries, and maintenance of other offshore communities. For example, one of the critical features in the study of food webs in mangroves may be the transport of energy out of the system. This is a difficult but important component to measure since the amount of production extracted from a mangrove community may in fact be an important consideration for understanding offshore community dynamics like coral reef development, fisheries population dynamics, and other important ecological phenomena.

The picture emerging from limited data seems to be that mangrove ecosystems operate as an energy trap, excess energy being utilised by temporary residents. This produces a large energy surplus in mangroves and results in an energy drain later in the year. For example, northern Australian mangrove fringed estuaries support juvenile populations of some abundant species such as banana prawns (*Penaeus merguiensis*) and greasyback prawns (*Metapenaeus insolitus* and *M. eboracensis*). These prawns grow from postlarvae to sub-adults in mangrove fringed estuaries and then migrate out of these estuaries in huge numbers into offshore marine communities, carrying with them much of the energy assimilated in the proximity of the mangrove community. Clearly migratory animals such as these remove a large portion of the assimilated energy of a mangrove ecosystem and fuel other communities elsewhere.

In addition to this active transport of energy away from the mangrove estuaries there is a large passive transport of material out of the system. Mangrove leaves, twigs, and seeds are flushed out of the rivers and estuaries during flooding in the wet season and can be found as far as 40 nautical miles to sea (personal observation). The effect of this flushing of energy to offshore areas is not known. But mangrove forests may be a keystone community, responsible for processing the fuel to keep the machinery of other offshore communities functioning.

Mangrove communities are clearly important to the stability and maintenance of many important marine systems of northern Australia. A thorough understanding of the trophic functioning in these systems will help to unravel many of these functional complexities of the systems. This, in turn, will give us greater understanding of the role mangroves play in the ecology of northern Australia's fringing zone ecology.

References

Beumer, J.P., 1978. Feeding ecology of four fishes from a mangrove creek in north Queensland, Australia. *Journal of Fish Biology* 12, 475-90.

Davies, J.M., J.C. Gamble, and J.H. Steele, 1975. Preliminary studies with a large plastic enclosure. In L.E. Cronin (ed.), *Estuarine Research*. Academic Press, New York, Vol. I, pp. 251-64.

de Silva, D.P., 1975. Nektonic food webs in estuaries. In L.E. Cronin (ed.), *Estuarine Research*. Academic Press, New York, Vol. I, pp. 420-77.

Holling, C.S., 1973. Resilience and stability of ecological systems. *Annual Review of Ecology and Systematics* 4, 1-24.

Krebs, C.J., 1978. *Ecology*. 2nd ed. Harper and Row, London.

Liem, D.S., and A.K. Haines, 1977. The ecological significance and economic importance of the mangrove and estuarine communities of the Gulf Province, Papua New Guinea. *Purari River (Wabo) Hydroelectric Scheme Environmental Studies*. Papua New Guinea Government, Office of the Environment and Conservation, Vol. 3. 35 pp.

Lugo, A.E. and S.C. Snedaker, 1974. The ecology of mangroves. *Annual Review of Ecology and Systematics* 5, 39-64.

Macnae, W., 1968. A general account of the fauna and flora of mangrove swamps and forests in the Indo-West Pacific region. *Advances in Marine Biology* 6, 73-270.

Malley, D.F., 1978. Degradation of mangrove leaf litter by the tropical sesarmid crab *Chiromanthes onychophorum*. *Marine Biology* 49, 377-86.

Odum, E.P., 1974. Halophytes, energetics and ecosystems. In R.J. Reimold and W.H. Queen (eds.), *Ecology of Halophytes*. Academic Press, New York, pp. 599-602.

Odum, W.E. and E.J. Heald, 1972. Trophic analysis of an estuarine mangrove community. *Bulletin of Marine Science* 22, 671-738.

Odum, W.E., and E.J. Heald, 1975. The detritus-based mangrove community. In L.E. Cronin (ed.), *Estuarine Research*. Academic Press, New York, Vol. I, pp. 265-86.

Onuf, C.P., J.M. Teal, and I. Valiela, 1977. Interactions of nutrients, plant growth and herbivory in a mangrove ecosystem. *Ecology* 58, 514-26.

Paine, R.T., 1966. Food web complexity and species diversity. *American Naturalist* 100, 65-76.

Part V

RESOURCE STABILITY AND MANAGEMENT

Introduction

B.F. CLOUGH

Although the importance of mangroves as a coastal resource is widely recognised, the particular significance attached to them is often a matter of individual perspective. To some, the importance of mangroves lies in their contribution to coastal fisheries, in their role of stabilising shorelines and enhancing water quality in coastal streams and estuaries, or in their potential as a forest resource to be developed and managed for sustained yields of timber or other forest products. Others see mangroves as a unique ecological niche, a habitat for a diverse variety of insects, birds, small animals and fish. For yet others, mangroves represent an unusual group of plants which have become adapted to withstand inundation by saltwater, a genetic resource which could be used in future years by plant geneticists as a gene pool for developing new types of salt-tolerant plants. All are valid and important points of view. It is not surprising then, to find t at goals and strategies for the management, conservation and utilisation of n angroves are often as diverse as the reasons for which mangroves themselves are valued.

Irrespective of their goal, management strategies must be based on a thorough working knowledge of the way mangrove systems function, and of the factors, both natural and man-induced, which influence their stability and function. The first chapter in this section deals with the stability of mangrove systems, bridging the gap between their biological and ecological attributes, discussed by earlier contributors, and the two later chapters dealing with their utilisation, conservation and management. In it, Bird and Barson discuss the concepts of zonation and stability in relation to natural and man-induced changes of the coastal environment.

The remaining two chapters in this section consider the conservation, management and utilisation of mangroves from different geographic perspectives. Both trace the history of exploitation of mangrove wetlands in Australia and both discuss the present state of coastal management and planning guidelines with particular reference to mangroves. Neither offer radical proposals for conservation and management. Rather, the authors draw attention to the deficiencies of present management guidelines and suggest a general framework within which to develop more effective goals and strategies for management.

Goals for the management of mangrove systems, and the strategies for achieving them, will be a continuing source for debate in Australia in the years ahead. The three contributions to this section provide a valuable and positive contribution to this debate.

16

Stability of Mangrove Systems
E.C.F. Bird and M.M. Barson

Introduction

Mangroves occupy the upper part of the intertidal zone in low-wave energy environments around the Australian coast, particularly on the shores of estuaries, tidal lagoons, and sheltered embayments. Typically the substrate is muddy, particularly in areas of active accretion, but mangroves can also occupy sandy and even rocky habitats. Where mangroves are present, the transverse profile of the coast often takes the form of a depositional terrace with a slight seaward slope that steepens at the outer edge; in places the outer margin has been cut back to form a minor cliff exposing mangrove roots and substrate sediments.

A mangrove system can be considered stable as long as it occupies the same area of intertidal land, and unstable if its boundaries are advancing or retreating. The seaward margins of a mangrove system often show evidence of advance, indicated by an abundance of seedlings and young plants, a sustained advance being indicated by an unbroken rising canopy of mangroves that increase in age and size landward. On the other hand, a sharp margin in which exposed trunks of mature mangroves are undermined and falling on to the shore is evidence that recession is taking place.

Where the seaward margin is advancing there is often a compensating migration of the inner margin as the result of mangrove die-back and replacement either by other forms of vegetation, such as rainforest or saltmarsh, or by unvegetated, usually hypersaline plains, so that the mangrove zone as a whole is moving seaward. Occasionally the reverse is the case, with young mangroves spreading landwards from the inner margin as the outer mangroves are cut back. Corresponding changes occur within a mangrove zone where tidal channels are migrating laterally, undermining mangroves on one bank and depositing sediment that is colonised by mangrove seedlings on the other.

Such changes can sometimes be detected by comparing the pattern and extent of mangroves on historical maps and air photographs with the modern outlines, but vagaries of scale, map accuracy, and interpretation rarely permit the determination of horizontal changes of less than a metre, and a more satisfactory method is to institute monitoring of changes in relation to inserted markers on and around mangrove boundaries. Such studies should be continued over several years to build up a picture of trends of change that can be related to physiographic and ecological factors.

There have been few attempts to measure such changes (Chapman, 1976). In Cairns Bay, Bird (1972a, b) traced the advance of the seaward margin of mangroves by comparing air photographs taken in 1942, 1960 and 1970, and in Westernport Bay, Bird and Barson (1975) described changes in the extent of mangroves detected from comparisons of nineteenth century maps and charts with modern air photographs. More recently, Blacker (1977) has traced changes in the extent of mangroves in Pittwater, Cowan Creek and Middle Harbour, Sydney, since 1940. Further reference will be made to these studies subsequently.

Apart from the question of boundary changes it is necessary to consider the changes that occur in the structure and species composition of a mangrove system. Although the general structural characteristics of mangrove communities around the Australian coast have been documented (Saenger *et al.*, 1977) little attention has been given to the internal dynamics of these ecosystems. Stability of mangrove systems should really be considered in terms of variations from year to year of such attributes as the standing crop of mangroves, or the total biomass of a mangrove ecosystem, but although the biological productivity of mangroves is often quoted in textbooks as being high in comparison with most other natural ecosystems (cf. Golley *et al.*, 1962, who found short-term productivity of 8 grams per square metre per day), we have been unable to find records of the regular measurements needed to assess mangrove stability. Indeed, Chapman (1976) considers that the productivity of mangrove swamps is still really an unexplored field.

In these terms mangrove systems must be naturally dynamic rather than stable, because of secular changes related to the growth and replacement of individual plants within the mangrove community. Little is known of the life span of mangroves, partly because of the difficulty of dating them: the growth rings of *Avicennia,* for instance, are not annual (Gill, 1971). Where a mangrove system consisting of a single species has consistently occupied the same area over a century or more it may be presumed that some of the individual plants have died and been replaced by younger descendants. Shore sectors that have carried a mangrove fringe continuously through the 6000 years since the Holocene marine transgression established present sea level (cf. Thom and Chappell, 1975) must have had repeated *in situ* regeneration. We have been unable to find information on the rates and patterns of such regeneration, but this could be obtained by long-term monitoring of sample quadrats to measure rates of growth, trace the canopy changes that occur as individual mangroves die and are replaced, and determine how regeneration occurs, and what factors and processes influence it.

Where several mangrove species are arranged in zones parallel to the shoreline, the pattern may either be static, with each species occupying a preferred habitat zone, or a plant succession may be in progress, one species being replaced by another in a seaward progression (e.g. Macnae, 1967). The latter is probably the case where the seaward margin is advancing, and accretion is in progress as on the northern shores of Cairns Bay, but no detailed studies have been made of the rates of such successions or the factors that influence the replacement of one species by another. Evidence of successional changes and the migration of zones dominated by one or more mangroves in the past may be obtainable from stratigraphical and palaeobotanical studies of sediment sequences underlying the existing mangrove systems.

Our examination of literature on mangroves in Australia and elsewhere available to us has thus indicated major gaps in available knowledge of the internal and external dynamics of mangrove systems. Existing accounts of mangrove dynamics have rarely been based on detailed research, a situation which probably reflects the difficulties of working in mangrove environments and the problems of instituting and maintaining long-term research and monitoring in these areas. Given this situation, the best we can do is to indicate some of the topics that should be investigated, and draw attention to some relevant published work.

Zonation of mangrove communities

Mangroves may occupy well-defined zones dominated by a single species, or a group of similar species, arranged parallel to the shoreline, or to the margins of estuaries (Chapman, 1976), but the pattern is often more complex, as in some of the North Queensland estuaries, where up to 27 species are intricately distributed in extensive mangrove swamps (Jones, 1971). Where mangrove species and communities are zoned, their distribution is often related to variations in substrate characteristics, or in terrain level within the mangrove area, correlated with depth and duration of tidal submergence, or exposure to atmospheric conditions, including rainfall. The implication is that the establishment of each mangrove species is optimal within slightly differing ranges of ecological conditions related to tidal submergence, and that competition restricts each species to one zone. As the variations in terrain level are generally only a few centimetres, this zonation of mangroves implies a close sequence of narrowly defined ecological conditions optimal for successive species.

According to Macnae (1966), salinity is one of the factors that influences the establishment and zonation of mangroves. Variations of salinity occur in relation to the level of the substrate and the frequency of inundation by seawater, as well as the patterns of inflow of freshwater by seepage from the hinterland and stream flow into tidal creeks. Farrell and Ashton (1974) found that *Avicennia marina* has a wide range of salinity tolerance, but shows optimal growth at the salinity of seawater. This would explain its success as a pioneer on advancing mangrove margins in such areas as Westernport Bay. In Cairns Bay, *Avicennia marina* is again the main pioneer species, but upstream along the Barron River it passes behind a fringing stand of *Aegiceras corniculatum,* a mangrove that grows well in water less saline than the sea (Hegerl and Davie, 1977). Macnae (1966) deduced that *Sonneratia alba,* also a frequent pioneer species, prefers water of sea salinity. In the Cairns district these pioneer species are backed by a *Rhizophora* zone, then communities of *Bruguiera, Ceriops* and *Lumnitzera*; the *Rhizophora* and *Bruguiera* species grow best in soils which do not become hypersaline, which is often the case in the upper rearward parts of a mangrove swamp. *Avicennia marina* is also capable of growing in freshwater alongside rivers as well as in hypersaline sites where the soil water is up to 90 parts per thousand (Farrell and Ashton, 1974);

thus it is found on the fringes of salt pans above mean high spring tide level on the central Queensland coast.

Natural changes in soil and water salinity may facilitate the replacement of one mangrove species by another as succession proceeds on accreting substrates (Chapman, 1966). Any change in sea level, in the pattern and quantity of freshwater inflow, or in the rate of sediment supply that leads to variations in soil and water salinity within the mangrove system is likely to result in the die-back of some mangrove species and their replacement by others. If the changes are extreme, the mangrove vegetation may be lost altogether.

It has been suggested that the invasion of the *Avicennia* fringe by *Rhizophora* is related to the fact that *Avicennia* seedlings cannot develop in shaded situations; indeed, they cannot survive beneath a canopy of mature *Avicennia* (Macnae, 1966). *Rhizophora* seedlings, more tolerant of shade, are thus able to establish under the *Avicennia* canopy and to grow up and displace it. However, this does not explain why the *Rhizophora* zone advances gradually forward into the *Avicennia* fringe in such areas as Cairns Bay. Since *Rhizophora* propagules are widely dispersed by currents as the tide rises and falls, it might be expected that they would germinate and grow sporadically through the *Avicennia* fringe. Some other factor therefore prevents *Rhizophora* acting as a pioneer species on muddy shorelines and permits the *Avicennia* to grow seaward of it. Possibly wave scour inhibits *Rhizophora* establishment on muddy shorelines, for along the margins of brackish tidal creeks (as in Trinity Inlet at Cairns) the *Avicennia* fades out, and *Rhizophora stylosa* occupies the muddy banks.

The problem of how one species of mangrove can displace another can be analysed by means of transplant experiments of the kind carried out by Rabinowitz (1974), who used *Rhizophora, Avicennia, Pelliciera,* and *Laguncularia.* Her results indicated that species zonation may not be controlled by physiological preferences for habitats at particular levels, and that tidal sorting of propagules may provide a mechanism for zonation. A case of pioneer mangroves (*Rhizophora racemosa*) developing on substrate conditions less favourable for its own regeneration than for colonisation by *Avicennia germinans,* which thus moves in to replace it, was documented from the Gambia estuary in West Africa by Giglioni and Thornton (1965). Much more investigation is clearly needed of the ecological conditions that determine mangrove zonation and promote species succession in Australian mangrove swamps. We suggest that the inference that zonation of mangroves represents a succession be investigated by stratigraphic and palaeobotanical studies of cores taken beneath the inner zones; in North Queensland the *Melaleuca leucadendron* swamp forest should be underlain by a vertical sequence of sediments containing relics of each successive mangrove zone, through *Bruguiera* down to *Rhizophora* and *Avicennia,* with a basal layer of tidal mudflat sediments dating from the phase prior to mangrove encroachment. Some evidence for such a sequence was found under freshwater swamps on the Malaysian coast by Wyatt-Smith (1954), but such studies have apparently not been carried out in Australia.

Mangroves and changing sea levels

Each mangrove species grows between specific tidal levels, and the mangrove community as a whole is restricted to part of the upper intertidal shore zone. It is possible that some short-term changes that occur within mangrove communities, including patchy die-back of certain species, or the sudden advance of pioneer mangroves on to mudflats, are a response to the variations of sea level that occur from year to year, for annual mean sea levels can vary up to 5 per cent of the mean tide range (Easton, 1970).

Longer-term variations in sea level should lead to a migration of mangroves to maintain their position relative to tidal levels. The literature on sea level changes is voluminous and controversial; it has been briefly summarised by Bird (1976). A world-wide Holocene marine transgression between 20,000 and 6000 years ago has been followed by a phase of relatively stable sea level, during which there may have been an episode of higher sea level. If there has been a phase of sea level 1 to 2 metres above the present within the past 6000 years, mangroves should then have occupied higher levels, while the succeeding emergence would have stimulated a marked seaward spread, with migration of mangrove zones, and a succession to other vegetation at the landward margin. Critics of the concept of an episode of higher Holocene sea level may point to the absence of any confirmation of this vegetation oscillation from stratigraphic evidence in Australian mangrove areas.

On the other hand, a rise of sea level should lead to a reduction in the seaward spread of mangroves, to erosion of the seaward margin, and to a regression of mangroves to landward, with recolonisation of the immediate hinterland. An example of this was described by Scholl (1974) from the Ten Thousand Islands region of Florida, where mangroves are migrating inland on a submerging coast, and we have observed similar evidence of landward spread of young mangroves in the saltmarshes to the rear of mangrove swamps, particularly in Westernport Bay.

Such modern responses to a rise or fall in sea level deserve closer attention in Australia. Over long periods there have certainly been major changes in mangrove distributions. During the Last Glacial low sea level phase, mangroves must have occupied sites along a coastline 100 to 150m below present sea level, close to the outer edge of the continental shelf, and during this cooler phase lower sea temperatures presumably resulted in a migration of mangrove species equator-wards. In the ensuing Holocene marine transgression, mangrove communities migrated to suitable habitats as the sea advanced, taking up their present distributions only within the past 6000 years (Bird, 1972c). However, as Beard (1967) has described an inland occurrence of mangroves (*Avicennia*) in the arid hinterland south of Broome, it is possible that some mangroves persisted locally on the emerged sea floor during the Last Glacial low sea level to act as sources of dispersal as the Holocene transgression brought the sea back over such enclaves.

Mangroves and sedimentation

Since the attainment of present sea level, changes in the extent of mangroves have been related to such factors as the lowering or raising of their substrate by processes of erosion or deposition. In some cases there has been a reduction of substrate level by the winnowing away of sediment previously deposited: at Port Clinton in South Australia, such lowering is leaving mangroves without support, and as they die they are not being replaced (Butler *et al.*, 1977).

Vertical changes of substrate level in and around a mangrove fringe were studied by Bird (1971) at Yaringa in Westernport Bay between 1966 and 1971, with measurements on implanted stakes and probing to find marker horizons made by laying brick dust on accreting surfaces. A pattern of variable accretion and erosion was demonstrated on the adjacent tidal mudflats, which were either unvegetated or carpeted with a sparse *Zostera* cover, and sustained vertical accretion of up to 1.6 cm per year within the area occupied by mangroves.

The only species present here is *Avicennia marina,* which develops radial networks of vertical pneumatophores, among which there are related patterns of accretion of mud and organic litter. Simulation of a typical pneumatophore network by wooden pegs implanted at 10 cm intervals on eight radial lines from a central point set up at mean high neap tide level produced a similar pattern of localised mud accretion, and it was deduced that mangroves were here responsible for trapping and fixing sediment that would otherwise have remained mobile (as on the tidal mudflats), as well as adding organic materials (leaves, twigs etc.) from the mangroves to the accumulating sediment.

In Westernport Bay the vegetation zones associated with transverse profiles suggest that once *Avicennia* has spread on to tidal mudflats, the mangroves trap sediment and build up a relatively stable depositional terrace close to mean high spring tide level, on which they are successively replaced by saltmarsh communities, and eventually *Melaleuca ericifolia* swamp scrub. The initiation of this process depends on preliminary accretion of the mudflats to a level suitable for initial colonisation by *Avicennia*; in Westernport Bay, to around mid-tide level. Each year, numerous *Avicennia* seedlings take root in the mudflats seaward of the mangrove fringe, but only survive on areas where the mudflats have accreted to above mid-tide level. Elsewhere, the seedlings soon die, but the physiological reasons for this failure are uncertain: it is possible that vertical fluctuations due to erosion and deposition on the mudflats destroy some seedlings by uprooting, and others by rapid burial in soft mud. In this connection Macnae (1966) suggested that a layer of fine mud deposited on *Avicennia* seedling leaves would have the same effect as deep shade, and thus kill the seedling.

The role of mangroves in stabilising and protecting a shoreline requires careful analysis. In environments where the tidal rise and fall is accompanied by only minor wave action, mangrove substrates are more stable than unvegetated mudflats, where the sediments remain relatively mobile, but where wave action becomes stronger (for example as the result of the deepening of nearshore water or the removal of a protective sand spit) mangrove-covered terrain is soon eroded away. The actual or potential stabilising role of mangrove systems is thus confined to low wave energy situations (Savage, 1972).

Mangroves and man's activities

Some of the changes that have recently taken place in and around mangrove areas are related directly or indirectly to man's activities. Examples of this have been documented from Westernport Bay, where Bird and Barson (1975) indicated a sequence of shoreline changes related to changes in the mangrove fringe.

These changes were of various kinds, some resulting from dieback, others from deliberate clearance. Dieback has occurred on sites where sand eroded from other shoreline sectors or carried in from drainage channels has drifted in and buried pneumatophores. Accumulations of dead *Zostera* are also thought to have played a role in mangrove dieback at several sites. Damage to mangroves by frost action and high summer salinities has also been reported (Ashton, 1972). Gaps have formed, notably where the mangroves were cut to create boat landings, build jetties or harbours, or allow runoff to escape from drainage canals and ditches excavated to carry water off swampy hinterlands. In some places the mangrove fringe has been embanked and infilled to reclaim land bordering the bay shore.

The spread of mangroves has continued only in a few sectors of Westernport Bay, such as the inlet north-east of Tortoise Head on French Island, where muddy sediment is accumulating on either side of a sheltered tidal creek that was formerly a more exposed strait. In such an environment as Westernport Bay the presence of a stable (or advancing) mangrove fringe helps to maintain deeper areas free from sedimentation, whereas the destruction of mangroves results in shore erosion, liberating and mobilising sediment that was previously trapped, and leading to sedimentation and shallowing elsewhere. This is of much significance in an estuarine area where port development requires the maintenance of navigable depths in approach channels.

Blacker (1977) has examined changes in mangrove distribution in the Sydney region since 1940, and found an increase in the extent of mangroves related to an accelerated sediment yield from fire-damaged bushland and urbanising areas in their hinterland. After 1961 the mangrove area became stable, except for losses due mainly to clearing and reclamation. Hutchings and Recher (1977) related the reduced area of mangroves in Sydney's Georges River to the reclamation of land for housing and industry.

Apart from the obvious destruction of mangrove systems buried by landfill in the course of reclamation projects there are indirect impacts of man's activities. An example is seen adjacent to the attempt to reclaim about 640 ha of mangroves south-east of Cairns as land for sugar cultivation. In the early 1970s a large embankment constructed to exclude tidal flooding ran across several tidal creek systems, and completely modified the extent and regime of tidal action as well as the pattern of freshwater inflow to the wetlands south-east of the Trinity Inlet. As was expected mangroves were killed within the area enclosed by the embankment as soon as tidal inundation was excluded, but Hegerl and Davie (1977) found evidence of changes seaward of the embankment, where there was die-back of an 18 ha stand of 10-12 metre high *Rhizophora stylosa* forest, still subject to tidal inundation, but deprived of the freshwater flow that had previously come down an adjacent creek. The importance of salinity dilution for this species was confirmed by its persistence alongside the embankment close to a flood-gate which permitted the overflow of freshwater after heavy rains.

There is also evidence of morphological changes within the beheaded tidal creek systems adjacent to the embanked area, some sectors shallowing and narrowing by deposition as the channel network begins to adjust to the changed tidal regime within artificially truncated creek catchments. Such an adjustment will probably take several decades, and be accompanied by changes in the pattern of mangrove species that would not have occurred in the absence of this interference. There is little doubt that the reclamation project could have been designed to have much less impact on the mangrove system, and it is understood that the enclosed area is now subject to severe drainage problems produced by runoff from the adjacent Murray Prior Range, and it seems that an environmental assessment would have shown that the project was not viable.

Conclusions

We conclude that there are substantial gaps in knowledge of the various factors that contribute to the stability or instability of mangrove systems in Australia. Little is known of rates of erosion or accretion on transverse profiles across intertidal zones where mangroves are present, or of rates of advance or recession of the seaward margin of mangroves, the boundaries between mangrove zones, and the landward margin of mangroves accompanying such changes. Stratigraphical and palaeobotanical data on sediment sequences beneath mangroves are needed to establish past successional stages, their date and duration, and hence the historical rate of development of the mangrove system and its associated upper intertidal landforms.

Information is scanty on the processes which permit the establishment of pioneer mangroves on tidal mudflats, the displacement of these by other mangroves as succession proceeds, and the eventual development of other communities, such as swamp forest or saltmarsh, or of unvegetated saline plains to the rear of the mangrove fringe. It is necessary to know more about the factors that favour or inhibit seedling establishment and growth to maturity, and more about the life span of mangroves, and the factors that aid or impede the replacement of a dying mangrove by another individual of the same species, or the establishment of another species. In broader terms, we need data on the biological production of mangrove systems, and the changes in standing crop or total biomass that proceed with time.

On the basis of such information, it would be possible to determine the degree of stability of a mangrove system, and to decide the extent to which changes in progress are natural, or a response to man's activities. Without such information, any program for the conservation and management of mangrove systems rests largely upon speculative inferences.

References

Ashton, D.H., 1972. Mangroves in Victoria. *Victoria's Resources* **13**, 27-30.

Beard, J.S., 1967. An inland occurrence of mangrove. *Western Australian Naturalist* **10**, 112-15.

Bird, E.C.F., 1971. Mangroves as land builders. *Victorian Naturalist* **88**, 189-97.

Bird, E.C.F., 1972a. Mangroves and coastal morphology in Cairns Bay, North Queensland. *Journal of Tropical Geography* **35**, 11-16.

Bird, E.C.F., 1972b. Recent changes on the shoreline of the Barron delta. *North Queensland Naturalist* **157**, 6-8.

Bird, E.C.F., 1972c. Mangroves on the Australian coast. *Australian Natural History* **17**, 167-71.

Bird, E.C.F., 1976. *Coasts*. Australian National University Press, Canberra, pp. 32-58.

Bird, E.C.F. and M.M. Barson, 1975. Shoreline changes in Westernport Bay. *Proceedings of the Royal Society of Victoria* **87**, 15-26.

Blacker, J.R. 1977. Changes in mangrove distribution in Pittwater, Cowan Creek and Middle Harbour, Sydney, since the early 1940's. Unpublished B.Sc. (Hons.) thesis, University of Sydney.

Bulter, A.J., A.M. Deepers, S.C. McKillup and D.P. Thomas, 1977. Distribution and sediments of mangrove forests in South Australia. *Transactions of the Royal Society of South Australia* **101**, 34-44.

Chapman, V.J., 1966. Some factors involved in mangrove establishment. *Scientific Problems in Humid Tropical Zone Deltas*. UNESCO, Paris pp. 219-24.

Chapman, V.J., 1976. *Mangrove Vegetation*. J. Cramer, Vaduz. 447pp.

Easton, A.K., 1970. *The Tides of the Continent of Australia*. Horace Lamb Centre, Flinders University of South Australia, Bedford Park. 326pp.

Farrell, M.J. and D.H. Ashton, 1974. Environmental factors affecting the growth and establishment of mangroves in Westernport Bay. *Westernport Bay Environmental Study*, Ministry for Conservation, Victoria. pp. 361-5.

Giglioni, M.E.C. and I. Thornton, 1965. The mangrove swamps of Keneba, Lower Gambia river basin. *Journal of Applied Ecology* **2**, 81-103 and 257-69.

Gill, A.M., 1971. Endogenous control of growth-ring development in *Avicennia*. *Forest Science* **17**, 462-5.

Golley, E., H.T. Odum, and R.F. Wilson, 1962. The structure and metabolism of Puerto Rican red mangrove forest in May. *Ecology* **43**, 9-19.

Hegerl, E.J. and J.D.S. Davie, 1977. The mangrove forests of Cairns, Northern Australia. *Marine Research in Indonesia* **18**, 23-37.

Hutchings, P.A. and H.F. Recher, 1977. The management of mangroves in an urban situation. *Marine Research in Indonesia* **18**, 1-11.

Jones, W.T., 1971. The field identification and distribution of mangroves in Eastern Australia. *Queensland Naturalist* **20**, 35-51.

Macnae, W., 1966. Mangroves in eastern and southern Australia. *Australian Journal of Botany* **14**, 67-104.

Macnae, W., 1967. Zonation within mangroves associated with estuaries in North Queensland. In G.H. Lauff (ed.), *Estuaries*. American Association for the Advancement of Science Publication No. 83, pp. 432-41.

Rabinowitz, D. 1974. Planting experiments in mangrove swamps of Panama. In G.E. Walsh, S.C. Snedaker and H.J. Teas (eds.), *Proceedings of the International Symposium on Biology and Management of Mangroves*. Institute of Food and Agricultural Sciences, University of Florida, Gainesville, Florida, Vol. I, pp. 385-93.

Saenger, P., M.M. Specht, R.L. Specht and V.J. Chapman, 1977. Mangal and coastal salt-marsh communities in Australasia. In V.J. Chapman (ed.), *Ecosystems of the World*. I. *Wet Coastal Ecosystems*. Elsevier, Amsterdam.

Savage, T., 1972. *Florida Mangroves as Shoreline Stabilizers*. Florida Department of Natural Resources, Marine Research Laboratory, Professional Paper 19.

Scholl, D.W., 1964. Recent sedimentary record in mangrove swamps and rise in sea-level over the south-western coast of Florida, *Marine Geology* **1**, 344-66.

Thom, B.G. and J. Chappell, 1975. Holocene sea levels relative to Australia, *Search* **6**, 90-3.

Wyatt-Smith, J., 1954. Mangrove flora replaced by freshwater forest. *Malayan Forester* **17**, 25-6.

17

Mangrove Management in Australia
Edward J. Hegerl

Introduction

At first sight, mangrove swamps may not seem to have any particular significance. In fact, the general view is more likely to be of a foul-smelling swamp, rich in muck and ooze, with strange animal noises, snakes, mosquitoes and a myriad other queer forms of creeping and crawling creatures. No wonder they are used for refuse and sewage or, preferably, reclaimed by herbicide and pump, power shovel and dredge, to make way for industrial installations, harbours, marinas, runways and summer cottages. HRH Prince Philip, Australian Conservation Foundation President, 1972.

In all fairness, Philip then went on to say that mangroves really are very important, even if they don't look that way (Australian Conservation Foundation, 1972). His comments provide an appropriate opening to any discussion of mangrove management, as they reflect a common view of mangroves that has only recently begun to change under the onslaught of well-informed natural history documentaries on television. The Australian image of mangrove forests as useless wastelands probably evolved in the nation's colonial history, where mangroves gained notoriety as 'alligator' and mosquito-filled obstacles to famous explorers like Edmund Kennedy.

Australian Aborigines appear to have utilised the flora and fauna of the mangroves extensively, but it is unlikely that any useful record exists of the environmental impact of their activities. Maiden (1889), however, provided Aboriginal names for some mangrove species and noted that in Queensland, Cleveland Bay Aborigines baked and ate *Avicennia* fruit, and that other Aborigines used *Excoecaria* sap to cure 'certain ulcerous diseases, e.g. leprosy'. Cribb and Cribb (1975) reported that, at least as late as 1933, Aborigines of Princess Charlotte Bay, Queensland, baked, and after considerable preparation, ate the hypocotyls of *Bruguiera gymnorhiza*. Maiden (1889) recorded many other uses of mangroves by the natives of India and Fiji, but did not mention any uses by European settlers in Australia. Jones (1971) listed uses of most species known from Australia, but did not indicate if these uses occurred within Australia or elsewhere in the region. As European settlers had convenient access to better quality wood from terrestrial forests, they do not appear to have made extensive use of mangroves.

According to Gutteridge, Haskins and Davey (1975), minor use was made of *Avicennia marina* wood for transom knees in small boats, and bark from unspecified species was used for tanning.

Sticks from *Aegiceras corniculatum* were used as cultch material in the oyster industry, particularly in New South Wales. Macnae (1966) listed 'the bark of the *Rhizophora* and *Bruguiera* mangroves' as useful for tanning and also for making fibre fishing nets more durable.

Today, *Aegiceras* provides an important commercial honey source in southern Queensland, and *Avicennia marina* is 'a useful supporting species' (Blake and Roff, 1958).

As Philip's quotation suggested, twentieth century Australians have also found a variety of new ways to utilise the continent's mangrove forest resources. These uses have resulted in extensive mangrove destruction, which has catalysed a growing awareness of the need for conservation and management. The purpose of this chapter is not to present a review of the literature on management of mangroves, but to consider the recent human activities which make management a necessity, and then to examine the goals and scope of Australian mangrove management as well as to suggest methods for better protecting the continent's resource.

The threats to the mangroves
The human population of Australia is still increasing and is expected to continue to do so until at least the turn of the century. Eighty per cent of the present population live within 160 km of the coast, and sixty per cent live directly at the mouths of estuaries (Rooney *et al.*, 1978).

During this century the magnitude of Australian industrial and agricultural activity, and the affluence and lifestyle of most Australians, have had a considerable impact on mangroves and tidal marshes. The human activities which constitute threats to the survival of mangroves are numerous and in many cases overlapping and destructively synergistic in their effects.

Filling for Dry Land Use
The most widespread destruction of both mangroves and tidal marshes has resulted from filling the tidal wetlands to create dry land sites for industrial areas, airports, harbour facilities, waterfront housing, dumps and sporting fields. Occasionally fill is brought in from terrestrial sources, but more commonly dredging of adjacent tidal or sub-tidal areas takes place instead. American examples suggest that three hectares of surrounding waters may have to be dredged to create one hectare of filled land (Odum, 1970).

The estuarine areas from which the fill is taken may be excavated to depths below the photic zone which prevents later colonisation by light-requiring benthos and organisms which they might support (Lindall, 1974). Silt and clay stirred up by dredging operations is likely to affect marine life well outside the dredged area (Ellway and Hegerl, 1972).

The elimination of intertidal areas may also alter current patterns and velocities, which can result in accelerated erosion or accretion in remaining mangrove stands on other parts of an estuary. Scouring or siltation of channels may result, and provoke political pressure for corrective measures which are likely to cause further damage to estuarine organisms.

Estuarine landfill can modify the local tidal range and patterns of tidal inundation within an estuary which may, in turn, result in gradual, but pronounced, changes to the affected mangrove flora and fauna elsewhere within the estuary.

After a filled area has been put to use, other environmental problems usually follow. Stormwater runoff from the developed area is likely to carry silt from road verges, and non-point source pollutants from vehicles, factories or residential areas into adjacent waterways. Accidental spills of pollutants frequently occur from harbour facilities or industrial sites, and industries may exert political pressure to permit the discharge of treated or untreated factory wastes.

The establishment of one development project on reclaimed tidal wetlands often creates the demand for other reclamation projects to follow. Botany Bay, New South Wales, provides a good example. There the establishment of an oil refinery and tanker loading facilities directly led to the establishment of other noxious industries in the area, and increased residential development. These projects involved additional reclamation of mangroves and tidal marshes in the area adjacent to the refinery. The increased residential development then created a demand for sporting fields which eventually led to more mangrove destruction in nearby Woolooware Bay. Part of the Woolooware Bay reclamation included a garbage dump situated in an intertidal area cleared of mangroves. This tip was closed in 1966 and converted to sporting fields, but is still believed to be leaching pollutants into Woolooware Bay, a major oyster-farming area (Australian Littoral Society, 1978).

Intertidal areas in estuaries along the eastern Australian coast are frequently used for garbage dumps and water pollution problems usually result (Co-ordinator General's Department, 1973; Hegerl and Tarte, 1974; Hegerl et al., 1976). Silt runoff from intertidal dump sites may cause mangrove mortalities in adjacent areas.

Where extensive filling is permitted on estuarine floodplains, flooding problems may be accentuated in upstream areas and, on occasion, the filled areas may themselves be subject to flooding, as well as erosion.

Canalisation

Canal estate housing projects have destroyed large areas of mangroves in southern Queensland. On Queensland's Gold Coast, the Nerang River's original extensive mangrove forests have been almost totally replaced by Australia's largest system of canalised waterways. Most other southern Queensland estuaries now have one or more canal systems, and a number of canal developments have been permitted along the shores of Moreton Bay. Canals have also been constructed in a number of areas along the New South Wales coast.

In southern Queensland deficiencies in siting and in engineering design have led to flooding and erosion problems, as well as water stagnation in canals with poor circulation. These problems, coupled with public concern at continuing mangrove destruction and the discovery that canals were creating a biting midge problem, prompted the Queensland Government to commission the Coastal Management Investigation in March 1974. This study summarised existing knowledge of the environmental problems associated with canal estate housing developments. While recommending engineering improvements for any future canals, the consultants came out strongly for the protection of most of the remaining mangroves, saltmarshes and seagrass beds in southern Queensland (Gutteridge, Haskins and Davey, 1975).

Westman (1975) has discussed problems common to both Australian and American canal developments, and Saenger and McIvor (1975) have studied fish populations in two Gold Coast canals, but, relative to the United States (e.g. Lindall and Trent, 1975), we have little Australian documentation on either the capability or inability of canals to support healthy estuarine biota.

Canal estates are now being cut into terrestrial areas or freshwater swamps. These inland or 'upland' canals can still damage estuarine wetlands in a number of ways. They may modify the estuary's tidal range and substantially alter patterns of inundation, and also alter freshwater and nutrient inputs to the estuary. Water quality can be expected to diminish if storm drains are allowed to flush urban runoff through the canal system into the estuary.

In the more common canal development involving dredge and fill operations in intertidal areas, the environmental impacts are those which have already been described under filling for dry land use, except that the canals themselves can create a severe biting midge problem.

Biting insect control

The biting midges common to most tropical and subtropical Australian mangrove estuaries breed in a narrow band closely related to the mean neap high water level. Within this band each species has very restrictive habitat requirements. Suitable conditions are found only in very small areas within the intertidal zone. Only one pest species seems dependent on mangroves and, as with mosquitoes, felling mangroves can create extremely favourable conditions for midge infestations to develop (Reye, 1973, 1977).

Ironically, real-estate developers who have claimed that they would rid areas of 'sandflies' (i.e. biting midges) have created optimal breeding conditions for these insects on the sandy beaches of man-made canals. In southern Queensland serveral hundred kilometres of suitable habitat have been created (Reye, personal communication, 1977).

While biting midges are not known to transmit any diseases to humans in Australia, they are potentially vectors of disease to man or to domestic animals. A number of midge species have been introduced to various Pacific islands by aircraft, and the danger exists that disease-carrying species could be introduced to Australian airports bordering intertidal areas, for example Cairns, Mackay or Brisbane (Reye, 1977). Diseases could also be introduced by human visitors from outside Australia. Where human populations are dense in the vicinity of midge breeding areas (e.g. Queensland's Gold Coast), the possibility exists that midges will bite more than one human host. Blood diseases may be transmitted if infected humans are bitten first (Reye, personal communication, 1977).

Most midge species will rarely travel more than 400 metres from their breeding site unless inadvertently carried further by humans (e.g. cars or aircraft). Unfortunately, waterfront housing places humans where they can be greatly bothered by midge bites. Individuals who react severely to midge saliva may be incapacitated (Reye, 1977).

The saltmarsh mosquito *Aedes vigilax* is a common pest species around most of the northern Australian coastline from Sydney to Perth (Marks, 1973). Mass migrations of *A. vigilax* occur for distances of 32 or more kilometres from the breeding site. Breeding and larval development of this species generally occurs in saltmarsh pools, while other pest species may utilise brackish or freshwater pools (Marks and Mabbett, 1977).

In normal circumstances there is no mosquito breeding among mangroves inundated by daily tides. Breeding only occasionally occurs among less frequently inundated mangroves. However, when mangroves are felled and left on the substrate, or bund walls are constructed to prevent tidal inundation, extremely favourable conditions for mosquito breeding may be created (Marks and Mabbett, 1977). Emerging adults will shelter in any dense coastal vegetation during the daytime.

When coastal development is permitted close to estuaries, a demand for biting insect control is usually created. Aerial spraying or ground fogging are the most visible and newsworthy forms of control so they are sometimes employed by local councils in preference to larval control, which is much more effective, but less conspicuous. Aerial mosquito spraying has caused fish kills in the Brisbane area (Connell, 1970).

At present, Abate (0,0,0',0'-tetramethyl 0,0'-thiodi-p-phenylene phosphorothioate), an organophosphorous compound with low mammalian toxicity, is proving quite successful as a larvicide for biting midges and mosquitoes in southern Queensland. On present information, Abate seems less toxic to marine organisms than alternative chemicals, but few local species have been tested.

There is now some concern among entomologists that, if Abate is used too widely, resistance will develop and eliminate what may be the most effective chemical available for controlling any outbreaks of biting insect borne diseases.

Bund wall projects

Bund walls are sometimes constructed around mangrove or saltmarsh areas to prevent tidal inundation. The mangroves are then cleared and the area can be put to some other use—often to provide effluent ponds for industry. The bund walls are vulnerable to breaching by floods, and effluents may overflow the walls or leach through the substrate.

Bund walls have also been used in central Queensland saltmarshes to creat lower salinity pasture for cattle grazing. In Trinity Inlet, opposite the city of the Cairns, Queensland, 726 ha of mangroves and saltmarshes have been bunded in an attempt to grow sugarcane on intertidal soils. The project does not appear to be economically viable, but additional mangroves may still be cleared for this purpose.

In South-east Asia, bund walls are constructed in mangrove areas for mariculture projects (Macnae, 1968). Hopefully, this practice will not become widespread in Australia for, as Pollard (1973) concluded: 'Alteration of estuarine areas by construction of levee banks or by other means should be avoided in order that culture practices supplement and not endanger production from natural resources'. As Turner (1977) has shown, the construction of fish ponds in mangrove areas can, in some cases, result in a substantial net loss of fisheries production.

Estuarine dredging

The purpose of estuarine dredging may be flood mitigation, the creation or maintenance of navigable channels, or the recovery of sand, gravel or metals. Environmental impacts include destruction of habitat and benthos in the dredged area, altered currents and scouring of channels and riverbanks, and hence increased erosion, and increased turbidity and siltation. Dredging may also permit tidal waters to penetrate further up the waterway.

Dredging operations for flood mitigation often result in the removal of river or creek fringing mangroves. Engineers do this to speed up the runoff of floodwaters. However, even when the mangroves are replaced by expensive retaining walls, collapse of the banks may result. This shallows and broadens the waterway and, unless remedial dredging is undertaken, may then result in flooding of surrounding properties.

When dredging is undertaken to create or maintain navigable channels, dredging spoils are often pumped on the nearby mangroves or tidal marshes, or they may be carried offshore and dumped. Dredging channels through the mouth of an estuary may have severe environmental consequences, particularly when an entirely new, trained river entrance is constructed. As well as changing currents and tidal inundation characteristics within the estuary, the surf bar zone may be eliminated. Spawning of some commercial fish species is believed to take place in these areas (Gutteridge, Haskins and Davey, 1975).

When sand or gravel are mined from estuaries, the washing processes usually result in the return of silty water to the estuary, which intensifies silt pollution problems. Rutile mining adjacent to estuaries has also created problems. In particular, Cudgen Creek in northern New South Wales, which was once a productive mangrove estuary supporting fourteen commercial fisherman, has been virtually destroyed by dredging spoil.

Alterations to freshwater and nutrient inputs

For many Australian rivers, human activities have substantially altered natural drainage patterns and movement of nutrients and sediments from the land to the sea. Riverflow may be reduced by the construction of dams and by water use for agriculture or other purposes along the waterway. However, runoff during rain may be intensified as runoff from fields, pastures and urban areas is usually much greater than from natural systems. The net effect on mangroves and other estuarine biota may be to intensify the effects of severe periods of drought or flood, and to vary the prevailing conditions to which the organisms within the estuary have adapted.

The changes these human activities inadvertently produce within the estuary may be perceived as undesirable if they cause apparent death to mangrove forests or reduce populations of fish, crabs, prawns or other organisms deemed valuable within a time scale that attracts the attention of scientists or the public.

Similar problems may arise from alteration of freshwater and nutrient flow from human disturbance of terrestrial areas or freshwater swamps adjoining mangroves. Tall mangrove forests developed under conditions of high freshwater runoff would seem particularly vulnerable (Lugo and Cintron, 1975). In Florida, Reark (1975) has shown how tall mangrove forests which were destroyed by hurricanes have not re-formed where areas have been deprived of freshwater inputs. Similarly, Hegerl and Davie (1976) described mortality of an 18 ha homogeneous stand of 10-12 m high *Rhizophora stylosa* forest in Cairns as a result of a bund wall blocking freshwater inputs to the area. The mortalities in Cairns were probably the result of a rapid change in the prevailing salinity range.

On a longer term basis, reduction in nutrient input may be of corresponding significance. Lugo and Snedaker (1974) saw the importance of nutrient input in these terms:

> The export of mangrove-produced detritus carries with it proportionate amounts of the incorporated mineral nutrients; each unit exported reduced the nutrient stock of the producing system by that amount. In order for mangroves to remain productive, in the broadest context, they must receive equivalent inputs of mineral nutrients from other sources. The rate of in situ organic matter decomposition and remineralisation is insufficient to replenish this stock internally. Based on field measurements and analog computer modelling studies of south Florida mangroves, Lugo *et al,* (1976) determined the probable response of mangrove production to reductions in upland runoff and the associated mineral nutrient burden. Reductions in such inputs to approximately 50% of normal reduced mangrove production proportionately. Nutrient input reductions below 50% induced declines to production levels similar to those observed for the scrub mangroves. The response time was of the order of ten years.

Improving access
Improvements in access to estuaries may involve the construction of elevated roads or cleared tracks through mangroves or tidal marshes, and the construction of launching ramps, jetties or marinas on the shoreline. In some cases it may simply involve clearing mangroves along the waterway to provide an unimpeded view. The environmental impacts extend beyond the clearing of mangroves in the path of these activities.

Elevated roads can substantially alter tidal inundation patterns and freshwater seepage through the local tidal vegetation with resultant damage to flora and fauna. Wheel ruts along cleared tracks can produce the same effect, although usually on a smaller scale (Australian Littoral Society, 1978). Similarly, pedestrian tracks or horse-riding tracks may create this problem on a still smaller scale. Tracks through tidal wetlands can also become breeding sites for midges or mosquitoes (Reye, personal communication, 1977, and author's personal observations, 1968-79), and midges may breed on cleared creek or river banks (author's personal observations, 1968-79).

Some dredging and/or filling is usually necessary to build and maintain marinas. This may result in direct mangrove or tidal marsh destruction, but, even where it does not, environmental problems may result from alteration to local water movements. Erosion or accretion may adversely affect estuarine life in surrounding areas. Jetties and launching ramps may produce similar effects on a smaller scale.

Improved access may also result in over-exploitation of recreationally or commercially important species of fish, crabs or prawns. The Mud Crab *Scylla serrata* seems particularly vulnerable.

Improved access may lead to some deterioration in water quality as a substantial proportion of human visitors will deposit faecal material in waterways or intertidal areas. Where visitation rates are high and people use the channels for swimming (e.g. 'The Bedroom' in Southern Moreton Bay, Queensland) health problems may result. In addition, visitors often spill small quantities of boating fuel, and metal rings from drink containers and other litter may be ingested by fish or birds. These are problems of little consequence until recreational use becomes intense, but this is now the case in most estuaries near Australia's coastal cities.

Tidal wetlands are also becoming increasingly popular as sites for teaching biology, and care needs to be exercised to ensure that habitat damage and over-collecting of organisms do not occur, At present little is known of the educational carrying capacity of tidal wetland (Australian Littoral Society, 1978; Shine *et al.*, 1973).

Water pollution
Although many Australian mangrove estuaries are polluted, the impacts of the pollutants on mangrove flora and fauna remain largely conjectural and would seem an area of mangrove research requiring a high priority for future investigations.

While mangrove mortalities attributable to water pollution sometimes occur, mangrove stands of healthy appearance often survive in badly polluted estuaries. For example, in tidal tributaries of the Brisbane River a variety of pollutants, including low levels of toxic chemicals and excessive nutrients, generally do not seem to kill mangroves, but there is little or no intertidal invertebrate fauna present.

The apparent tolerance of mangrove and marsh vegetation to high levels of nutrients has prompted some scientists to suggest that mangroves should be used as effluent disposal areas for treated or untreated sewage wastes. Some American biologists have even cited this potential use as another reason for protecting tidal marshes from destruction (Gosselink *et al.*, 1974).

According to Nedwell (1974a), 'a suitable tertiary treatment may well be obtained by simply discharging secondary effluent into shallow retaining ponds in mangrove areas, with overflow weirs from the pond finally discharging into the mangroves or mangrove-lined water channels'. He also suggested stocking the effluent ponds with fish to remove algal build-ups, and added that, 'a worthwhile return of protein to the human population may be an incidental benefit'. Nedwell (1974b) noted in a subsequent letter to *Search* that, 'When there is a danger of toxic bioaccumulation because of industrial contamination of domestic sewage then obviously the suggested use of mangrove areas may be discounted'.

Secondary sewage treatment does not remove most toxic wastes which are potentially harmful to both marine life and human consumers of contaminated seafood, nor does it remove most viruses which are potentially harmful to swimmers (Westman, 1974; Miller, 1978).

However, even where there is little industrial contamination of sewage wastes, secondary sewage effluent might still have important and undesirable effects on mangrove biota. Clearly this is one area where detailed environmental studies are needed before this becomes a much more widespread means of effluent disposal.

The goals and scope of management
In much of South-east Asia management of mangroves means controlling exploitation for firewood, timber or woodchip production, or utilising their modified habitat for agriculture or mariculture (Walsh, 1977).

In Australia quite different management goals have been publicly advocated (Australian Conservation Foundation, 1972; Australian Marine Sciences Association, 1977). Rooney *et al.* (1978) have summarised contemporary reasons for establishing marine reserves in Australia, and their publication provides a useful list which, with only minor additions, suggests some goals for Australian mangrove management:

1)   the preservation of the natural processes of the ecosystem;
2)   the preservation of not only rare and endangered species and habitats, but also the common 'representative' species and habitats;
3)   the protection of commercial and recreational fisheries;
4)   the establishment of reserves for scientific study;
5)   the establishment of reserves for educational study;
6)   the preservation of the aesthetic and recreational qualities of natural shorelines;
7)   the protection of the coastline and estuaries from erosion and/or siltation; and
8)   the containment of floodwaters within natural floodplains.

In at least two Australian cases these goals already have been employed to develop mangrove management strategies (Gutteridge, Haskins and Davey, 1975; Australian Littoral Society, 1978).

While the establishment of one or more reserves may be a key feature in any mangrove management plan, some degree of management control over adjoining land and water is essential . In any mangrove area the flora and fauna may be strongly dependent on the continued well-being of adjoining tidal wetlands habitats, which could include tidal marshes, seagrass beds, mudflats and sandflats. Thus, a management plan may need to provide a comparably high degree of protection to these associated habitats, as well as to exercise some control in adjoining waters on the seaward side of the mangroves, and in a terrestrial buffer zone on the landward side of the mangroves. The Australian Marine Science Association (1977) suggests that this terrestrial buffer zone should be at least 200 m wide.

Ideally, a mangrove management plan should attempt to minimise all potentially harmful impacts within the catchment, but in practice, those who manage mangroves are seldom given this opportunity.

Management plans must be based on a thorough understanding of local biophysical and hydrological conditions. Mangrove forests that have developed under conditions of high rainfall and prevailing low salinities will clearly be very different, and present differing management problems, from mangrove forests developed under lower rainfall regimes and higher prevailing salinities. However, even from one estuary to the next, there is often surprising variation in forest structure and floristics, as well as in dependent fauna. Management plans appropriate to one estuary may be quite inappropriate to the next, because of variations in management goals (such as the desire to protect sites harbouring unusual species or associations) or because of differential susceptibility to man-induced stresses.

To develop good management plans it is necessary to have sufficient field data from each mangrove estuary to know what processes and organisms we are trying to protect and specifically how they may be vulnerable to human activities.

Protecting Australia's mangroves

Probably the first Australian reference to suggest that tidal wetlands should be protected appeared in the Queensland Littoral Society Newsletter (Anon., 1965), while the first published statement of concern specifically for Australian mangroves appeared two years later (Harrison, 1967). Since then, a growing number of public organisations throughout Australia have attempted to save threatened areas of mangrove forests, seagrass beds and tidal marshes from destruction. Marine scientists have played an important role in fostering public concern by focusing attention on the natural values of the tidal wetlands. In little more than a decade, conservation of this resource has become an important public issue in Australia. As a result, destruction of some areas has been prevented.

Along the Queensland east coast twenty-three Fisheries Habitat Reserves have been created primarily to protect mangrove forests. Other mangrove areas have been fortuitously protected in Queensland and other Australian states where coastal parks have been created with the primary intention of safeguarding adjacent terrestrial habitats. Unfortunately, too little effort has yet been made to minimise or control developmental impacts in adjacent areas, hence the future of many of the present mangrove reserves is uncertain.

The failure of the governmental organisational processes in Australia to achieve satisfactory coastal zone planning and management (Cullen, 1978) has meant that the mangroves have frequently been undervalued as a resource when developmental projects are being considered. For most development proposals involving mangrove destruction, a government department will undertake its own environmental study or evaluate a report from another department or private consultant. This may be called an environmental impact statement even though few of the probable impacts will be properly investigated. Such studies will seldom involve comprehensive field surveys to determine what wetlands resources will be affected by the development proposal, nor do they commonly give adequate consideration to how the development will interact with the enviromental perturbations caused by other existing or proposed developments within the estuary.

Although politicians may pay lip service to the need for an environmental impact study, the political realities are that a decision to proceed with a development may have been taken even before the study begins.

Thus, it appears that two of the main reasons for continued loss of Australian mangrove resources are:

1) Required evaluations do not adequately define losses; and
2) Politicians often do not feel compelled to accept or be guided by environmental impact studies.

To find a way out of both of these dilemmas requires the active participation of a greater number of mangrove researchers concerned with social responsibility in their science. Frequent public comment on the inadequacies of environmental impact statements would do a great deal towards having more rigorous investigations become a properly considered requirement in decision-making.

In addition, the Australian Marine Science Association (1977) has advocated a number of measures to protect estuaries and estuarine wetlands which could be of considerable importance to mangrove conservation. These can be summarised as:

1) Government departments presently controlling estuarine wetlands in each state should prepare comprehensive resource and land-use inventories.
2) Until such inventories are compiled and the mechanisms for conducting multi-disciplinary studies are established, further development within the estuary or its wetlands should not be permitted.
3) Regional and local planning practice should seek to protect estuaries and estuarine wetlands from developmental pressures. Planning authorities should accept that estuarine wetlands need to be zoned in a special category of rural area which guarantees environmental protection, as has been the policy in New South Wales since 1977.
4) Estuarine wetlands and estuaries which by their size, special features or proximity to urban centres merit special protection should be designated as national parks or nature reserves.

5)   Privately owned areas of estuarine wetlands should be zoned as open space. Funds should be provided by the Federal and State Governments to pay fair compensation for re-acquisition of these areas according to a priority list established for each state.

6)   The Federal and State Governments should establish a joint committee of ministers and experts to develop a comprehensive and complementary non-partisan legislative program aimed specifically at the conservation and management of estuaries and estuarine wetlands, based on the Australian Marine Science Association's guidelines.

7)   An appropriately staffed coastal authority should be established in each state and given powers and the responsibility to ensure the protection of estuaries and their wetlands.

8)   The Federal and State Governments through the Council of Conservation Ministers should provide funds on a contract basis for existing organisations involved in marine and estuarine research to conduct research related specifically to the development of policies and methods for coastal zone management.

9)   The Council of Conservation Ministers should initiate a national program of public education on the need for the conservation of estuaries and estuarine wetlands.

These recommendations are not new, as all have been put forward over the last five years by various Australian scientists or scientific organisations. Clearly, there are still major social, as well as scientific, problems to be overcome if Australians are to learn to properly manage the continent's substantial mangrove resources. However, looking back on the last decade, it seems that each year we have progressed a little more toward the day when no-one will regard mangrove forests and tidal marshes as 'worthless swamplands'.

References

Anon., 1965. The wetlands — fertilizer for the sea. *Newsletter of the Queensland Littoral Society* **3**, 2-3.

Australian Conservation Foundation, 1972. *Mangroves and Man.*Viewpoint No. 7. Australian Conservation Foundation, Melbourne. 12 pp.

Australian Littoral Society, 1978. *An Investigation of Management Options for Towra Point, Botany Bay*. Australian National Parks and Wildlife Service, Canberra. 396 pp. + 46 pp. appendixes.

Australian Marine Sciences Association, 1977. *Guidelines for the Protection and Management of Estuaries and Estuarine Wetlands*. Australian Marine Sciences Association. 12 pp.

Blake, S.T. and C. Roff, 1958. *The Honey Flora of South-Eastern Queensland*. Government Printer, Brisbane. 199 pp.

Connell, D.W. 1970. Fish kill in Cribb Island area. *Newsletter of the Queensland Littoral Society* **36**, 15-16.

Co-ordinator General's Department, 1973. *Cairns Region Waste Disposal Study*. Co-ordinator General's Department, Queensland. 82 pp.

Cribb, A.B. and J.W. Cribb, 1975. *Wild Food in Australia*. Collins, Sydney. 240 pp.

Cullen, P., 1978. Coast management options for Australia. In Institution of Engineers, Australia, *Managing the Coast*. Fourth Australian Conference on Coastal and Ocean Engineering, Adelaide, pp. 1-7.

Ellway, C.P. and E.J. Hegerl, 1972. Fishes of the Tweed River estuary. *Operculum* **2**, 16-23.

Gosselink, J.G., E.P. Odum and R.M. Pope, 1974. *The Value of the Tidal Marsh*. Publication No. LSU-SG-74-03. Centre for Wetland Resources, Louisiana State University, Baton Rouge, Louisiana. 30 pp.

Gutteridge, Haskins and Davey, 1975. *Coastal Management Queensland-New South Wales Border to Northern Boundary of Noosa Shire*. Volumes 1-4. Co-ordinator General's Department, Queensland.

Harrison, G.G.T., 1967. Conservation of the marine life of mangrove swamps, estuaries and coastal swamps. In *Caring for Queensland*, Australian Conservation Foundation, Melbourne, pp. 27-30.

Hegerl, E.J. and J.D. Davie, 1976. The mangrove forests of Cairns, northern Australia. *Marine Research in Indonesia* **18**, 23-57.

Hegerl, E.J. and D.M. Tarte, 1974. A reconnaissance of the Capricorn Coast tidal wetlands. *Operculum* **4**, 50-62.

Hegerl, E.J., P. Shanco and R.D. Timmins, 1976. Some Problems of Siting Rubbish Tips in Intertidal Areas, with Particular Reference to Eli Creek, Hervey Bay, Queensland. Duplicated report, Australian Littoral Society, Brisbane. 9 pp.

Jones, W.T., 1971. The field identification and distribution of mangroves in eastern Australia. *Queensland Naturalist* **20**, 35-51.

Lindall, W.N., 1974. Alterations of estuaries of South Florida: a threat to its fish resources. *Operculum* **4**, 63-9.

Lindall, W.N. and L. Trent, 1975. Housing development canals in the coastal zone of the Gulf of Mexico: ecological consequences, regulations and recommendations. *Marine Fisheries Review* **37**, 19-24.

Lugo, A.E. and C. Cintron, 1975. The mangrove forests of Puerto Rico and their management. In G.E. Walsh, S.C. Snedaker and H.J. Teas (eds.), *Proceedings of the International Symposium on Biology and Management of Mangroves*. Institute of Food and Agricultural Sciences, University of Florida, Gainesville, Florida, Vol. II, pp. 825-46.

Lugo, A.E. and S.C. Snedaker, 1974. The ecology of mangroves. *Annual Review of Ecology and Systematics* **5**, 39-64.

Lugo, A.E., M. Sell and S.C. Snedaker, 1976. Mangrove ecosystem analysis. In B.C. Patten (ed.), *Systems Analysis and Simulation in Ecology* Vol. IV. Academic Press, New York. pp. 114-45.

Macnae, W., 1966. Mangroves in eastern and southern Australia. *Australian Journal of Botany* **14**, 67-104.

Macnae, W., 1968. A general account of the fauna and flora of mangrove swamps and forests in the Indo-West-Pacific region. *Advances in Marine Biology* **6**, 73-270.

Maiden, J.H., 1889. *The Useful Native Plants of Australia*. Facsimile edition, 1975. Compendium, Melbourne. 696 pp.

Marks, E.N., 1973. Saltmarsh mosquito control. *Operculum* **3**, 87-8.

Marks, E.N. and J.D. Mabbett, 1977. A mosquito survey and assessment of potential mosquito problems of the Brisbane airport development and environs. In *Brisbane Airport Development Project Environmental Study*. Australian Government Publishing Service, Canberra, Vol. III, pp. 71-5.

Miller, G.J., 1978. Critical review of proposed Gold Coast sewage outfall. Unpublished report. Queensland Commercial Fishermen's Association, Brisbane. 93 pp.

Nedwell, D.B., 1974a. Sewage treatment and discharge into tropical coastal water. *Search* **5**, 187-90.

Nedwell, D.B., 1974a. Letter to the editor. *Search* **5**, 368.

Odum, W.E., 1970. Insidious alteration of the estuarine environment. *Transactions of the American Fisheries Society* **99**, 836-47.

Pollard, D.A., 1973. Estuaries: development and 'progress' versus commonsense. *The Fisherman* **4**, 28-32.

Reark, J.B., 1975. A history of the colonization of mangroves on a tract of land on Biscayne Bay, Florida. In G.E. Walsh, S.C. Snedaker and H.J. Teas (eds.), *Proceedings of the International Symposium on Biology and Management of Mangroves*. Institute of Food and Agricultural Sciences, University of Florida, Gainesville, Florida, Vol. II, pp. 776-804.

Reye, E.J., 1973. Midges and mangroves. *Operculum* **3**, 31-4.

Reye, E.J., 1977. Biting midges — the problem as at October 1972. In *Brisbane Airport Development Project Environmental Study*. Australian Government Publishing Service, Canberra, Vol. III, pp. 65-70.

Rooney, W.S., F.H. Talbot and S.S. Clark, 1978. *Marine Reserves: the Development of Policy for Marine Reserves*. Environmental and Urban Studies Report No. 32. Centre for Environmental Studies, Macquarie University, Sydney, Vol. I. 502 pp.

Saenger, P. and C.C. McIvor, 1975. Water quality and fish populations in a mangrove estuary modified by residential canal developments. In G.E. Walsh, S.C. Snedaker and H.J. Teas (eds.), *Proceedings of the International Symposium on Biology and Management of Mangroves*. Institute of Food and Agricultural Sciences, University of Florida, Gainesville, Florida, Vol. II, pp. 753-65

Shine, R., C.P. Ellway and E.J. Hegerl, 1973. A biological study of the Tallebudgera Creek estuary. *Operculum* **3**, 59-83.

Turner, R.E., 1977. Intertidal vegetation and commercial yields of penaeid shrimp. *Transactions of the American Fisheries Society* **106**, 411-16.

Walsh, G.E., 1977. Exploitation of mangles. In V.J. Chapman (ed.), *Ecosystems of the World*. I. *Wet Coastal Ecosystems*. Elsevier, Amsterdam. pp. 347-62.

Westman, W.E., 1974. A new strategy for clean waters. *Operculum* **4**, 27-32.

Westman, W.E., 1975. Ecology of canal estates. *Search* **6**, 491-7.

18

Utilisation and Conservation of Western Australian Mangroves

Kevin F. Kenneally

In Western Australia there is almost no published information on the utilisation of mangals by Aborigines (see Campbell 1915; Love 1936; Akerman 1975; Moore 1978). Observations by the author in the Broome-Dampierland Peninsula area have shown that fish traps on the tidal flats and fishing platforms within the mangal are common. Many Aboriginal children use the mangal as a food-gathering or recreation area especially on the incoming tide. Interviews with the elders of the Bardi tribe at One Arm Point have revealed that mangroves are utilised to make rafts for turtle fishing (*Camptostemon schulizii*) and for wood carving (*Sonneratia alba*). The flowers of *Sonneratia* provide nectar for children while the fruits of *Avicennia marina* are collected, buried in mangrove mud for two days until they go black, then roasted and eaten. They are reported to have a 'sour taste'. A list of Bardi names for mangroves in given in Table 18.1. More ethno-botanical work remains to be done.

It is interesting to note that one of the appendixes to Gardner's 1923 Kimberley report contains a short note on mangrove exploitation for tanning purposes between Broome and Wyndham prepared by Head Forester McVicar. In it McVicar warns that 'In issuing permits to strip mangrove bark, adequate regulations should be formed so that only a proportion of the trees are killed, otherwise great damage to the foreshore will result'.

The occurrence of *Avicennia marina* on the Houtman Abrolhos is of particular importance. Here the trees act as nesting platforms for the Lesser Noddy (*Anous tenuirostris*), the only other breeding colony in the Indian Ocean being on the Seychelles.

In Western Australia there is fortunately relatively little exploitation of mangals apart from the solar salt production at Lake McLeod. With the recent industrial expansion of the State the mangroves at Bunbury and those of the Pilbara coast are under threat. Harbour developments at Bunbury and along the north-west coast, as well as off-shore gas deposits in the Pilbara, will all have a direct effect on the mangal. At Broome there is a long-established practice of cutting channels through the mangal in order to 'beach' pearling luggers. In some areas where mangals are located adjacent to townsites the dumping of rubbish within them is common.

At the present time there is no environmental protection directly afforded to safeguard mangroves in the State. However, in the conservation report on National Parks and Nature Reserves (1975) the Committee made strong recommendations concerning the importance of carrying out biological and sedimentological surveys on the tidal and supra-tidal flats. With respect to the

Table 18.1 Aboriginal (Bardi) names for mangroves

Avicenniaceae	
Avicennia marina	* tree; ranja
	* fruit; ngoor-ngoor-loo
Bombacaceae	
Camptostemon schultzii	* julbu
Rhizophoraceae	
Ceriops tagal	kurilee
Bruguiera exaristata	* bindune
Rhizophora stylosa	
Sonneratiaceae	
Sonneratia alba	* jolor

* Also recorded by Metcalfe, 1974.

solar salt production it was urged that: 'further development be restricted to the supra-tidal zone landward of the mangrove thickets and that any extension required the approval of the Environmental Protection Authority'. These recommendations were endorsed by State Cabinet on 9 February 1979.

Following the presentation of the first report by the Conservation Through Reserves Committee (CTRC) to the Environmental Protection Authority in January 1975, the Committee began an investigation of the National Park and Nature Reserve requirements of the Kimberley region of Western Australia. The findings of this study have now been forwarded to the Environmental Protection Authority for its consideration and review (Conservation Reserves in Western Australia, 1977). Because mangroves are an important feature of the Kimberley coast the report made special mention of them. The Committee considered that 'mangrove communities should be retained and protected wherever practicable. Some areas are already in existing or proposed reserves, but other areas large and small are not'. The Committee recommended that 'any proposed developments which would affect an area or areas of mangroves on the Kimberley coast be referred to the Environmental Protection Authority for assessment'.

Even Wildlife Reserves adjoining the coastline may afford no protection to mangals unless the reserve is specifically gazetted to extend to low-water mark. Unless specified, reserves extend only to high-water mark. The declaring of Aquatic Reserves such as those recommended by the CTRC (1977) for Prince Frederick Harbour and St George Basin would extend protection to the mangal as well as safeguarding the habitat of the Salt-water Crocodile.

Different mangrove areas seldom have the same zonation of mud flats and adjoining supra-tidal area because of soil type, salt deposits, rainfall, tidal range erosion and/or deposition. Thus there is a need then to conserve a wide range of mangrove habitats.

It is hoped that until they can be adequately studied mangals will receive protection or at least management that will ensure their survival. There is an urgent need to develop biological monitoring systems which will indicate changes in the mangal before the mangroves die. The work of George and Davis on the Australian Fiddler Crabs (see Kenneally, 'Mangroves of Western Australia', this volume) may provide such a system.

Acknowledgments

Peter Bindon (Archaeology) and Mancel Lofgren (Anthropology), Western Australian Museum, kindly provided assistance with ethno-botanical references.

References

Akerman, K., 1975. The double raft or Kalwa of the west Kimberley. *Mankind* **10**, 23.

Campbell, W.D., 1915. An account of the Aborigines of Sunday Island, King Sound, Kimberley, Western Australia. *Proceedings of the Royal Society of Western Australia* **1**, 55-82.

Conservation Reserves in Western Australia, 1975. Report of the Conservation Through Reserves Committee as recommended by the Environmental Protection Authority. Systems 4, 8, 9, 10, 11, 12.

Conservation Reserves in Western Australia, 1977. Report of the Conservation Through Reserves Committee on System 7 to the Environmental Protection Authority.

Gardner, C.A., 1923. *Botanical Notes. Kimberley Division of Western Australia.* Western Australian Forests Department Bulletin **32**, 1-105. Government Printer, Perth.

Love, J.R.B., 1936. *Stone Age Bushmen of To-day.* Blackie & Son Limited, London. 220 pp.

Metcalfe, C.D., 1972. Bardie Verb Morphology. Ph.D. thesis, Australian National University, Canberra.

Moore, D.R., 1978. *Islanders and Aborigines at Cape York.* Australian Institute of Aboriginal Studies, Canberra.

Part VI

Epilogue

Future Directions

The central theme of this volume has been to assess, in an Australian context, current knowledge of the environment in which mangroves grow, their distribution, biology and management, and to identify those areas where further work is required. It will be obvious from the contributions herein that there is now a considerable body of information on species of mangrove and their distribution in Australia. Progress has been made, too, in characterising the types of mangrove communities and their vegetational associations. By contrast, much less is known about the way in which specific enviromental and edaphic factors mediate growth processes in mangroves and the flow of organic materials, nutrients and energy through mangrove ecosystems.

It could of course be argued with some justification that our knowledge of the character of mangrove ecosystems and how they function is still rudimentary and that a great deal more work is needed on every facet of mangrove ecology if this valuable resource is to be husbanded wisely. Notwithstanding this view, a number of key areas can be identified where further research is urgently needed to provide the quantitative information so essential to assess the importance of mangrove ecosystems at both a local and national level. The final, 'synthesis' session of the National Mangrove Workshop was devoted to discussing these needs. It is appropriate that this volume should conclude with a brief statement summarising the conclusions reached in that final session.

Research needs

Mangroves are an important natural resource in Australia, which is close to the centre of evolution of these unique species; mangrove communities occupy about 22 per cent of the Australian coast and they are associated with many important commercial fisheries. Although some prominent work is being done on mangroves in Australia, activity is low compared with other fields of research in the biological sciences. An increase in the amount and cohesion of research needs to be encouraged.

To understand the behaviour of mangrove ecosystems it is imperative to adopt a parallel, two-level approach. At one level broad scale investigations focusing on distributional and environmental problems are required. At a second level detailed investigations, carried out both in the laboratory and at selected field sites, are needed of physiological and ecological processes in mangrove ecosystems.

Within these two major levels three key areas in which further research on mangroves is needed have been identified.

1. The co-ordination of information on mangrove resources and their environments
2. Research on growth processes in mangroves
3. Quantification of the trophic relationships and population biology of mangroves and their associated offshore ecosystems.

Co-ordination of information

Around Australia, mangroves occupy diverse climatic, tidal and geologic environments. Patterns of mangrove distribution (species and structure), species-habitat relationships, and plant community changes through time are areas of investigation which require co-ordination of existing and future information. It is recommended that a national inventory be established which can provide answers to distributional and environmental questions concerning Australian mangrove resources. The framework for such an inventory already exists in the efforts of various organisations, but is fragmented at present. The inventory program may consist of personnel and facilities which could:

1. Co-ordinate nationally a reference specimen collection;
2. Develop a data bank on location, species characteristics, and habitat conditions for mangroves in Australia at different spatial scales;
3. Promote the exchange of information on national and international research in mangrove ecology and associated disciplines (e.g. via a newsletter);
4. Develop guidelines and a repository of baseline (benchmark) information on 'representative' mangrove communities;
5. Prepare and maintain a bibliography of mangrove literature related to Australia; and
6. Establish the means for providing climatic information relevant to mangrove environments.

Research on growth processes

Mangroves are a unique group of tree species which grow predominantly in a tidal environment where the water ranges from brackish to a salinity of up to three times that of seawater, and where the sediments in which their roots exist are generally anaerobic. The elucidation of the physiology which enables them to function in such an environment is crucial to our understanding of the behaviour and stability of mangrove communities, and may yield fundamental information about biological processes in a wider range of higher plants. Thus research, both in the laboratory and at selected sites in the field, on the mediation of growth in mangroves by salinity and oxygen should be encouraged. There is presently a nucleus of such research in institutes and universities, but its extent is not commensurate with its importance. Specific aspects of the problem which should be emphasised are:

1. Culture of mangroves in artificial environments, particularly in relation to salinity, aeration, temperature, and nutrition;
2. Ion exchange and water transport in mangrove roots;
3. Effects of salinity, oxygen, temperature, and nutrition on metabolism in mangroves;
4. Allocation of carbon in mangroves under varying conditions of salinity, aeration, temperature, and nutrition;
5. Field studies of carbon fixation and water loss in relation to species, leaf age, salinity, and microenvironment;
6. Microclimatic structure of mangrove canopies as it affects leaf metabolism, water loss, and salt accumulation;
7. Effects of salinity on reproduction and seedling establishment in mangroves;
8. Transfer and transformation processes in anaerobic sediments as they affect growth of mangroves.

Community relationships

The most important area in which research is needed is the quantification of the microbial link in the transfer of organic matter from primary producers to animals. As the protein content of the plant detritus is too low for adequate nutrition of most marine animals, decomposition of detritus by bacteria and fungi, which can concentrate nutrients from additional external sources, is an essential process and should be quantified. Microbial biomass and productivity should be determined and related to litter fall, root production and exudation. The relative importance of meiofauna in the food chain compared to the direct utilisation of micro-organisms by large animals should be measured. Concurrent research on biomass and production of higher trophic levels are necessary in order to quantify energy flow through mangrove ecosystems and associated offshore ecosystems.

Other important areas of investigation are studies on the population biology of the key components in the system. In particular, studies of the demography, population stability, life-history adaptations, physiological and genetic variation of these key components would answer many questions about the stability and adaptability of these systems. Studies such as these may provide an indication of the impact of perturbation on the component species and their associated offshore components.

Conservation needs

Research on the environmental and biological aspects of mangrove wetlands will not necessarily ensure their protection. Elucidation of many of these will be time consuming and, although the importance of Australia's mangrove resources are widely recognised in qualitative terms, it may be many years before they are fully evaluated quantitatively. If current trends continue, however, mangrove and other coastal wetlands will be seriously depleted in some coastal regions by the end of this century. At greatest risk are those areas along the densely-populated, subtropical and temperate south-eastern and southern coastlines, where the occurrence of mangrove wetlands is already limited.

At the present time, responsibility for zoning, planning and conserving coastal wetlands in Australia is shared by various State and local government authorities, often with conflicting policy objectives. In consequence, decisions concerning the protecting and management of mangroves are often unco-ordinated and lack regional and national perspective. It is therefore suggested that the protection and management of mangrove and other coastal wetlands be co-ordinated nationally. Specific aspects which could be emphasised include:

1. Establishment of policy relating to the protection and management of mangrove and other coastal wetlands at national, regional and local levels;
2. Establishment and management of coastal wetland national parks or nature reserves which include substantial areas of mangrove.
3. Development of a program of public education on the need for conservation of mangrove and other coastal wetlands.
4. Provision of advice to Federal and State Governments and to private organisations on the need for, and funding of, research related specifically to the development of policies and methods for the management of coastal wetlands.

I.R. Cowan
B.G. Thom
J. Redfield
J. Imberger
B.F. Clough

Index

216; sorting propagules, 182, 268; West
Australian coast, 37, 38
Torres Strait, Qld, 43
Townsville, Qld, 25, 74
transpiration, 156, 201
Tuross River, NSW, 48
turtles, 133
Tweed River, NSW, 70

Van Diemen Gulf, 40, 50, 57, 75, 149
Vernon Islands, NT, 40
Victoria River, NT, 39, 42, 60, 70
Victorian coast, 48-9; *see also* under place
names e.g. Mallacoota Inlet
vivipary, 175, 177

water: pollution, 282-3; relations, 199-
200, 201, 207; table, 27; temperature
32-3; *see also* freshwater; xeromorphy
waves: damage by, 171, (Roebuck Bay) 37,
(Franklin Harbour) 50; New South
Wales, 48; Queensland, 47, 80; resistance to, 34, 270; shelter from, 34;
South Australia, 50
weather patterns, *see* climate
Western Australia, 289-91; distribution,
97, 101, 103, 104, 106; *see also* under
place names e.g. Cambridge Gulf; King
Sound; Ord River
Western Australian Museum, Perth, 149
Whitsunday Islands, 45, 48
wind, 24-6, 80-1; and evaporation, 26;
and tides, 28; damage, 171, 173, *see
also* crown damage
wood: anatomy, 172: production, 218-19
Woolooware Bay, NSW, 277

xeromorphy, 153-9, 167, 171
xylem sap, 195, 196
Xylocarpus australasicus, 60t, 75-6, 85*t*,
86*t*, 99*t*; litter fall, 226*t*
X. granatum, 57, 60, 60*t*, 76, 85*t*, 86*t*,
99*t*; litter fall, 226*t*
X. moluccense, 81, 86*t*